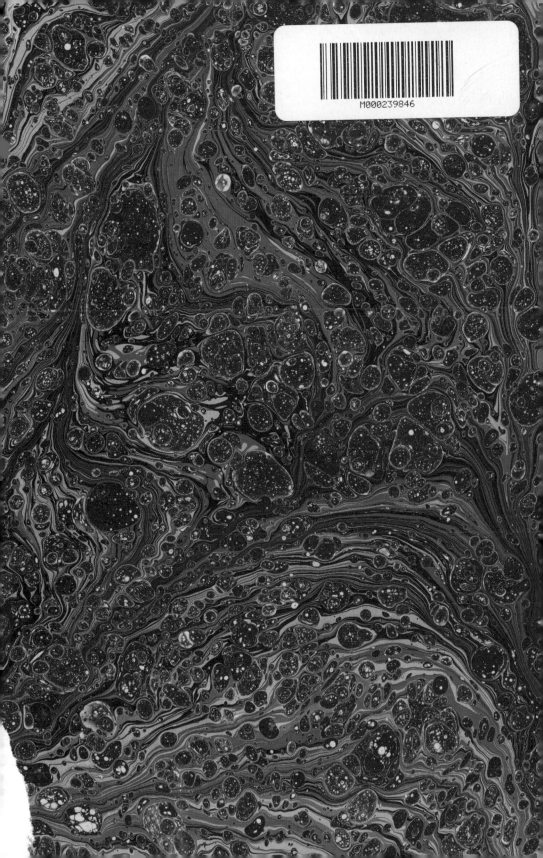

CAMP WILLIAM PENN

To the men of Camp William Penn – whose exemplary acts of courage forever changed the course of American history.

CAMP WILLIAM PENN

1863-1865

Donald Scott, Sr.

Schiffer Military History
Atglen, PA

Book Design by Ian Robertson.

Copyright © 2012 by Donald Scott, Sr.
Library of Congress Control Number: 2012940772

Printed in China.
ISBN: 978-0-7643-4253-0

We are interested in hearing from authors with book ideas on related topics.

Published by Schiffer Publishing Ltd.
4880 Lower Valley Road
Atglen, PA 19310
Phone: (610) 593-1777
FAX: (610) 593-2002
E-mail: Info@schifferbooks.com.
Visit our web site at: www.schifferbooks.com
Please write for a free catalog.
This book may be purchased from the publisher.
Try your bookstore first.

In Europe, Schiffer books are distributed by:
Bushwood Books
6 Marksbury Avenue
Kew Gardens
Surrey TW9 4JF, England
Phone: 44 (0) 20 8392-8585
FAX: 44 (0) 20 8392-9876
E-mail: Info@bushwoodbooks.co.uk.
Visit our website at: www.bushwoodbooks.co.uk

Contents

Acknowledgments

This project was made possible by the truly generous and enthusiastic support of family, colleagues, friends, researchers, archivists, historians, institutions, agencies, historical societies, community organizations, and the descendants of the soldiers.

Sincerest appreciation is extended to remarkable and gifted historians James Elton Johnson, Charles L. Blockson, James Spina, Andy Waskie, James M. Paradis, David B. Rowland, Thomas Wieckowski, James Mundy, Leon Clemmer, and William Chambrés for unselfishly giving of their knowledge and expertise.

The author is extremely indebted to Thomas I. Dawson, Cicero Green, and Lee Carol Cook, who generously shared items of significant historical value from their own personal family collections.

Additionally, kindly assisting the author with extraordinary talents and skills were V. Chapman-Smith, Director (National Archives, Mid-Atlantic Region, Philadelphia); Rodney Foytik and Steve Bye, Research Historians (U.S. Army Military History Institute); Philip Lapansky, Curator, African American Collections and Nicole Joniec, Print Department Assistant and Digital Collections Manager (The Library Company of Philadelphia); Laurie Zierer, Assistant Director and Pam Shropshire, Director and Communications & Programs Coordinator (Humanities Council of Pennsylvania); Robert Hicks, Director (Mutter Museum); Hillary S. Kativa, Rights & Reproductions Associate (Historical Society of Pennsylvania); and Leslie Willis-Lowry, Archivist and Diane D. Turner, Curator (of the Charles L. Blockson Afro-American Collection).

Community leaders, educators, scholars and theologians Bishop Jeffrey Nathaniel Leath, Rev. Dr. Mark Kelly Tyler, Joyce Werkman, Dorothy Spruill, Joseph Certaine, Sheila Jones, Molefi Kete Asante, Brian Chepulis, Jack and Mary Washington, Lise Marlowe, Cheltenham Township Commissioners, and the 3rd Regiment of Re-enactors in Philadelphia provided immense support which was deeply appreciated.

The author is especially grateful for the useful information and valued documents, portraits, photographs, and manuscripts supplied by numerous organizations and institutions dedicated to preserving historical treasures, which included the Citizens for the Restoration of Historic LaMott (CROHL); Cheltenham Township Historical Commission; Old York Road Historical Society; Jenkintown Library; Historical Society of Montgomery County (Pennsylvania); Historical Society of Pennsylvania; Pennsylvania Museum and Historical Commission; Civil War and Underground Railroad Museum, Philadelphia; Grand Army of the Republic Civil War Museum, Philadelphia; St. Paul's Episcopal Church of Elkins Park; Mother Bethel African Methodist Episcopal Church; Shiloh Baptist Church; Atwater-Kent Museum of Philadelphia History; Union League of Philadelphia; Free Library of Philadelphia; Adams County Historical Society, Gettysburg; The Lester S. Levy Collection of Sheet Music at The Johns Hopkins University; Rare Books and Manuscripts, The Sheridan Libraries; Pennsylvania State Archives; New Jersey State Archives; National Archives; National Park Service; and the African American Civil War Museum and Memorial, Washington, D.C.

This project finally came into fruition with the boundless love and encouragement of the author's wife, Billie; mother, Grace Scott; son, Donald Scott, Jr.; brothers, David Scott, Henry Scott, and Glenn Scott; nephews, Kristopher H. Scott (photo editor, as well as his proofreading wife, Bonnie) and Joshua Roderick Scott; friend Gerald T. Jenkins; and father-in-law, Lt. Cmdr. Wesley A. Brown, retired, the first African American graduate of the U.S. Naval Academy, Class of 1949.

Finally, deepest gratitude is expressed for the late Dr. Henry Scott, M.D. (father) and colleagues Perry Triplett, Arnold Snyder, and Philip Kind–for their stalwart dedication and tireless commitment to the betterment of humankind that has left an enduring legacy.

Introduction

The proudest moment of my life

The Reverend Jeremiah W. Asher hovered near death in Wilmington, NC, likely suffering from typhoid or "malignant fever," otherwise known as malaria. It was steamy hot in late-July 1865, as the country emerged slowly from the dreadful Civil War, climaxing with the Union troops' bloody charge through much of the South. Those forces included Asher's 6th United States Colored Troops (USCT) regiment of Pennsylvania as part of the 25th Corps' "operations on the North Carolina coast" (Taylor 1913, 6). During those final dire days it's probable that Asher, the chaplain of the regiment and one-time pastor of the Shiloh Baptist Church, consisting of a congregation of free blacks and former slaves in Philadelphia, PA, thought about his beloved grandfather, Gad Asher, a black "replacement" soldier in the Revolutionary War almost a century earlier. He likely recalled the story of Gad in about 1730 being "stolen from the coast of Guinea when four years of age," (Asher 1850, 15) as Jeremiah put it in his 1850 memoir, *Incidents in the Life of The Rev. J. Asher*, and destined for enslavement in colonial Connecticut.

And despite the betrayal of his so-called master, who reneged on an immediate promise of freedom after Gad courageously replaced him during the Revolutionary War following almost 40 years of servitude (Asher 1850, 18), Grandfather Gad would pass the burning torch of his Old Testament religious fervor to his grandson, Jeremiah (Asher 1850, 28-29). And that, in part, likely inspired Jeremiah later to pursue the ministry, as well as serve in Connecticut, Rhode Island, and Washington, D.C. as a Baptist preacher, eventually ending up in Philadelphia. That was before supporting the recruitment of black Civil War troops and becoming a respected citizen and clergy person of Philadelphia's African American community. He'd soon sign on as chaplain of one of the mightiest and earliest federal black regiments of the Civil War to be trained at Camp William Penn, "the centerpiece of black recruitment in the North from its inception to the end of the war," (Johnson 1999, 96) as well as the first and largest of 18 U.S. facilities to exclusively train such Northern-based black soldiers during the war:

This color lithograph, engraved by P.S. Duval and Son in Philadelphia and depicting soldiers and an officer of the 25ᵗʰ USCT on the grounds of Camp William Penn, was used to recruit African American troops. It was developed from an earlier black and white image of the unidentified soldiers and officer. *Courtesy of the Library Company of Philadelphia.*

...With the recommendation of a number of Philadelphia clergy he was appointed by regimental officers to the chaplain position on November 1, 1863. Asher had been a principle supporter of black enlistment in the Philadelphia region. Before accepting the chaplain's appointment he was pastor of the Shiloh Baptist Church in south Philadelphia. Dated August 1, 1863, his letter of recommendation read: "This certifies that the Rev. Jeremiah Asher is a regularly ordained minister of the Baptist Denomination – that he has been for fourteen years the pastor of the Shiloh Baptist Church in the city – that he is an earnest & faithful man and that as such we recommend him for appointment as a Chaplain in the army." (Johnson 1999, 89-90)

According to his pension file at the National Archives, the letter was signed by "J. Wheaton Smith, Thomas S. Malcom, Howard Malcom, Reuben Jeffery, Jonathon H. Castle, James Cooper, Daniel C. Eddy, and James B. Simmons" (90). The official date of Reverend Asher's enlistment, according to his online service record, was December 4, 1863 (*American Civil War Soldiers about Jeremiah Asher*, 2011).

The Reverend Jeremiah Asher, the fourth pastor of the Shiloh Baptist Church in Philadelphia, volunteered as a chaplain for the 6ᵗʰ USCT, one of the fiercest units to train at Camp William Penn. An ardent abolitionist who would travel to England on an anti-slavery lecture tour and write two autobiographies, Asher died of disease in Wilmington, NC, leaving his wife and children. *Courtesy of Donald McMurray.*

Born about half-a-century earlier on October 13, 1812, as America waged its second war of independence from the British (the War of 1812), Asher's name appeared on Civil War recruiting posters for African American soldiers starting in 1863 throughout the Philadelphia region with top anti-slavery abolitionists. They included the likes of Frederick Douglass, Octavius Catto, Robert Purvis, and ministers of the African Methodist Episcopal Church, including Reverend Elisha Weaver, editor of *The Christian Recorder* newspaper (Paradis 1998, 11). Many of Asher's soldiers wrote Weaver from the front lines to tell black Philadelphians and others around the country, via the paper that was distributed to troops throughout the south and eastern seaboard, of battle events and conditions, as well as concerning their general welfare.

That was the case when a black soldier identified as "Arnold," likely in the 3rd or 4th USCT, described the black soldiers of the regiment and other accompanying units, such as the 6th USCT, triumphantly marching into Wilmington, NC, on President George Washington's February 22, 1865, birthday commemoration:

> April 15, 1865
> *The Christian Recorder*
> Philadelphia, Pennsylvania
> For the Christian Recorder.
> THROUGH THE CAROLINAS.
>
> February 20th – We had something of a skirmish with one of General Bragg's "bad men," General Hoke, and, as usual be fell back. On the 21st we built a line, and bivouacked for the night; being only four miles from the largest and oldest city in the State. We asked ourselves as well as others, "How would you like to march through Wilmington tomorrow, February 22d, the anniversary of the birth-day of Washington?" The answer was, "It would be the proudest moment of my life!" But little does a soldier know when, or at what time, he may be ordered to "fall in." We slept behind our works that night. The 22nd came, and a more lovely day I never saw. By half past six o'clock we were on the move, as General Hoke had evacuated during the night, and one hour's march brought us on the corporation line of Wilmington, when large volumes of smoke were seen rising in the eastern part of the city. For a time, we thought Hoke had set fire to the city as he went through. But not so. It was the burning of cotton and turpentine at and near the Wilmington and Weldon rail-road. The column halted for a few moments, when the mayor met General Terry, and begged for protection. We finally moved, and entered the blockaded city of the confederacy – the place where all the southern and some of the northern men have made their piles of money – the once thriving city of the confederacy; the place noted for its slave-market! But now, alas! We march through these fine thoroughfares, where once the slave was forbid being out after nine p.m., or to puff a 'regalia,' or to walk with a cane, or to ride in a carriage! Negro soldiers! – the colored division of the 25th army corps, commanded by General Charles J. Paine. It would be a mere attempt for such a one as myself to describe the manner in which the colored people of Wilmington welcomed the Union troops – cheer after cheer they gave us – they had prayed long for

their deliverance, and the 22nd day of February, 1865, realized their earnest hopes. Were they not happy that day? Free, for evermore? The streets were crowded by them, old and young; they shook hands with the troops, and some exclaimed, "the chain is broken!" "Joy! Freedom to-day!" "Hurrah, for Uncle Abe!" (Redkey 1992, 166)

Then the giddy soldier, according to Redkey, described the utter joy that Reverend Asher must have felt too, though perhaps, from time to time, asking his flock of men to simmer down their celebratory antics a bit. Still, Asher and the 6th couldn't help but soak in the jubilation of the black townsfolk gazing at the spectacle of African American men parading with loaded weapons, many of them former slaves who had labored in the North Carolina tobacco and cotton fields for white masters:

> "There goes my son!" said a lady. "Which one," asked a corporal. "That one, just gone ahead!" And, sure enough, it was her son. She overtook him, and embraced him; and how proudly she felt, none but those similarly situated can ever feel. The man knew that his mother was living when he entered the service for some friend and so informed him. He had left his home a slave, but had returned in the garb of a Union soldier, free, a man. Similar incidents have happened in other colored regiments. At one corner, near the market, the colored people had boxes of tobacco, which they distributed to the troops as they passed. At almost every door was a bucket of water; and, in many places, ladies gave bread and meat to the boys, saying, "Tis the best we have." The farther we advanced, the more numerous the people. At one corner, my attention was attracted to a crowd who were "jumping for joy!" One old man among them, said he was nearly ninety-three years old, and had not been in the street since last July; but hearing the music of the Union troops, it had revived him, and he felt so happy that he came out; and there he stood, with his long, white locks and his wrinkled cheeks, saying, "Welcome, welcome."
>
> We passed out of the town, and were soon on Hoke's track. We came up with him at North-East Bridge, or Station, nine miles from town – the 4th, 6th, and 30th U.S.C.T., Gen. Duncan's Brigade, gave him battle at this place, and during the night – as usual – Gen. Hoke retreated. (ibid.)

In fact, it was Asher's zeal for religion and black rights, also sparked by his grandfather's tragic enslavement and blindness due to his War-of-Independence injuries received at Bunker Hill, which probably helped to propel Asher to bravely leave his wife and children, over and above the comforts of his Philadelphia home.

Indeed, according to the 1860 federal census, Asher's home was a place where Elizabeth Taylor Greenfield, "the Black Swan," a former slave and well-known singer famous for entertaining African American troops to raise funds at Shiloh and other venues, was listed as a 40-year-old "servant." She also performed for Queen Victoria of England on May 10, 1854 at Buckingham Palace (Hine 1993, 1). Greenfield had been born to "enslaved Indian and African American parents in Mississippi and … came to Philadelphia at a young age with her mistress, who freed her after joining the Society of Friends. Largely self-educated

The former slave Elizabeth Greenfield helped to raise funds for the black regiments by singing in concerts, eventually reaching great notoriety in the U.S. and England, where she sang for Queen Victoria. She resided for a while with the Reverend Jeremiah Asher according to census reports. *Courtesy of the Library of Congress.*

in piano, harp, guitar, and voice, Greenfield thrilled a Buffalo, New York audience in 1851 and soon became a popular concert artist in eastern cities" (Nash 2002, 199-200).

Asher had been so convinced of the righteousness of the Union cause, without doubt a cause completely dedicated to eradicating slavery, that he was one of just 14 black chaplains during the war. He furiously recruited African Americans when he arrived in Wilmington, NC:

> Pursuant to Special Order No. 15 issued on February 26, 1865 at Department of North Carolina Headquarters in Wilmington, "Permission is hereby given to Captain G. P. Riley and Chaplain J. Asher with three privates and two musicians[...]to remain in Wilmington six (6) days for the purpose of recruiting." Asher maintained a grueling schedule recruiting in the south, providing spiritual support for his embattled Sixth regiment and tending to his family and church back in Philadelphia. He had earlier written "The last month has been one of constant excitement and fatigue." Full agenda notwithstanding, Asher and his small recruiting party may well have enlisted the nearly one hundred soldiers who joined the regiment over the next two weeks. (Johnson 1999, 90)

Asher kept up his searing pace, according to the "regimental surgeon, Leeman Barnes, who on July 21, 1865, wrote: 'I have carefully examined this officer and find that he is suffering from the effects of remittent fever and that a change of location is necessary for his recovery and to prevent loss of life. I further certify that in my opinion he will not be able to resume his duties in a less period than thirty (30) days" (90). The question is, would that help come too late?

Indeed, as Asher lay on his probable deathbed, he had to also be very concerned about the welfare of his wife, Abigail, and their children (Thomas, about age 19, and John, near 10, in 1865) (Asher 1850, 27). He undoubtedly missed them as he drifted off to the next world after frantically trying to nurse his ailing flock of 6th USCT soldiers battling the ravages of Yellow Fever or typhoid.

The regiment, not long before marching into Wilmington, had been sorely tested, fiercely fighting at the bloody Battle of New Market Heights in September 1864 and suffering very heavy casualties, despite a few earning the prestigious Congressional Medal of Honor for valor by saving the regimental colors. That feat is remarkable, given that 16 blacks out of almost 200,000 earned the honor by the end of the war. Departing October 14, 1863, from Camp William Penn, located in Chelten Hills or Camptown, about 10 miles northwest of central Philadelphia, the 6th "had a more active part in a field of operations

THE RESURRECTION OF HENRY BOX BROWN AT PHILADELPHIA.
Who escaped from Richmond Va in a Box 3 feet long 2½ ft deep and 2 ft wide.

Henry "Box" Brown escaped to Philadelphia in 1849, one year before the notorious Fugitive Slave Act of 1850, allowing pro-slavery forces to unilaterally enslave or re-enslave African Americans. Abolitionists who would be associated with Camp William Penn more than a decade later actually helped him escape in a railway box that was shipped by train to Philadelphia. *Courtesy of the Library of Congress.*

covering a large portion of two States [Virginia and North Carolina] than any other colored regiment originating from Pennsylvania." (Taylor 1913, 6)

Remarkably, the stories of the 6th USCT and 10 other Camp William Penn regiments as America's first Northern-trained federal black soldiers – as well as the Asher family's saga and the establishment of Camp William Penn – are central to the greatest American historical contradiction: the perpetuation of slavery during the colonial period by many of America's founders, although they yearned and fought for liberation from England during the American Revolution, unequivocally lit the fuse to the U.S. Civil War less than a century later.

The Camp William Penn saga is essentially a poignant reminder of African American warriors, magnified via a black family's incredible sacrifices, to save the Republic from its inception to its agonizing war-between-the-states salvation. It's the story of how Camp William Penn became the center and symbol of the black liberation movement in America: because of its vital central geographical location on the East coast, in a city (Philadelphia) with the largest black population in the United States; how it was organized in conjunction with Lincoln's Bureau for U.S. Colored Troops and thereby became the first and largest federal facility to train black soldiers in the North during the Civil War; and how it drew to its grounds most of America's top anti-slavery abolitionists and Underground Railroad operators – from Frederick Douglass and Harriet Tubman to Lucretia Mott, Sojourner Truth, Robert Purvis and William Still.

The Asher family's giving of blood from the country's inception reflects the paradoxical essence of the camp's historic founding and its namesake, Governor William Penn. After all, Penn established Pennsylvania in 1683, almost 100 years before the Revolutionary War, espousing religious and political freedom for European immigrants while quickly taking over lands of the Native Leni Lenape ("original people"), despite his initial so-called good intentions.

President Lincoln's Emancipation Proclamation actually only freed a minimal number of slaves in Rebel held territories and not in the neutral border states. Regardless, African Americans rejoiced at the news because the Proclamation allowed for the recruiting of black Federal troops. *Courtesy of the U.S. Army Military History Institute.*

Furthermore, and also very striking, Penn, a persecuted Quaker in England, was a slaveholder, one of the earliest practitioners of America's great contradiction that several generations later exploded in the lap of a young politician from Illinois, Abraham Lincoln.

Indeed, following President Lincoln's Emancipation Proclamation that took effect on January 1, 1863, which allowed – for the first time – the recruitment of black federal soldiers, the 6th USCT was second of the 11 regiments, consisting of almost 11,000 black soldiers, to train at the legendary camp in Chelten Hills. It was nestled amid a mostly anti-slavery community of rolling hills and farmland led by the abolitionist and women's rights advocate Lucretia Mott, a Hicksite Quaker who lived next door to the sprawling 13-acre facility (Scott 2008, 9).

Mott, a distant cousin of the colonial leader Benjamin Franklin via her mother's Folger line, was a legendary theologian who often drew parallels between the struggles of blacks and women, despite realizing the differences and competitive elements of the groups. In an 1864 speech during the "third decade" birthday commemoration of the American Anti-Slavery Society in Boston, Mott provided a sampling of her oratory skills that made her the most recognized woman in America during much of the 19th century:

> Some of us women can perhaps more fully sympathize with the slave because the prejudice against him is somewhat akin to that against our sex; and we ought to have been more faithful than we have been, so that when we hear the words applied to us, "Come, ye blessed of my Father," we might be ready to ask, "When saw we thee an hungered, or athirst, or in prison, and ministered onto thee?" It seems to me, therefore, as has been recommended here to-day, that we should keep on our armor. It may not be necessary to continue our operations in precisely the same way; but it will be necessary to multiply our periodicals, and scatter them, as we have done heretofore with good effect ... Many have come, and made their acknowledgements, that when we have, been mobbed, when Pennsylvania Hall was burned, they were in the wrong, that they were in the mob; but now they say, "Whereas I was blind, I now see, and I am willing, now to be faithful to what I see." Let us welcome them, hail them in their coming, and gladly receive them.[1]

Meanwhile, at Mott's "Roadside" estate, which also served as a major stop of the Underground Railroad, she'd sometimes entertain such guests as Frederick Douglass, Harriet Tubman, Sojourner Truth, William Lloyd Garrison, and even William Still ("father of the Underground Railroad"), who operated a supply center or store at the camp (8).

Lucretia Mott and other abolitionists supported the release of Anthony Burns, a fugitive enslaved African man from Virginia that had been re-captured. Their pressure during the 1850s on pro-slavery forces, as well as fund raising, helped to free Burns, who became a symbol of black liberation, even for many of the soldiers who'd one day train at Camp William Penn. *Courtesy of the Library of Congress.*

Sojourner Truth was among the abolitionists, including Frederick Douglass, Harriet Tubman, and Lucretia Mott, who encouraged President Abraham Lincoln to recruit black troops during the Civil War. *Courtesy of the Library of Congress.*

The January 30, 1864, edition of *The Christian Recorder* noted Still's ascendancy to post sutler:

> Mr. William Still, of this city, has been elected post sutler, at Camp William Penn, and has been appointed the same by the Secretary of War; so we have been informed. And Mr. Ellis Peer, one of our best cake and confectionery dealers of this city, is his partner. We wish them great success in their noble undertaking. Mr. Still is also a stove and coal dealer, in 5th, above Arch St. It will be found by his advertisement in another column, that the price of coal is reduced. This will suit this year for the poor widows and old men, as well as those who are in pretty fair circumstances.[2]

The black activist and Underground Railroad icon William Still was appointed post sutler at Camp William Penn, despite some controversy that followed regarding his treatment of the soldiers. Despite charges of classicism, Still was instrumental in combating the segregation of the day, as well as likely guiding more than a few enslaved Africans to the gates of Camp William Penn and Lucretia Mott's nearby "Roadside" estate. *Courtesy of the Library of Congress.*

Still's base of operation, in fact, included his business and residence at "No. 105 NORTH-FIFTH STREET, PHILADELPHIA," according to an advertisement in the Saturday, May 16, 1863, edition of the *National Anti-Slavery Standard*, in a small display ad indicating: "A General Assortment of Cooking, Parlor and Chamber Stoves, Ranges, Heaters, Etc., constantly on hand." Still also made repairs, the ad said.

Perhaps Still was appointed to the position due to his reputation as being honest, and perhaps the most important person in the local black anti-slavery movement. And he was also the unmistakable head of the Underground Railroad system. The apparent possibility of greed by those with avarice intentions may have also contributed, despite Still himself being accused of such by members of the 25th USCT. The following correspondence indicates that Camp William Penn became a target of swindlers from all walks of life:

War Department,
ADJUTANT GENERAL'S OFFICE

Washington, D.C. Dec. 21st 1863
Lieut Col. Louis Wagner
Comdg Camp Wm Penn
near Philadelphia Pa.

Colonel,
The Department having been informed that there are two white men at Camp William Penn acting as sutlers of said Camp, and pretending to have authority therefore from the Secretary of War to direct men to have the aforesaid pretended sutlers removed forthwith from the Camp and not permit them to enter again within the limits of the Post.

You will immediately report to this office by what authority said persons were allowed to enter your lines as Sutlers, and also the action taken by you under this order.

I have the honor to be

Very Respectfully
Your Obd't Servant
Lew Foster
Assist Adjt Genl Vols.[3]

However, the appointment of a post sutler for Camp William Penn, at first, was not such a great idea to superior officers in Washington, according to correspondence exchanged between Commander Wagner and the Adjutant General's Office in Washington. Wagner initially sent the following correspondence to Major Foster:

Head Quarters Camp William Penn,
CHELTEN HILLS, PA.

November 18th, 1863
Major L.W. Foster AAG
Chief of Bureau for Col'd Troops
Washington D.C.

Sir:

It is my intention to appoint a sutler for this post as soon as the barracks are completed, provided the Department would endorse such an appointment. My reasons for making such an appointment is the desire to accommodate the men and also to raise a Post Fund.

Should a sutler be appointed for the Post and should a regiment at the Post appoint a sutler before leaving the Post, how could the difficulty be abbreviated? Would a regiment have the [right] to introduce a sutler while at the post?

Hoping that you may give me early information, I have the honor to be

Very Respectfully
Your obt servant
Louis Wagner
Lt. Col. 88. P.A.
Comg Post[4]

Major Foster, however, responded with a very terse and objectionable correspondence that seemed to actually admonish Wagner:

War Department AGO
Nov. 21st 1863

Respectfully returned to
Lt. Col. Louis Wagner, Comdg.
Camp William Penn, Near Philadelphia Pa.

Post Sutlers are appointed by the War Department. Camp William Penn being a temporary Post, such an appointment is not considered necessary.

By order:
Lew Foster
Asst. Adjt. Gen. Vols. [5]

However, ultimately Wagner must have been able to convince his superiors of the need for a post sutler. Yet, according to James Elton Johnson and other historians, controversy regarding the issue would arise again when members of the facility's 25th USCT would charge Still with short-changing them, even leading to a major disturbance and the destruction of property at Camp William Penn. Judged by some historians to be a major misunderstanding, perhaps due to the classist friction between the soldiers and Still, it's clear that fences were ultimately mended and the soldiers, in general, had great respect for such black abolitionists. Indeed, it's quite possible that Still actually helped some of those very soldiers to be liberated and join regiments at Camp William Penn.

Many of those great abolitionists actually addressed the camp's soldiers, including Frederick Douglass, near the start of their service in late July 1863 (Scott 2008, 8), and in April 1865, the celebrated Underground Railroad matriarch, Harriet Tubman (10). After the war she'd marry Nelson Davis of Camp William Penn's 8th USCT, suffering extremely heavy casualties in Olustee, Florida, during a clash with seasoned Confederate soldiers from Texas. Tubman spoke not long before the war ended and Abraham Lincoln, the president, was cut down on April 14, 1865, by a pistol shot of John Wilkes Booth, a Confederate and Rebel sympathizer, leading to his pursuit by the 22nd USCT of Camp William Penn (Scott 2011). The 22nd USCT also was the first black regiment to participate in a presidential funeral – Abraham Lincoln's – while other soldiers from the camp earlier helped to capture Confederate General Robert E. Lee and the president of the Rebel states, Jefferson Davis. Regiments from the camp – including the 3rd, 6th, 8th, 22nd, 24th, 25th, 32nd, 41st, 43rd, 45th, and 127th – fought and died in many of the war's most bloody battles, from Florida's February 1864 Battle of Olustee to Virginia's horrific Battle of the Crater in July of the same year, despite too often being relegated to menial or laborious duties.

For instance, the 6th USCT men had also fought with General Benjamin F. Butler's Army of the James in May 1864, participating in the Virginia sieges of Petersburg and Richmond, as well as New Market Heights or Chaffin's Farm in late September 1864. One company at New Market Heights "led by Capt. John McMurray, went into the charge with thirty-two men and returned with but three," amounting to "the greatest average company loss recorded of any troops in the course of the war" (Taylor 1913, 6).

So the Rev. Jeremiah Asher, a tall, muscularly-built man with a medium-brown complexion, parted bushy hair, and long sideburns attached to a beard running under his chin at the start of the war, was likely a very worn-down soul on July 27, 1865 as the "bilious disease" drained the life from him. In all probability the reverend spent his last hours in bed at the residence of Thomas Day, Jr., a well-known black activist in the Wilmington, NC, area. "Bro. Asher was well cared for while lingering in his afflictions. The ever hospitable Mr. and Mrs. Day took him into their own home during his illness. Wilmington, North Carolina," noted the July 30, 1865, edition of the Philadelphia-based *Christian Recorder*.[6]

Also likely living at the residence and monitoring the dying preacher was Thomas' aging mother, Aquilla, whose late husband Thomas Sr. piled up a tremendous fortune making furniture before his insolvency in 1857 due to a nationwide financial panic. That was not long before the Civil War erupted in 1861 and about the time of the death of the senior Thomas, who was a black owner of several slaves himself as an entrepreneur owning a very popular furniture-building factory earlier in Milton, North Carolina (Logan, Winston 1982, 162). In 1865, in fact: "Aquilla Day, and two of her children (Thomas Jr. and Mary Ann) are living in Wilmington, NC in the activist free black community there. Mary Ann helps found a school for recently freed black children with other free black teachers" (Thomas Day Timeline, 2010).

Asher, though, "worked as a minister throughout his entire life." Prior to "the Civil War, he traveled to England to raise funds for his Shiloh Baptist Church of Philadelphia. He enlisted on December 4, 1863, as a chaplain for the 6th USCT Regiment" (Sailer, 2010). The first chaplain appointed by President Lincoln himself, was Rev. Henry McNeal Turner (1834-1915) of the 1st USCT, which was based in Washington, D.C. Rev. Turner, who was crucial in helping to convince the president to recruit black troops, would become a bishop of the Philadelphia-based African Methodist Episcopal Church in 1880 (Gates, Higginbotham 2004, 825).

Now, as his strength sapped, Reverend Asher, "born in the town of North Brandford, county of New Haven, state of Connecticut," (Asher 1850, 15) likely looked forward to the heavenly embrace of his African progenitor, Grandfather Gad. Jeremiah probably remembered the dramatic story of his grandfather being captured, a narrative that Jeremiah poignantly expressed in his autobiography of 1850, when the horrible Fugitive Slave Act was passed. Indeed, it wouldn't be surprising if that narrative was written, in part, to gather public sentiment against the federal law that allowed pro-slavery forces to enslave or re-enslave countless blacks throughout the country, even in the North, including such cities as Philadelphia.

Jeremiah wrote that in Africa, about 1735, grandfather Gad's "father cultivated a small portion of land not far distant from his dwelling" in Guinea, "the produce of it my grandfather believed to be rice, though on account of his youth could not be certain," (15) Asher wrote, before continuing:

> The ground being prepared, and the seed broadcast upon it – it was then the employment of the small children to watch it for a season, to prevent the birds, which are so numerous, from devouring the seed. This department of labour fell to his brother whom he supposed to be next older than himself, and about twelve or fourteen years of age; he had been accustomed to take his younger brother into the field with him for company, while he was employed in watching, which was effected in the following manner: In the centre of the plantation a stage was erected, elevated about six or eight feet so as to possess a commanding view of the

field, and upon this was brought a large quantity of stones which, when the birds alighted were slung at them to scare them away. (15-16)

Then, as the two young brothers at some point were in the field, stationed on the platform, looking out for birds, Asher wrote "two men were observed coming out of a thicket, and making towards the stage, the elder brother suspecting their object, immediately took his younger brother and descended the stage, running with all possible haste to make their escape from these men-stealers," Asher wrote. The two brothers ran together for home, as fast as possible, but the younger Gad, "poor little fellow, soon tired, and began to lag" (16).

> His [older] brother then took him upon his back, and ran as fast as he could; but seeing their pursuers would soon overtake them, he was at last, though not without the deepest reluctance, obliged to abandon his little charge in order to make his own escape, and bear the melancholy tidings to his heart-stricken mother. (ibid.)

Next, these chilling words, mindful of many similar episodes of the trans-Atlantic slave trade that so many of Camp William Penn's soldiers were probably all too familiar with, came pouring from Asher's pen concerning the despair of countless African mothers suffering such losses: Gad's mother, he wrote, "doubtless felt as mothers only can feel [...] that her darling little boy was stolen away, and that they would probably see him no more in this world" (ibid).

Even Asher, in his account, seems to be overtaken by the gravity of the event. "Here I feel tempted to linger for a moment, to gaze upon and attempt a description of this heart-rending, God-provoking, heaven-daring, hell-deserving crime" (15-16). And then his emotions explode:

> But alas! For me, I have neither power of imagination to conceive, or eloquence to utter the nature or amount of punishment due to such transgression. But the Lord will repay, vengeance is his, and he will one day most assuredly make inquisition for blood. Neither can I give any idea of the awful solemnity of that moment when the intelligence was received that the poor little boy was stolen. This I must leave for an abler pen than mine to delineate, and content myself with a simple narrative of the subsequent events in the history of the little captive. (16-17)

It's clear that Asher realized in 1850, when his narrative was originally published in London by Charles Gilpin, with the financial help of sympathizing English abolitionists (including Wilson Armistead, who wrote the book's introduction), that some kind of violent debacle was eminent. That's even if it did not occur until more than a decade later in 1861. The Civil War, in fact, also followed the monumental prediction of the anti-slavery martyr John Brown just before his execution after leading a small band of whites and liberated slaves in the 1859 raid on the U.S. arsenal at Harper's Ferry, Virginia. And some of the very prominent black abolitionists and Underground Railroad icons who associated with

Lucretia Mott at her "Roadside" home, adjacent to land where Camp William Penn would rise, helped to devise the doomed raid. They included Harriet Tubman, "who participated in planning the Harper's Ferry raid." In fact, prior to "putting his plan into action, Brown had sought [in May 1858] a 'general convention or council,' of free Africans to 'aid and contenance' his activities in Chatham, Ontario, such as Martin Delany" (Geffert 2002, 594), who would eventually become the highest ranking black (as a major) in the Army. Meanwhile, when Brown had disclosed his plans to Frederick Douglass in 1847, the former Maryland slave argued that such a raid would not likely be successful, and that the massiveness of slavery had to be solved with "federal force" (599). Douglass' prediction proved to be correct. The raid on Harper's Ferry, although arguably a symbolic victory for the soon-to-be martyred Brown, was a failure in its attempt to create a massive slave insurrection. However, it was a major spark that lit the Civil War fuse, ultimately leading to the liberation of blacks that Brown had envisioned. As Brown and some of his conspirators were hung, his wife, Mary, was harbored at the estate of Lucretia Mott, in Chelten Hills, next to where Camp William Penn rose several years later during the summer of 1863. Brown's raid sparked the revolution against slavery that the likes of Asher and Brown had so accurately foretold.

John Brown's raid on Harper's Ferry, Virginia, helped to spark the Civil War. Brown also resided for a while in Philadelphia and Chambersburg, PA, as well as corresponded with Lucretia Mott, who lived in Philadelphia and Chelten Hills, adjacent to Camp William Penn. *Courtesy of the Atwater-Kent Museum of Philadelphia History.*

1

'Emotions ran very high'

At the moment John Brown's neck snapped by the force of his body plummeting downward at the end of a military rope on December 2, 1859, his wife, Mary, was in the clutches of northern anti-slavery advocates, most notably Lucretia Mott (Scott 2008, 34). As the anxious days of Brown's trial passed, Mott's heart went out to Brown's wife, who had lost two sons in the battles of Harpers Ferry. Through Miller McKim [a well-known abolitionist and journalist for the Anti-Slavery Standard, as well as corresponding secretary and general agent of the Pennsylvania Anti-Slavery Society] she arranged for Mary Ann Brown to stay at Roadside until the trial ended, giving her the comfort of the Mott household and what spiritual solace she could (Bacon 1980, 172). It was adjacent to her home, on about a dozen acres of land owned by her son-in-law, Edward M. Davis, where Camp William Penn would rise in 1863.

Meanwhile, eyewitnesses to Brown's death were President Lincoln's future assassin, John Wilkes Booth, as a low-level federal soldier, and Robert E. Lee, an arresting officer. But from a distance, the community of Chelten Hills certainly monitored the happenings via the press and the empathetic eyes of fellow abolitionists – similar to other such communities throughout the United States. In nearby Philadelphia, the Rev. Jeremiah Asher conducted a vigil service at his Shiloh Baptist Church. And the area's black activists declared December 2, 1859, "Martyr Day," the date of Brown's execution. In fact, as "six hundred Negroes and sixteen white sympathizers crowded into Shiloh Baptist on South Street to sit in vigil" emotions ran very high. "A visiting black minister took pains to explain why his church denounced the 'truckling' of some local blacks to whites in this crisis time. When Shiloh's pastor, Jeremiah Asher, said members of his own family were still trapped in slavery, shouts went up from every pew: 'So is mine!' 'So is mine!'" (Biddle, Dubin 2010, 233).

One of the letters that Mary Brown wrote to her children while she organized at Mott's "roadside" home, after corresponding with her husband, was dated November 28, 1859, just a few days before his death: "I am here with Mrs. Lucretia Mott where I expect to stay until your dear father is dispose of," the distraught woman wrote. "Oh what a terrible thought [...] But may the god of all peace be with us all as he is with him" (Scott 2008, 34).

Exemplifying the closeness of the abolitionist community, even though Mott, as a staunch Quaker, certainly did not condone Brown's violence, the two had met earlier in Boston, according to a letter that John Brown sent to Mary at Mott's home, dated November 25, 1859:

> I remember the faithful old lady well, but presume she has no recollection of me. I once set myself to oppose a mob at Boston, where she was. After I interfered, the police immediately took up the matter, and soon put a stop to mob proceedings. The meeting was, I think, on Marlboro Street at a Church, or Hotel, perhaps. I am glad to have you make the acquaintance of such old "Pioneers" of the cause. (Redpath 1860, 361)

While at Mott's home, it's very likely that Mary Brown met son-in-law Edward M. Davis, who owned the land where Mott's home stood, and additionally greeted by the likes of William Still and other principles of the Underground Railroad. At some point, it's likely

Mary Brown is pictured with two of her children. She was harbored by William Still and Lucretia Mott when her husband was executed on December 2, 1859. *Courtesy of the Library of Congress.*

that Mary Brown and her children were also harbored by Still. Still, known as the "father of the Underground Railroad," was the author of the epic book *The Underground Railroad* that described his slave-sheltering activities.

As Still harbored runaway slaves well before and during the opening salvo of the Civil War on April 12, 1862, when Confederate forces bombarded Fort Sumter in South Carolina's Charleston Harbor, various people in the Philadelphia area, and certainly some of Lincoln's army commanders, were considering the use of black troops. General John C. Frémont, in fact, earlier commanded Edward M. Davis (a captain and assistant quartermaster who rented his land to the federal government for the erection of Camp William Penn) in Missouri during the war, decreeing that blacks enslaved by Confederate sympathizers in that territory be freed and allowed to join the Union cause, an order that Lincoln thought premature and illegal, rescinding it and reassigning Frémont. That was consistent with Lincoln's initial hesitancy to recruit black troops due to "political exigencies" (Wert 1979, 335).

However, other observers and historians clearly sided with Lincoln's power play:

In September 1861 Lincoln overruled General John C. Frémont's proclamation granting freedom to slaves in Missouri. Frémont was already well known for his expeditions in the West when Lincoln, partly in deference to Frémont's politically influential relatives, installed him as the military commander of the entire western theater. The President stationed him in St. Louis with orders to keep a lid on the volatile situation in Missouri, one of the four border states that Lincoln was desperately trying to keep in the Union. This was an assignment that required both military and political skills, neither of which Frémont possessed in any measurable degree. His heavy-handed policies and arrogant demeanor alienated Missouri's Unionists, while the secessionists went on a rampage throughout much of the state. Unable to defeat the disloyal element by rallying those loyal to the Union, Frémont resorted to high-handed declarations of martial law. He established military tribunals and empowered them to execute those deemed traitors, and he had very broad notions of who counted as a traitor. On August 30 he went even further by announcing not only that the property of all traitors would be confiscated but that their slaves would be freed. (Oakes 2007, 150)

Davis' mother-in-law, Lucretia Mott, did not respect Lincoln's position or maneuvering, not in the least: "Old Abe seemed to her more than ever a miserable compromiser, sacrificing young lives and then firing Frémont for 'personal and partisan effect'" (Bacon 1980, 180). And Mott was not alone, because Frederick Douglass "could not help noticing Lincoln's very public repudiation of Frémont and his equally public concern for the loyalty of the border states." In fact, as 1861 came to an end, "Douglass had begun to argue that Lincoln, far from being an antislavery President, was actually determined to thwart the destruction of slavery. Such, at least, was the stance he took. And it was probably just as sincere as Lincoln's continued disavowal of any intention to interfere with slavery in the states" (Oakes 2007, 160).

Historian James Oakes, though, in his award-winning book *The Radical and the Republican*, concerning the unique relationship between Frederick Douglass and the

President, asserts that Lincoln actually used cunning and deft political skills to outmaneuver pro-slavery forces: "Far from inhibiting emancipation, Lincoln actually paved the way for it by carefully securing the loyalty of the border states," Oakes contends, noting that Lincoln was masterful at shielding his true anti-slavery intentions and ultimate distaste for slavery. "By late 1861, as it became clear that Missouri, Kentucky, and Maryland would remain loyal, Lincoln began pressuring them to emancipate their slaves on their own," according to Oakes. "Abolition by state legislatures was still the only legally certain route to emancipation. Everyone knew that as soon as the first slaveholder sued his way to the Supreme Court, the chief justice – Roger Taney, author of the Dred Scott decision – would instantly declare that contraband and confiscated slaves could not be freed by any power of the federal government, congressional or executive. The same fate would have awaited Frémont's attempt to free slaves by martial law had Lincoln himself not blocked it first" (153).

Regardless, several of Lincoln's commanders persevered: "David Hunter, commander of the Department of the South, enlisted nearly 150 blacks in early April 1862 at Hilton Head, South Carolina. Following early successes Hunter's program faltered; and on 10 August the general ended it, after failing to secure the administration's support" (Wert 1979, 335).

Despite that temporary setback, the U.S. Congress took action via the Militia Act of July 17, 1862, allowing Lincoln to accept African Americans in the military. As a result, several high-ranking officers made their moves. For instance, "Rufus Saxton, who succeeded Hunter, received orders in late August to enlist 5,000 blacks, and on 7 November 1862 the First South Carolina Volunteers were mustered into service" (336). It was the "first slave regiment mustered into the service of the United States during the late Civil War," wrote Thomas Wentworth Higginson in his account about that brigade in the book, *Army Life in A Black Regiment.* "It was, indeed, the first colored regiment of any kind so mustered, except a portion of the troops raised by Major-General Butler at New Orleans" (Higginson [1869], 2009, 3). In fact, according to Higginson, despite some seemingly contradictory evidence, "my regiment was unquestionably the first mustered into the service of the United States," making it the first federal unit, with "the first company muster bearing date, November 7, 1862, and the others following in quick succession" (221).

Nevertheless, those first dominoes seemed to knock down more than a few more pieces:

> In Louisiana, Benjamin Butler went ahead and by September formed the First Regiment Louisiana Native Guards, composed of freedmen. Senator James Lane, an amateur soldier, also began a campaign to enlist blacks in Kansas. Ordered by Secretary of War Edwin Stanton to cease such activities on 23 August, Lane persisted and, by the end of October, had raised two regiments. Clearly, the question of arming blacks had largely resolved itself as these activities in the field continued. (Wert 1979, 336)

And there were other substantial pressures placed on the Lincoln administration, according to the historian, James Elton Johnson, as discussed in his 1999 University of Pennsylvania doctoral thesis, *A History of Camp William Penn and Its Black Troops in the Civil War, 1863-1865*. Those pressures, Johnson believed, began to *really* build up when enslaved black Southerners in mass "withdrew their labor from the Confederate rear," an idea he crystallizes based on a passage (page 121) in the book, *Black Reconstruction in America*, by the preeminent black scholar, W.E.B. Du Bois: "... these slaves had enormous power in their hands. Simply by stopping work, they could threaten the Confederacy with starvation," wrote Du Bois, who'd ultimately end up being hired as a professor at Atlanta College by a white officer of the 43rd USCT of Camp William Penn, Horace Bumstead, who was destined to become president of that institution following the war. "By walking into the Federal camps, they showed to doubting Northerners the easy possibility of using them as workers and as servants, as farmers, and as spies, and finally, as fighting soldiers" (Johnson 1999, 8).

Johnson, in fact, asserts that a combination of such pressures finally convinced Lincoln to recruit African Americans for the military, despite very fierce opposition from broad elements of the white community and politicians, excluding the likes of Salmon P. Chase, "Lincoln's most radical cabinet member" (26):

A fourfold combination of domestic pressures and international considerations forced the Lincoln administration to begin recruiting black troops for the war. These forces were generated first by the unexpected contributions of thousands of blacks who escaped enslavement and supported the Union in such positions as cooks, teamsters, and construction laborers. Since early in the war their suitability for combat had been heralded by Frederick Douglass and other activists. A second and third pressure on the White House came from pro-enlistment blacks and Northern whites who sought to avoid military service in a conflict viewed as a "rich man's war and a poor man's fight." If drafted under the conscription act of July, 1863, a man "could hire a substitute, which exempted him from this and any future draft; or he could pay a commutation fee of three hundred dollars which exempted him from this draft but not necessarily the next one." Consequently, poor whites and blacks frequently served as substitutes in the place of such economically independent businessmen and professionals. In addition, white advocates of black recruitment stood to benefit from the fact that the inclusion of black men in the Union army meant that fewer whites would be called upon to meet the state's enlistment quota. The fourth pressure on the White House derived from international relations. European powers, especially Britain and France, were concerned about the intricacies of post-war diplomacy in the event of a Confederate victory. Thus, by the early summer of 1863, international recognition of the South was an increasing possibility with each Confederate advancement on the battlefield. (22-23)

And despite some very early wavering on the issue of recruiting black troops, Secretary Stanton soon became convinced that using African American warriors was mandatory, according to Johnson:

> Contrary to Lincoln's reluctance on the matter, Secretary of War Edward M. Stanton advocated the arming of black men. "Almost from the time he became Secretary of War, Stanton was far ahead of Lincoln in his thinking on the matter of utilizing Negroes in the war effort." Having been won over to this view by Salmon P. Chase, Lincoln's most radical cabinet member, Stanton's position reflected a changing direction of national sentiment and policy on the recruitment of African Americans. At this juncture, however, Chase was the only other cabinet member who supported Stanton's position on black enlistment. Writing in his diary on Tuesday, July 22, 1863 Chase penned his thought on the matter. "Went to cabinet at the appointed hour […] The question of arming the slaves was then brought up and I advocated it warmly." (25-26)

WANTED IMMEDIATELY!
100
Colored Teamsters!
For the Army of the Potomac.
WAGES,
$20 PER MONTH
AND RATIONS.
FRANK PFEIFFER,
Master Mechanic.

U. S. Steam-Power Book and Job Print, Ledger Buildings

During the Civil War blacks often worked as teamsters assigned to transport huge loads for the Union Army. *Courtesy of the Library Company of Philadelphia*

In the interim, most black leaders ferociously supported the recruitment of black troops, according to Johnson, in conjunction with white abolitionists. Like Frederick Douglass, most believed that blacks fighting in the war would lead to emancipation, citizenship, and equal rights (26).

Harrisburg, PA, native Thomas Morris Chester, the first black correspondent for a major metropolitan newspaper (*The Philadelphia Press*), seemed to side with Douglass. That was despite Chester earlier advocating that blacks reserve the option to immigrate to Liberia (where he initiated a newspaper, *The Star of Liberia*) to start their own nation:

> At a meeting in Harrisburg, presided over by Chester, blacks made their position abundantly clear. They would not shrink from meeting in battle "desperate men who are struggling to destroy free institutions upon this continent," including "secession sympathizers in the north, who have been industriously attempting to reason themselves into the belief that black men will not fight." But they would do so only "when legitimately called upon by the proper authorities, that will not involve our self-respect." If, as one New Yorker insisted, the government wanted their services, then blacks should be guaranteed all the rights of citizens and soldiers. The demands were revolutionary, and no one in Washington was willing to take that leap. All Douglass could do in answer to these demands was please the potential: "Remember Denmark Vesey of Charleston; remember Nathaniel Turner of Southampton; remember Shields Green and Copeland, who followed noble John Brown, and fell as glorious martyrs for the cause of the slave. Remember that in a context with oppression, the Almighty has no attribute which can take sides with oppressors." While few questioned Douglass' assessment of the war's ultimate consequences, many were determined to seize the opportunity to wrest concessions from the government. But the authorities resisted, and such demands as black officers for black regiments were systematically denied. Andrew was able, however, to do something about matters of pay and bounty. In February he sent one of his representatives to consult with the black "Philadelphia Committee to Recruit Colored Troops." Douglass visited a few weeks later. By April, there were reports of increased recruitment in the state. Chester headed the drive in Harrisburg. In early June, 135 recruits left the city, 45 from Harrisburg, the rest from neighboring towns and Cumberland County, to join the 55th Massachusetts Regiment. (Blackett 1989, 33-34)

Still, there were some elements of the black leadership who believed that African Americans should not rush to the aid of the Union, angered by Lincoln's hesitancy to implement the Emancipation Proclamation, the president's initial vacillating with recruiting black soldiers, and the poor treatment that blacks received generally, even if they were not legally enslaved. They were also incensed about the higher pay for white soldiers compared to black warriors. Many Northern blacks had to endure lower pay (regardless of profession), segregation, and racism on almost every front that increasingly translated to devastating violence, such as the "draft" rioters attacking deprived blacks in such Northern cities as Philadelphia and New York City during the Civil War. African Americans were blamed for the war and for replacing wealthy white men with enough money to pay for the substitution services. Some of the blacks were slaves who were promised liberation, often bogusly, in exchange for military service, similar to Jeremiah Asher's grandfather, Gad, during the Revolutionary War. Poor white Irish immigrants without such replacement or substitution options and often castigated to the lower realms of the social totem pole with blacks, were especially angry and brutal towards African Americans. The "public outcries of Northern whites" came just "after the first national draft was authorized by the conscription act passed by Congress on March 3, 1863" (Johnson 1999, 24):

> This anti-draft frustration disrupted home front society in demonstrations that were largely led by poor urban whites. Anti-draft activity was often violent and nearly always directed against the African American community. Although this social upheaval did not initiate the debate over black enlistment it was a basis for continued discussion of the issue by the Federal government. Incidents of white civilian riots had previously occurred in Ohio, Indiana, and other northern home fronts. (25)

So some blacks, including those of the African Methodist Episcopal (AME) Church, did not quickly advocate that African Americans pick up arms, according to Johnson (17):

> In October, 1861, for example, William H. Parham of Cincinnati, Ohio took a representative stand against the idea of black military participation. In Parham's view it was pure folly to think that participation in the war would change the denizen status of African Americans. An emigrationist, Parham also believed in the principal of self-defense against racial oppression. Self protection, he argued, should be the sole purpose of any military training for African Americans in the United States. (27)

The AME Church was officially dedicated in 1794 by a group of African Americans angered by bygone segregationist policies of St. George's Methodist Episcopal Church in Philadelphia. It was founded by Bishop Richard Allen, a former slave of Pennsylvania's Supreme Court Justice Benjamin Chew, and had roots to the Free African Society that was established in 1787 to advance blacks' civil rights in Philadelphia. The church "followed the precedent set by the uplift projects of the Free African Society [black rights' group], and was influenced by the emergent philosophies of Black Nationalism and Pan-Africanism" (Appiah and Gates 1999, 28). The church became the center of black culture in Philadelphia and other cities with large black populations, and by default often had the strongest historical voice combating racial segregation, hatred, and even violence that was often directed against anti-slavery abolitionists; such violence many times did not occur far from where the church's main sanctuary was ultimately built at 6th and Lombard streets:

> In 1833 a demonstration took place against the Abolitionists, and in 1834 serious riots occurred. One night in August a crowd of several hundred boys and

men, armed with clubs, marched down Seventh street to the Pennsylvania Hospital. They were joined by others, and all proceeded to some places of amusement where many Negroes were congregated, on South street, near Eighth. Here the rioting began, and four or five hundred people engaged in a free street fight. Buildings were torn down and inmates assaulted on Bedford and St. Mary streets and neighboring alleys, until at last the policemen and constables succeeded in quieting the tumult. The respite, however, was but temporary. The very next night the mob assembled again at Seventh and Bainbridge; they first wrecked a Negro church and a neighboring house, then attacked some twenty Negro dwellings; "great excesses are represented as having been committed by the mob, and one or two scenes of a most revolting character are said to have taken place." That the riots occurred by prearranged plan was shown by the signals – lights in windows – by which the houses of the whites were distinguished and those of the Negroes attacked and their inmates assaulted and beaten. Several persons were severely injured in this night's work and one Negro killed before the mayor and authorities dispersed the rioters. (Du Bois 1899, 27-28)

It was at this point that blacks, likely supported by the Free African Society and its members affiliated with the AME Church, Black Baptists, and Absalom Jones' Free African Church of St. Thomas (Episcopal), realized self-defense was in order, according to Du Bois:

> The next night the mob again assembled in another part of the city and tore down another Negro church. By this time the Negroes began to gather for self-defence, and about one hundred of them barricaded themselves in a building on Seventh street, below Lombard, where a howling mob of whites soon collected. The mayor induced the Negroes to withdraw, and the riot ended. In this three days' uprising thirty-one houses and two churches were destroyed and Stephen James "an honest, industrious colored man" killed. (28)

In 1838 in fact, "on the dedication of Pennsylvania Hall, which was designed to be a centre of anti-slavery agitation, the mob, encouraged by the refusal of the major to furnish adequate police protection, burned the hall to the ground and the next night burned the Shelter for Colored Orphans at Thirteenth and Callowhill streets, and damaged Bethel Church, on Sixth Street," wrote Du Bois (29).

Yet following the near destruction of Bishop Allen's Mother Bethel, there was a culminating event for this phase of rioting in pre-Civil War Philadelphia history that actually required heavy armor to quell the debacle. "The last riot of this series took place in 1842 when a mob devastated the district between Fifth and Eighth streets, near Lombard street, assaulted and beat Negroes and looted their homes, burned down a Negro hall and a church; the following day the rioting extended to the section between South and Fitzwater streets and was finally quelled by calling out the militia with artillery" (29-30).

MEN OF COLOR

OF PHILADELPHIA!

The Country Demands your Services. The Enemy is Approaching. You know his object. It is to Subjugate the North and Enslave us. Already many of our Class in this State have been Captured and Carried South to Slavery, Stripes and Mutilation. For our own sake and for the sake of our Common Country we are called upon now to

COME FORWARD!

Let us seize this great opportunity of vindicating our manhood and patriotism through all time. The General Commanding at this post is arranging for the

DEFENCE OF THE CITY!

He will need the aid of every Man who can shoulder a musket or handle a pick. We have assured him of the readiness of our people to do their whole duty in the emergency. We need not ask you to justify us in having made this assurance. The undersigned have been designated a Committee to have this matter in charge. Members of this Committee will sit every day at

BETHEL CHURCH, cor. of 6th & Lombard Streets

AND AT

UNION CHURCH, Coates Street below York Avenue

Their business will be to receive the Names of all Able Bodied Men of Color who are willing to share with others the burdens and duties of Entrenching and Defending the City. Men of Color! you who are able and willing to fight or labor in the work now to be done, call immediately and report yourselves at one or the other of the above named places.

E. D. Bassett,	Wm. D. Forten,	Fred. Douglass,	John P. Burr,	Jas. R. Gordon.
Wm. Whipper,	Rev. S. Smith,	Rev. J. Asher,	Rokt. Jones,	Samuel Stewart,
D. D. Turner,	N. W. Depee,	Rev. J. C. Gibbs,	O. V. Catto,	David B. Bowser,
Jas. McCrummell,	Dr J. H. Wilson,	Daniel George,	Thos. J. Dorsey,	Henry Minton,
A. S. Cassey,	J. W. Cassey,	Robert M. Adger,	I. D. Cliff,	Daniel Colley,
A. M. Green,	P. J. Armstrong,	Henry M. Cropper,	Jacob C. White,	J. C. White, Jr.,
J. W. Page,	J. W. Simpson,	Rev. J. B. Reeve,	Morris Hall,	Rev. J. P. Campbell,
L. R. Seymour,	Rev. J. B. Trusty,	Rev. J. A. Williams,	James Needham,	Rev. W. J. Alston
Rev. J. Underdue.		Rev. A. L. Stanford,		J. P. Johnson,
John W. Price		Thomas J. Bowers,		Franklin Turner.

The historic Mother Bethel African Methodist Episcopal Church, founded by Richard Allen in 1794, became a primary place where funds were raised to support and recruit black soldiers. The AME Church also published *The Christian Recorder* newspaper, which presented first-hand accounts of the black soldiers' activities in the field and was circulated in many areas of the battlefront. *Courtesy of the Library Company of Philadelphia.*

It's clear that some members of the AME Church absolutely agreed with Parham concerning the right of self-defense during potential draft riots of the Civil War era, as indicated by Johnson in his reference to Matthew Galman's 1990 book, *Mastering Wartime: A Social History of Philadelphia during the Civil War*:

> "Our citizens are expecting every day that a mob will break out here in Philadelphia. And if so, it is thought, they will not only resist the draft, but will pounce upon the colored people as they did in New York, and elsewhere, and if so, we have only this to say to the colored citizens of Philadelphia and vicinity: Have plenty of powder and ball in your houses, and use it with effect, if necessary, in the protection of your wives and children." (Johnson 1999, 4)

Despite the racial animosity that blacks had to deal with, most were convinced by leaders such as Frederick Douglass and their local leader, Octavius V. Catto, that serving in the armed forces to save the Union and liberate fellow African Americans was the best long-range plan. Douglass, in fact, responded to black Philadelphians who were angered about the lower pay that black soldiers were supposed to receive compared to their white counterparts. According to Johnson, who quoted Douglass:

> There are obviously two views to be taken [...] a broad view and a narrow view [....] The narrow view [...] respects the matter of dollars and cents. There are those among us who say they are in favor of taking a hand in the tremendous war, but they add they wish to do so on terms of equality with white men.
>
> They say if they enter the service, endure all hardships, perils and suffering – if they make bare their breasts, and with strong arms and courageous hearts confront rebel cannons, and ring victory from the jaws of death, they should have the same pay, the same rations, the same bounty, and the same favorable conditions every way afforded to other men.
>
> The only question I have, and the point at which I differ from those who refuse to enlist is whether the colored man is more likely to obtain justice and equality while refusing to assist in putting down this tremendous rebellion than he would be if he should promptly, generously and earnestly give his hand and heart to the salvation of the country in this its day of calamity and peril. (44-45)

By June 27, 1863, African Americans, supported by the Institute for Colored Youth, Black Baptist preachers such as Jeremiah Asher, and Underground Railroad principals, including Jacob C. White, Robert Purvis, and William Still, organized to start the "all-black" group, Philadelphia Committee to Recruit Colored Troops, noted Johnson (41):

> Reflecting the views of Frederick Douglass and fifty-four other black committeemen, the message urged African American men to seize 'our golden moment' in the long fight for equality by joining the Union army. A number of black committeemen lived in Philadelphia's Seventh Ward where the city's largest percentage of African Americans also made their home. In addition, the process

Black leaders and politicians, such as Frederick Douglass, Robert Brown Elliott, Blanche K. Bruce, J.H. Rainey, P.B.S. Pinchback, and William Wells Brown, as well as Professor R.T. Greener, were featured in black broadsides to increase black pride and solidarity, ingredients that propelled many of the African American warriors. *Courtesy of the Library of Congress*

of convincing their brethren to enlist in sufficient numbers was facilitated by a network of social relations already enjoyed in their community. (41)

Indeed, blacks from Philadelphia's Seventh Ward seemed to be particularly enthusiastic about enlisting, according to Johnson. And it seems they came from all sectors of the area where most of the city's blacks resided, relying on more than a few social and religious institutions, including the influential and historic Mother Bethel African Methodist Episcopal Church:

> From their doorstep on Ludlow Street in Philadelphia's Seventh Ward, Abram Elsey and Emeline Harris Elsey watched the departure of many neighborhood men as they left to join the army. The [Elseys] had taken their marriage vows in 1845 at Mother Bethel AME. Church. They had been married for eighteen years and living on the same street. They probably had a chance to say so-long to their neighbor and fellow church member Isaac Wilmore, a stevedore, of 1017 Barley Street. Wilmore simply walked the few blocks from his home to enlist at the Seventh and Emiline Streets recruiting office. Already married for nine years, Wilmore was appointed the regimental commissary sergeant. He came home to Ludlow street after the war and, with his family, moved to Atlantic County, New Jersey in the post-Reconstruction era. (75)

Wilmore was not alone, Johnson notes. The desire to recruit had reached such a fever pitch that even juvenile Seventh Ward residents joined regiments at Camp William Penn:

> Another Seventh Ward recruit was John Thompson who was one of at least two underage enlistees to enter Camp William Penn on June 26. Just sixteen years old in 1863, the youngster rose to the rank of Sergeant a few months before mustering out with the rest of his company on October 31, 1865. "I always lived in Gatzmer St. 1 rear, 123 before I enlisted and [after] I was mustered out of service." Thompson remained a bachelor until 1869 when he married Angelina Bailey of Philadelphia.
> In the final months of the war on February 14, 1865, Abram Elsey also enlisted. He was assigned to the 127th regiment – the eleventh and last regiment formed at the post [although the 24th USCT reportedly departed the camp after the 127th]. Like Issac Wilmore, Elsey came home after the war and moved to southern New Jersey in the late 1880's. (75-76)

That's not to say that conditions for blacks in New Jersey were any better. "In the neighboring state of New Jersey socio-economic and political conditions were just as grim for African Americans," Johnson noted. "New Jersey held strong Southern sympathies. In fact, it was the only state in the North which Lincoln failed to carry in 1864." With the state legislatively curtailing the immigration of blacks to its territory, African Americans were also "totally disenfranchised by 1860," similar to social and political sentiments in Pennsylvania (83).

Although some New Jersey soldiers of the 3rd USCT were trained at Camp William Penn during mid-summer 1863, blacks hailing from the so-called Garden State enlisted in primarily two time periods. "From early December, 1863, to the spring of 1864, among the state's first wave of black enlistees were volunteers assigned to the Eighth, Twenty-second, Twenty-fourth, Twenty-fifth, and Thirty-second Regiments." However, the initial "recruits arrived in early December, 1863 and were assigned to Company K, Eighth Regiment." More than a few of the men hailed from Salem County's Mannington Township (84).

The 22nd USCT of Camp William Penn was especially noted to have a very heavy New Jersey contingent, perhaps the most of the 11 regiments at Camp William Penn, but also spread to other units:

> At least half of the Twenty-second Infantry Regiment came from across the Delaware River [from New Jersey], between early December, 1863 to early January, 1864. Similarly, about one third of the men in the Twenty-fifth Regiment were New Jerseyans. This regiment was devastated by a disease epidemic at Camp William Penn. Between February and May, 1864, twenty-two New Jersey recruits assigned to the Twenty-fifth Regiment died of sickness or disease at Camp William Penn. Enlistment from New Jersey appears to have slowed in the wake of the deadly epidemics. (85)

Still, Camp William Penn's commander, Louis Wagner, couldn't help but notice the influx of recruits originating from the Seventh Ward and marching through the gates of his training complex. Johnson related:

> In the post-war years Louis Wagner recalled the first time that recruits left the Seventh Ward homefront for Camp William Penn. Speaking at a Union League affair near the turn of the century, Wagner stated, "The few officers who established Camp William Penn [...] conducted the first company, recruited and mustered at Seventh and Emiline Streets, unarmed to the North Pennsylvania Railroad depot, at Third and Berks Streets [...]" Their departure from the recruiting station at Seventh and Emiline Streets in South Philadelphia was reported in the Philadelphia Inquirer[:] "they enlisted for three years or the war, and, accompanied by a fife and drum, paraded the streets in the pitiless storm [...] utterly unmindful of the beating rain." Eighteen year old laborer, Richard Smith, who was missing a finger on one hand, may have been one of the recruits producing those harmonic sounds on an instrument. Smith, of West Chester, held the rank of musician throughout his tenure of military service. His missing finger resulted from a gunshot accident four years earlier. (76)

Nevertheless, despite the push for black enlistment, some blacks "remained pessimistic about the eradication of racism as a reward for black military service," according to Johnson. A June 27, 1863 broadside produced by the group was laced with "desperation" as it tried to rally African American men to the cause: "Brothers and fathers [...] by all your desire for citizenship and equality before the law, by all your love of country [...] stop at no subterfuge, listen to nothing that shall deter you from rallying for the army" (42).

Some of the most active abolitionists supporting the recruitment of black soldiers, despite many being pacifist Quakers, posed for this photograph. Standing left to right are: Mary Crew, Edward M. Davis (son-in-law of Lucretia Mott), Haworth Wetherald, Abigail Kimber, Miller McKim, and Sarah Pugh. Seated are: Oliver Johnson, Margaret Burleigh, Benjamin C. Bacon, Robert Purvis, Lucretia Mott, and her husband, James Mott. *Courtesy of the Library of Congress.*

Meanwhile, white abolitionists and power holders began to idealistically and financially support the establishment of black Civil War troops. Edward M. Davis (Lucretia Mott's son-in-law), who would join a Supervisory Committee to organize the raising of black troops and Camp William Penn, was to become very powerful in the Union League of Philadelphia, which would provide much of the financial seed money for the facility. Davis was very well connected politically as well as economically, indicative of an advertisement he apparently took out in the Saturday, May 16, 1863, edition of the *National Anti-Slavery Standard* concerning his "STOCK AND EXCHANGE BROKER" enterprise. Located at "No. 39 South Third street, SECOND FLOOR, PHILADELPHIA, PA," Davis revealed:

I have this day [April 1st, 1863] opened an office for the transaction of a general EXCHANGE and BANKING BUSINESS, and the sale of Bonds and other Securities on Commission.

Particular attention will be given to GOVERNMENT SECURITIES, as the most reliable investments [...] As I have a prompt and reliable correspondent in New York, connected with the Broker's Board, I can execute orders there with dispatch.

Any business entrusted to me will be attended to promptly and faithfully.[1]

The league was one of many such organizations of white privileged men, started around the country to support Abraham Lincoln's policies after his rise to the presidency.

The Union League also drummed up support by publishing pamphlets extolling the bravery of blacks in the military. The Supervisory Committee eventually raised over $33,000, which paid most of the expenses of raising eleven regiments of United States Colored Troops in Philadelphia (Paradis 1998, 11).

One of the more effective broadsides published on June 27th by the "predominately white Union League Supervisory Committee to Recruit Colored Troops," according to Johnson, appealed to the historical contributions of blacks participating in previous American wars, but also expressed an annoying reality: "In two wars with Great Britain your strong arms aided to beat back the foe and Washington and Jackson acknowledged the services which you so willingly rendered. You failed in your reward then [...] there is even yet inequality of reward, and you are offered no bounty by the Government" (Johnson 1999, 41).

In fact, though, some black soldiers did receive private bounties from rich whites desiring "replacements":

> Some recruits earned a bounty that was paid by white men of means seeking to avoid the draft. Large numbers of conscripts and substitutes started arriving at Camp William Penn in September, 1864. Nearly fifty percent of the men in the second wave of recruits were either draftees or substitutes. These soldiers were assigned to the Forty-first, Forty-third, Forty-fifth, [and] 127th regiments. (85-86)

Meanwhile, such general unfairness did not stop blacks overwhelmed and inspired by the January 1, 1863 Emancipation Proclamation of Abraham Lincoln to begin organizing their group, encouraged by Lincoln's declaration that they could join the Union Army and the Confederate Army's invasion of Pennsylvania during the summer of 1863. In fact, initially, "forty-six prominent black Philadelphians had formed a committee to recruit volunteers of their race to defend the city," wrote James Paradis, in his book about the 6th USCT, *Strike the Blow for Freedom.* "William D. Forten, Octavius Catto, the Reverend Jeremiah Asher, and a host of other prominent black Philadelphians signed their names to a circular exhorting their brothers to enlist" (Paradis 1998, 11).

After all, the Confederate army had penetrated western Pennsylvania and was moving towards a town called Gettysburg, snatching African Americans back into slavery along the way. It wouldn't be long before they threatened Philadelphia itself. Many free blacks, who had never worn shackles or been enslaved, were also carried into bondage. Pandemonium swept the countryside as African Americans tried to escape in droves, many of the young men heading for Philadelphia in hope of joining Union forces:

> Salome Myers lived on West High Street in Gettysburg, adjacent to the black section of town. On the night of June 15, as Myers remembered in her diary, "the Darkies made such a racket up and down by our house that we could not sleep."

Gettysburg's African American population was hurriedly making preparations to evacuate the town. On that day, Brig. Gen. Albert Gallatin Jenkins' Confederate cavalry crossed the Potomac River at Williamsport, Maryland, and rode as far as Chambersburg, Pennsylvania, twenty-three miles west of Gettysburg. The black residents of Gettysburg and all of south central Pennsylvania were fleeing northward, correctly fearing that if they were caught by the Confederates, they would be taken to slavery [...] On July 1, Lt. Gen. James Longstreet reminded his division commander George Pickett that "the captured contraband had better be brought along with you for further disposition" when Pickett left Chambersburg for the march to Gettysburg. (Vermilyea 1996)

The Confederate army virtually left no stone unturned to capture blacks, regardless of age or sex:

One of the exciting features of the day was the scouring of the fields about town and searching of houses for Negroes. These poor creatures, those of them who had not fled upon the approach of the foe, concealed in wheat fields around the town. Cavalrymen rode in search of them and many of them were caught after a desperate chase and being fired at. In some cases, the Negroes were rescued from the guards. Squire Kaufman and Tom Pauling did this, and if they had been caught, the rebels would have killed them.

The best-known incident in which the Confederate army captured blacks occurred on the afternoon of June 16 in Greencastle, Pennsylvania, twenty-five miles southwest of Gettysburg. Between thirty and forty black women and children who had been captured at Chambersburg were brought into town in wagons. A Confederate chaplain and four soldiers guarded this caravan. As the wagons came through the town, the residents surprised the guards, disarmed them and locked them in the town's jail. The captives were freed. When Jenkins received word of this, he demanded $50,000 in compensation for the blacks, who he claimed were his property. The town leaders refused, prompting Jenkins to threaten to return in two hours to burn the town. After Jenkins rode out of town, fourteen of the blacks whom the townspeople freed met with the town leaders and offered to give themselves up to Jenkins to spare the town. The town leaders refused their offer, and the town ended up being spared as Jenkins never returned. Despite the happy ending in Greencastle, no less than fifty blacks from the Adams County area ended up on auction blocks of the southern slave markets, brought south while "bound with ropes" as "the children were mounted in front or behind the rebels on their horses." (ibid.)

A young resident, 12-year-old Mary Elizabeth Montfort, wrote a very moving passage regarding local blacks fleeing: "Today we saw Aunt Beckie. She is the colored lady who helps mother with the wash. Jennie and I love Aunt Beckie. She and some other colored people were pulling wagons or pushing wheel barrows and carrying big bundles. (ibid.)"

Aunt Beckie allegedly responded: "Yo ol' Aunt Beckie is goin' up into de hills. No rebel is gonna catch me and carry me back to be a slave again."

Another tragic story was recalled by an unidentified Gettysburg resident, concerning:

> A nigger named Jack who worked on a farm near the town. At the time when a troop of raiders was known to be swooping in our direction he said, "they'll kill all us niggers, or take us back to slavery." He was a bow-legged nigger who couldn't make much speed and he didn't have any confidence in his ability to outrun the rebels, so he crep' under a haystack and stayed without a morsel to eat for three to four days. He almost starved. (Vermilyea 1996)

The Philadelphia Inquirer, a newspaper derived from the earlier *Public Ledger* and *The Philadelphia Press* that was destined to hire the nation's first African American correspondent, Thomas Morris Chester of Harrisburg, reported in its June 30, 1863, issue:

> There is scarcely a negro left in any of the border counties of Pennsylvania.... The cooks in the kitchen and the knights of the razor have fled. At Mechanicsburg yesterday we made a dinner of peanuts, the hotel proprietor declaring that his assistants had vanished. At York the same story was told, and at Carlisle there was no variation.... Along the turnpike roads they go in gangs, seldom asking favors and nearly always having sufficient money to pay for their meals. They find no shelter from white citizens. (Johnson 1999, 39)

Yet there were many close calls, including an especially moving incident that historian Johnson noted, found in an article at the Adams County Historical Society, "Gettysburg: A Boy's Experience of the Battle," appearing in *Eyewitness Accounts: Battle of Gettysburg*:

> A number of colored people lived in the western part of town, on the first day a great many of them were gathered together by the Confederates and marched out of town... We never expected to see "Old Liz" again, but the day after the battle ended she came walking in... We all crowded around her anxious to know how she got away.... She was marched with the rest down the street and there was such a crowd that when they were opposite the Lutheran church, in the confusion she slipped into the church without being seen and climbed up into the belfry: she stayed there for two days without anything to eat or drink. (40)

The celebrated Philadelphia diarist Sidney George Fisher described the intense situation, which seemed almost unbelievable, in a June 16, 1863 entry of his diary:

> The news is that the rebels have entered Penna. in large force & have taken Chambersburg. They are said to have 18,000 men. Went to town. Attended to business. The streets were crowded, the State House bell was tolling to call the people together to enroll for the defense of the state. Telegrams came from the governor urging strenuous efforts to send men forward to Harrisburg, which the rebels, after taking Carlisle, were rapidly approaching. (Fisher 1864, 469)

By June 29th Fisher's tone was even more alarming: "The news is that Lee has invaded Penna. with his whole army, 100,000 strong, in different divisions and that his headquarters are in Chambersburg" (471). Then, in an apparent reference to the great battle of Gettysburg, Fisher continued in a July 3, 1863, entry:

> In the paper an account of the affair at Gettysburg. An advanced corps of Meade's army were attacked by a superior force of the enemy & were forced to retire after a severe contest in which our troops behaved admirably. Unfortunately, Gen'l Reynolds was killed. The whole of Lee's army and of Meade's are now confronting each other and a great battle is expected to come off, probably is now going on. It will have much influence on the result of the war. (472)

About the same time, blacks were used en masse to defend Pennsylvania's capital from the Rebels. They hailed from such places as nearby Lancaster County, most notably the town of Columbia, where blacks had repelled southern slave catchers trying to capture a runaway enslaved African about the time of the 1850 Fugitive Slave Act. In fact, "black militiamen of Columbia" who were commanded by Colonel Jacob G. Frick, "prevented a Rebel detachment from crossing the Columbia bridge in order to reach the east bank of the Susquehanna River" (Johnson 1999, 36), a development that could have led to the capture of Harrisburg and the demise of even Philadelphia:

> Although the Battle of Columbia Bridge on June 28 has been properly overshadowed by the historic engagement at Gettysburg from July 1 to 3, the significance of the former event in saving Harrisburg from capture merits scholarly attention. As suggested by battle reports of the Gettysburg campaign, only the defense and destruction of the bridge by Pennsylvania militia saved the day. A section of Lee's report on the campaign outlines the Confederate rationale for advancing against Harrisburg. A breakdown within the Rebels' communication network led to Lee's mistaken belief that the Union's Army of the Potomac was in Virginia when, in

Thaddeus Stevens was a well connected Lancaster abolitionist and politician whose name appears on Civil War recruitment posters for black soldiers. Lydia Hamilton Smith, a black woman of mixed race, helped him with much of his administrative work, serving as an executive assistant. *Courtesy of the Library of Congress.*

fact, the Yankees were crossing the Potomac into Maryland and heading north to meet the enemy in Pennsylvania.(37)

The intention of the Rebels, according to scholars, was to interrupt the railroad line between Harrisburg and Baltimore thus impacting the communication and supply lines of the Union, as well as separating Northern combat forces. Johnson cites from official records the Confederate commander Jubal Early's own disappointment in not taking the bridge, while acknowledging the incredible contributions of those black militiamen:

> I regretted very much the failure to secure this bridge, as, finding the defenseless condition of the country generally, and the little obstacle likely to be afforded by the militia [...] I had determined, if I could get possession of the Columbia Bridge, to cross my division over the Susquehanna, and cut the Pennsylvania Central Railroad, march upon Lancaster, lay that town under contribution, and then attack Harrisburg in the rear while it should be attacked in front by the rest of the corps, relying, in the worst contingency that [...] my division from the immense number of horses that had been run across the river [...] move to the west, destroying the railroads and canals, and returning back again to a place of safety. This project, however, was entirely thwarted by the destruction of the bridge. (38)

Early's views were paralleled by observing a resident of Columbia, John B. Linn, among neighbors who believed the battle at the bridge and its destruction by the black militiamen led to the withdrawal of the Rebel forces from Pennsylvania. An excerpt of a letter written by one of Columbia's citizens was very much to the point:

> The burning of our fine bridge was the turning point in the great invading Army – this the enemy have acknowledged [...] It was hard work to arouse the citizens [...] however, we got a regiment of new Militia from Harrisburg and about three hundred Citizens. 100 of them negros who did nobly and succeeded in throwing earth works in Wrightsville (the town [...] at the other end of the bridge) and with the above force – Held the bridge until the enemy came on about 5000 strong. (38)

The Rebel invasion, indeed, had fired up many black men to seek retribution and halt the Confederate onslaught. Randolph Johnston, who later joined the 24th USCT of Camp William Penn with neighbor Lloyd Watts, recruited locals to join the black Massachusetts regiments:

> Randolph Johnston wanted to fight back. This twenty-two-year-old, dark-skinned, dark-eyed man had grown up in Gettysburg and seen his family struggle for respectability. His father was Upton Johnston, one of the black church's toughest cases – recalcitrant with alcohol and notorious with women. Randolph never crossed those kinds of boundaries, but he had not been an easy case for church leaders. He had occasionally violated church discipline – it seems he played cards – and he had been, with a company of others, a "total neglecter" of

religious instruction. But the war meant something new for Johnston. Since the first days of the conflict, he had put together a company of soldiers, had drilled them, had achieved the rank of captain, and had accrued "considerable military notoriety." In the early summer of 1863, Johnston offered this "colored company" to Governor Andrews of Massachusetts, who had organized the Fifty-fourth and Fifty-fifth Massachusetts infantry regiments. But Pennsylvania wouldn't let the company go; it would sponsor its own troops of color, eventually. Johnston, however, was ready. With rumors of invaders circulating, he offered the services of his soldiers – about sixty men – to the governor of Pennsylvania. (Creighton 2005, 217)

Young black men in Philadelphia were also upset with Pennsylvania's early stance regarding the recruitment of black soldiers, including Octavius Valentine Catto. He was a very well respected professor at the Institute for Colored Youth (ICY), dedicated to providing a classical, college-level education for African Americans desiring to become teachers. The ICY, in fact, was the first such institution of higher learning in the country, headed for many years by the legendary Fanny Coppin and today is known as Cheyney University, located southwest of Philadelphia:

It was during the Civil War that Catto first began to attract public attention. In June of 1863, General Robert E. Lee's army moved northward toward an eventual showdown with the Union army at Gettysburg. The Philadelphia newspapers were filled daily with the events of the northward movement. Governor Andrew

Fannie Muriel Jackson Coppin was a former slave who became the head of the Institute for Colored Youth in Philadelphia, where many Camp William Penn recruits were students, inspired by brilliant teacher and administrator, Octavius V. Catto. *Courtesy of the Library of Congress.*

Curtin and Mayor Alexander Henry issued proclamations calling for new recruits to bolster the state militia. Ignored by most Philadelphians, the call to arms caused great excitement in the black community. Meetings were held in the black churches of the city, fifers and drummers paraded in the streets, and orations of patriotism occurred throughout the day. (Silcox, *Nineteenth-Century Philadelphia Black Militant: Octavius V. Catto (1839-1871)* 1997, 203)

The ICY, according to Silcox, served as a center for organizing the potential black warriors:

> Headquarters were opened at the Institute for Colored Youth at 715-717 Lombard Street for the expressed purpose of recruiting a black company. The students at the institute were in the center of the recruiting activity. Catto was among the first to volunteer and immediately was selected to lead the newly formed company. The institute students followed Catto almost en masse – Lombard L. Nickens, William T. Jones, Martin M. and Joseph White, Joseph B. Adger, Andrew Glasgow, Henry Boyer Jr., Joseph G. Anderson Jr., and Jacob R. Ballard leaving school to go off to fight Lee's army. (203)

The company paraded to the train station in West Philadelphia, met by crowds of jubilant blacks wishing them their best. Yet, the virulent racism in Pennsylvania that Frederick Douglass once described as the worst in the United States repelled the men's efforts to defend the Union. "Upon reaching Harrisburg, they were fully mustered in and issued equipment, but Major General Darius N. Couch, of the Department of the Army in the Susquehanna area, refused to allow them to be inducted." Couch claimed that blacks could not be enlisted for a short-term emergency because Congress had made provisions for troops to serve a minimum of three years. "Since this company was an emergency militia unit enlisted for limited services of a few months, they could not serve. Considering the dire state of the nation, Couch's view indicates his prejudice" (ibid.).

Regardless, the Secretary of the Army, Edwin M. Stanton, sent a blazing telegraph to Couch after reading about the decision in the June 18, 1863, edition of the *North American and U.S. Gazette*: "You are authorized to receive into the service any volunteer troops that may be offered, without regard to color," Stanton's telegraph declared (ibid.). However, Catto's unit had already returned to Philadelphia, according to historian Harry Silcox.

The black community and white abolitionists were furious:

> Scarcely a week elapsed after Catto's return from Harrisburg before he attended a mass meeting at Franklin Hall to protest Couch's actions. Speeches by blacks and whites decried the treatment of Catto's recruits. Major George Stearns, one of the few whites in favor of enlisting the black regiment sent to Harrisburg; William D. Kelley, the Republican congressman; Ebenezer D. Bassett, the principal of the institute; and [...] David E. Gipson spoke out for the necessity of enlisting black troops. The rally produced resolutions in which Philadelphia blacks offered to [brush] "aside unpleasant memories of the past," to look to the

future, and to ask only the same guarantees and fair play received by whites. They also reiterated their "willingness and readiness to defend the union" (203-204).

During this period many whites were happy about black men being repulsed to serve. There was rampant indignation in local Caucasian communities concerning the use of such black warriors with loaded weapons. Furthermore, many unfairly believed that African Americans could not learn the intricacies of combat, as well as lacked the conviction and courage to withstand the horrors of war.

Barred from starting and joining local regiments, potential black recruits began to look out of the state.

Months before Camp William Penn's establishment, some local blacks had learned that African American men were being recruited for two new state regiments in Massachusetts, the Massachusetts 54th and 55th. Frederick Douglass and two abolitionist-leaning brothers of the Hallowell family recruited in the Philadelphia and Boston areas. Philadelphia natives Norwood Penrose Hallowell and Edward Needles Hallowell ultimately served as top officers in the 54th and 55th and suffered terrible injuries. Their father, Morris L. Hallowell, was a very prominent Philadelphia businessman who had actually conferred with President Abraham Lincoln during the war about his huge fabric enterprises, including cotton holdings in the South that had been seized by Southerners angered by his anti-slavery stances. And Douglass' sons, Lewis N. Douglass and Charles Douglass, served in the Massachusetts 54th too (Scott, 2011).

An absorbing account of how Edward Hallowell was injured appears in the Saturday, August 8, 1863, edition of *The National Anti-Slavery Standard* in a column entitled, "Personal":

Among the wounded who arrived here from South Carolina last week was Lieut.-Col. E.N. Hallowell, of the 54th Massachusetts. The reporter of The Tribune, who saw him after his arrival, wrote:

Lieut.-Col. Hallowell was on the parapet at Fort Wagner at the time he received his first serious wound. He fell into the ditch, and while scrambling out of it he was wounded again. He crept along the beach under a shower of iron and fire, until he was picked up by his Surgeon, Dr. Stone, and his Quartermaster, John Ritchie. He was then taken to Beaufort. This gallant young officer, though suffering from his severe wounds, was calm as a Summer morning. His father, a tall, noble-looking man, in Quaker costume, was by his side, attending to his wants with parental solicitude. Lieut-Col. Hallowell says he shook hands with Col. Shaw when near the Fort, and wished him success. Saw him again just as he was about to climb the parapet. He says he has been in many engagements, but he never saw a better display of courage and dash, and all the qualities that constitute a true soldier, than the colored troops exhibited at the time of their charge on Fort Wagner. Col. Hallowell is a member of the Society of Friends, and a resident of the city of Philadelphia. The report that he gave up his sword has no foundation in fact. We saw the trusty weapon lying behind his pillow, and it showed signs of having rendered good service.[2]

Another account in the *Pennsylvania History* journal indicates:

> It was E. N. Hallowell who commanded the left wing of the Fifty-fourth during the night attack on Fort Wagner. The assault was repulsed and the Fifty-fourth suffered grievous casualties. Hallowell was hit three times and was carried to safety by his men. An editorial in *The Press* called the repulse at Wagner a moral victory for the Negro troops and commended the splendid action of Color Sergeant Carney [the first African American during the Civil War to earn the Medal of Honor], who planted his flag on the enemy's parapet and when forced to retreat, though wounded, crawled back to his own lines still clutching the colors. In the opinion of this paper, at any rate, the Fifty-fourth had proven itself in the field and the editorial therefore concluded with a plea for more white officers 'to lead these gallant men.' (Binder 1950)

Remarkably, Charlotte Forten-Grimke, a black Philadelphian whose grandfather, James Forten, was a wealthy sail-maker, business person, and pioneering civil rights' activist, founding the Free African Society in 1787 with black theologians Richard Allen and Absalom Jones, had actually met Hallowell and Shaw just two weeks before Shaw's demise. Traveling to the Sea Islands (primarily St. Helena in Beaufort County) of South Carolina to educate newly-liberated blacks during the "Port Royal Experiment," Forten-Grimke was deeply hurt by the circumstances of Shaw's death, according to a Thursday, July 2, 1863, entry in her diary:

> Col. Shaw and Major H[allowell] came to take tea with us, and afterward stayed to the shout [African American spiritual celebration and rhythmic religious dance] […] I am perfectly charmed with Col. S[haw]. He seems to me in every way one of the most delightful persons I have ever met. There is something girlish about him, and yet I never saw anyone more manly. To me he seems a thoroughly lovable person. And there is something so exquisite about him. The perfect breeding, how evident it is. Surely he must be a worthy son of such noble parents. I have seen him but once, yet I cannot help feeling a really affectionate admiration for him. (Billington [1953], 1981, 211-212)

That's not to say that Col. Shaw was perfect. In fact, there's evidence that he too may have carried "racial baggage", based on correspondence to his family and friends during the war:

> In the letters to Charley Morse we see Shaw as a white man of his times. There he refers to the debate over the use of black troops as 'the nigger question' and plays up racial stereotypes. In one letter, for example, Shaw draws upon the white man's caricature of blacks and claims that physical differences interfere with a black soldier's ability to drill: 'The heel question is not a fabulous one – for some of them are wonderful in that line – [.] One man has them so long that they actually prevent him from making the facings properly.' (Glatthar 2011)

Nevertheless, following the July 18, 1863, assault on Fort Wagner, initial reports indicated that Shaw had, in fact, survived and was taken prisoner. However, that was not to be. The colonel had been killed and buried in a mass grave with his black comrades. Grimke-Forten was clearly disappointed and wrote in her Friday, July 24th entry:

> To-day the news of Col. Shaw's death is confirmed. There can no longer be any doubt. It makes me sad, sad at heart. They say he sprang upon the parapet of the fort and cried "Onward, my brave boys, onward"; then fell, pierced with wounds. I know it was a glorious death. But oh, it is hard, very hard for the young wife, so late a bride, for the invalid mother, whose only and most dearly loved son he was, – that heroic mother who rejoiced in the position which he occupied as colonel of a colored regiment. My heart bleeds for her. His death is a very sad loss to us. I recall him as a much loved friend. Yet I saw him but a few times. Oh what must it be to the wife and the mother. Oh it is terrible. It seems very, very hard that

THE GALLANT CHARGE OF THE FIFTY FOURTH MASSACHUSETTS (COLORED) REGIMENT,
On the Rebel works at Fort Wagner, Morris Island near Charleston. July 18ᵗʰ 1863, and death of Colonel Robᵗ G. Shaw

The 54th Massachusetts Infantry, led by Col. Robert Gould Shaw, fought in South Carolina at the battle for Fort Wagner of July 18, 1863, about the time that the abolitionist Frederick Douglass spoke to the 3rd United States Colored Troops at Camp William Penn. Two of Douglass' sons served with the 54th and 55th regiments of Massachusetts. A large number of black Philadelphians traveled to Massachusetts to join those regiments before federal soldiers were recruited in Pennsylvania. Shaw and many of his courageous black soldiers died during the assault but received national praise. This lithograph was originally designed by Currier and Ives in 1863. *Courtesy of the Library of Congress*

the best and the noblest must be the earliest called away. Especially has it been so throughout this dreadful war. (Billington [1953] 1981, 216-217)

Following the battle, the Saturday, August 22, 1863, edition of the *National Anti-Slavery Standard* reported that Hallowell had been promoted: "Lieut.-Col. Hallowell, of the Massachusetts 54th regiment, has been promoted to the place made vacant by the death of Col. Shaw. He is said to be fast recovering from the wound received in the late attack on Fort Wagner, and he will doubtless be found at the head of his regiment at an early day."[3]

Many of the men (up to 1,500) who enlisted in those out-of-state regiments were from the Philadelphia area, including Lancaster County, where the Confederates had been rampaging just before the bloody Gettysburg engagement in July 1863:

> Twenty-six Lancaster Countians served in the Massachusetts Fifty-fourth Volunteers, and perhaps the most famous of these was Stephen Swails, a native of Columbia who was enrolled in Elmira, New York, and because of bravery in battle was recommended for two promotions. Racial prejudice delayed his promotions to first lieutenant almost to the end of the war. (Hopkins 1997, 182)

Swails and other Pennsylvania blacks had to be encouraged by Lincoln's Emancipation Proclamation, which took effect seven months earlier on January 1st, despite initial reservations by black and white abolitionists, including Lucretia Mott:

> Radical abolitionists, Lucretia among them, were not appeased by Lincoln's Emancipation Proclamation of January 1, 1863. Read closely, it freed slaves only in the rebel areas, over which the federal government had no control. It specifically exempted all areas under federal military occupation and did nothing to disturb slavery in the loyal border states. Still she felt hopeful that 1863 might become the year of Jubilee, despite her lack of faith in the carnal weapons. (Bacon 1980, 182)

And with the Union seemingly on the retreat so often since the proclamation that provided for the recruitment of black troops, despite the government very slowly recruiting, by June 7, 1863, black troops at Milliken's Bend, near Vicksburg, Mississippi, on the Mississippi River, performed courageously defending a "post," despite their minimal training:

> This post was defended mainly by two new regiments of contrabands. Untrained and armed with old muskets, most of the black troops nevertheless fought desperately. With the aid of two gunboats they finally drove off the enemy. For raw troops, wrote [General] Grant, the freedmen "behaved well." Assistant Secretary of War Dana, still with Grant's army, spoke with more enthusiasm. "The bravery of the blacks," he declared, "completely revolutionized the sentiment of the army with regard to the employment of negro troops. I heard prominent officers who formerly in private had sneered at the idea of negroes fighting express themselves after that as heartily in favor of it." (McPherson 1997, 634)

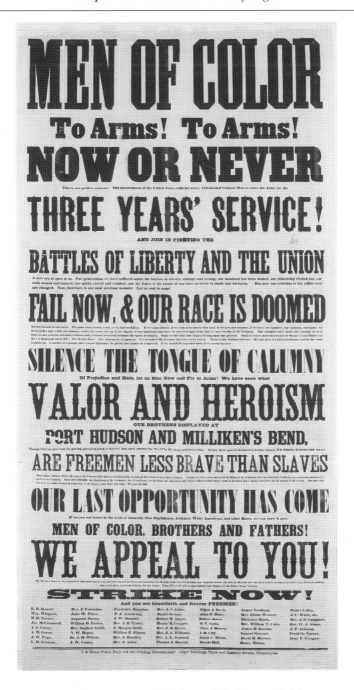

The battle at Milliken's Bend, fought June 7, 1863, featured black troops fighting courageously during the Vicksburg Campaign. Their bravery received praise from General Grant. Such developments were often displayed in the recruiting broadsides for African American soldiers. *Courtesy of the Library Company of Philadelphia.*

Yet, the 54th Massachusetts' valor at the battle for Fort Wagner in South Carolina on July 18, 1863, would also convince authorities that blacks were essential to their Union cause, an event portrayed in the 1989 motion picture *"Glory"*. But black soldiers had to deal with the double-edged sword of racism within the Union army and combating Confederate forces on the field:

> The effects of prejudice are dramatically portrayed in the film *Glory*, which underscores the inequity of the pay which black soldiers were offered. Although the government had reneged on its promise of equal pay, the men of the Fifty-fourth did not allow their anger to affect their devotion to duty. The regiment entered battle and acquitted itself quite well at the disastrous attack on Fort Wagner, which claimed the life of their commander, Colonel Shaw. Subsequent engagements turned skeptical observers into reluctant admirers of the colored troops' bravery under fire. The mood on the home front was, however, unchanged. (Hopkins 1997, 182)

For instance, a local newspaper (*Examiner & Herald*), in June 1863, wrote about the men marching off to join their Massachusetts brethren:

> As they passed by the different stations, they loudly cheered (themselves) but, with few exceptions, received no response; but instead thereof, insulting and scurrilous remarks respecting "nigger soldiers." Even the remarks of good Union men were, in the highest degree, unfeeling, such as – "That's the right way to get rid of the darkies," "I would rather see them sent off to be killed than white men." (Hopkins 1997, 182)

Black soldiers from several Pennsylvania locales had to endure such insults, including Albanus S. Fisher of Norristown, PA, who'd eventually rise to the rank of sergeant in Company I of the 54th under the leadership of Col. Shaw, the regimental commander who was killed at Fort Wagner. However Fisher, "a 32-year old married laborer at the time of his enlistment" on April 22, 1863, apparently survived the battle (Meier 1994, 33).

Fisher had been a long-time resident of southeastern Pennsylvania: "Albanus Fisher first appeared by name in the 1850 census of Port Kennedy, Upper Merion Township, when he was a 17-year old boatman living with Leah Hector, a 60-year old black woman, and Joanna Hector, 2" (34). And 10 years later, just before the outbreak of war in 1860, he was listed in the census of that year as a 30-year-old laborer (34).

In fact, six months after Colonel Shaw's death Fisher was noted in the January 14, 1864, edition of the *Mercury* newspaper covering a "Solemn Convention" attended by black troops on Morris Island in Charleston Harbor, where the tremendous battle had occurred the previous year in July, according to the book *On the Altar of Freedom: A Black Soldier's Civil War Letters from the Front*, by Corporal James Henry Gooding, which is edited by Virginia M. Adams. He apparently spoke, but likely with so much emotion, that some in the audience had difficulty following him (33):

Sergeant Fisher was the next one announced, but as he was very much like a ship at sea, without a compass, the world will remain a blissful ignorance of his sentiments. After Sergeant Fisher's homily, the Chaplain ascended the forum and gave a very interesting exposition of the Constitution as regards slavery. (34)

Private Solomon Hazzard, "a 22-year old single farmer from West Chester," PA, enlisted in Company B of the 54th Massachusetts, "and was wounded in the left leg," likely during battle and possibly at some stage in the fight to capture Fort Wagner.

George Price, 30, of Montrose, in Susquehanna County, was a farmer when he enlisted "under Col. Hallowell, at Readsville, Massachusetts, on March 21, 1863, mustered in at Camp Meigs on March 30, and was reported missing since July 18. It was assumed that he was killed on July 18 during the assault on Fort Wagner, South Carolina. His body was never recovered and was presumed to have been burned or buried by the Rebels" (99-100).

Likely in an effort for Price's widow to gain pension benefits following the war, several of his fellow warriors testified "that they had known George Price and his widow since before the war" and were members of the 54th Massachusetts' Company C:

[The men] were engaged in the attack upon Fort Wagner, Charleston Harbor, S.C., on the 18th day of July, 1863, with their Co. & Reg. & other Regts., that when they marched out of camp and went to the Island, and when they commenced the attack upon the Fort, marching up from the beach and storming said Fort, he said George Price was with them side by [side] and his Co. & Regt. fighting [...] as bravely as any one could – they distinctly recollect seeing him on the march up towards the Fort in his proper place in the Ranks – but in the darkness and hurry of the hour they did not see him again, nor see him actually fall but they firmly believe and have no doubt that he was killed then and there while storming said Fort, and his body fell into the hands of the rebels and was buried or burned by them, as they have never seen or been able to hear from or learn anything about him from that night to the present time. (100)

The detailed description continues, as the testimony is clearly in support of Price and his widow, with many survivors of black soldiers finding it exceedingly difficult to obtain pensions following the war, including many from Camp William Penn:

Four other members of the Regt. were taken prisoners, and afterwards exchanged and returned to the Co., and they said he was not among the prisoners – that he was a brave, steady soldier, doing his duty faithfully, and they have no doubt whatsoever that he fell and died on the night of the 18th day of July 1863 at Fort Wagner, S.C., and so close up to or on the rampart or parapets that his body could not be recovered by his friends and fell into the hands of the Rebels, that some two weeks afterwards the Rebel prisoners then taken from the Rifle Pits told deponents that on the morning of the 19th (after the night of the battle) they buried Col. Shaw and twenty three other of the Colored Regt. (54th Mass.) who were killed in the attack – and witnesses believe that the body of George Price was among the number. (100)

Although very few, if any blacks fought at the battle of Gettysburg in early July, the 54th's valor and Northern realization that the Union was severely jeopardized, propelled Lincoln to expedite the recruitment of black federal soldiers at Camp William Penn:

> Until the Battle of Gettysburg, Negro troops had not played a prominent part in the northern armies. Pennsylvania had had no colored units enlisted, and in Philadelphia as elsewhere there had been strong prejudice against recruiting Negroes. But the invasion crisis changed this picture [...] One Negro company which had been rejected a week previously and had returned to Philadelphia was now accepted at Harrisburg. (Calderhead 1961)

President Lincoln, near the end of the first week in July, had already realized the significance of the Confederate's defeat at Gettysburg, as described on July 6, 1863, by the diarist Sidney George Fisher:

> The news is that Lee's army was signally defeated on Friday and on Saturday was withdrawing to the South Mountain pass, pursued by Meade and also Couch from Harrisburg with 18,000 men. It is supposed that Lee will try to escape to the South Mountain into Virginia, but his pontoon train at Williamsport has been burnt by Gen'l French & the rains have swollen the Potomac. Gen'l Longstreet is a prisoner in our hands. The battle was a dreadful one – loss on our side said to be 20,000, on the other 30,000, tho these figures were probably exaggerated. We have taken from 10,000 to 15,000 prisoners. (Fisher 1864, 472)

Fisher, in fact, wrote a lengthy article entitled "Our Black Army," showing his vehement support for recruiting blacks to fight in the war. Yet, he also asserted that African Americans would be fighting the war for the primary purpose of winning their liberty:

> We are fighting for an empire; they wish to fight the same battle for freedom. We are fighting that we may have a government worthy of the name, able to protect us in our civil and political rights; they ask to be permitted to fight in the vague and uncertain hope that they may be regarded as men, and not as merchandise; that they may henceforth belong to themselves, and not be bred for sale and bought and sold like the beasts of the field. Is not their purpose and hope as lofty as ours? Let us then fight side by side in this war. (*North American*, June 24, 1863)

In fact, most African Americans – and more than a few white prominent citizens – began to move cohesively together to muster black troops, mindful of the incredible Confederate threat to the Union and the country's destiny:

A group of white citizens of Philadelphia – a city of 'strong, widespread anti-Negro sentiment' – met on 23 March 1863 to organize a committee to recruit for black regiments. Colonel William Frismuth, a former cavalry officer, was selected as chairman. 'All appeared very enthusiastic in the new understanding,' a newspaper correspondent reported. Five thousand circulars were ordered to be distributed to blacks and several letters from wealthy blacks offering $60,000 to finance the drive were read. Frismuth asserted that he had assurances of support from Lincoln, Stanton, and Curtin. (Wert 1979, 337)

James Logan, an influential delegate, was asked to travel to Washington in order to secure the permission in writing. A couple of days later Governor Curtin, while visiting Philadelphia, said that "immediate authority would be forthcoming to form a brigade of 5,500 men" (ibid.).

Logan returned a day or two later with great news for the committee, indicating that written authority would be soon granted. "Logan also reported that he spoke with a Mr. Holmes, a black from the interior of the state, who claimed that many of his people were willing to enlist" (ibid.).

In reality, committee members began to fear that Massachusetts recruiters were poised to accept Pennsylvania blacks who might otherwise be pleased to join a local regiment. "After Colonel Frismuth related an encounter with a Massachusetts recruiter at the Colored Institute, the committee moved to ask the Pennsylvania legislature to prevent the outside recruiting of its blacks" (ibid.).

And then, perhaps the most important development that would bode extremely well for the establishment of Camp William Penn came: "To coordinate these diverse programs by army officers and Northern states, the War Department eventually established the Bureau for Colored Troops on 22 May 1863." (336)

As anxiety began to build for the long-awaited order:

> Stanton finally conferred the department's official blessing in June 1863 on the Supervising Committee for Recruiting Colored Troops, the organization which created and governed Camp William Penn A number of local leaders now formed a committee for raising colored regiments, and on June 23 Camp William Penn was set up beyond the city limits in Cheltenham Township as a rendezvous for the new Negro recruits. Several days later Governor Curtin indirectly aided this recruitment by sending word to Philadelphia that although he did not favor employing Negro soldiers, the need for men at this time was so overwhelming that he would now agree to their use [...] In the remaining months of the war nearly 11,000 men (from all over the state) were mustered at Camp William Penn. (Calderhead 1961)

Stanton's authorization "coincided with the Federal government's establishment of a Bureau of Colored Troops" (Wert 1979, 338). Just as important, because of "this official endorsement to coordinate the raising of black regiments, the War Department actively sought volunteers. No person or group of persons could recruit blacks without specific authorization from the War Department. The Bureau appointed federal recruiters [including Frederick Douglass] and authorized the creation of recruiting stations and depots" (338-339).

The Saturday, June 6, 1863, edition of the *National Anti-Slavery Standard* reported that Special Order No. 143 indicated:

1. A bureau is established in the Adjutant-General's office for the record of all matters relating to the organization of colored troops. An officer will be assigned to the charge of the bureau, with such number of clerks as may be designated by the Adjutant-General.

2. Three or more field officers will be detailed as Inspectors, to supervise the organization of colored troops at such points as may be indicated by the War Department in the Northern and Western States.

3. Boards will be convened at such posts as may be decided upon by the war Department to examine applicants for commissions to command colored troops, who on application to the Adjutant-General, may receive authority to present theirselves to the Board or examination.

4. No person shall be allowed to recruit for colored troops except specifically authorized by the War Department; and no such authority will be given any one person to raise any more than one regiment.

5. The reports of boards will specify the grade of Commission for which each candidate is fit, and authority to recruit will be given in accordance. Commissions will be issued from the Adjutant-General's office when the prescribed number of men is ready for muster into service.

6. Colored troops may be accepted by companies, to be afterwards consolidated in battalions and regiments by the Adjutant General. The regiments will be numbered seriatim in the order in which they are raised, the numbers to be determined by the Adjutant-General. They will be designated "Regiment of U.S. Colored Troops."

7. Recruiting stations and depots will be established by the Adjutant-General, as circumstances shall require, and officers will be detailed to muster and inspect the troops.

8. The non-commissioned officers of colored troops may be selected and pointed from the best men of their number in the usual mode of appointing non-commissioned officers. Meritorious commissioned officers will be entitled to promotion to higher rank if they prove themselves equal to it.

9. All personal applications for appointments in colored regiments, or for information concerning them, must be made to the Chief of the Bureau. All written communications should be addressed to the Cadet of the Bureau, to the care of the Adjutant-General.

> By order of the Secretary of war.
> E D. TOWNSEND, Asst.-Adjt.-Gen.[4]

A vigorous program was put together by organizers to filter through good officers, initially with imperfections. However, after a bit of trial and error, it seems that an efficient process was activated to achieve the wanted goal of matching empathetic officers with the black troops, despite eventual and obvious mistakes that had heavy consequences:

> Candidates entered the USCT officers' corps via one of three ways: 1. By application to one of the special examining boards set up in Washington, D.C., Cincinnati, St. Louis, Davenport, New Orleans, and, after the war, in Richmond. 2. By application through "one of the divisional examining boards established by Ad. Gen. Lorenzo Thomas"; or 3. By completion of the short-lived officers' training program at the "Free Military School" in Philadelphia. Before the third system was developed many of the officers reporting for duty at Camp William Penn were viewed as substandard by the camp commander. (Johnson 1999, 72)

One such officer was Captain Girard P. Riley, who Wagner had singled out in the fall of 1863 as being quite insufficient, despite his great rapport with the black soldiers:

> Procuring qualified white officers for these men was an important goal of the camp's commander and the white Supervisory Committee. Hence, new officers at Camp William Penn were sometimes personally evaluated by the commander who greatly respected military protocol and combat experience. Most USCT officers met the basic qualifications. As [historian] John Blassingame explains, however, some unqualified officers slipped through the system, albeit infrequently. '[…] many of the officers did not live up to these high expectations. Some were dishonest […] Several were charged with drunkenness.' (92)

In an effort to appear unbiased and without favoritism for choosing the white officers, the bar may have been lowered too low with respect to the relatively brief training period to qualify. Still, it appears that a reasonable amount of applicants of different socioeconomic backgrounds were permitted to take the exam if they had white skin, many standing more than a 50 percent chance of being assigned:

> When the Government adopted the policy of organizing colored troops, it constituted a Board of Examiners, whose duty it is to examine all persons, whatever their rank, who make application for commissions in that branch of the public service. Major-General SILAS CASEY is permanent President of the Board. The other members of the Board, consisting of two Colonels, one Lieutenant-Colonel, one Surgeon, and one Lieutenant, who is ex officio the Recorder, are changed from time to time, according to the exigencies of the public service, but the President being permanent, the utmost regularity and uniformity of examination and decisions are secured.

Up to December 26th, one thousand and fifty-one applicants had been examined; of these, five hundred and sixty were passed, and four hundred and ninety-one were rejected.

The applicants are first examined in Infantry Tactics, Army Regulations and in regard to their general information. They are then turned over to the Surgeon for physical examination. If found capable, they are recommended to the War Department, to be appointed to such positions as they have respectively been adjudged competent to fill. Every candidate stands upon his merits – the most obscure corporal or private stands an equal chance with the most favored and influential citizen. No recommendations, however high, are regarded as any compensation for lack of qualifications, and while the best testimonials that can be offered are the evidence of faithful and competent military service in the field, it is not to be understood that actual experience in the service is an indispensable pre-requisite. A large number of the successful applicants have had no such experience, having but recently left the school, the college, the desk, farm or workshop, and by a few weeks' diligent study of the elementary books, fitted themselves for command, as Lieutenants or Captains, and in some instances as Majors and Lieutenant-Colonels. (Taggart 1864, 3-4)

And quite interestingly, a precise paragraph stating that political and social pressure to get an officer appointed would not be tolerated:

No talents, no zeal, no sympathy for the colored race, unless attended with military knowledge, and power to command men in battle, can avail; and no amount of pretence or number of testimonials of influential friends will answer the purpose; the applicant must give reasonable evidence of his ability to command. If pretence without merit, or zeal without knowledge, or mere recommendations of personal and political friends would be sufficient evidence of fitness to command, an examination would be an idle and useless ceremony. It is the obvious duty of the Board of Examiners to select the best officers possible from those who come before it. (7)

Teachers at the school were carefully chosen, at least according to the manual, based on experience and competency. Those instructors were likely told to be especially sensitive to applicants from humble backgrounds. According to Taggart:

The Committee has secured the services of well recommended and experienced officers [...] and professors competent to faithfully instruct applicants in Infantry Tactics, Army Regulations, Mathematics, and thoroughly prepare them for successful examination. The School is amply supplied with books and everything necessary to its complete organization. The Committee invites young men in civil life, who are physically sound, and especially privates and non-commissioned officers in service, who may aspire to command colored soldiers, to avail themselves of the facilities which this free military school offers. (ibid.)

TO MEN of COLOR.

Authority has been received to Raise a

REG'T OF MEN OF COLOR

FOR 100 DAYS.

RALLY, MEN OF COLOR, AT ONCE FOR YOUR COUNTRY!

Arm for the Defence of your Homes! Enroll yourselves for the Emergency. A Regiment ought to be raised within **TWO DAYS.** Chester and Delaware Counties will send **3** Companies, Bucks and Montgomery will do as well. What will Philadelphia do?

COL. TAGGART,

Late Colonel 12th Regiment Pennsylvania Reserves, will command, and the Officers will be the Graduates of the Military Board at Washington.

$50 CITY BOUNTY

Will be paid Each Man. Come, then, to Head-Quarters,

1210 CHESTNUT STREET

And Enroll Your Names.

Steam -power Job Printing Establishment, S. W. Corner of Third and Chestnut Streets, Philada.

As this poster indicates, a bounty was offered to black soldiers initially if they enlisted to fight in the Civil War. That's despite many charges of lower pay after they joined Union forces. *Courtesy of the Library Company of Philadelphia.*

And in a clear acknowledgement that Camp William Penn was the largest state or federal facility to train black soldiers during the Civil War, in an area where the standard of living was attractive, the manual for soldiers, officers and other interested folks, entitled "Free Military School for Applicants for Command of Colored Troops, No. 1210 Chestnut Street, Philadelphia," noted that an internship of sorts was also available:

> Camp William Penn, the largest camp existing for the organization and disciplining of Colored Troops, is in the immediate vicinity of the city, of easy access at low rates of fare. Arrangements have been made with Colonel Wagner, Post Commander, by which Students of this School, upon the recommendation of the Preceptor, will be allowed to sojourn temporarily at the camp and exercise the functions of officers, in assisting to drill and train the Regiments that may be organizing there.
>
> The superior comforts and cheapness of living, remarkable in Philadelphia, offer special attraction to all who may seek the advantages of the School, and especially to those of moderate means. Good board can be had at from $3.50 to $5 per week. (7)

Further, appealing to the patriotism of applicants, the manual continued:

> The Committee trusts that its efforts, by means of a Military School, to provide what the country so urgently needs at the present time – namely, applicants competent to be officers in the Colored Regiments – will be handsomely responded to by the spirited young men of the country – by those in the army, as well as those in civil life, and that it may be able to speedily furnish the Board of Examiners a sufficient number of applicants well-grounded in the knowledge of tactics, and otherwise fitted to command troops, who may pass examination and thus largely relieve the War Department from the great pressure now existing for officers to organize and train the hosts of colored men now seeking to enter the service of their country. (7-8)

Apparently, special furloughs were granted to soldiers and officers interested in applying to the school. Applicants came from many corners of the country, noted Taggart, including the young and aging:

> The rapid influx of students, from the hospitals, the army, and from almost every section of the country, varying from eighteen to forty-eight years of age, and from nearly every profession, trade and calling, has been highly gratifying to the Committee. Increased accommodations and additional preceptors in the different branches of study were promptly provided to meet the large increase of the school. (9)

For instance, George W. Baird, age 24, born in Connecticut and listed occupationally as a student in the manual, was previously served as a private in Company A of the 13th Vet. Res. Corps, but up to that point had seen no action. Entering the school on January

26, 1864, he was appointed to the rank of colonel after graduating and was destined to command the 32nd USCT of Camp William Penn. Meanwhile, Henry W. Barry, 22, of Kentucky, was listed as a teacher and served previously as a 1st Lieutenant of the 10th Kentucky. Entering the officers' school on March 3, 1864, Barry had seen action at Mill Spring and matriculated from the school as a colonel too. He'd serve with the 8th USCT Heavy Artillery unit. Then there was Delos T. Stiles, 36, of New York, who enrolled at the school January 7, 1864, listed professionally as a "Stereotyper." He had served as a captain of the 1st USCT, serving at Port Hudson and reclaiming the rank of captain after graduating, but was destined to resign for an undisclosed reason (29).

Still, at least 40 percent of the officer candidates hailed from Pennsylvania – candidates who were only given a month to pass the courses and apply for acceptance:

> Only thirty-day furloughs were available for soldiers to attend the school. This time limit meant that the student body was confined to civilians and men from the Army of the Potomac. Since Pennsylvania was the nation's most populous state in 1860, it is not surprising that nearly 40 percent of the soldier-students came from Pennsylvania regiments, many of them organized in Philadelphia itself. The school's brochure boasted that ninety of its first ninety-four graduates passed the examining board, but according to the list of names, only seventy-three received appointments. Of the 205 names listed as still attending at the end of March 1864, fewer than half appear in the volume of the Official Register of the Volunteer Force that includes the Colored Troops. It would appear, therefore, that the graduates' rate of success was less than the school's brochure intimated. Most graduates' appointments were in one of the regiments formed at Camp William Penn or in one of the Kentucky regiments that began to form rapidly in 1864 as federal armies penetrated so far south that there was little need any longer for the Lincoln administration to placate the slaveholders of that state. Nearly all these regiments served in Virginia and the Carolinas. The school's influence, therefore, was mainly regional. (Dobak 2011, 16-17)

Interestingly, the former clerk Christopher McKey, 32, was a native of Ireland and had served as a private in the U.S. Engineer Corps, putting in time at the siege of Yorktown. He

White officers were trained at this headquarters in Philadelphia to command black troops during the Civil War. Many of them were assigned to Camp William Penn following stringent exercises and lessons. The center was known as the Free Military School for Applicants for the Command of Colored Troops at 1210 Chestnut Street. *Courtesy of the U.S. Army Military History Institute.*

enrolled at the officers' training school on January 4, 1864, yet his follow-up assignment has been difficult to ascertain. Still, attendance at the school for most recruits seemed to be decent:

> The average daily attendance at the school, by the consolidated morning report, is one hundred and ninety-four. Strict military government is enforced, and the School is also formed as a battalion of four companies under command of students appointed by the Chief Preceptor to act as officers, and twice each day is exercised in the school of the company and the school of the battalion, in an excellent parade ground a short distance from the head-quarters. (Taggart 1864, 9)

Meanwhile, the manual also noted that the recruitment of black non-commissioned officers and soldiers, even from the slave state of Maryland, had certainly picked up not long after the training headquarters for white officers was founded:

> A short time since it was found, on inspection, that of over three thousand colored troops – chiefly the late slaves of rebels, enlisted in Maryland – not one could 'read, write and cipher' well enough to correctly discharge some of the duties of non-commissioned officers. At the suggestion of the chief mustering and recruiting officer for Colored Troops for that State, Col. S.M. Bowman, of 84th P.V., and late a member of the board for examining applicants for command of Colored Troops, the Committee invited active, intelligent, educated young men of color in Maryland, to enlist, with the view of becoming non-commissioned officers in regiments to be raised in that state, promising to them military teaching and training at this School. Twenty-one spirited young men of color have responded to the invitation, and have been mustered in and sent hither for that purpose. The Preceptors and the more advanced Students have volunteered to teach these colored patriots, and the auxiliary School has been commenced in the Head Quarters for the purpose of teaching and training colored soldiers for the posts of non-commissioned officers. (12-13)

In the intervening time, as the black recruits prepared at Camp William Penn in the Chelten Hills countryside, officers were also required to study, drill, and even parade:

> DAILY SESSIONS AND DRILLS.
> I. On and after March 1st, 1864, there will be THREE sessions of the School held daily, (except Sundays, and on Saturday evenings,) viz.: The First Session will commence precisely at 9, and end at 10:30 a.m., at which hour the several companies of the Free Military School Battalion will assemble in their respective armories, when the roll of each Company will be called, and absentees noted. At 10:45, the Battalion, under command of a Student, will march to the Parade Ground, on Locust street, west of the Academy of Music, where the Battalion will drill until 12 [pm], after which the dress parade will take place, the General Orders read, and the Battalion dismissed.

The Second Session will commence at 2 p.m. precisely, and continue until 3:30 p.m., when the companies will meet at their armories for roll call, after which the Battalion will march to the Parade Ground, and be drilled until 5 p.m., after which dress parade will take place, orders read, and Battalion dismissed.

Commanding officers of Companies will present their morning reports to the Post Adjutant every evening, previous to 6 o'clock, with a list of all members of the company present and absent during the day, at either session. These reports must be attested by the signatures of the Captain and First Sergeant, as required by Army Regulations.

The Evening Session will be confined chiefly to the study of Mathematics, and will be in charge of the Professors and their assistants instructing that Department. This session will commence at such hours as may be announced, from time to time, in General Orders.

An Evening Class, of Students exhibiting a high degree of proficiency and advancement in the School of the Battalion, will meet in the evening for instruction, by the Chief Preceptor, in Evolutions of the Brigade. This Division will be designated as the First Class. (18-19)

Following their overall officers' training, Washington, D.C. would be the next stop, where the candidate would appear before an examining board:

VII. It is required that all students admitted to this School shall pledge themselves to apply to the Board of Examiners, in session in Washington City, for permission to appear before that Board for examination as to their qualifications for commands in Colored Regiments, and to accept commands in the same if conferred on them, and this pledge is made on signing these rules.

When Students are passed by the Preceptor, as competent to appear before the Board at Washington, they will proceed thither without delay, as soon as permission to appear before said Board has been obtained. (22)

In fact, despite the initial formation of the 1st USCT in Washington, as well as the 2nd in South Carolina, the first official and largest federal camp dedicated to the training of Northern-based black Civil War soldiers would be Camp William Penn. That's despite evidence that some officers of the facility's first regiment, the 3rd USCT, would at first receive some training in the Washington, D.C. area, likely at Camp Casey.

However, as mentioned earlier, blacks had been fighting in the Civil War before the establishment of Camp William Penn. "Before the Emancipation Proclamation, five black regiments were in uniform," according to the historian William A. Gladstone. "They were the 1st Regiment of the South Carolina Volunteer Infantry (African Descent), mustered in federal service on January 31, 1863; the 1st, 2d, and 3d Regiments of the Louisiana Native Guard, mustered into federal service in September and November of 1862; and the 1st Regiment of the Kansas Colored Infantry, mustered into federal service on January 13, 1863." Gladstone explained that the "five regiments were eventually redesignated and amalgamated into the United States Colored Troops. The 1st South Carolina and the 1st Kansas Colored were redesignated the 33d and 79th (new) Regiment Infantry, United

States Colored Troops." Meanwhile, the "1st, 2d, and 3d Louisiana Native Guard were redesignated into the Corps d'Afrique first, and then into the 73d, 74th, and 75th Regiments of Infantry, United States Colored Troops" (Gladstone 1993, 1).

Simultaneously, there were other important early developments. "General Order No. 1, issued on January 2, 1863, from the War Department, was President Lincoln's Proclamation of Emancipation," William Gladstone points out. "The seventh paragraph gave the military the authority to 'such persons of suitable condition, will be received into the armed service of the United States, to garrison Forts, positions, stations, and other places, and to man vessels of all sorts in said service.'" Meanwhile, Rhode Island was granted permission "on January 15, 1863, to raise an infantry regiment of volunteers of African descent. This became the 14th Regiment Rhode Island Volunteer Heavy Artillery." The regiment was "redesignated the 8th Regiment U.S. Colored Heavy Artillery and then the 11th Regiment U.S. Colored Heavy Artillery." Then permission was granted for Massachusetts to raise black troops on January 26, 1863, leading to the formation of the 54th and 55th Massachusetts regiments. Ultimately, in May 1863 the Bureau of Colored Troops was officially designated (3), allowing for the mass mustering of the most federal black troops in a given Northern location at Camp William Penn and near the heart of the city.

Regardless, more black recruits began to pour into Camp Casey and Camp William Penn, many of them motivated by the Confederate onslaught that threatened Philadelphia and Washington, D.C. There were many poignant examples of Camp William Penn recruits:

Twenty-two year old Private Martin Ewing, for example, came from rebel infested York County. In the postwar period he resided in Merchantville, New Jersey and later Downingtown, Pennsylvania. James Lee's home town of Carlisle, Pennsylvania was occupied by Confederate troops on the day he enlisted. At age forty, Lee was one of the oldest members of Company A, Third regiment.

Privates John E. Dickerson and Charles Brooks had scarcely left Franklin County, Pennsylvania to enter Camp William Penn on June 26 when Rebel forces moved in. The county seat, Chambersburg, was occupied by Confederate troops on the following day, June 27. About one dozen men in the group entering on June 26, were born in the county of Lancaster which was also threatened by the Confederates. Filling out the rest of Company A were recruits from Philadelphia, West Chester, Pennsylvania, and Delaware.

Company B of the Third Regiment was organized out of the more than eighty men who arrived on Tuesday, June 30. From this group would emerge Henry James, a superb twenty-five year old soldier who was quickly appointed Sergeant-Major, the Union army's highest rank for black soldiers throughout most of the war. James, who led raids into enemy territory in Florida demonstrated superior leadership in the field, is discussed by Samuel Bates in *A History of Pennsylvania Volunteers*: 'On one occasion, a body of twenty-nine enlisted men of the Third and one private of another regiment, all under the command of Sergeant Major Henry James, proceeded about sixty miles up the St. John's in boats, rowing by night, and hiding by day, marched thence thirty miles into the interior, gathered together fifty or sixty contrabands, besides several more horses and wagons, burned store-houses and a distillery ... and returned bringing their recruits and spoils safely into camp.' (Johnson 1999, 76-77)

Still, there were others from Pennsylvania's interior who found Camp William Penn to be a tremendous magnate. Some of them, including soldiers in the Third USCT, according to historian Johnson, would make "the ultimate sacrifice" during the Battle of Olustee, in Florida on February 20, 1864:

Joel Benn of Lancaster County, Pennsylvania, for example, was assigned to the unit after bidding goodbye to his wife Philina, and their two sons Joseph and Joel, Jr., who were seven and five years old respectively. Joel Benn's parting from his family, however, was a permanent one. An excellent soldier who demonstrated leadership on the battlefield, Corporal Benn died in Florida on March 10, 1865, from wounds received at the Battle of Olustee. (77-78)

Johnson noted that at the minimum, "a dozen New Jersey Blacks were killed in the late Saturday afternoon engagement" at Olustee, and "several more were wounded," including Henry Benson, just age 18 and a native of Mannington Township, NJ, when he "was hit by a bullet in the inner thigh near his crotch. As Benson writhed on the ground in pain Samuel Robins of the same New Jersey township tried to get to the soldier but a withering Confederate assault drove off his neighbor and comrade." Sadly, and tragically, "Benson was captured by the enemy and sent to the infamous Confederate prison at Andersonville, Georgia where he spent more than a year" (84).

And Benson certainly was not alone:

At Andersonville, the wounded Benson recognized the familiar face of John S. Peacock among the prisoners. Peacock, a White acquaintance since boyhood, also recognized Benson. Decades later, at the end of the nineteenth century Peacock recalled the surprise encounter at Andersonville. 'I was in Andersonville prison […] when Henry Benson was brought in […]' Peacock also remembered the miserable conditions to which the helpless Benson was subjected. "While there he [was] laying on the ground without shelter or bed […]' Although he carried the rifle ball that struck him at Olustee, Benson survived the wound and Andersonville. Benson returned to Salem county [New Jersey] after the war and married Frances Boyar. Together they had ten children. Benson passed away in 1909. (85)

There were stories of triumph and miracles, and even betrayal, including the sordid tale concerning a soldier hailing from just outside of Philadelphia in Chester County:

Tillman Valentine, of West Chester, Pennsylvania would also fail to return to his family which consisted of his wife of seven years, Annie, and three small children Elizah, Clara, and Ida. Respectively, the Valentine children were ages five, three, and one year old. Although Tillman visited his family several times before leaving Camp William Penn for the southern warfront he may have been unaware that his wife was in the first weeks of a new pregnancy. On March 3, 1864, eight months after Tillman's enlistment, Annie gave birth to little Samuel Valentine.

When Tillman first departed from Coatesville to begin training at Camp William Penn his friends and neighbors gathered with Annie and the children as they wished the volunteer Godspeed. Elizabeth Tin, a long time family friend, was among the well wishers. Years after the event she described Tillman's sendoff: 'I saw him the morning he left to go to the war and he gave (Annie) an affectionate goodbye.' Such parting warmth notwithstanding, Tillman never returned to his family after his regiment went south but the permanence of this separation had nothing to do with physical wounds or death.

Tillman was alive and well when the war ended. Like Richard Smith of Company A and other veterans, Valentine elected to remain in the South. He was part of a post-war migration and settlement in the South by a number of black soldiers from the North. Tillman mustered out with his unit at Jacksonville, Florida on October 31, 1865. By this time, however, the Jacksonville region already held irresistible attractions for Sergeant Valentine. He stayed and became a successful building contractor. Even more interesting is the fact that Tillman married two other women without benefit of ever divorcing his first wife, Annie. Thus, Mary Susan Alford became Tillman's second wife in either 1870 or 1871. Four children issued from this union before Mary Susan died on November 24, 1880. At her passing Tillman and Mary's youngest child was just large enough to crawl around. In a marriage ceremony eleven months later Edith Keys became the third Mrs. Valentine. This union lasted until Tilman's death from pneumonia on March 12, 1895. Edith's claim for a widow's pension, however, was challenged. (78-79)

And that challenge undoubtedly came from one of his other wives:

By April 3, 1895, when the grieving Edith finally applied for the pension in Jacksonville, Annie's rival claim had already been submitted in Philadelphia. Annie's claim was filed on March 25, less than two weeks after Tilman's passing. Three months later, however, Edith would also die at the age of forty-five. Thus ended the brief counter-claim for a widow's pension by Tilman Valentine's third wife. Now Annie had to only prove that her marriage had never been terminated. (79-80)

Such situations were not all that uncommon, with more than a few USCT soldiers restarting their lives, often in areas where they had been discharged.

There were so many others who returned home to wives, children, extended family and friends, but too often were not able to acquire pensions. Yet, they returned with the inner knowledge and peace of serving their country, looking forward to better lives for themselves and their families.

This popular broadside was used to recruit black soldiers, including many for Camp William Penn, featuring the names of leaders they identified with: Frederick Douglass, Octavius Catto, his father the Reverend William Catto, and Robert Purvis, a rich entrepreneur who was close to Lucretia Mott and her family. *Courtesy of the Library Company of Philadelphia.*

Such soldiers were originally inspired by publicity concerning the courageousness of earlier black soldiers who had not received the official backing of the federal government, but nonetheless, experienced fierce combat.

The Saturday, June 20, 1863, edition of the *National Anti-Slavery Standard* reported in the column, "The Army and the Negroes," making special note of the courageous fighting of black, state-sponsored soldiers in Louisiana at Port Hudson:

Washington, Thursday, June 11, 1863: Two companies were added to the colored regiment yesterday. This makes four regiments now mustered into the United States service here. Steps are taking to raise a full brigade of colored troops in the District of Columbia. The government is receiving numerous applications from officers commanding white troops to be transferred to colored regiments, with commissions of higher rank. The applications of some four hundred are already filed before the Examining Board here. The bloody fighting of the 1st Louisiana colored troops before Port Hudson has given a fresh impetus to enlistment.[5]

Then, under the same column, a Washington story, dated Friday, June 12, 1863, said:

The War Department to-day granted authority to Col. Wm. Birney to receive recruits for colored regiments in Philadelphia, where a working committee has been formed for the purpose, who promise two regiments when organized under officers who have passed before the Examining Board. They will be placed in a camp of instruction near Washington, with the District regiment, of which the fifth company, not regiment, as the telegraphs last night made it, is well under way.[6]

Meanwhile, Major George L. Stearns, the managing recruiter for the Mid-Atlantic States, "opened headquarters at the Continental Hotel in Philadelphia in early June." His initial funding totaled $5,000, allowing Stearns to seek "black volunteers and citizen support" (Wert 1979, 339).

In fact, the June 20, 1863, edition of the *National Anti-Slavery Standard* noted in an article "BLACK ENLISTMENTS – PHILADELPHIA" that Stearns was working hard, and with the help of its journalist, J.M. McKim:

Mr. [Stearns] is now in Philadelphia, where his presence and cooperation have been solicited by a number of leading gentlemen of that place. A memorial, signed by upwards of two hundred Philadelphians, including some of the most prominent and conservative citizens, has been forwarded to Washington, praying the government to commence at once the work of organizing black regiments in Pennsylvania, and asking for such facilities as will make the work effective. A Committee is in the process of formation to raise funds to defray recruiting expenses.

Mr. Stearns is assisted, we understand, by our friend J.M. McKim, whose relations to the cause, and the fact of his enjoying alike the confidence of the white and black communities, makes him a valuable auxiliary. Mr. McKim, though an eminently peaceable man, is not a peace-man in any technical sense of the word. He has taken an active part in the subject of black enlistments, from the beginning, and in this he has been true to his own sense of duty as an Abolitionist.[7]

Actually, the governance of the forthcoming training facility in Philadelphia had already begun to take shape:

> Prior to Stearns' arrival, a group of Philadelphians, designated as the Citizen's Bounty Fund Committee, petitioned Secretary Stanton to recruit black troops. Stanton telegraphed on 17 June that 'proper orders have been issued for raising the troops. The views of the department will be explained to you by Major Stearns.' The committee met in the evening of 19 June at the Sansom Street Hall, and it was moved that a Supervising Committee for Recruiting Colored Troops be formed. Twenty-seven men joined the committee with Thomas Webster as chairman. Sub-committees of Finance, Auditing, and Visiting were created. The Visiting sub-committee was constituted to keep minutes and to visit the training camp that would be erected, devising means of helping the black soldiers. The civilian organization which would administer Camp William Penn had been officially established. (Wert 1979, 339)

Several days later, according to Wert, the long awaited official written orders arrived by telegraph: "I am instructed by the Secretary of War, the telegram read, to inform you that you are hereby authorized as the representative of your associate petitioners to raise in Philadelphia, or the eastern part of Pennsylvania, three regiments of infantry, to be composed of colored men, to be mustered into the service of the United States for three years or during the war" (ibid.).

The potential black recruits had to be embittered or very concerned by the following stipulations:

> The orders then listed certain specifics – no bounties would be paid; troops would receive ten dollars a month, three of which will be in clothing (white soldiers received thirteen dollars); an officer would be detailed to muster them into service; and finally, one regiment would be recruited at a time. (ibid.)

Regardless, it's likely that the sweetness of the order outweighed its bitterness, at least for the moment:

> The troops raised under the foregoing instructions will rendezvous at Camp William Penn, Chelten Hills, near Philadelphia, where they will be received and subsisted as soon as they were enlisted, and an officer will be assigned to duty at that post to take command of them on their arrival and make the necessary requisitions for supplies. (339-340)

Although several sources indicate that the original site for the camp was the estate of Jay Cooke, the "financier of the Civil War" for the Union and head of his preeminent brokerage firm Jay Cooke & Co., a more level area was deemed necessary, according to some accounts:

> Whoever selected the site chose wisely. Eight miles north of Philadelphia and beyond the city limits, the training site was located near "Roadside," the home of abolitionists James and Lucretia Mott in the modern community of LaMott. The camp encompassed an elevated piece of land commanding a splendid view of the cultivated, rolling countryside with nearby streams supplying the necessary water. In addition to the physical advantages, the camp rested only a half mile from Chelten Hills and the depot of the North Pennsylvania Railroad, thereby facilitating travel between the city and the installation. (340)

Nevertheless, there were certainly other considerations, given the racial climate of the day:

> One historian, on the other hand, stated that the camp was located to keep the black recruits out of Philadelphia. Considering the pervasiveness of anti-black feeling in Philadelphia during the war, this was plausible. However, the availability of the land, the physical attributes, and its strategic location near a railroad probably governed its selection. (339)

The July 4, 1863, edition of the *National Anti-Slavery Standard* summarized a "private" correspondence that it had received from McKim, apparently so busy that he was not able to file his regular report as the newspaper's Philadelphia correspondent:

The work of black enlistments goes on bravely here. Our most prominent citizens take a leading part in it. They give liberally and work earnestly. A committee is engaged raising funds to defray the extraordinary expenses of recruitment. They have already raised $10,000

Jay Cooke, who financed the Union's war machinery during the Civil War by selling bonds, lived near Camp William Penn. In fact, his land was originally considered for the camp, but was deemed to be too hilly. His neighbor, Edward M. Davis, a former officer under Gen. Frémont and son-in-law of Lucretia Mott, leased his nearby more level land to the Federal government to establish Camp William Penn. *Courtesy of St. Paul's Episcopal Church.*

and expect to make the amount of $50,000. T.M. leads off with a subscription of $1,000. Other Quaker Abolitionists have also given liberally. It is expected that anti-slavery men of every class, all over the State, will contribute to the funds. In what better way can they promote the great cause?

A camp, called Camp William Penn, has been established for the black recruits, and about 150 men have already enlisted. Its location is at Chelten Hills, on property of our friend E.M. Davis, and near the residence of our friends James and Lucretia Mott.

The colored people of the city are offering themselves by hundreds "for the emergency," and their services are gladly accepted. Nothing could exceed the dignity and decorum of our colored friends in this crisis.[8]

Then McKim displayed, as an example of the progress and mentality of local abolitionists, the "MEN OF COLOR OF PHILADELPHIA" recruitment poster likely produced by members of the "all-black committee." It poignantly stated that "The enemy is approaching. It is to subjugate the North and enslave us. Already many of our class in this State have been captured and carried South to slavery, stripes and mutilations," the poster noted, appealing to the men's sense of outrage and quest for justice. "For our own sake, and for the sake of our common country, we are called upon now to come forward. Let us seize this great opportunity of vindicating our manhood and patriotism through all time."[9]

Signers of the document met at "Bethel Church, SIXTH and LOMBARD streets, and at Union Church, COATES street, below York avenue," including: E.D. Bassett, William D. Forten, Frederick Douglass, William Whipper, Rev. Stephen Smith, Rev. Jeremiah Asher, David B. Bowser, and Octavius V. Catto.[10]

Indeed, the overall recruitment campaigns were quite effective:

The examination of recruiting campaigns reveals the following initial facts: In 1860, the aggregate African American population for Pennsylvania, New Jersey, and Delaware numbered 103,912 persons. More than ten percent of this aggregate population served at Camp William Penn. Fifteen percent of Pennsylvania's African American population answered the call to arms while Blacks in uniform from New Jersey and Delaware respectively represented 4.7 percent and 4.4 percent of their statewide racial group. Most of these men underwent their initial military experience at Camp William Penn.

Eighty six hundred twelve recruits officially enlisted from Pennsylvania. This was the highest number of Black soldiers raised in states above the Mason-Dixon line and the sixth highest number raised in any state during the war. Camp William Penn's first troops were recruited in Philadelphia where 22,185, nearly forty percent, of Black Pennsylvanians resided. This was the largest population of Blacks in the urban north until the end of the twentieth century.

Eleven hundred eighty five men came over from New Jersey. Beginning in late 1864, many New Jersey recruits enlisted as substitutes for economically secure White citizens seeking to avoid the Federal draft. A similar campaign in the slave state of Delaware helped to send nine hundred fifty-four Blacks to Camp

William Penn. Numerous other recruits came from states as far away as Maine and Indiana. Such geographical diversity at the camp was enhanced by the presence of foreign born enlistees who came from such places as Canada, West Indies, and Africa. Although a small number of recruits came from the elite strata of Black community life, most of the enlisted men were economically impoverished prior to joining the service and they remained so in the post-war years. (Johnson 1999, 91-92)

Indeed, a sampling of the soldiers in the 24th USCT of Camp William Penn, one of the last to leave the facility for war in the spring of 1865 before being sent off by none other than the Underground Railroad matriarch Harriet Tubman, reveals the incredible diversification of native nationalities. Hailing from the Caribbean island of St. Vincent was Thomas Jones, a sailor who mustered in on September 27, 1864. The 19-year-old, described as having "colored" skin with black hair and eyes, had enlisted for one year in Company A. In fact, Jones may have known Company A's Callis Duncan, also a sailor, but from South America, who opted to desert the camp on April 24, 1865. Records show, though, that he was returned to the facility later that day. Company B's Edward McMillan, 30 years old and standing about five feet, five inches, with a "yellow" complexion and black hair and eyes, hailed from Cape De Verde, but apparently died at Islington Hospital in Pennsylvania of an unidentified injury or illness. Charles Jones, 25 years old, stood about five feet, five inches and hailed from Barbados, in the West Indies. He was apparently mustered in at Norristown, Pennsylvania, on March 25, 1865, mere weeks before the war ended.[11]

Points of origin within the United States, however, were certainly also diverse. Company A's Peter Fuller, 18 years old, rising about five feet, four inches, had arrived from Savannah, Georgia, working there as a waiter and enlisting on August 13, 1864. The 44-year-old John Francis, described with a "light" complexion and of the same company, came from Canterbury, New Hampshire, where he had worked as a seaman. The former Evansville, Indiana, resident, Alexander Moses, age 39, with "dark" skin, hair and eyes, standing about five feet, nine inches, had previously worked as a fireman. He enlisted on January 2, 1865, for a one year term. Charles J. Johnson, 43, medium height and a laborer by trade, came from Salem, New Jersey, similar to many from the 22nd USCT of Camp William Penn. Enlisting on March 16, 1865, into Company I, Johnson reportedly died at a post hospital in Richmond, Virginia, that July following the war, but was able to make his "final statements" before expiring.[12]

There were more than a few Pennsylvanians in Camp William Penn regiments, including Samuel Morris, 44 years old and with Company G of the 24th USCT. Hailing from Holmesburg, and racially described with black "wool" hair and a dark complexion, Morris enlisted on March 10, 1865. There was also Herbert Dull, an 18-year-old from Lancaster, whose occupation had been "sailor." Enlisted into the 24th's Company K on April 4, 1865, only days before the war would end and Lincoln was assassinated on April 14th, Dull was granted a 14-day furlough for an undisclosed reason.[13]

By July 8, 1863, Fisher, the diarist, seemed elated that the Union army had garnered significant victories and was impressed with the establishment of Camp William Penn, as well as the recruitment of its first official federal soldiers into the 3rd USCT, despite great reservations concerning blacks achieving full equality:

Papers full of news of the surrender of Vicksburg, the flight of Lee, & rejoicings in Phila […] The abolitionists are trying to make what they can out of the enlistment of Negro soldiers & are likely to cause a reaction & injure their own cause & the real interest of the Negro. There is a camp of a colored regiment at Chelten Hills & speeches have been made to them by Kelly, Fred. Douglass, &c. [etc.], reported in today's paper. The orators claim equality for the Negro race, the right of suffrage, &c. All this is as absurd as it is dangerous. (Fisher 1864, 473)

Regardless, Fisher and others had to accept the incredible news of the day:

When the camp officially opened on 26 June the response by blacks was immediate. That day Colonel Louis Wagner, a former officer in the Eighty-eighth Pennsylvania Volunteers and recently appointed commander of the training site, mustered in the first company from Philadelphia. Designated as the Third Regiment of U.S. Colored Troops, the volunteers paraded with fife and drum in the streets during a 'pitiless storm.' Three days later a second company entered the army. Blacks throughout the Commonwealth and adjoining states hurried to enlist. In Pennsylvania, they came from cities of Scranton and Norristown and the counties of Schuylkill, Huntingdon, and Bedford. Two recruits walked from Lancaster. On the evening of 3 July, ninety-six blacks arrived from Buffalo, New York. By 24 July the ranks of the first regiment were filled and recruiting for a second regiment was undertaken. (Wert 1979, 340-341)

Wagner, a major while in the 88th, had the right combination of experience and frame of mind, advocating the abolition of slavery, to command such an ambitious enterprise, according to a Boston speech that he gave to the American Anti-Slavery Society. Further, Wagner believed slavery absolutely must not be extended to Western territories or states. And his early advocation of a presidential proclamation and constitutional amendment to end slavery were visionary. Excerpts of his potent words were printed in the January 15, 1864, edition of *The Liberator* newspaper, edited and published by the renowned white abolitionist William Lloyd Garrison:

I stand here this brief moment, then, that I may utter an exhortation to you who

Commander Wagner, a native of Germany, became the commanding officer of Camp William Penn after he was injured at the Second Battle of Bull Run. He received a severe leg injury, causing him to limp for the rest of his life. Wagner staunchly defended black rights and was a member of the Union League of Philadelphia, which supported the establishment of Camp William Penn. *Courtesy of the U. S. Army Military History Institute.*

are the immediate members and friends of this Society, to continue your efforts, recognizing the new opportunities, and remembering our increased responsibility to make one last, best effort for the complete overthrow of the common enemy of the country, human slavery[.] If there is that fidelity which there ought to be; if there is an appreciation of the importance and significance of this hour, this transition period, there will be engrafted in the Constitution of the country the simple amendment, when slavery has been abolished by a general emancipation act, that there shall be neither slavery nor involuntary servitude in any State or Territory of this Union, as explicit as the ancient prohibition in the Territories of the North-west.[14]

And Wagner clearly expressed his belief that the blood spent and lives lost during the war must result in complete liberation for blacks, and in essence, the nation:

At the outset of this rebellion, there was assembled at Washington a Peace Congress, supposed to contain the wisdom and statesmanship of the country, outside the Halls of Congress. And what was that wisdom in that hour? How was it proposed that we should avert this great calamity of national war? Charles Francis Adams, to the disgrace of that noble name, offered a resolution proposing an amendment to the Constitution, an amendment in the interest of slavery. And now, with three hundred thousand graves between us and slavery, with the industry and economy of the country disarranged, and with mourning and lamentation in every household in the land, in Heaven's name, may we not end this conflict by amending the Constitution so that it may be as explicitly in the interest of liberty, as in the beginning it was proposed to make it in the interest of slavery? (Applause)[15]

Undeniably, before moving on to command Camp William Penn's officers and soldiers, Wagner's toughness was proven when a Confederate bullet slammed into his right shin on the afternoon of August 30, 1862, at the Second Battle of Bull Run. The fighting had been particularly intense since about noon that day, as Rebel fire relentlessly poured onto Union troops commanded by Major General John Pope. By evening, the forlorn and defeated Northern army moved back to the relative safety of Washington, D.C., leaving behind Wagner, who was among 16,000 casualties (Scott 1999, 44).

Only age 24 and born in Germany, Wagner "had been a shining star ever since he enlisted at the outbreak of the war, rising steadily in rank and prestige. By the time he was wounded at Second Bull Run, he had already fought valiantly at Cedar Mountain, Rappahannock Station, Thoroughfare Gap and Groveton" (ibid.).

However, even before his leg wound made him unfit for duty, Wagner was compelled to return to the front just before the Battle of Chancellorsville. Unfortunately, his return was premature and the wound was aggravated, requiring Wagner to return to Philadelphia. And although it was determined that he was not ready for field duty, the young officer refused to take refuge in his civilian job as a lithographic printer, but instead took command of Camp William Penn (ibid.).

Wagner's appointment and the developments at Camp William Penn thrilled the African American community:

> During these initial weeks of enthusiastic volunteering, black citizens in Philadelphia lent their support. Mass meetings of blacks had been held in the days prior to the establishment of Camp William Penn. These activities reached a climax on the evening of 6 July at the National Hall, where a large gathering met to encourage black recruiting. A band, playing 'national airs,' preceded the addresses of distinguished speakers. Congressman William D. Kelly spoke, the first time an elected politician addressed a group of black Philadelphians. On the platform with Kelly was Frederick Douglass, who spoke at length and concluded by saying: 'Young men of Philadelphia, you are without excuse. The hour has arrived, and your place is in the Union Army. Remember that the musket – the United States musket with its bayonet of steel – is better than all mere parchment guarantees of liberty.' (Wert 1979, 41)

In fact, Wagner was often the center of activities, especially flag raisings, at Camp William Penn, as described by the August 1, 1863, edition of *The Christian Recorder*. Such episodes would send the black community virtually into a frenzy, with many whites almost just as excited, prompting them to visit the facility often via segregated public transportation:

> Last Thursday evening an immense crowd of colored and white ladies and gentlemen left the city of Philadelphia in carriages, hacks, omnibuses, and cars, for the camp of the colored soldiers to see them drill, and to see a flag hoisted. We are free to say, that no troops who have volunteered command more attention or receive more respect than the colored soldiers. They are under one of the best drillers in the country [Commander Louis Wagner] [...] The [3rd] regiment has been a comparatively short time in forming, and has evinced a degree of enthusiasm and discipline that would do credit to older troops. The camping ground is delightfully situated on an eminence of country, commanding a full view of many miles of the neighborhood. To the large number of people who were assembled yesterday afternoon to witness the drill and stamina of the regiment, a most favorable opportunity was offered. A long train left the depot of the North Pennsylvania Railroad at half-past three, filled with colored people, and another train with white persons, ladies and gentlemen, who have evinced not a little interest in the formation of colored companies. On reaching the grounds the regiment went through a regimental drill, and it is only the truth to say, that the manner in which every evolution was effected, was characterized by military correctness, and none were more emphatic in the expression of that judgment than military officers of other volunteer regiments who were present. Brig. Gen. Owen was among the officers who took part as a participant in the ceremonies. At the close of the drill, the flag was raised to the mast-head, Hon. William D. Kelley and acting Colonel Wagner, of the 88th P.V., performing that part of the day's programme. The bands, two in number, struck up, simultaneously with the

raising of the flag, "The Star Spangled Banner," which occasioned repeated hearty cheers. The flag being raised, Mr. George H. Earle came forward and addressed the soldiers and people in a thrilling and patriotic speech. He said he was very happy to have the opportunity of speaking on this occasion in the colored regiment. The reflections which their appearance occasioned, the emotions excited in him by the events of this day, were such as to prevent a flow of words that might aptly express his feelings. The spot from which he now addressed them was a consecrated one, dear to the memory of every friend of his country. Along this road marched Washington's troops, to engage the enemy at Germantown. The inspiration of the moment is divine; the inspiration of the moment is like the voice of the great Creator pointing to this last day as the commencement of the redemption and salvation of America – a day on which America has consented to accept your services to defend her life in the death struggle in which she is now engaged. Our country now calls upon the colored men to defend the flag you have just raised. That flag which is at this time especially the flag of freedom.[16]

And in reference to the black soldiers' contributions to the Civil War up to that point, Earle pointed out their heroism at "Port Hudson, Milliken's Bend and Morris Island," as he hailed the 3rd Regiment warriors' mission:

> Your enemies have said you would not fight. You have already shown how base was that charge. Could you not fight for freedom? Could you not feel for your own children? Do you not realize that when you struggle for the Union, there would be a feeling of gratitude for your hereafter? If you have not fought Heretofore, it was not from want of courage, nor from want of loyalty, nor honesty of purpose. I have been told since I came here today, in refutation of the charge of dishonesty, that no farmer in this neighborhood has had cause to complain that you have done him injury in any particular. Nothing destroyed, nothing has been stolen by any soldier in the regiment. (Applause.) I would like to see another regiment that can say as much. [The speaker congratulated the troops on the splendid fame won by the colored soldiers at Port Hudson, Milliken's Bend, and Morris Island.] Why should they not fight? The white soldiers are in a manner policemen suppressing a riot, but the colored soldiers are impelled by other motives which are additional. They are a body of men fighting for liberty, fighting for the elevation of their race, so long trampled upon by a cruel and relentless tyranny. They are moved with the spirit which found utterance from the lips of Patrick Henry: 'Give me liberty or give me death!' Therefore, I shall expect in every engagement you may chance to be in, that you will be distinguished by a courage as bold and as daring as any that has been displayed since the opening of the war. As I look upon you, I can see the light of battle in your faces, and I feel assured that you will realize all the expectations which have been formed of you. You will go forward to meet a God-defying bond of conspirators, arrayed against human progress, against democratic government, against the rights of the poor man, against every thing that is good – a rebellion in the interest of every thing that is bad. Your enemies charge that you are armed there would be no end to the outrages you would commit. I cannot

see that this false charge was sustained in any sphere of action in which you have yet been placed. Port Hudson and Morris Island have proven that you know your duty as soldiers, and as anxious to maintain a good reputation as any soldier of our army. Though your regiment is called on at the close of the fight, may your conduct be the reverse of that which your enemies predicted would characterize you. You will go forward to do battle in a great and holy cause, to sustain a noble Government, and fight for the right and for human freedom. May you always sustain that cause with courage and honor; may your strong arms hasten the day of peace; may God, who looks, I trust, approvingly on this scene, keep you in his holy keeping, and preserve this country for a future of liberty, freedom, and righteousness. [17]

For sure, within six months of 1863 the primary apparatus that would allow black troops to serve and likely save the union was institutionalized:

The accomplishments of the first half of 1863 were numerous and of outstanding importance. The recruitment of Negro soldiers had been systematized under War Department control; officer procurement had been regularized; centers had been established in the North for the reception and training of Negro recruits; and in Washington the Bureau for Colored Troops had been established to control the whole widespread machinery. The main outlines of the colored troops program had emerged. While there were to be departures from these outlines in some details, organizational and procedural decisions made during the first half of 1863 were to serve as guideposts for the raising of Negro regiments for the rest of the war. (Cornish 1987, 231)

This rare image of Camp William Penn shows the hilly panorama of Chelten Hills, likely on the property of Jay Cooke, who financed the Union's cause. Scholars have pondered whether the site above is on Cooke's property or adjacent to Lucretia Mott's "Roadside." The pathways of soldiers leading to a nearby creek are evident, along with a series of tents that dotted the landscape before the camp was relocated to Edward M. Davis' land. *Courtesy of the Library of Congress.*

The Setting, Routine, and Base Life at Camp William Penn

Situated on almost a dozen acres at the rear of Lucretia Mott's "Roadside" estate, the camp consisted initially of shelter tents for recruits and wall tents for the officers, all "neatly arranged along intersecting company streets. A headquarters tent accommodated Colonel Wagner and his staff." In fact, a "large flag pole, secured by a recruit, was erected on 15 July, the event being celebrated with a parade on the parade ground situated behind the camp area" (Wert 1979, 342). "The campground sat on a rectangular shaped plot of land which measured six hundred feet across the front and rear fences by eight hundred feet along the side barriers. Its geographical configuration followed a common pattern of real estate tracts in Cheltenham township" (Johnson 1999, 53).

Mott, in fact, was also impressed with the camp's establishment, despite her reservations as a Quaker pacifist:

> Soon eleven black regiments were drilling within sight of Lucretia's parlor window. Despite her strong feelings against war, she could not help but be interested. "The neighboring camp scene is the absorbing interest just now. Is not the change in feeling and conduct toward this oppressed class, beyond all that we could have anticipated?" (Bacon 1980, 183)

By July 12, 1863, Mott, a very well known speaker and at one point known as the most recognized woman in America:

> [Mott] accepted an invitation to preach at Camp William Penn. Whatever she thought of war, she believed these young black soldiers, too, needed her spiritual comfort. On July 12 she walked over to the camp from Roadside and was shown by the commanding officer [Wagner] where she could stand on some boxes (local legend has it that it was a drum) so that, small as she was, she could be seen and heard. Then some six hundred soldiers were marched in formation before her. She spoke to them stressing the theme of the one true religion and her own faith that the time would come when war would be no more. (185)

Camp regulations for the soldiers were identical to their white counterparts at other similar facilities (Wert 1979, 342), despite contrary charges that black soldiers sometimes did not receive as extensive and potent training as did Caucasian warriors.

Training, in fact, was said to be intense for most Camp William Penn soldiers. "The men themselves soon fell into the camp's regular training routine: 5:00 a.m. Reveille, followed by drilling throughout the day until Taps at 10:00 p.m." (Trudeau 1998, 125). And that was despite the abbreviated time periods over weeks, and sometimes a couple of months, being a severe problem for several of the regiments once they were on the battlefield:

> Most of the eleven regiments organized and trained at the camp for only two months. Military requirements at the front permitted only this brief period of rudimentary soldiering [...] As a regiment's ranks were filled and training begun, another regiment mustered in recruits. This practice continued throughout the camp's existence. Usually only two regiments shared the camp's facilities at the

same time, each in a different state of organization and training. (Wert 1979, 340-341)

The specific routine for soldiers at Camp William Penn, according to September 8, 1863 roster information, included (according to General Order no. 5), reveille and roll call in the morning at 6, surgeons' call at 6:30, breakfast at 7, sergeants roll call at 7:30, drill at 8, adjutants roll call at 9, guards mounting at 10:30, another sergeants' roll call at 11 and then lunch or "Dinner" at noon. By 3 p.m., drills were held followed by evening dress parade at 5:30, supper at 6, tattoo about 7:30 and taps, finally, at 9 p.m. (Johnson 1999, 74).

Saturday's schedule did not include the battalion drill, but companies formed at 1:30 p.m. to "Clean Camp." At 8:30 a.m. on Sunday came inspection, noted Johnson, followed by church at 4 p.m. and dress parade at 5 p.m. (74).

As with most military camps of the period, there were concerns about behavior, and even mutinous conduct, as well as desertion. For instance, Jacob Wilson of the 25th USCT's Company A, described as a 32-year-old cook from Harrisburg, Pennsylvania, enlisted in Norristown on January 13, 1865, for one year; however, he apparently deserted February 14th while on pass in Philadelphia.[18] Such circumstances may have been magnified at Camp William Penn given the racial dynamics, as well as the brutal enslavement experiences of the black recruits:

> Desertion by the recruits persisted as the most serious problem in the camp. Numbers of men deserted, either leaving army life entirely or reenlisting at another location to collect a bounty. One unfortunate deserter from the camp traveled to Delaware, enlisted as a substitute, collected his money, and, much to his chagrin and surprise, found himself returned to William Penn for training, his bounty money still in his pocket. His punishment probably consisted of being placed on barrel heads at the entrance to the camp, the usual method discomforting these

Soldiers on sentry duty at Camp William Penn seem to withstand the frigid cold weather of late 1863 or 1864. *Courtesy of the Historical Society of Pennsylvania.*

absconders. No method proved effective. If a Civil War soldier wanted to desert, he simply walked away, relatively certain that he would not be caught. (Wert 1979, 342-343)

There are several vivid desertion examples pertaining to the 24th USCT, the last regiment to depart Camp William Penn during the spring of 1865. Sergeant Elliwood W. Stevens of Company B apparently "deserted while on pass" on March 22, 1865, despite a month earlier being promoted to that rank on July 17, 1865. Josiah Allen, 25, described as standing about five feet, five inches with a dark complexion, eyes and hair, had worked as a laborer in Wheeling, Virginia, but apparently deserted Company K on May 18, 1865. A report indicated that he owed the U.S. government $36.17 for "clothes received." Twenty-year-old Charles Cooper, a Philadelphia "seaman" in Company K, mustered in April 5, 1865, just days before President Abraham Lincoln's assassination on April 14th, took off on May 18, 1865, "indebted to the U.S. government for clothing received" totaling $3.80. Yet he "returned from desertion" on July 8, 1865, "endured a trial," but was "acquitted and to receive all back pay due," obviously being able to provide superior officers with a suitable excuse. And there was Jeremiah Dorsey, a 24-year-old Pennsylvania laborer who was "apprehended as a deserter." He apparently survived his punishments, likely including a Court Martial, but was discharged before making "final statements" on June 26, 1865, following the war. Finally, Nova Scotia native James Gardner, a 21-year-old standing just five feet, three inches and a barber by profession, scrammed on May 7, 1865, owing the government $38.15 for clothing, as well as $23.86 for "ordinance lost."[19]

Apparently the desertions were also an issue with respect to the 3rd USCT, the first unit to be raised at Camp William Penn, according to correspondence that Commander Wagner received from the Washington, D.C.-based Major Lewis Foster in November 1863. The letter regards how Wagner was advised to deal with several deserting soldiers, as well as a horse and flag that were involved:

War Department,
Adjutant General's Office,
Washington, D.C., November 9, 1863

Lieut. Colonel
Louis Wagner,
Comdg Camp William Penn,
Near Philadelphia, Pa.

Sir,
In reply to so much of your letter of the 6th instant, as refers to deserters and stragglers, men in your camp from the 3rd Regiment U.S. Colored Troops,

I am directed to say that you will turn them over to the military commander at Philadelphia, to be forwarded to the regiment. This course will be pursued in all similar cases.

The flag should be sent by Express, or any other private conveyance. [It] would be in great danger of injury if sent with Quarter Masters stores. The parties forwarding, or receiving it will of course have to pay any expenses incurred.

The horse referred to cannot be transported at public expense. An officer is only entitled to transportation for his horse when moving with his command.

I have the honor to be,

Very Respectfully,
Your Obdt Servant
Lew Foster
Asst Adjt Gen'l Vols. [20]

In fact, Wagner had to even chastise officers who had gotten into the habit of residing outside of the camp, presumably to live in more accommodating housing and to escape unpleasant conditions at Camp William Penn. The following correspondence that was sent to Wagner from his commander, Foster, illustrates the issue:

War Department,
Washington, D.C.

November 17, 1863

Lieut. Col. Louis Wagner
88th Reg't Pa. Vols
Comdg Camp William Penn
Near Philadelphia Pa.

Sir,
I […] acknowledge the receipt of your letter of the 15th instant, in reference to the issue of forage to officers residing beyond the limits of the post, and am directed in reply thereto to say that all officers assigned to duty with the troops at Camp William Penn will reside at the Post, as required by the Regulations of the Army.

If it is necessary that officer's horses be kept without the limits of the Post you will issue the forage to which they may be entitled; but of this necessity you must, as commander of the Post, be the judge.

Any officer disobeying, or resisting, your orders should be at once placed in arrest and the proper charges and specifications forwarded to this office. It is of course expected that your authority will be exercised with discretion and all unnecessary causes of irritation avoided.

I have the honor to be

Very Respectfully
Your Ob'dt Servant
Lew Foster,
Assist Adjt Genl Vols.[21]

Indeed, Commander Wagner tried to contain the desertion problems at Camp William Penn as much as possible. He decided to take preventative, but very strong action, indicative, perhaps, of his personality:

> Vigilance against intruders and deserters was maintained by armed sentries who were stationed at eleven sentry posts around the perimeter of the camp and at three positions inside the campground. A parade ground of fifteen acres lay immediately outside the camp's huge front gate which faced southeast. From such positioning the sun rays would generally travel over the camp in a [cater-cornered] fashion striking first near the horse stables before passing over the field officers' quarters at the rear of the post.... (Johnson 1999, 54)

All and all, matters at Camp William Penn, even just after the first week of operation, were surely moving in the right direction, according to the July 7, 1863, edition of *The Philadelphia Inquirer*:

> A visit to Camp William Penn, at Chelten Hills, will well repay any one who takes an interest in the military operations of these stirring times. He will there see the first results of a movement which can hardly fail to prove of great importance in the arduous task imposed upon us by the Rebellion. Nearly four full companies

This lithograph of Camp William Penn shows its construction after many of the initial tents were gone. There appears to be a reasonable amount of activity, with an officer patrolling by sentries and soldiers marching in formation on the parade grounds. *Courtesy of the U. S. Army Military History Institute.*

of colored men, enlisted for the war, are there, fully equipped for service, and busily perfecting themselves, with all the apt docility of their race, in the mysteries of the school of the soldier. Scarcely more than a week has now elapsed since that enterprise was begun, yet its first fruits are already apparent, and Colonel Wagner, the commandant of the camp, is no less gratified with the progress of his men in learning the duties of their new position than with the unexampled rapidity with which recruits are pouring in upon him. [22]

In fact, recruitment efforts were quite widespread, as the following notation in the July 10, 1863, issue of the *Delaware County Republican* newspaper indicates, even in one of that county's boroughs and beyond:

COLORED TROOPS FOR THE WAR. – It will be seen, by our advertising columns, that a mass meeting of the men of color will be held in our Borough, on Monday evening next, in furtherance of enlisting colored men for the war. It is contemplated to run an excursion train, at very low fare, from Elkton, Maryland, and from St. George, Delaware, stopping at Wilmington and other stations, for the accommodation of the colored people on this occasion. A detachment of the Third Regiment, U.S. Colored Troops, now forming at Camp William Penn, near Philadelphia, will be present. The great attraction, however, will be the intrepid and eloquent orator, Frederick Douglass. We hope every encouragement will be given to this movement. [23]

That's not to say there were no complaints from the officers and men about Camp William Penn and its conditions. Indeed, the ensuing cold weather with autumn and winter made it necessary for Commander Wagner to at least coordinate the building of wooden structures for officers, meals, and eventually even schooling. "On January 2, Charles M. Fribley, the commander of the Eighth Regiment noted in his diary that it 'was a decidedly cold day. Had the companies ordered out but it was too cold for drill,'" Fribley wrote, with Wagner, who "viewed with alarm the inclement weather and a shortage of proper housing for the increasing number of recruits entering the camp" (Johnson 1999, 55).

It wasn't long before a "complex of forty-nine wooden structures had been built by the fall of 1863," with the majority having "rectangular bases and A-frame roofs," despite "a critical housing shortage" that "remained for the rank and file who were bunked in twenty barracks. The overflow was bunked in wedge tents" (ibid.). With the officers primarily housed in the wooden structures, Colonel Wager sent a pleading letter to the head of the U.S. Bureau of Colored Troops, Charles W. Foster, asking for additional center-poled Sibley tents, which he argued were larger and capable of housing at least 16 men or recruits (55-56).

Otherwise, the men were susceptible to a variety of illnesses due to the inclement weather and even exceptionally unsanitary conditions if housed in the smaller, less secure tents, Wagner contended.

As the researcher and historian James Elton Johnson noted in his dissertation, Camp William Penn was taking on the form of a vibrant and virtually self sufficient "village," replete with command accommodations, soldiers' barracks, kitchen areas, and much more:

> An observer, upon entering Camp William Penn through its front gate, which was nearly thirty eight feet in width, could immediately see the elongated sides of three of the six buildings that were controlled by the post commander. Respectively, from left to right the three structures were utilized for the combination schoolhouse/church (which was privately sponsored), the fenced-in post headquarters, and post quartermaster's unit which included a carpenter shop and stables. In linear foot measure the elongated sides (or lengths) of these buildings respectively measured one hundred twelve, one hundred twenty-five, and one hundred forty-five feet. Each of these structures also had a width (or depth) of twenty-eight feet. In addition, the post headquarters had an eight foot porch extending from three sides of its exterior walls. (62)

Augmenting the campgrounds were buildings controlled by the post command, used to take care of the sick, and to maintain horses and livestock, as well as a special well-used place for the unruly. The Guard Report Book of the 22nd USCT of Camp William Penn indicates that a soldier identified as "J. Rickets" of Company D was confined at the guardhouse the entire day for "theft" on February 21, 1864. His punishment: "To be bucked & gagged two hours on and two hours off for 4 days," actions that would later wear on the patience of the black soldiers, many of them ex-slaves forced to endure such treatment while in bondage.[24]

Other camp structures, of course, received considerable use:

> The three other buildings which fell under the post commander's control were located in the rear area of the camp. These structures included the blacksmith shop, post hospital and a building which functioned as both a guardhouse and a prison. Smithing operations were conducted in a twenty by twenty-nine feet shop that was set up near the target shooting gallery at the western rear corner of the camp. The post hospital occupied the center portion of the grounds at the rear area while the guardhouse-prison complex was situated about one hundred sixty feet away near the northern corner of the campground's rear area.

> Within the one story hospital, which roughly measured eighty-five by twenty feet, there were five sections. A twenty-four bed dormitory for patients, a surgeon's ward, an apothecary, a kitchen, and quarters for the ward master made up the entire facility. A porch extended six feet from the elongated side of the hospital which faced southeast toward the front of the camp.

> At the detention center inmates were either confined in the guardhouse which measured seventy by twenty feet or they were incarcerated in the draconian twenty square foot prison section. It would be the hospital and guardhouse/prison around which much controversy would swirl during the final eighteen months of Camp William Penn's existence. Other facilities completing the rear area of the camp included a daguerreotype gallery, a bathing pond, a creek in which clothes were

washed, and the sutler's concession where soldiers could purchase necessities and novelties. (Johnson 1999, 63)

There were a total of 44 buildings at Camp William Penn that housed two regiments. "More than two thousand men lived, ate, and performed most of their training camp duties from within these units," Johnson noted. "When fully manned, a Union infantry regiment consisted of 1,016 soldiers who were divided into ten companies – each numbering 101 men." (ibid.) Hence, Johnson remarked, barracks for the soldiers seemed to inundate the camp:

> Barracks for housing the rank and file were the most numerous structures in the camp. Completed in November, 1863, wooden barracks accounted for nearly half of the forty-four structures controlled by regimental authorities. Each regiment had ten barracks – one for each company. Sharing a common wall between them, barracks – like most regimental structures – were connected in two's. Each barrack measured approximately one hundred six by twenty feet [including] seventy-five soldiers who slept in four-man billets which measured five feet wide by twelve and a half feet long. These bunks were arranged in tiers which were three high and permanently affixed, lengthwise to the wall. A space of four feet existed above and below the middle tier. With this arrangement each man was provided a sleeping space which measured about thirty inches by six and a quarter feet [...] At one end of the structure, and occupying more than one third of the barracks, were a kitchen, mess hall, and store room. (64-65)

Line officers, compared to the average recruits, had better and larger accommodations, according to Johnson:

> The quarters for company officers (also called line officers) stood about fifteen feet away from one end of its corresponding troop barracks (the end of the barracks facing the center of the campyard.) Each of the company officers' quarters were twenty-five by seventeen and three quarter feet. Unlike the barracks system, however, adjacent line officers' quarters did not share a common wall. Instead, adjacent line officers' quarters shared a yard five feet wide. Paired line officers' quarters did share a porch, however. This was an accommodation which the rank and file barracks lacked. (65)

Apparently, notes historian Johnson, the rank-and-file soldiers would encroach on areas (including porches) reserved for line officers. That was perhaps a way to combat perceived racism, causing some controversy and at least one general order (Number 2), specifically by the commander of the 41st USCT regiment, Lewis L. Weld, to curtail or hamper such unruliness (65-66). Yet, there were areas where soldiers and officers were forced to be in the very same vicinity, despite various restrictions:

> The central building including its mess halls was one hundred eighty-five feet long by thirty feet wide. Nearly one hundred forty-six feet of the central building

was segmented into quarters for the field officers and staff of two regiments. Placed on opposite sides of the rectangle's impressive length, each field and staff officer lived and operated out of individual quarters which measured twelve and a half by fifteen feet. A flag pole surrounded by a flower garden was contiguous to the southeast end of the central building (the end pointing toward the front of Camp William Penn). Placement of the flagpole was done by enlisted men of the Third regiment which predated the construction of permanent wood framed regimental headquarters. […]

Attached to three sides of the regimental headquarters, was a porch which extended eight feet from the exterior walls. On the fourth side of regimental headquarters, at the end of the building which pointed toward the rear area of the camp, were the entrances to two officers' mess halls. Both mess halls were forty by fifteen feet. As the largest structure at Camp William Penn, the field officers' quarters had an orientation that made it perpendicular to the company officers' quarters and parallel to the porches of these latter units. The porches attached to each lengthwise side of the central building were separated from the company quarters by a one hundred feet wide courtyard upon which daily marching drills were probably conducted. Finally, completing the array of forty-four buildings set aside for the regiments were two one hundred by twenty feet units reserved for the quartermasters' officers and storerooms. The quartermasters' facilities were situated between the company quarters and the structures taking up the rear portion of the campground. (66-67)

Despite the greatly improved facilities, according to Johnson, disease still was a constant threat at camp. "In fact, disease was the most threatening of all the dangers facing new recruits," Johnson wrote. "The so-called 'camp diseases,' diarrhea and dysentery as well as malaria, and typhoid fever, were 'common to all armies before the twentieth century […] Like its counterparts, Camp William Penn would also endure the ravages of infectious disease" (56-57).

To help alleviate the problem, a very concerned Wagner issued General Order Number 10 in January 1864: "As a sanitary measure it is ordered that companies be required to use at least one fourth the ration of vinegar issued them by the government. Regimental Commanders will hold Co. Commanders strictly responsible for the execution of this order" (57).

However, Johnson asserts that Wagner's mightiest efforts were no match for the rampant disease, and remedies were all too often ineffective: "despite such preventive measures Camp William Penn recruits fell ill and died at an alarming rate during this period." Johnson points out that almost "forty recruits from the Garden State [New Jersey] died from illness within this period [winter of 1864]," many undoubtedly from infectious diseases (57-58):

The spread of camp disease and other infectious maladies were facilitated by overcrowded tents and wooden barracks that were often poorly heated and unsanitary. Sleeping either in twelve man Sibley tents or double bunked upon straw in wooden barracks with eighty or more recruits, pediculosis (lice infection) became nearly universal among the rank and file. "The big central training and distributions camps exposed every regiment that passed through." (58)

Horrific personal sanitation practices at such camps, regardless of ethnicity, were prevalent, noted Johnson and other historians, including the improper disposal of human waste:

> In late spring 1864, a damaging report by a U.S. Army medical inspector cited the numerous kitchen areas at Camp William Penn for being unclean and causing a blockage of the drainage system. Army inspector John L. Leconte's analysis focused on the relation between ineffective supervision of kitchen personnel, an apparently inadequate drainage system, and finally, the linking element of poor barracks design. Submitted to headquarters at the Department of the Susquehanna, the report stated that "the company officers do not pay sufficient attention to the police of the grounds behind the kitchens, or I would not have to record the fact that the drainage is obstructed in some places by small quantities of offal."
>
> The manner in which the quarters are built with separate mess rooms and kitchens for each company leads undoubtedly to bad cooking, waste of food, and filth, and unless the cooking is closely looked after by the commissioned officers of the companies, will fail to produce the only good effects which are desirable; viz: the instruction of the cooks and the establishment of Company [unclear]. (59)

The August 29, 1863, edition of *The Christian Recorder* reported:

> There has been complaint made of late by the colored soldiers encamped at Camp William Penn, Chelton Hill, of the bad quality of bread which was given to them. The complaints thus made induced the persons in charge of the camp to bring the matter before the Visiting Committee of the Supervisory Committee on Colored Camps. Accordingly, the Committee held a meeting yesterday morning, at the headquarters of the colored regiments, in Chestnut street, above Twelfth, when it was resolved to visit the persons who are engaged in the manufacture of the bread, and investigate the matter. Some of the bread was exhibited, which had been baked but a few days, and it was found to be so hard that a hatchet would scarcely break it. There was also a substance mixed with the dough which was not very pleasant to the sight or taste. It appears that the Government furnishes the flour, for which a good price is paid, but by some means a very bad article has been sent to the camp in return. Some of the bread shown yesterday looked as though coal dust had been mixed in the flour. [25]

The soldiers, too, complained of inferior medical treatment. In fact, one recruit was so angry about how he was being cared for at Camp William that he penned a letter to President Lincoln. He was very concerned about white soldiers being granted adequate leave for illness and home visits while the black recruits often, he said, had a much tougher

DEPARTMENT OF THE SUSQUEHANNA,

MEDICAL INSPECTOR'S OFFICE,
Philadelphia, Pa.,
March 5, 1864.

CIRCULAR.

The following extracts from Circular No. 6, Medical Inspector General's Office, Washington, D. C., Feb. 22, 1864, are published for the instruction and advice of all Officers who are so situated as to profit by the suggestions contained therein:

*   *   *   *   *   *

The exercise of a little energy and foresight on the part of Officers, in establishing Gardens for early Vegetables near their Posts, Hospitals, and even Camps, would enable them to obtain a supply of rapid growing esculents, and, at the same time, afford a healthful pastime for the men.

Many of the choicest vegetables come to perfection in six weeks from the time of planting, so that even troops in the field could often have it in their power to supply themselves with corrective articles of diet, which they could not obtain by purchase. It is earnestly recommended that Officers in localities suitable for the enterprise be requested to prepare for planting, in due season, a quantity of lettuce, radishes, carrots, &c., and some of the leguminous plants, especially bunch beans; also, squashes, cabbages, onions, corn and potatoes. A few of the condimentary and corrective herbs, such as parsley, pepper grass, spinach and mustard, which grow with great rapidity, would be valuable additions to the soldiers' garden.

(Signed)   JNO. M. CUYLER,
Acting Medical Inspector General U. S. Army.

The Medical Inspector of the Department trusts that the importance of the suggestions made by the Medical Inspector General will be appreciated, and that speedy attention will be given to the planting of a good supply of early Vegetables, in such grounds as are available for the purpose, at the Hospitals and Military Posts.

John L. Leonte

Medical Inspector U. S. A.
For the Department of the Susquehanna.

This correspondence represents the concern that some officers had about health conditions at Camp William Penn, advocating that gardens be grown to increase morale and the supply of good, clean food. *Courtesy of the National Archives, Mid-Atlantic Region, Philadelphia.*

time getting such permission. "We had boys her that died and wood gout [would have gotten] well if thy could go home," the soldier wrote. "[They] can come back as well as a white man" (Scott 1999, 48).

Another recruit reported: "My left leg is very badley affected from an old cut and the surgent here have bin giving me […] Leinament to rub it with ad it is well mixt with turpentine," he wrote. "I hav bin using it until I have almost lost the use of my leg. I have tole hm often that it was getting worse, but he will driv me off like a dog and say that he can't do anything for me" (ibid.).

The conditions at the camp were of great concern to the black populace in Philadelphia, to the degree that organizations had been setup early to try and alleviate the problems. One such organization, the Soldiers Circle Society, consisting primarily of black women associated with the Bethel AME church, was extremely active:

> This Society was formed in response to a call of the 55th Massachusetts Regiment, at Camp Meigs, Readville, July 15th, 1863. This regiment having a great number of sick in camp, called on the public for articles of nourishment; a list of necessaries was sent by this Society, for which acknowledgement was made in the *Anglo-African*, October 13th, 1863. A Committee of the society visited the Hospital at Camp Wm. Penn, making distribution of articles of nourishment to the sick soldiers therein, such as crackers, rice, sugar, oranges, lemons, and pickles.[26]

The women made up the committee that served such soldiers, and were essentially the backbone of these endeavors:

> The Committee consisted of – Mrs. Sarah Scott, Mrs. Harriet Bacon, Mrs. Mary A. Campbell, Mrs. Jane L. Johnson, President, Mrs. Esther Armstrong, Secretary. The Committee made their second visit to the Hospital at Camp Wm. Penn, March 22d, 1864, when they distributed among the sick soldiers, oranges, lemons, sugar, sweet and other crackers, pickles, canned peaches, and rice. The third visit was made to the Hospital at Camp William Penn, June 20th, 1864, when distribution was made of oranges, lemons, tamarinds, prunes, apples, crackers, and sugar.[27]

And that organization was not alone. The Colored Women's Sanitary Commission also helped out immensely. Headquartered at 404 Walnut Street in Philadelphia, its officers included the Reverend Jeremiah Asher, before he joined the 6th USCT as chaplain, as well as "Mrs. Caroline Johnson, President; Mrs. Arena Ruffin, Vice-President; Reverend Stephen Smith [a very well-known black abolitionist from Lancaster County]" (*Historic La Mott PA* 2007). Another black women's group was the Ladies Sanitary Association of St. Thomas's African Episcopal Church, the congregation that Octavius Catto's father, the Rev. William Catto, had been affiliated with after he moved his family from Charleston, South Carolina, to Philadelphia (Frank 2008, 286).

Women, in fact, were an integral part of camp life, from the aging motherly types to the younger females interested in romance, and even vice. "Despite its male centered orientation, however, it is interesting to note the assertion made by Civil War historian Mary Elizabeth Massey: "To the common soldier, the most exalted individuals in military camps were the older, more motherly souls who looked upon them as they would their sons" (Johnson 1999, 103).

Meanwhile, Camp William Penn's 45th USCT's Captain Wilhelm Von Bechtold "attempted to extinguish sexual liaisons between his troops and some of the women frequently present in the camp" via a general order of July 1864, demanding that "no woman (except the authorized laundresses) will be allowed in the Company Quarters. 1st Sergeants and Acting 1st Sergts will be responsible for their leaving the quarters as soon as their business is transacted," the order said. "During the hours that women are allowed in camp a guard will be stationed at each door of the quarters whose duty it will be to strictly enforce this order" (108).

Although the presence of some women who may have been prostitutes was alarming, it's likely that camp officers and even members of the Supervisory Committee used too broad of a brush to paint all black women visitors with devious intentions, reflecting the upsetting racist views of that society. Indeed, Johnson wrote, the committee certainly suffered public relations problems with Camp William Penn's soldiers during this period:

> Simultaneously however, the Supervisory Committee's popularity waned at Camp William Penn in late March, 1864. At that time Thomas Webster elected to cast a blanket of suspicion on black women visitors. Webster, as Captain Bechtold of the Forty-fifth regiment had earlier expressed, viewed the presence of black women among the rank and file in similar terms. Writing to the head of the Bureau of Colored Troops, Webster sought the establishment of a firm policy challenging the presence of women at Camp William Penn: "I visited Camp Wm. Penn this afternoon in company with one of the most active members of our committee. I found not less than one hundred and twenty colored women visiting it, ninety five percent of whom were harlots and half of them more or less under the influence of liquor." Revealing class antagonisms in the black community, Webster's letter also boasted support for his controversial position among "decent" African Americans. "The behavior of these women – of this class of women has been the subject of great complaint by the decent of their own color – and by all respectable persons of both sexes and of all colors under whose observation they have fallen." (115)

The researcher Johnson, in fact, insists that "Webster's missive made clear that the committee's goal was to gain control over a community of blacks who had apparently developed a flourishing underground economy and social structure which was not unlike the environs of training camps for white regiments." He cited Camp Curtin, near Harrisburg, as having the same issues that were generally overlooked (115).

Meanwhile, it's likely, according to Johnson, that an underground economy at Camp William Penn was unavoidable, since black soldiers received much less pay compared to white warriors. Furthermore, the rampant employment discrimination in nearby Philadelphia and elsewhere in the region helped to cause such illicit or unconventional behavior, attracting black and white opportunists (116):

Although a percentage of those women observed by Webster were probably working in the world's oldest business, there was a connective between such activities and the economic impoverishment of free blacks. Its practice was exacerbated by the unequal pay they received (less than half the pay of white soldiers). Such economic discrimination had natural consequences such as that detailed by Webster... From the purely economic matter Webster moved to an attack on the women's social class. 'The behavior of these people at the depot and on the cars is blasphemous and obscene to the last degree – besides they introduce syphilitic disease and demoralization into the camp. I cannot speak too strongly against the practice of allowing female visitors in the camp, whether white or colored. I therefore respectfully ask that you issue positive instructions to the Post Commander to forbid female visitors from entering the camp.' (116)

However, it seems that Webster's efforts were in vain. His criticisms caused the white officers and their black recruits to unify, at least regarding this matter concerning sexual gratification. In the end, Camp William Penn became quite similar to other such facilities, both North and South, noted Johnson:

On this one important occasion the officers and men found common cause in dealing with the authoritarianism of the white run Supervisory Committee [for] the Recruitment of Colored Troops. Following Thomas Webster's attempt to bar women from the camp, a number of officers in defense of the women and their men promptly challenged his accusations. Their views on the matter had apparently been solicited by Colonel Wagner and the officers' responses reflect support for the status quo from at least three perspectives. Several officers affixed their names to a letter containing the following statement relating to the post's military preparedness:
"Having been requested to express our opinion of the discipline and condition of this camp we beg to state that we believe it to be in as good or even better condition in every respect than we know of." From a public health standpoint Ali Waterhouse, surgeon for the Forty-third regiment, stated that there was "less syphilis in the 43rd Rgt. than in any others in similar circumstances." Signed by several officers, another letter was strongly critical of Webster's actions. In addition it suggested the social benefits of having women present in the camp. "Webster's statements are unjust & exaggerated. Our men in camp, about 2300 presently, have many female relatives and on the whole their behavior is excellent. *Only* Webster has requested that no females be allowed to visit." In the aftermath of such rebuttal Webster was effectively silenced on the women's question and they appear to have continued their visitations till the camp's closing. (117)

Meanwhile, fires at such camps were a constant threat, with arson sometimes being a possible cause. Johnson noted that "an effective fire prevention system was employed in January, 1864" at Camp William Penn:

Issued by the commander of the Twenty-fifth Infantry Regiment on January 17, General Orders number 6 directed that: 'A number of fire buckets will be placed in various parts of the camp as a safeguard against fires. Orderly sergeants of companies, Regt'l Q.M. Sgts., the Hosp. Steward at the post hosp. Sergeant of the guard at the guard house and sergeant [sic] of the post at H,Q. will be held responsible for having those buckets filled at all time. The officers of the day will inspect all the fire buckets immediately, after Guard Mounting each day and state their condition in his report. (62)

Despite the improvements, Camp William Penn still faced immense pressures from within and externally, most notably about nine months before the end of the war with the passing of the Conscription Act of July 4, 1864, according to Johnson (100). Such pressures would ultimately contribute to the facility's closing, despite lasting beyond the end of the war. Perhaps its ultimate social and operational decline was endemic to the war's culmination, which certainly was not a panacea for the tremendous civil rights and political ills that faced the nation:

A provision in the act permitted northern states to recruit soldiers in the Confederate states and to credit such enlistees against their own quotas for the draft. "Any State governor could send recruiting agents into states still in rebellion and credit all secured to any quotas within their States to which they chose to assign them." More importantly, however, an increasingly obvious uselessness of Camp William Penn reflected the changing nature of the black soldier's role as the war ground to a halt in the winter of 1864-1865. (ibid.)

Despite its eventual closing, things began to gradually improve at Camp William Penn in some areas as several notable visitors observed, including two female visitors from Allegheny County, according to an article published in *The Christian Recorder*:

On last Monday morning we paid a visit to Camp William Penn, in company with two ladies from Allegheny City, who are esteemed members of Rev. Samuel Watts' congregation. The husbands of both these ladies are at the present time in the service of 'Uncle Sam,' both of them having enlisted into the ranks of the Union army by their own free will and consent – both noble volunteers. We arrived on the camp-ground at about 11 o'clock, a.m., and there met Colonel Wagner and several other officers connected with the regiment, who were [on] their way to the city. The appearance presented by the barracks would remind one most forcibly of some little village or town in the country. Every thing looked clean and trim, the barracks being neatly whitewashed, as was the entire surroundings, the walks were smooth, and all combining to present a healthy and neat aspect. The entire campground is kept in the very best order possible under the circumstances. The visitors at the camp are composed of persons of all kinds, hues, grades and conditions – many of them having husbands, fathers, brothers, uncles, or other relations in the United States service – friends who have enlisted to aid Uncle

Sam in putting down this most wicked and unjustifiable rebellion, and to restore or bring peace to this great and once prosperous and happy nation.[28]

The visitors, including the correspondent of *The Christian Recorder* – likely its editor, Rev. Elisha Weaver, who likely associated with the accompanying Rev. Samuel Watts – noted the enhanced intellectual atmosphere too, despite some disturbing observations that clearly angered the writer:

> We noticed while at the camp a most remarkable display of intelligence and literary taste among both white and colored; while, on the other hand, we could not fail to observe the apparent indifference exhibited by others in reference to intellectual improvement, who presented a dull and indolent appearance. It is quite probable that these truly unfortunate ones never had the opportunity afforded them of possessing themselves of the advantages to be derived from a liberal education. We can only sympathize with them. But, be this as it may, these noble men have left their homes, their wives and children, and every thing that was near and dear to them, to do battle for the righteous cause of humanity and justice. Especially is this the case with colored men, who have been and are still deprived of their rights – and the question now comes up as to what these people are fighting for? They have none of the most important rights of human beings accorded them. Hence we ask, what will be the result or true condition of the colored people when the war shall have ended?[29]

The writer then insisted that the black soldiers, and African Americans in general, be treated with fairness, and if assaulted, must receive the protection of the law and its enforcers:

> The man who would dare to insult a colored person, when they have shed their best blood on the field of battle – blood equal to that of the white man, to save their country from ruin, and who, at the same time, do it under adverse circumstances, such as no other people in the world would have stood up under, does but show his own brutality and want of good sense and real decency. But the brave colored people bore up under their load of oppression with heroic fortitude – and when the Government made a requisition upon their patriotism, they sprang to arms with all lightning-like rapidity with which the royal Bengal tiger emerges from his native jungle, and took upon themselves the solemn obligations to fight for the Stars and Stripes, and to defend a Government that – won't defend them! Their bayonets gleam like the noon-day sun on every field of blood and carnage, while their ghastly corpses and bleaching bones strew the ground and whiten every plain in "bloody Dixie's land," martyrs fallen at the shrine of Liberty. And still they must be crushed beneath the Juggernaut wheels of prejudice and oppression. The brave heroes, the illustrious dead who have fallen in the strife, turn uneasily in their bloody shrouds at this continuous backward tread. Shame! Eternal shame! Ask Fort Sumter, Fort Pillow, and various other places, whether these men have not fought with brave and manly courage, and let history sing praises to their

fame and tell her story – and then will it be found that the colored soldiers of America have fought as bravely as any who ever trod her shores. This is a plain and undeniable fact. [30]

The writer then suggests penalties for the offenders:

In view of all this, we say that the man who would insult the right and dignity of the colored people, should be sentenced to a fine of not less than five hundred dollars, and made to undergo an imprisonment of ten days, for the first offence, and, for the second offence, the fine should be two thousand dollars, and imprisonment for not less than two years, nor more than four. This would teach the offender how to respect his fellow-men. In England you can have any man arrested for insulting you, or calling you out of your name. The same law should be made and enforced in this country. The example is a good one. The Democrats are saying many hard things about the colored people, which goes to show that they are our enemies, or they would never make such statements as many of them do make, and that without a shadow of truth or provocation. But as they have no other course to resort to, they think that by misrepresenting the true condition

Black recruits and African Americans in general enthusiastically supported their leaders, despite friction and differences of opinion from time to time. The "heroes" included the likes of Frederick Douglass, as well as the former U.S. senators Blanche Kelso Bruce and Hiram Rhoades Revels. *Courtesy of the Library of Congress.*

of the colored people, they can thus prey better upon the minds of ignorant and stupefied white men.[31]

The correspondent, after releasing his or her anguish, then returned to matters at Camp William Penn, acknowledging meeting a very special worker at the facility named William Still, the patriarch of the Underground Railroad:

> But let us return to the camp. We found there many of our old friends, who had enlisted. We found them all in good health, and doing well. We also had the pleasure while there of meeting with our old and much esteemed friend, Mr. William [Still], who is acting in the capacity of post-sutler. Mr. [Still] has, indeed, quite a neat and tasteful little place out there, and transacts business in his own peculiar and energetic style. His corps of assistants are indeed models of politeness and refinement, and very accommodating to their customers.[32]

Of paramount importance, Still and other abolitionists associated with Camp William Penn clearly made the Chelten Hills area earlier an epicenter of Underground Railroad activities, and fought the rampant segregation in the Philadelphia area via a fierce civil rights campaign to desegregate local public transportation. Still, in fact, was outraged when he became the victim of the apartheid-like policy while traveling to Camp William Penn, as he indicated in a letter that appeared in *The Philadelphia Daily Press*, and published in *The Christian Recorder* on December 27, 1863:

> Briefly the circumstances were these: Being under the necessity of going out to the Camp William Penn, to-day on business, I took the North Pennsylvania Railroad, and reached the ground about 11 o'clock. Remembering that pressing duties required my presence at my store by a certain hour in the early part of the afternoon, I promptly attended to my business at the camp, but as I could not return by the way I came without waiting two and two and a half hours for the down train, I concluded that I would walk over to Germantown, and come to the city by the 1 o'clock steam cars. Accordingly, I reached Germantown, but too late for the train by about five minutes, as the cars had just gone. To wait another hour I felt was out of the question; hence, I decided to take the city passenger cars. Soon one came along, with but few passengers in it, and into it I walked with a man who had been to the camp with me, (but fortunately he happened to be of the approved complexion,) and took a seat. Quickly the conductor approached me, and I tendered him the fare for us both (the man alluded to being in my employment.) The conductor very cordially received the money, but before he took time to hand me the change that was due me, invited me to "step out on the platform." "Why is this?" I remarked. "It is against the rules," he added. "Who objects?" I inquired. "It is the aristocracy," he again added. "Well, it is a cruel cult! And I believe this is the only city of note in the civilized world, where a decent colored man cannot be allowed to ride in a city passenger car. Even the cars which were formerly built in Philadelphia for New Orleans, were not devoid

of accommodations for colored people inside," I continued. And now, with regard to the aristocracy, I do not believe the blame rests with them; for I happen to be one of a committee who sometime back brought this question before the public in the shape of a petition, and it was very freely signed by hundreds of the most respectable citizens; by leading clergymen, lawyers, doctors, editors, merchants, &c., amongst whom were Bishop Potter, Hon. Horace Binney, &c., and some of the railway presidents besides. Of course the conductor declared that he had no objections himself, but continued to insist that it was "the rules."[33]

At this point, instead of backing down, Still became even more persistent, likely causing more than a few onlookers to become quite concerned:

"Who is the president of this road?" I inquired. After pausing a comment, (what he meant I know not,) he answered by saying he believed his name was "Mr. Whartman." "A former president," I remarked, declared to a committee that "no such rules had ever been made on this road." I told him that I paid taxes, &c., but of course it was all of no avail. Riding on the platform on a bitter cold day like this I need not say is almost intolerable, but to compel persons to pay the same as those who enjoy comfortable seats inside by a good fire, seems quite atrocious. Yet I felt, under the circumstances, compelled to submit to the wrong, for the sake of arriving at my place of business in due time. But before I arrived at my destination it began to snow, which, as I was already thoroughly chilled with the cold, made the platform utterly intolerable; hence, I concluded to walk the rest of the distance, and accordingly got off, feeling satisfied that no where in Christendom could be found a better illustration of Judge Taney's decision in the Dred Scott case, in which he declared that "black men have no rights which white men are bound to respect," than are demonstrated by the "rules" of the passenger cars of the City of Brotherly Love. The Judge's decision and the "rules" have harassed me every moment since. I try to think of cannibals in heathen lands and traitors in the South, and wrongs generally, but it is all to no purpose – this car inhumanity sticks to me.[34]

In the letter to the editor, Still skillfully noted that his case transcended to a much greater cause:

But this is only an individual case, hence but a trifling matter, you may think, Mr. Editor. Far from it, sir. Every colored man, woman, and child of the entire 23,000 inhabitants of this city, many of whom are tax-payers, and as upright as any other class of citizens, are daily liable to this treatment. The truth is so far, as my case is concerned, I fared well, compared with the treatment some have received. A long catalogue of injuries and outrages could be recounted, but suffice it to remind your readers of only one or two instances: A venerable old minister of the Gospel in going from here to his home at Frankford, one dark, cold, and rainy night last winter, while occupying the only place on the platform assigned for colored people, was killed. Who has forgotten this fact? One more instance, I will relieve you. One evening, in going home from a lecture, two elegantly dressed young women stepped into a car, and took seats. The conductor courageously brought the rules forward, and one of them instantly stepped out, while the other remained. The car was stopped, and actually by physical force, thrust her out of the car. The father of this young woman pays several hundred dollars taxes annually; helps his horse and carriage, and lives as nicely as most respectable citizens. But the God-given hue of the skin of his daughter rendered her obnoxious to the rules of the railway company, and she had to meekly submit to the outrage. Respectfully, WM. STILL. PHILADELPHIA, Dec. 11, 1863.[35]

Still, Lucretia Mott, and the camp's commander, Louis Wagner, with other local abolitionists, fought heartily when soldiers from Camp William Penn were discriminated against while traveling in a city that too often mimicked segregated life in the South:

Life in nineteenth century Philadelphia, which was known as "the most rigidly segregated city above the Mason-Dixon line" made it very difficult for black workers to reach Camp William Penn via the public street cars system. "Even black soldiers returning to their camps [...] were rejected from the horsecars." From these circumstances resulted a vigorous struggle for the right of black people to ride public streetcars. Begun in the 1850s, this fight existed throughout the life of Camp William Penn, which, along with the Philadelphia hospital wards reserved for black soldiers, stood symbols of equal sacrifice in the face of inequality of rights. (Johnson 1999, 103)

Johnson elaborated more:

A portrait of those conditions of racial exclusion and the emergent black-led struggle to end racist discrimination on the Philadelphia street cars is found in the correspondence of contemporary Philadelphians. A white clergyman chronicled the following event in 1865: "A few minutes before six o'clock on Monday evening two non-commissioned officers of the United States army, belonging to a regiment now forming at Camp William Penn, stepped on the front platform of a fifth car [...] on their way to the Berks-street depot of the North Pennsylvania Railroad. It was the last car by which they could reach the train to convey them out to their camp that night. When these well-dressed and well-behaved colored soldiers stepped on the platform there was no one else on it except the driver. They were almost immediately seen by the conductor, who rushed through the car and ordered the men to "get off." One of the soldiers replied, "We want to reach the train to get out to the camp tonight." "I can't help that, you can't ride on this car," was the answer. As the men did not move at once, the conductor put [them] off. The men, without resistance, but with indignation they could not express, were forced from the platform [...] They were then on the sidewalk, within a short distance of us, but the conductor would not listen to their being allowed to stand on the vacant platform [...] We reached the Berks-street station just in time to take the train on the North Pennsylvania Railroad, and the two soldiers were left behind." (104)

Johnson, citing a 1973 article by Philip Foner, also pointed out how black women, presumably trying to visit Camp William Penn soldiers who were friends or kin, being treated at local Philadelphia hospitals, also faced hard times:

> In 1864, one black [woman] fought the problem by submitting a letter to the Philadelphia Press newspaper. Speaking up for her people she wrote, '... These ladies, whenever they desire to visit their brethren at the hospitals, either to minister to their wants or attending them when dying, are constrained to pay for carriage hire, at an expense of six or seven dollars, thus expending money that would be otherwise appropriated to the soldiers were they permitted to ride in the cars. [...] Now we do think this is a great outrage, not only upon us but upon the men who [...] have at the call of their country rushed forth to aid in putting down the rebellion, and now they are wounded, many disabled for life, are deprived of seeing those dear to them, because the directors of the city passenger cars refuse to let colored people ride." (104-105)

Frederick Douglass and other anti-slavery abolitionist leaders noted the perniciousness of Philadelphia's racism:

> Little wonder black Americans hated Philadelphia. "There is no more regard shown by the whites for the common and natural rights of the colored people here, than there is at Richmond," wrote John Oliver in 1863. "The city of Philadelphia generally has no sense of justice, where colored peoples rights are concerned, or no disposition to do justice to that despised race," the Reverend B.F. Barrett declared in a fiery sermon delivered at his church at the corner of Broad and Brandywine Streets on September 23, 1866. But it was Frederick Douglass who most frequently and bitterly heaped scorn upon the city "for the insult and degradation offered to the colored citizens of Philadelphia." In 1849 he pointed out that Philadelphia had long been "the scene of a series of most foul and cruel mobs, waged against the people of color," and noted that for the colored man and woman it was "one of the most disorderly and insecure cities in the Union." "Shame upon the guilty city!" Douglass cried. "Shame upon its law-makers and law-administrators!" (Foner 1973)

Regardless, such men of the 3rd Regiment in general dealt with the hardships and persevered, including Josiah Walls, born a slave in Winchester, Virginia, in 1842, more than likely the biracial son of a Dr. John Walls, his so-called master. Private Walls, however, did not actually know his black mother's identity, or was silent about the topic throughout his fascinating life (Logan, Winston 1982, 629).

Remarkably, Walls was pressed to serve in the war, initially as a Confederate valet for an artillery battery, soon to be captured in spring 1862 by Union forces and educated for a year in Harrisburg, PA, before joining the 3rd USCT at Camp William Penn during the summer of 1863. Following the war and after service with the 3rd USCT, his acumen and intelligence would elevate Josiah T. Walls to remarkable political and business heights. Walls' ascension would even allow him to purchase the Florida plantation of an ex-Confederate general and hire some of his former Union commanders as editors for one of the Florida newspapers he would one day own and publish (Logan, Winston 1982, 629).

By the time Walls, who'd one day become a U.S. congressman, joined the ranks of the 3rd USCT Regiment, his life had already been full of intrigue and great challenges. However, the worst, as well as the best, was yet to come.

2

The 3ʳᵈ United States Colored Troops
Fortunes of the whole race

When the great anti-slavery abolitionist Frederick Douglass strode in front of the 3ʳᵈ USCT Infantry to speak on or about July 24, 1863, he had to be mighty proud, but also alarmed. That's because as he entered the sprawling camp he saw several black recruits standing atop barrels with their arms tied across long wooden poles, as if they were being crucified. They were likely being punished for various infractions, some undoubtedly rebelling due to the reported incidents of unfair treatment by some of the white officers, unsanitary conditions, and concerns about unequal medical treatment and leave time compared to white troops at other camps (Scott 1999).

So Douglass, who bore the scars of a slicing whip on his back, similar to some of his 3ʳᵈ USCT brethren, asked these first federal black troops to consider the larger picture. He warned that it was vital for blacks with great discipline to take to the battlefield and prove their courageousness, similar to those at Milliken's Bend and Fort Wagner. He told the 3ʳᵈ USCT:

The fortunes of the whole race for generations to come are bound up in the success or failure of the 3ʳᵈ Regiment of

Frederick Douglass was in the Philadelphia area some time during the week of July 18, 1863, likely speaking at Camp William Penn on the 18ᵗʰ or 24ᵗʰ, depending on the source. *Courtesy of the Library of Congress.*

100

MEN OF COLOR

IN CONSEQUENCE OF

INDISPOSITION,

OF

FRED'K DOUGLASS

The Meeting for Promoting Recruiting for

3d REGIMENT

U.S. COLORED TROOPS

IS POSTPONED UNTIL

FRIDAY, JULY 24, 1863.

This recruitment poster is evidence that Frederick Douglass planned to speak at Camp William Penn in the latter part of July when one of his sons was likely recovering from wounds suffered at the Battle for Fort Wagner, off the coast of South Carolina. *Courtesy of the U. S. Army Military History Institute.*

colored troops from the North. You are a spectacle for men and angels. You are in a manner to answer the question, can the black man be a soldier? That we can now make soldiers of these men, there can be no doubt! (Scott 1999)

Douglass predicted that their brave combat and willingness to risk life and limb for the Union would win them their long-sought liberty and elevate African Americans. Their service, Douglass believed, would set blacks on an irreversible path to equal rights: "It is for you to justify that reply, which I certainly believe you will do, but in order to [do] this you will have to prove that you cannot only parade and drill, but equal the white soldiers in deportment, in neatness of person, in the brightness of your arms, in orderly deportment, and scrupulous obedience to orders" (ibid.).

Many of the men, in fact, had been recruited by Catto, Douglass, and other abolitionists. So it's likely that Douglass, a paid recruiter for the Union army, also felt that he had a personal and professional stake in the black troops performing well.

Douglass knew that, although Philadelphia at that time had the largest free-black community in America, racism was alive and well in the city that sat smack in the middle of the eastern seaboard, a gateway to the South and North. The city's split political sentiments reflected that geographic reality. In fact, slightly more than two decades earlier, in 1842, Douglass "had been pulled from his train seat by an irate white passenger after giving a speech in nearby Norristown [...] After reaching the state capital at Harrisburg, Douglass was attacked by a white mob and barely escaped with his life" (ibid.).

Organized in June, July, and August 1863, most of the 3rd Regiment hailed from Philadelphia and Pennsylvania's interior towns. (Bates 1871, 925)

And the most prolific recruiter for soldiers of the 3rd was likely George L. Stearns, "the recruiting agent originally appointed by [Massachusetts] Governor John Andrew to collect men for the 54th and 55th Massachusetts" (Cornish 1987, 235).

> Stearns had set up a widespread recruiting organization made up of salaried agents in most of the larger Northern cities and of sub-agents paid a per capita fee for the men they brought into the service. Stearns offered the services of this organization to the War Department, and on June 13, 1863, he went to work as recruiting commissioner for colored troops with the rank of major. He began in Philadelphia and in four weeks had raised eight hundred men for the Third U.S. Colored Troops. (ibid.)

Josiah Walls, the future congressman, meanwhile "enlisted as a private in the Third Infantry Regiment, United States Colored Troops, in July 1863 [by way of Harrisburg]. He was mustered in for three years on July 9 at Philadelphia," when the city – especially the African American community – was abuzz with news about Camp William Penn's establishment for black warriors (Klingman, 1976, 7). "Walls' military service included almost the entire agenda of the regiment's movements, from its inception to its disbandment in Florida in 1865" (ibid.).

Walls, promoted to corporal in October 1863 (9), would participate in action at Fort Wagner with his 3rd compatriots, as well as early 1864 campaigns in Florida (Logan,

Winston 1982, 629), where six of the Third's members immediately following the war would become embroiled in a racial controversy with local townsfolk and white officers commanding the soldiers. This led to charges of mutiny and their hanging following a military tribunal. Black comrades, defending the six, insisted at least two to three of the men were completely innocent and the others did not deserve such a fate. "They were the last servicemen in the American Armed Forces to be executed exclusively for this [mutiny] offense" (Bennett 1991, 167).

Walls, though, before that debacle, would during the war be "appointed heavy and light artillery instructor to the troops defending Jacksonville and St. John's River" (Logan, Winston 1982, 629).

The regiment was led by Colonel Benjamin C. Tilghman, who had commanded the 26th Pennsylvania until he was wounded at the battle of Chancellorsville. Yet, indications are Tilghman was very concerned about "the general health condition of his troops" and the abbreviated training that they received:

> The medical records indicate that the proportion of sickness among black soldiers, which according to Tilghman stood at 12.2 per cent, was 1.74 times greater than among their white counterparts. Walls himself was afflicted at this time with a severe case of diarrhea, hemorrhoids, and an unknown eye disease that continued to plague him for the rest of his life. One cause of the poor health among the members of Walls' regiment was the long hours they spent in the swamps surrounding the fort at Morris Island, cutting sod in the cold and wet. (Klingman 1976, 8-9)

The observant commander noted that such conditions eventually had a negative psychological impact on his men:

> The 'rough and dirt' work wore out shoes and clothing at a rapid pace, hardship upon men who received no special clothing allotment. Tilghman pointed out that these conditions lowered morale and were of greater import to the men than either poor health or lack of military instruction: 'They begin to believe that they are not intended for soldiers, but merely drudges to do the hard and dirty work; whereas to make them reliable troops their self respect and pride in their profession should be cultivated in every reasonable way.' (9)

The other 3rd commanders were Lieutenant Colonel Ulysses Doubleday and Major Frederick W. Bardwell. Serving as adjutant was S.S. Marseilles, formerly of the 6th New Jersey and acting quartermaster was Second Lieutenant John McCaughan, who had been serving in the 75th Ohio, as well as Surgeon John W. Lyman. (Bates 1871, 925)

There were also several black noncommissioned officers, including Sergeant-Major Henry James, Quartermaster's Sergeant Henry S. Roberts, and Commissary Sergeant Isaac Wilmore (925-926).

And as they trained, it wasn't unusual for hordes of black and white onlookers to view them parading and drilling, especially during weekends. Many of their female companions, including proud wives, would embark on the segregated trolleys or trains for the trek to

Activities at Camp William Penn were bustling during weekends, when the regiments would often parade for curious crowds, most coming from Philadelphia on segregated trains. *Courtesy of the Union League of Philadelphia.*

Camp William Penn. Local abolitionists, such as the Motts, and even Commander Wagner actively fought against such discrimination:

> Many of the visitors to Roadside were black, and nearby Camp William Penn attracted the wives and sweethearts of black soldiers. The horse-drawn cars that brought visitors to Chelten Hills did not allow black passengers to ride with the whites but reserved every fifth car for them. Otherwise, they had to ride outside. Lucretia was riding home from Philadelphia one cold rainy day, when the conductor ordered an elderly black woman to ride outside in the rain. Lucretia was so indignant that she insisted on riding with her, until the other passengers protested and the conductor reluctantly permitted both women in. A few months later James [her husband] caught cold because he rode outside in the rain with some black workmen he had hired to help him at Roadside. (Bacon 1980, 187)

The marching bands and music were also potent draws to the facility, in spite of the exciting scene of marching soldiers dressed in full uniform (Scott, 1999). Optimism was, during the initial establishment of Camp William Penn, quite prevalent. "Fueled by excitement over Union victories at Gettysburg, Vicksburg, and Chattanooga, the first six months of Camp William Penn's existence were generally upbeat" (Johnson 1999, 96).

And although the white press would generally characterize the black soldiers as docile at first, it wouldn't be long before that stereotype or myth would be refuted by the men's general refusal to accept substandard treatment. Johnson, in fact, cites a July 7, 1863, report in *The Philadelphia Inquirer* that "reflected a public mindset which viewed African Americans [including those at Camp William Penn] as passive members of society" (ibid.).

Meanwhile, the August 4, 1863, edition of *The New York Times* marked the momentous presentation of an American flag to the "colored regiment," the 3ʳᵈ USCT:

Yesterday afternoon the Third Colored Regiment, now encamped at Camp William Penn on Chelton Hill, about eight miles from the city, and a mile from the North Pennsylvania Railroad, were the recipients of a large and handsome American flag, presented to them by the Committee who were instrumental in raising the regiment.

The occasion was celebrated by a flag raising, [during] which speeches [were] made by Geo. H. Earle, Esq., and Judge KELLEY.

A special train left the depot of the North Pennsylvania Railroad at 3 ½ p.m., consisting of fourteen cars, well loaded with colored persons, and among them a sprinkling of white ladies and gentlemen, all bent on witnessing the ceremony. A band, composed of colored musicians, escorted the excursion party.

Shortly after the arrival of the excursion train at Chelton Hill, the regiment was formed and taken to an adjoining field, where they were put through a series of […] maneuvers, which were executed with commendable promptness and witnessed by about fifteen hundred spectators, comprising all colors, ages and sexes.

After an hour spent in drilling the regiment, they were marched to the camp-ground near by, and formed into a hollow square around a lofty flag-pole, at the peak of which the emblem of our nationality was destined to float to the breeze. About 5 ½ o'clock the raising of the flag took place, the colored band attached to the regiment playing the "Star-Spangled Banner." Immediately afterward Col. Lewis [sic] Wagner, the commander of the camp, mounted a rough stand, and proposed three cheers for the Star-Spangled Banner.[1]

Although the regiment's official colors were not completed until November when most were in the field, enough of its Camp William Penn representatives and area spectators, many from the black community, were on hand to witness the presentation of the second flag that was designed and made by the very talented David Bustill Bowser. The November 21, 1863, edition of *The Christian Recorder* reported:

A presentation of a flag took place at Sansom St. Hall, Philadelphia, on last Tuesday evening. The hall was filled to overflowing with both colored and white people, on which occasion the presentation of a flag to the 3d Regiment of the United States Colored Troops took place. The flag was painted by our excellent

The 3rd Regiment, the first to leave Camp William Penn, lived by its motto, "Rather die freemen than live to be slaves." The flag, designed and created by David Bustill Bowser, represents what one historian has called the most radical black expression of the century. *Courtesy of the Library of Congress.*

and gentlemanly Mr. Bowser, who is a colored man and an artist No. 1. It was prepared by the special order of our patriotic colored ladies of Philadelphia, who contributed funds for that purpose. The stage or platform was filled. Our young and gentlemanly Mr. John Quincy Allen, a graduate of the colored high school [likely the Institute for Colored Youth], had been chosen by the ladies to present the flag in their behalf. There were some two speeches made before he spoke. Rev. Mr. Slicer, who has been chaplain in the army, spoke very fluently. Mr. Walker also spoke very fluently. Next came our young (orator) J.Q. Allen, who delivered an address which was a credit to his head and heart. When we see young men who can acquit themselves as he did, we are made to say that Ethiopia is stretching

The reverse side of the 3ʳᵈ USCT's colors features the great American eagle and evidence that a "a committee of ladies" paid for its production. Women's groups associated with various black churches often supported the black regiments at Camp William Penn. *Courtesy of the Library of Congress.*

forth her hands to God. Colonel Wagner, commander of Camp William Penn near Chelten Hills, made a brief but short speech. Mr. Wm. Nichols, a very staunch Abolitionist, delivered a very excellent speech, and set the whole house on fire. His remarks were greeted by all. This meeting was creditable to our race.[2]

Bowser, whose cousin was the famed abolitionist Frederick Douglass and "grandfather was a baker in the Continental Army" led by George Washington, in fact designed and made virtually all of the flags and colors for Camp William Penn regiments. Bowser received an impressive education at a private school led by his cousin, Sarah Mapps Douglass. He "had studied art with his cousin Robert Douglass, Jr., an African American pupil of Thomas Sully," the renowned artist. "When his cousin moved to Haiti in 1837, Bowser probably went west to work as a barber, a trade he began to practice in Philadelphia in 1842." (Explore PA History 2011) His grandfather, Cyrus Bustill, also became "one of the first black teachers in Pennsylvania." Forty-one years old when the Civil War erupted, Bowser "was an established artist and painter of signs in Philadelphia." Indeed, the "flags were of regimental size and often contained the national arms on the reverse and an allegorical painting depicting various scenes of the black man in uniform." Bowser also designed and made flags for black regiments outside of the Philadelphia area. Further, Bowser "sold albumen photos of both sides of the flags in carte de visite format." He "took pride in having painted live portraits of Abraham Lincoln and John Brown" (Gladstone 1993), despite some sources indicating that the paintings were not live. Nevertheless, the white abolitionist, before the war, lived with Bowser as a boarder. For sure, Bowser's activities expanded beyond his artistry to anti-slavery work, while he developed his enterprises with ingenuity. "Bowser's landscapes were not commercially successful among white Philadelphians for prejudice among the upper classes against black artists was as deep as working-class prejudice against black craftsmen. However, Bowser was highly regarded among Philadelphia's black bourgeoisie, and his commercial work – elaborately decorated fire engine panels, fire company parade hats, and commercial signs – was in demand" (Nash 2002, 199-200).

Regardless of the positive attention, the 3rd Regiment's members often faced hostile whites if they ventured too far from the camp. In fact, there were reports of the black soldiers being repeatedly accosted by white mobs and even jailed by racist police (Scott 1999).

David Bustill Bowser was a very well connected artist who painted images of the abolitionist martyr John Brown and President Abraham Lincoln. He was also a sign painter and barber with family ties to Frederick Douglass and Sarah Mapps Douglass. Cyrus Bustill, David's grandfather, baked bread for George Washington's Continental Army. *Courtesy of the Library of Congress.*

Still, despite such hardships the men persevered, but were not permitted to participate in a full parade into battle from Philadelphia due to authorities being concerned that the spectacle of black men with weapons marching through the streets would incite white riots.

The August 8, 1863, edition of *The Christian Recorder* newspaper told of the local black community's great disappointment, as well as the soldiers' anger:

> At the latter part of last week several of our daily papers published the gratifying intelligence that the Third Regiment of Philadelphia Colored troops would come into the city from Camp William Penn, to go through the evolutions of a street parade. The day came, but with it also came the postponement of the promised treat indefinitely. This has been a source of grievous disappointment to a great many, both colored and white. (ibid.)

The paper continued:

> Not only were the friends of the regiment disappointed, but when the intelligence reached the encampment it caused a great commotion amongst the men, amounting, as we have been told, almost to a state of mutiny, which had been the consequences of so frequently disappointing the men on this account

> [...] What right any man has to interfere with colored, more than with white troops, we cannot conceive. Does the government want to get them up in some dark corner, and prepare them to do just what white men are prepared to do in the dark? It should be remembered, that these men are human beings, and have their five senses, and feel just as well as the whites do. They are not ignorant of the manner in which they are treated; and of course they know what they are, and the kind of treatment they deserve. And the men who would interfere with, or molest them in any way, deserve the severest punishment. We, therefore, hope that both the Government and Philadelphia will redeem themselves from last week's doings. (ibid.)

John Brown, who lived with the artist David Bustill Bowser as a boarder, was actually painted by Bowser as a kind and empathetic figure. *Courtesy of the Atwater-Kent Museum of Philadelphia History.*

So, the men had to inconspicuously depart Camp William Penn after being ordered to Morris Island's Fort Wagner, in South Carolina, where the 54th had fought so valiantly, but failed to take the fort.

In fact, the departure of the regiment from Camp William Penn was even covered by *The New York Times* via a dispatch from *The Philadelphia Inquirer* on August 13, 1863.

Philadelphia's black community was enthralled by the ebony phalanx of warriors in blue, despite the limited parade route of the soldiers:

> At the Poplar-street wharf they were met by an immense crowd of colored friends and relatives, who had waited for over an hour to welcome them. The steamers did not leave the wharf until 11 ½ o'clock, during which time baggage, &c., was taken aboard. As the steamers moved away from the wharf, the regiment received a perfect ovation the people gave cheer after cheer, and the troops left amid great enthusiasm. They were also greeted with the heartiest cheers from the wharves and vessels along the river front, as they moved down the river. As the vessels containing the regiment moved down the river, the men crowded the decks, waving caps, handkerchiefs, &c., and singing the anthem of "John Brown's body lies mouldering in the grave."[3]

Once the troops reached their destination on Morris Island, not a moment was wasted:

> It was immediately put into the trenches, and shared in the hardships of that memorable trial of skill and endurance which resulted in the fall of the fort. The loss during attacks which resulted in the capture of a line of rifle-pits, a Corporal was reported missing. Two days after, the advance sappers came upon his dead body. Warned by previous experience, they were careful to examine it thoroughly before attempting to remove it. A small string was discovered attached to its leg, which led away to the trigger of a torpedo buried in the sand. Such was the warfare which this command was called to meet. (Gayley 2011)

The regiment had helped with the taking of forts Wagner and Gregg by September 7th, victories that had to be quite gratifying after the courageous, but unsuccessful, action of the black troops of the 54th Massachusetts. It had also participated in other operations in the vicinity of Charleston.

By early 1864 the 3rd ventured into Florida with Union forces led by General Truman Seymour. It was drilled in heavy artillery, then garrisoned near Jacksonville "at a fort on the St. John's River" and "one at Fernandina." (Gayley 2011) By late spring, specifically on May 29, 1864, Orderly Sergeant Thomas B. Rockhold of Company D penned a letter to *The Christian Recorder* newspaper that was published on June 25, 1864, providing a detailed account of the regiment's activities. In addition to expressing great satisfaction in capturing and holding Rebel prisoners, Rockhold was delighted to free and protect blacks who had been enslaved, folks he described as the regiment's "flesh and blood":

For the Christian Recorder.
FLORIDA CORRESPONDENCE
Head Quarters 3d U.S.C.T.
Jacksonville, Florida,

May 29th, 1864.

MR. EDITOR: – I, now, this beautiful Sunday afternoon, sit myself down, according to promise, to write a few lines to you, hoping they may find you and all your friends enjoying good health.

I will commence my correspondence with you by giving you my Florida Expeditions. Our regiment left Hilton Head on the 6th of February, for Jacksonville, Fla., and we arrived there on the 8th. Just as soon as we landed we were ordered to camp. Here we remained until the 8th of February, when we received orders, in the night, to surprise the rebel camp, called 'Camp Finagan,' about ten miles from Jacksonville. We got to the rebel camp about 1 o'clock at night, but were too late to do any good; but we had the pleasure of liberating some of our flesh and blood. There were about two hundred slaves at that place that had the pleasure of saying: 'We are free from the chains and fetters of slavery.' On the morning of the 9th we were ordered to fall in and march to the next station, called by the natives of the State, 'Ten Mile Station.' There our mounted infantry had a little skirmish with Gen. Finagan's men, and we captured four pieces of artillery from the rebels; and our regiment, of Col. Halley's brigade, was ordered to stay till the gallant 8th regiment came up to us.

On the morning of the 10th of February, we started to the next station, called Baldwin, the junction of all the railroads that lead to Georgia, Mobile, and Charleston. We arrived there about noon of the same day, and went into camp; some of us to do picket duty, and some to do provost guard duty; and, Mr. Editor, the best of all, that day there were two companies to go further on. Company G and D had to go to the next town, called Barber's Station, about fifty miles from Jacksonville. When we arrived there we found the 115th New York regiment, waiting for us to relieve them. We, after marching hard all day, had to go on duty for twenty-four hours; though tired and fatigued out, you may say, there was not a word said about our duties to our superior officers, for they all knew what soldiering was. We found, there, ten of our wounded soldiers, and two wounded rebels. One of them died while we were there, and we buried him with pleasure; although we were convinced in our own minds, if it were us, they would not even give us a drink of water. But we had a Christian spirit in us.

Company G, (F.W. Webster, Captain,) went out on the 11th of February, and was to return in a short time, but did not come until late in the night. We had given them up; but as God would have it, they came back all safe and sound.

On the 13th of Feb., we were ordered back to our regiment by Col. Barton, who was commanding the post at **Barber's Ford**, and we guarded down that day, three prisoners of war: one Lieut. Colonel, one Major, and one private; and the best of all, about fifty colored people, that Col. Barton had captured at Sanderson, about seventy miles from Jacksonville. About 6 o'clock in the evening, we got back to our regiment. Our Colonel met us and said: "How do you do, boys? I see the rebels haven't got you yet!" and we gave three cheers for Col. Tilghman and his regiment. There we staid one week, while that awful slaughter came off at Olustee; but as God knew best, we did not have to go up there to be murdered like dogs. (T.R. Rockhold 1864)

Rockhold and his fellow 3rd USCT warriors were tremendously impacted by the event, without being there, because their 8th USCT comrades, barely trained and new to the field, suffered tremendously during the debacle when they were ambushed by seasoned Rebel troops:

> On the 15th of Feb., the fight took place; and on the 16th, early in the morning the wounded came in by the wagon load, and ambulances loaded down. But the worse of all, was to see the poor soldiers come in with no hats on, and some with arm and hands off. Our regiment stayed at Baldwin till all of the wounded were off the field; and about 10 o'clock at night, we took up a line of march for Jacksonville, down the railroad, to keep the rebels from flanking us, and cutting off our communications with the army. We got as far as Camp Finagan that night, where we bivouacked. We rolled logs together and made up camp-fires; though tired and worn out, we made some coffee in our tin cups, and it tasted as good as if our mothers had made it. The next morning, at half-past eight o'clock, we started for, we didn't know where, but we went in camp on Stocklain's Road, and stayed two days; and on the third day, we were ordered on the railroad, about three miles from the main road.
>
> Last week Col. Shaw, of the 7th U.S.C.T., went out with his regiment, and some mounted infantry, and four pieces of artillery, and marched out on the railroad, about five miles from this place, and had a little fight with the rebels. They captured about fifty of them, and killed and wounded a large number, and did not lose a man, and but one of our number wounded; he belonged to the 7th U.S.C.T. They all got back to camp the evening of the same day.
>
> I suppose you have all heard about the destruction of the Mapleleaf, Gneral Hunter, and the gunboat Harriet A. Weed. The destruction of these three boats, occurred in three weeks' time. They were valued at $500,000.
>
> Since I have been staying at Jacksonville, I have attended four cotillion parties, given by the colored ladies of this place.
>
> I will bring my letter to a close, by bidding you good-bye. May God bless you, and may you be prosperous in all your undertakings.
>
> I hope to hear from you soon; and I hope the next letter I write may be better.

Yours until death,

THOMAS R. ROCKHOLD,
Orderly Serg't of Co. D, U.S.C.T.
(T.R. Rockhold, 3rd USCT Letter, 1864)

Even as spring arrived, the 3rd Regiment kept up a fierce pace, according to another writer to *The Christian Recorder*, Private William B. Johnson, of Company A, in a June 22, 1865, correspondence laced with humor and tragedy:

> Our regiment was ordered to Tallahassee on the 19th of May. On the evening of the 20th we marched to Baldwin, and on the morning of the 21st took the cars at Baldwin Station, en route for Tallahassee. Nothing of note occurred until we arrived at Olustee Station, where, one year before, we fought the Confederate forces. The cars stopped for wood, when the platforms of the cars were immediately crowded with white and colored persons, all eager to catch a glimpse of the "black soldiers." Some dee dyed villain made the remark that all the niggers should be – (a place of not very moderate temperature.) A moment afterward, twenty guns were pointed at his heart; and one man, more angry and revengeful than the rest, discharged his piece, the ball grazing the speaker's cheek; and if it had been a little closer, Johnnie would have been no more, and would, in all probability, have received a through-ticket for the locality which he named.
>
> For a period of about half an hour, the wildest excitement prevailed around the immediate vicinity. Finally, Brigadier-General B.C. Tilghman made his appearance upon the scene, and hastily demanded the cause of so much disorder and confusion, and in a little while I saw him lead the wounded man aside, with but little grace, and bid him depart in peace, lest a worse evil came upon him.
>
> About half-past ten o'clock, the same evening, we arrived at the Capitol. The place was wrapped in slumber, and a quietness as profound as that [...] o'er Godsmith's Deserted Village reigned around. No sound arose to break the dead silence, save the soft hissing of the steam as it escaped through the valves of the reposing engine.
>
> In the morning, however, we had plenty of visitors, and among them the most inhuman and brutal man that ever lived, in the person of the Hon. Benjamin Cheers, of Tallahassee; and if ever there was a demon in human form, he is one. The day before we came up, he took one of his slaves, a boy of twelve years, and laid upon his naked back Three Hundred Lashes! But, thank God, to-day he stands awaiting trial. Three cheers for General B.C. Tilghman; he has resigned and gone home, and we are left alone. He was a man much beloved and respected by the men in his command. He possesses in an eminent degree the qualities of soldier and gentleman. May prosperitiy [*sic*] ever attend him.

The rebs here seem to die very hard at the idea of having black troops to guard them, but they keep very quiet, and do not have much to say. How true is the saying that we know not what a day may bring forth! Great changes are being wrought.

On Monday last a man calling himself General Myers stabbed a colored man. He was immediately arrested, and is at this time awaiting his trial.

I must now draw my letter to a close. Remember as most kindly to the ladies of the Sanitary Commission. Tell them we thank them for the noble cause in which they are engaged. Fully do we appreciate the earnest labors of these modern Good Samaritans, and may we all soon be enabled to meet again. The war is over, the supremacy of the Government has been amply vindicated, our flag waves in triumph on land and sea, we have all done our duty, and we now want to go home. More anon.

> Yours very respectfully,
> WM.B. Johnson
> [Co.] A., 3d U.S.C.T.
> (W.B. Johnson 3rd USCT Letter, 1864)

Meanwhile, although he did not retire then, as Johnson indicates in the above letter, Colonel Tilghman was temporarily reassigned north, so command of the regiment fell to Lieutenant Colonel Doubleday. The regiment participated in several expeditions in Florida's interior led by General William Birney (Gayley 2011).

Sgt. Rockhold of company D described the regiment's activities during this period, as well as his feelings about the temporary departure of Colonel Tilghman, in a letter that was published in *The Christian Recorder* by its editor, Elisha Weaver:

For the Christian Recorder. ARMY CORRESPONDENCE.

Headquarters 3d U.S.C.T., Camp Jacksonville, Florida, September 16, 1864.

MY DEAR BROTHER WEAVER: - I will commence my letter by giving you a brief sketch of our regiment, now in Jacksonville, Florida. Although our Col. is north, we know not what his absence if for, but still know him to be a good man, and always looking for a good situation for his command. Our regiment is doing garrison duty at Jacksonville now, and all is quiet now around our lines. One company is doing duty at Fernandina, and my company is at Yellow Bluff, about fifteen miles below Jacksonville, where the army transport Harriet A. Weed was blown up last summer. The health of the regiment is good now, much better than what it has been since we have been out. Our chaplain is a thorough-going man, and always has a smiling countenance for the boys as he comes around through our streets. His name is Hobbs, of Lancaster City, Pennsylvania, and I must say he is both a gentleman and a religious man and tries to do what's right, I [think], both in preaching and teaching the men, and striving in giving them education, what time they have to do it in; for you know a soldier has no time hardly for any thing but soldier's duty. I must tell you a little of Company D, 3d U.S.C.T., now stationed at Yellow Bluff, commanded by Captain John L. Bruer. We are enjoying the best of health, and our company have nothing to do but guard duty at the fort, and some on the river. Our company can muster 60 men out of 81 that we had when we left Camp William Penn. I have been sick almost all the time since I left home. These few lines leave me well. – I remain your friend. I hope you will pray for me and my company. Respectfully yours, THOMAS B. ROCKHOLD, Orderly Sergeant Co. D, 3d U.S.C.T. [4]

However, by September 1864 Colonel Tilghman returned and patrols were organized to travel deep into the Florida wilderness, "for the purpose of bringing in contrabands, and destroying property belonging to the rebel government." In fact, at one point, about 30 "enlisted men of the Third" commanded by Sergeant Major Henry James trekked nearly 60 miles up the St. John's River by boat, "rowing by night, and hiding in the swamps by day, marched thirty miles into the interior, gathered together fifty or sixty contrabands, besides several horses and wagons, burned store-houses and a distillery belonging to the rebel government, and returned bringing their recruits and spoils all safely into camp" (ibid.).

Nonetheless, before they reached camp the men were engaged by Confederate cavalry, but put up a very good fight, carrying with them their wounded" (ibid.). Undoubtedly, a major incentive for fighting so fiercely was that if they were taken prisoner, such black soldiers and white officers often met grisly fates, including torture and hanging. Sometimes they were immediately shot:

> It was somewhat remarkable, that the regiment never lost a man as prisoner, though raiding parties not unfrequently were beaten, and driven by superior numbers. The general feeling among the men seemed to be, that immediate death was preferable to the treatment likely to be experienced as prisoners. On one occasion, a soldier who had been surrounded and driven into the river, stubbornly refused repeated calls to surrender, and was killed on the spot. (ibid.)

The regiment's motto, emblazoned on its colors that were designed by the Philadelphia black artist and activist David Bustill Bowser, was "Rather Die Freemen than Live to Be Slaves" (Davis, Pohanka, and Troiani 1998).

Yet, the Third's courageousness did not protect it from pay inequalities, even as they served on the front line, a matter that Tilghman officially protested:

> The Third Regiment, along with all other black organizations, suffered from unequal pay scales. The normal $3 clothing allowance, an addition to the pay of white soldiers, was subtracted from their regular $10 per month wages. Extra issues of clothing became necessary to "keep a soldierly appearance" while engaged in siege and fatigue details. In January 1864, Tilghman indignantly wrote his superiors that the extra clothing had amounted to $41 per man since the regiment had been formed, equaling 80 percent of its pay and allowances. Nine

of his men had been killed after only one month of service, but their clothing bills totaled $30 per man in that short space of time. This debt had to be assumed by their survivors before the federal government paid bounties or pensions. Moreover, black noncommissioned officers did not receive increased pay with their promotions. Walls was affected by this situation, as he had been promoted to corporal in October 1863. (Klingman 1976, 9)

Although the Third did not participate in the Battle of Olustee, Florida, where their comrades of the 8th USCT would face overwhelming odds, with many slaughtered and captured during an ambush, the Third returned to the Jacksonville area after the Rebels successfully stopped the Union forces' push across the state. "[Josiah] Walls' unit was then assigned to garrison the city until the close of the war and was bivouacked east of the city. The troops participated in many of the maneuvers and raids inland that were undertaken to weaken southern resistance" (Klingman 1976, 10). And, undoubtedly, one of the most satisfying aspects of the assignment was freeing their enslaved brothers and sisters. "During one raid near St. Augustine in March, a twenty-five-man patrol from the Third brought in seventy slaves" (ibid.).

However, there were certainly losses among the triumphs and defeats. The April 29, 1865, edition of *The Christian Recorder* referred to the above raid, as well as reported several deaths and injuries, including the wounding of Sergeant Thomas B. Rockhold of Company D, who had previously written to the newspaper about the 3rd Regiment's activities and action. And the remarkable act of heroism by Sergeant Joel Ben was also highlighted. The clerk of the regiment's Company A described the action to the editor, the Rev. Elisha Weaver, in a letter dated April 7, 1865:

MR. EDITOR: – Having a few leisure moments, I will employ them in writing a few lines to your most valuable paper, the *Christian Recorder*. I have no doubt but some of our friends [at] home would like to hear from the 3d regiment of U.S. Colored troops. I am happy to say that the men of the 3d have been blessed with very good health ever since they have been in active service.

A detachment of fifteen men, from our regiment, made a very successful raid into the interior of the State, on the 20th of March last. They destroyed some three hundred barrels of sugar, laid waste several large plantations, captured thirty head of horses, mules, wagons, &c., brought in thirty contrabands, and engaged the enemy in a severe fight, which lasted nearly two hours. The enemy had two men to our one. We lost one of the best sergeants we had, Sergeant Joel Ben. Israel Hall, guide, was taken prisoner; John M. Brown, son of Rev. John M. Brown, of West Chester, Pennsylvania, was wounded in the hand; he was also a guide. On the 6th of the present month, Sergeant Thomas B. Rockhold, of Company D, left Yellow Bluff with a party of men for the purpose of raiding among the secesh, who are pretty plenty hereabouts. They had not gone far before they came across a party of rebels, who after a small skirmish, skedaddled. Sergeant Rockhold was wounded and Samuel Brown killed.

A few words more and I am done. I am proud to say that Sergeant Joel Ben fought hard and faithfully for the Stars and Stripes, and when he received his death wound he was endeavoring to shield a helpless woman and her child from the hands of those God-forsaken traitors. Peace to his ashes.

Our thanks to the ladies of the Sanitary Commission. May the time soon come when peace shall again reign throughout the land.

Hoping you will excuse mistakes, I remain, very respectfully your obedient servant,

WILLIAM B.D. JOHNSON,
Clerk Co. A, 3d U.S.C.T.
April 7ᵗʰ, 1865. [5]

Earlier, however, in June 1864, Walls was transferred to the 35ᵗʰ USCT, "stationed in Picolata, a settlement on the St. Johns River near St. Augustine." In fact, his steadiness as a soldier, despite not earning meritorious medals, was apparently noticed by his superiors before he mustered out of the service:

He had been promoted to first sergeant in March, and was assigned as an artillery instructor with his new regiment. He mustered out on October 31, 1865, with a debt of $6.00 to the army and a credit of $18.66 in back pay plus his service bounty of $100.00. In general, Walls' military record is not very distinguished. He received no citations, either for merit or discipline, although he was considered responsible enough to command at least one prisoner detail escorting deserters from Picolata to the provost office in Jacksonville. (Klingman 1976, 10)

Meanwhile, following the war and General Lee's surrender, the regiment was assigned to Tallahassee, Lake City, and other Florida locales. Then, on May 16, 1865, Colonel Tilghman resigned, with Major Bardwell appointed to take his place. Lieutenant Colonel Doubleday had been previously promoted to colonel and commander of the 45ᵗʰ USCT of Camp William Penn the previous October. The regiment stayed in Florida until October, before it returned to Philadelphia and was mustered out of service on or about October 30ᵗʰ (Gayley 2011).

However, before returning to Pennsylvania, members of the 3ʳᵈ USCT would meet untimely fates via a combination of the racists from good 'ol Dixie and their own officers during what has been termed in Florida as the "Jacksonville Mutiny." Yet the visionary Josiah Walls, despite the adversity, would see opportunity in what he would later coin as the "sunny state" in order to attract congressional funding for tourism, among several of his major forward-thinking causes, including the need for nationwide public education. Where some of his compatriots met their doom, Walls would soon return to Florida and become resoundingly successful.

3

The 6th United States Colored Troops
'This momentous struggle'

When Captain John McMurray of Brookville, Pennsylvania, arrived at Camp William Penn on a Sunday morning (September 27, 1863), he likely anticipated a very amicable meeting with the commandant of the post, Lieutenant Colonel Louis Wagner. However, the reception was less than impressive, at least according to McMurray, who was poised to help command the 6th USCT, destined to become the most combat-driven regiment to graduate from the post:

> During a fifteen-minute interview he was kept standing, hat in one hand and gripsack in the other, in plain view of three or four officers. Fifty years later McMurray had not forgiven Wagner for what he considered a rude reception. Shortly after this embarrassing encounter, the young captain was assigned to command Company D, 6th United States Colored Troops, and conducted to his tent headquarters. (Montgomery 1961, 159)

McMurray, who undoubtedly knew Rev. Asher (the sole chaplain of the 6th,

Captain John McMurray of the 6th USCT, Company D, was a school teacher for a period before the war, seeing much action in Virginia. *Courtesy of the U. S. Army Military History Institute.*

who would leave his black Shiloh Baptist Church congregation and family to join the regiment), would be central to its very active history, despite his typical and humble start as a white soldier from Ligonier Valley, Westmoreland County, PA (ibid.).

Born June 12, 1838, "McMurray was still a child when his family moved to a farm in Pine Creek Township in nearby Jefferson County. Here he grew to manhood, learned the carpenter's trade, attended Brookville Academy, and taught school for three winters" (ibid.).

At about age 23, McMurray joined the 135ᵗʰ Pennsylvania Volunteers on August 14, 1862. However, the regiment was "disbanded" on May 24, 1863, but not before he obtained the rank of first lieutenant. Then, while serving the 57ᵗʰ Pennsylvania Militia "near Pittsburgh [...] McMurray learned that Major Stearns was organizing several regiments of Negro recruits. Applying at once for a commission, he was soon called to Washington where, upon approval by Casey's board, he was appointed by the Secretary of War to a captaincy in the 6ᵗʰ United States Colored Troops" (ibid.).

After his initial, unsettling meeting with Commander Wagner, McMurray, while walking towards his tent headquarters, "had his first meeting with regimental commander Lieutenant Colonel John W. Ames. Informal and brief, it left no distinct impression on McMurray except that Ames's behavior contrasted sharply with that of Wagner" (159). However, their war experiences would bind them steadfastly together:

> For almost two years McMurray and Ames were to lead their dusky soldiers through the swamps and onto the battlefields of the country of the York and James rivers and to conclude their efforts with the campaign against Fort Fisher in North Carolina. They were to witness death among their comrades, rejoice over the same victories, and deplore the same defeats. From these experiences grew a lasting personal friendship and a sincere admiration for the Negro soldier. (159-160)

The September 5, 1863, edition of the *National Anti-Slavery Standard* showed that the recruitment of the 6ᵗʰ was vigorous from the start:

> The second regiment at Camp William Penn (being the '6ᵗʰ Regiment U.S. Colored Troops') is steadily filling up, and an uncommonly fine-looking and well-behaving body of men it is said to be.

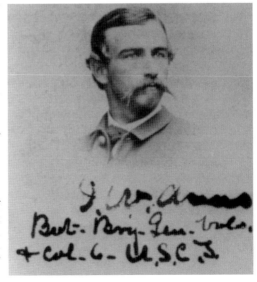

Colonel John W. Ames was the commander of the 6ᵗʰ USCT and led them into much action at the Battle of New Market Heights in Virginia, where three of his warriors earned the Medal of Honor. *Courtesy of the U. S. Army Military History Institute.*

A flag-presentation took place at the camp last Monday, which attracted a large crowd of spectators. The flag was a gift from ladies of color of Philadelphia, and was painted by Mr. David Bowser of that city, a colored man of fine skill in that line of art. It was presented to the regiment through Col. Wagner, the officer commanding, by Robert Purvis, who made it the occasion of a brief but eloquent speech. Col. Wagner replied happily in a strain that showed him to have been much touched by Mr. Purvis's remarks.[1]

And the African American newspaper *The Christian Recorder* published on September 5, 1863, a detailed report about a flag-raising ceremony for the 6th USCT. The program featured such dynamic speakers and black leaders as Robert Purvis, friends with Lucretia Mott, as well as the post commander, Louis Wagner, who also addressed the soldiers and citizen onlookers:

At five o'clock yesterday afternoon a flag was presented to the colored troops encamped at Chelton Hills. The flag was the gift of the troops, and a large number of ladies and gentlemen, who had left the city in a special train for their accommodation, were on the ground. The troops were paraded prior to the presentation, and their muscular frames elicited the admiration of those who witnessed the drill. They were then drawn up in line in the centre of the camp facing the south, and the flag was presented to them. It was a beautiful banner, made of the finest silk, with the American eagle in front, over it the words, "freedom for all," and under it the inscription, "Sixth United States Colored Troops." On the reverse was "Presented by all," and under it the inscription, "Sixth United States Colored Troops." On the reverse was "presented by the colored citizens of Philadelphia." Its dimensions are six feet square.[2]

The article then identified principle speakers and their powerful messages, mixed with pride, hope, and demands for equality:

MR. JACOB E. WHITE was the first speaker. He alluded to the history the colored men were making for themselves in the present war. – High upon the scroll of fame they were writing their names. Any post of honor is available if the effort for its securing is but put forth. Not by simply looking on, but by active participation, and by marching forward to the battlefields of the nation. The colored man's time is now, and by striking with a firm, strong hand for the privileges offered in the present hour, the black man's nationality will be secured for all coming time.[3]

Even black leaders associated with Camp William Penn via official capacities spoke that day:

ROBERT E. PURVIS, Aid de camp to Major STEARNS in the recruiting service, was then presented to the troops. His address was brief and pointed, and was received by the soldiers with marked deference. It was as follows: Soldiers of the Sixth United States Infantry: I have been selected as the representative of those who have procured for you this beautiful banner, to transfer it unto your charge, and on their behalf this splendid guidon, this glorious emblem of freedom, I present, through the commanding officer of the post, to you. You will prove yourselves worthy of the gift; you will see that the flag of your country suffers no dishonor at your hands. I am fully satisfied that the loyalty, prowess and devotion of the colored soldiers will take care of the interests committed to them by the country. What are the facts? Let Milliken's Bend answer.[4]

And there were more than a few praises for Colonel Robert Gould Shaw and the 54ᵗʰ Massachusetts, composed of many Philadelphians:

> Said Adjutant Gen. THOMAS, "the negro soldiers repulsed the enemy; to the brave black men we are indebted for the possession of that important post." – Let Fort Wagner answer! Led by the noble and heroic Colonel ROBERT G. SHAW, no men fought more bravely, no soldiers bore in hospitals their wounds more patiently. Let Port Hudson answer! Let no one who reads the official report of Major-General BANKS, bearing testimony to the valor of the colored soldiers, dare to scruple and say the black men will not fight, unless he belong to that tribe of the meanest of all God's creeping things, the copperhead. Soldiers, in this momentous struggle between freedom and slavery, in other words, between a true democracy and a tyrannical despotism, I thank God that the Government, from a sense of despotism, and therefore in the exercise of its highest wisdom, recognized your manhood, and evidences it calling on you to share the sacrifices necessary to establish the doctrine of equal rights. "Stand to your faith, America, Sad Europe, listen to our call, Up to your manhood, Africa, [T]his flag floats over all. Pure as its white our future see… Bright as its red is now our sky… Fixed as its stars is now our faith [t]hat nerves our hearts to do or die."[5]

At that point, apparently the powerful black abolitionist Robert Purvis became quite moved by the comments:

> Taking the flag in his hand, Mr. Purvis extended it to Col. Wagner, saying, "Receive this standard," and then, turning to the troops, concluded with – Soldiers, under this flag let your rallying cry be for God, for freedom and our country. If for this you fall, you fall the country's patriots, heroes and martyrs.[6]

Finally, the commander of the camp, Col. Louis Wagner, took center stage:

> Advancing in front of his men he waved the flag aloft, saying: – Mr. Purvis, Ladies, and Gentlemen: – It affords me pleasure, indeed, to receive this magnificent standard this day presented to the Sixth Regiment of the United States Colored Infantry. It will never be disgraced. Wherever the soldiers of the Sixth Infantry go they will with honor uphold and defend this banner. There are two regiments of colored troops now at Charleston, who left this city, and they have sustained the

reputation of their race by the conduct displayed before Fort Wagner. The soldiers to whom this flag is committed will be found true as they were true. They will follow it to victory, or falling, they will fall only when the flag falls with them. We will uphold it and preserve it; protect it honor and maintain its supremacy against all who would injure its folds.[7]

The September 10, 1863, edition of *The National Anti-Slavery Standard* published a similar story detailing the flag raising.[8]

The Christian Recorder newspaper of September 12, 1863,[9] even detailed the contributions (collected by black community leader Jacob C. White) of some of the region's most prominent citizens, many of them members of the black committee dedicated to supporting Camp William Penn. This included payment to David B. Bowser, who diligently designed and made the flags for the Camp William Penn regiments.[10]

According to the September 26, 1863, edition of the *National Anti-Slavery Standard*, plans were being made to construct barracks for incoming recruits, in a very brief story, "MUSTERING CAMP FOR COLORED SOLDIERS":

> Washington, Sept. 18 – Thomas Webster, Esq., and J.M. McKim, Esq., of Philadelphia, on behalf of the Supervisory Committee for recruiting colored troops in Philadelphia, had an interview with the Secretary of War this morning on that subject. The result will be the issue of an order to construct barracks at Camp William Penn, near Philadelphia for the reception of colored volunteers from New Jersey and Delaware, the States in which they are raised to be credited with them.[11]

It's likely that McMurray would have been soon accommodated in the barracks, since he was a line officer.

And one of the officers also headed for the barracks was Captain Girard P. Riley, acknowledged as "a friend" to African Americans in the October 3, 1863, edition of *The Christian Recorder*, while also providing an update on the Sixth USCT's activities and addressing soldiers of the regiment quite directly:

> This regiment has not been ordered to move yet. They are still under drill by Col. Wagner and Captain G.P. Riley. This gentleman has been chaplain in a regiment out in Kentucky, and has been promoted to the position of a Captain. We had the pleasure of meeting with Capt. Riley in Louisville, Kentucky, while we were out west, and before he came east as Captain over the 6th U.S. Colored Regiment. We may say to the regiment that he is from the West, (Ohio) and is of the right stamp you may be sure, or he would never have been appointed Captain over you. He is a gentleman, and beside all that, he is a Christian. The colored people in Louisville found him a friend to them when they were kept and driven like cattle, right under the eye of the government. We mean the freedmen of contrabands, whom they had no right to treat so in Louisville. We say again to the 6th regiment, that Capt. Riley is all right side up, and is unquestionably a staunch friend of the black man, so you need not entertain any fears whatever.[12]

Consistent with the primary message above, Capt. Riley during the war would rescue on February 20, 1864, two enslaved children owned by Thomas White of Mathews County, Virginia. Their mother had been sold at auction on February 13, 1864, after being "beaten and branded for being kind to Union Soldiers." The woman, left tied down in a cart, looked to the heavens for solace: "O! God send the Yankees to take my children away," she reportedly exclaimed. Riley made sure that they eventually landed at the Orphanage for Colored Children via help from the Quakers or Society of Friends. The story was retold in publications featuring an image of the children in tattered slave clothes before Riley's rescue, and then a short time later well dressed, but still with a deep sadness in their eyes (Scott 2008, 60).

Indeed, despite such orphanages being supposed safe havens for desperate black children, the "burning of such facilities by white mobs in Philadelphia and New York City before and during the Civil War likely rallied more black men to the Union's cause" (61).

And it seems Captain Riley sometimes doubled as a preacher while on Camp William Penn's grounds before his group marched to war. On at least one occasion he performed a marriage.[13]

Yet, not everyone at first held Riley in the highest esteem, including Commander Wagner:

> In early September, 1863 the camp commander, Louis Wagner, communicated his concern about [a] problem officer. "Examining a list of the officers appointed … I find Girard P. Riley, Aug. 26ᵗʰ, 1863. I feel duty bound to lay these letters before the Department with an earnest protest against this man as an officer in these Colored regiments. I cannot imagine how anyone so ignorant of the simplest rules of grammar and orthography as well as military affairs as this Chaplain Riley is, could ever receive the position he now holds much less that of Captain." (Johnson 1999, 92-93)

Despite obviously eventually accepting Riley as the months passed by, Wagner tied up his letter with very biting words: "I do not know whether this man has been before the Board of Examiners or not but am satisfied that his letters prove him unfit for any position in the service" (93).

By October 10, 1863, an unidentified correspondent of *The Christian Recorder* newspaper visited Camp William Penn and noted: "We were out there on Wednesday last, and found the place is alive with troops, and while we were there a squad of men were brought from the city."[14] So, even with the erection of the barracks, which eventually did provide shelter for some of the facility's enlisted men, recruitment continued at a brisk pace.

However, inside of "two weeks after McMurray's arrival at Camp William Penn, Ames's regiment was completely organized." With over 1,000 men filling the ranks of the 6ᵗʰ, it was made of 10 companies, including McMurray's Company D, consisting of almost 100 recruits (Montgomery 1961, 160).

When the regiment was ready to depart camp for war, local newspapers, such as *The Christian Recorder* via the reporting of its editor, the Rev. Elisha Weaver, covered the event in detail, even noting the participation of some of the warriors hailing from the next regiment to be established at Camp William Penn, the 8th USCT. The paper also noted some racial hostilities along the parade route. Unlike the 3rd USCT, the initial regiment to be organized and march to battle from Camp William Penn, the 6th was the first to fully parade through Philadelphia streets:

> The 6th United States colored regiment, and four companies of the eighth regiment, on last Saturday, the 3rd inst., came in from Camp William Penn, and formed a line on Master St., right resting on Fourth, facing south, and marched [...] down Washington [Street] to the Refreshment Saloon. Now we say, that no troops ever passed through the streets of Philadelphia, that made a better appearance. The uniformity with which they held their grounds, was the best we ever witnessed. Those who are the real friends of their country, and are loyal to the back-bone, cheered them either from their houses at the doors and windows, or on the streets, with handkerchiefs, flags, and pleasant countenances. These men give the lie to those men who are their enemies, and say they will never make soldiers. Some of these men who marched through the streets were better equipped than some of the white officers who were appointed to positions when the rebellion first broke out. The officers over these companies say the colored people learn much faster than the whites; the cause we suppose to be this: the colored people as a general thing are loyal, and they believe in freedom, &c. There was an immense crowd of white and colored followed them through the streets.[15]

The sight of so many black soldiers, however, was a bit too much for some in the crowd to bear, so they tried to react physically, demonstrating their racist disdain:

> We were somewhat amused while standing on the corner of Third and Walnut to hear some person remark, "Here comes the flag of distress." Some white men were in the crowd, and one well-dressed heavy-set gentleman, whom we took to be a German, although he spoke good English, exclaimed, "What did you say, sir? I'll let you know, sir, that it is the American flag, and it is time you had learned enough to that effect, and if you don't know it I can quickly teach you." The poor fellow looked bad and hung his head when he saw those who stood around him look upon him with such contempt; but the gentleman who addressed himself to him looked with as much indignation as to say if the poor ignorant fellow would have said so again he would have felled him to the ground. There were but a very few remarks made anywhere through the city, except between South and Lombard Sts., on the east side of the market house, and it was said by some who followed the regiment up and down all the streets, they heard no offensive remarks until they got there. They heard several offensive remarks, about the "nigger" line officers, but they said it so low that none of them could hear them; but they forgot that these were government officers over them as well as the negro regiments.[16]

The social upheaval of seeing so many troops marching armed through the city's streets, as well as being served food and refreshments at Philadelphia area eating establishments, was tremendous:

> They were marched down to the Union Volunteer Refreshment Saloon, at the foot of Washington St.; here the arms were stacked and guards stationed over them, while the noble-hearted soldiers went under a long shed erected for the accommodation of soldiers, where some hundred or so could wash, and a number of nice towels for them to dry themselves; they then marched in around the tables, which were bountifully spread, looking very well. The ladies and gentlemen, I say ladies and gentlemen because they proved themselves to be so, by waiting on those colored soldiers with interest and politeness, and a sense of feeling sympathy, as much to say, you have left your homes and your families, and all that was near and dear, and have given yourself to the government to aid in putting down the "rebellion," and striking an everlasting blow for freedom and liberty to all men. They were all white ladies and gentlemen.[17]

Reverend Weaver even described a chance meeting with Commander Wagner:

> We tried to note and observe everything. Col. Wagner and some ten or twelve of the officers had a table in the same room just at the upper part where there was just space wide enough to wait on them. This was the first time we were ever there, and of course we were a stranger to the committee, but they found out who I was, the editor of the *Christian Recorder*, and we could not have been treated better had we been the Mayor of the city, or Governor of the State, and nothing would do but we must take dinner or a cup of coffee any how. We were not thinking of such a thing, but took a cup of coffee, bread and butter, and thought it was the best we ever tasted, maybe because it came from those Christian ladies and gentlemen. The committee of this saloon has always been ready and willing to feed the colored soldiers on the very principle they feed the white, for they believe that they were just as much duty-bound to feed one as the other, hence [...] no difference.[18]

Weaver, in fact, noted a breaking down of the racial conventions of the day, as he continued to describe the apparent relenting of the Cooper Shop Refreshment Saloon in the Washington Street area:

> This saloon stands back farther from Washington street, and we did not know that it was there until just a little before it was time to leave. We went around and found four companies of the 8ᵗʰ regiment and the officers, who dined there. When the first company was raised here in Philadelphia, and the talk was that the colored company was coming into Philadelphia to parade through the streets and would be marched down to said saloon. It seems that a meeting was held at the Cooper

Shop Refreshment Saloon, and a vote was taken by the committee and managers, which was in substance, that if the negro soldiers came down, they would neither feed nor wait upon them. The Union Saloon prepared at once to feed them all, (nearly) but it seems that when the 6th regiment came in, they very kindly opened the doors, and had got quite a number of colored waiters, and he stated to me that the help he keeps on hand all the time waited on the colored soldiers; we were glad to hear this from his own lips, for we had, up to this time, an unfavorable opinion of Mr. Cooper and his saloon, but his conversation to me removed that state of feeling. He said more; they behaved just as well as any troops that he had ever fed there; this speaks volumes for the character of colored soldiers and their race. Everybody seemed to be pleased. We cannot say quite as much about Mr. Cooper's saloon as we can about the Union, because we were at the Union pretty much all the time, and was taken up stairs and shown the room for the poor sick soldiers, and the splendid view they have of the [Delaware] river.[19]

The spectacle of the black Camp William Penn troops marching off to war even caught the attention of publications based in New York City, who described the 6th's parading through downtown Philadelphia streets and its departure for Virginia:

Early in October its dusky troops moved along Walnut, Pine, and Broad streets on dress parade – "blacks in blue" with white gloves and fixed bayonets. The correspondent of the New York Tribune reported: "They made a brilliant appearance." On the 14th the regiment paraded again, this time from the North Philadelphia railroad station to a ship waiting at the wharf to take it to Fortress Monroe, Virginia. The next day it arrived at its destination, the first of the Camp Penn trainees to reach Virginia. For many of the Negro recruits the trip from Philadelphia to Fortress Monroe was a new experience. En route some were stricken with seasickness, but upon arrival all were able to begin immediately the march of some twenty miles up the Peninsula to a camp just below the historic village of Yorktown. Here Ames's men spent their first night on Virginia soil. Here, except for minor forays, they were to remain until the latter part of April, 1864. (Montgomery 1961, 160-161)

The Christian Recorder neatly summarized the embarking of the 6th USCT off to war in a follow-up October 17, 1863, article:

THE DEPARTURE OF THE 6TH U.S. COLORED REGIMENT.
On last Wednesday morning, the Sixth Colored Regiment of the U.S. came in from Camp William Penn, and marched down Chestnut St. to the head quarters all equipped for war: from there they marched down to Second St., and thence to Washington St., and to the refreshment saloon, where dinner was prepared for them all at the union saloon, and at the cooper shop, where they all fared sumptuously. There was an immense crowd of both white and colored who followed them so as to see the last of them. The boys all seemed very lively and in good spirits. About 5 o'clock, p.m., they commenced to embark on board the steamer Conqueror,

company after company, until they were all on board. At 10 minutes past six the steamer left the dock, at the foot of Washington St. The boys then gave three cheers for the Union, three for Colonel Wagner, and three for Governor Curtin and the war; and also three for Captain Sullivan of the steamer, that he might land them safely at their destination.[20]

The sights and sounds had to be very overwhelming to onlookers as the 6ᵗʰ broke out in song:

> They then sang the tune entitled "John Brown's body lies mouldering in the dust." The tears were standing in the eyes of mothers, sisters, and fathers; also wives and relations wondering if they ever should be permitted to see them again. The white friends who are really loyal and friends indeed, seemed to indicate sorrow, but would say from their suppressions, "You are going in a good cause – the cause of your country." Yes, bleeding as she is, you have left your homes and all that is near and dear, and have gone to help to rescue her from thralldom to freedom.[21]

In fact, the troops would now get the opportunity to fall in step with other black brigades. With Major General Benjamin F. Butler, an early proponent of using black Union troops, directed to oversee in Virginia and North Carolina the 18ᵗʰ Army Corps, preparations were being made to launch a huge attack against Richmond, the seat of the Confederacy. Butler was said to be "preoccupied with the physical, intellectual, and moral welfare of his blacks," even trying to provide equitable medical care and pay, despite the incredible challenges. (Longacre 1981) "The 4ᵗʰ and 5ᵗʰ regiments of colored troops were […] brigaded with the 6ᵗʰ. All three were assigned to Colonel Samuel A. Duncan and placed in Butler's 18ᵗʰ Army Corps" (Montgomery 1961, 161).

Yet, since the 6ᵗʰ Regiment's men barely had enough time to train, they were essentially "still raw recruits when they reached Virginia" (ibid.). So during the next 60 days Ames and his officers drilled the men very hard. "The weary round of camp life consisted of guard mounting in the morning, the interminable tramp of sentinels on their beats, the marching of men on the drill field, and 'dress parade' in the evening" (ibid.). Yet, the soldiers were getting stronger each day. "Trips up the peninsula toward Richmond and expeditions north of the York River in the direction of the Rappahannock River were frequently undertaken to give practice in marching. Often the troops covered thirty miles in one day" (ibid.). And that was despite, at times, being verbally accosted by Confederate-sympathizing women along the routes, who would "jeer and shake their fists" (ibid.). For the most part, noted Montgomery, the men shook off such behavior with giggles. "Jeers and clenched fists, and the laughter they provoked, helped to break the monotony of the repetitious drill and the long march" (ibid.).

In fact, there were increasing activities that interrupted the relative boredom, an indication that more than their share of excitement was not too far in the distant future. For instance, there were "preparations for reviews by such dignitaries as General Casey," then offset by the grueling "work on fortifications at Yorktown and Gloucester Point" in Virginia. But then there were raids "against a Confederate works farther up the Peninsula" that "gave the troops a taste of real warfare," according to Montgomery. In fact, as the year 1863 wound down, on December 12-14th Union forces aimed to "capture a battalion of Virginia Cavalry at Charles City" (ibid.). In fact:

> Early on the 13th the 6th left camp at Yorktown to receive and guard prisoners and horses, issue rations, attend the wounded, and do picket duty. After marching twenty-four miles it reached Twelve-Mile Ordinary. There a good defensive position was selected and pickets posted. Before the day had ended the entire Confederate command at Charles City was captured and turned over to Ames's men. The next day the 6th returned to Williamsburg, having lost only one man during the encounter. (ibid.)

And what really broke the monotony were the very much anticipated visits of the officers' family members, especially wives, not an uncommon practice during the Civil War. "Captain McMurray's wife and two children spent part of the winter of 1863-64 on the Peninsula. They lived in good quarters, had an abundance of wholesome food, and enjoyed the associations with the wives and families of other officers." The anguish between the spouses was evident when the officers were required to leave on patrols that could last several days (ibid.).

Meanwhile, the war and the Union occupation certainly had a deleterious impact on the surrounding communities. "By the fall of 1863 historic Yorktown was a shambles. Its few remaining buildings were occupied by poverty-stricken whites and negroes," according to Montgomery. And Williamsburg "was a dismal place of some four or five hundred whites and negroes." McMurray and his men likely found nothing in the towns that served as a release from the "military routine." Yet, McMurray "had a good sense of history and appreciated the opportunity to walk the streets of these two old Virginia towns" (162-163).

Still, there were incidents that certainly raised the soldiers' adrenaline:

> For McMurray the most exciting incident at Camp Yorktown occurred while he was once serving as Officer of the Day. The camp was on a forty-foot bluff overlooking the York River. Directly below and close to the river's edge was a spring of water. Colonel Ames ordered the men in the guardhouse put to work in constructing a path from the camp to the spring. McMurray passed the order to a corporal, who in turn commanded the prisoners to "fall in" and go to work. One of them refused to obey and McMurray was called to the scene. Upon arrival, he observed the prisoner prostrate before the guard tent. Commanded by the Officer of the day to "fall in," the refractory soldier again refused. McMurray then ordered him tied up and "bucked and gagged." As soon as he saw what was in store for him, the soldier sprang to his feet, drew a razor he had concealed on his person, and waving it in one hand rushed at the officer. Taken by surprise, McMurray seized a club and struck the soldier on the head. He fell to the ground and was promptly tied up. (163)

However, instead of McMurray quelling the matter, the situation became dangerously overheated, according to Montgomery:

> The news of what had happened electrified the camp and a hundred excited men quickly gathered around the guard tent. With the wildest rumors going through the camp, McMurray suddenly realized he was the symbol of those emotional ingredients which might easily explode into mutinous behavior. At this point he was rescued by a young lieutenant, who handed him a pistol. Pointing the weapon at the rapidly increasing crowd of colored troopers, the Officer of the Day explained what had happened and ordered every man to return to his quarters. The demonstration was convincing, and the crowd of milling solders turned and walked slowly back to their tents. (ibid.)

Consequently, the recalcitrant soldier faced a court martial for "insubordination," causing "great excitement" again for his concerned comrades. Indeed, three of those compatriots "had collaborated on an article which appeared in a Philadelphia paper." The piece "violently attacked McMurray," charging that the officer had used "brutality in the treatment of the Negro soldier." McMurray was called to the headquarters of General Butler at Fortress Monroe fearing almost certain chastisement or worse since the "command was recognized as the champion of the colored solder." But McMurray, said Montgomery, must have been surprised about Butler's polite questioning and ultimately dismissing the young officer without punishment (164).

Yet, the "first two weeks of December" in 1864 would bring a barrage of activities for the 6th USCT when:

> Brigadier General Isaac J. Wistar wrote his report of an expedition to Charles City Court House, Virginia, in which [...] the 6th U.S. Colored Infantry, had performed a humble role in a satisfactory manner. General Wistar merely stated, without rhetorical elaboration, the assignment given the colored troops participating in the expedition, a Union raid in brigade strength up the peninsula toward Richmond. "At 4 a.m. on the 13th instant, the 6th U.S. Colored Infantry, Col. J.W. Ames, marched from Yorktown, with ambulances and a wagon loaded with rations, with instructions to arrive at Twelve-Mile Ordinary, 24 miles distant, a sufficient time before dark, to select a good defensive position, and throw out pickets on both roads, which form at that point." The report disclosed that the assignment was "effected with complete success, notwithstanding a severe storm of wind and rain which commenced suddenly during the process of ... execution." Apparently General Wistar was pleased. "Col. Ames' colored infantry did what was required of them," he wrote, "which would be considered very severe duty (weather and roads considered), except in connection with the more arduous services of the other troops." His cavalry had moved some 76 miles in 44 hours, and his white infantry 67 miles in 54 hours "over deep and muddy roads." Still he thought the colored troops' position at Twelve-Mile Ordinary "in readiness to

receive and guard prisoners and horses, issue rations, attend to wounded, and do picket duty, on the return of the other exhausted troops, was found of extreme advantage." They had won no glory, but they had done their job to the complete satisfaction of the brigadier commanding. (Cornish 1987, 259-260)

In the interim, General Butler became very concerned about the Confederates' treatment of prisoners and exchanges with Union forces. Butler thus decided that "direct action was the answer," so "he devised early in [February] 1864 a plan to set at liberty the Union captives at Richmond's Libby and Belle Isle prisons." The 6th and 22nd of Camp William Penn, as well as the 4th and 5th black regiments were called upon, in addition to the white troopers of the 11th Pennsylvania Cavalry. On February 5th the soldiers "rendezvoused at Williamsburg under the command of Brigadier General Isaac J. Wister [also spelled Wistar]." By the evening of the 6th the brigade "had reached a point within two miles of Bottom's Bridge, which crossed the Chickahominy Creek about six miles east of Libby Prison." However, according to McMurray, a New York regiment soldier who escaped from the stockade in Williamsburg and faced a death sentence warned the Rebels "of the approaching raiders." The Confederates positioned artillery that surprised and repelled the Union troops, a development that must have greatly anguished and frustrated the 6th and other black regiments, since they had "marched forty-two miles in twenty-four hours." (Montgomery 1961, 164-165).

Wister's force, in fact, included more than six thousand, with the blacks hailing from several regions of the country:

> It consisted of twenty-two hundred cavalry and four thousand infantry, the latter evenly split among three white and three black regiments. The African American units comprised the 4th, 5th, and 6th USCT, forming a brigade under Colonel Samuel A. Duncan. Despite the anonymous utility of their USCT labels, there was a distinct regional character to each of the black regiments: the 4th had been organized in Baltimore, and the 5th was a product of Ohio's Camp Delaware, while the 6th had formed at Camp William Penn, near Philadelphia. (Trudeau 1998, 202)

The historian-writer Noah Andre Trudeau, a 6th USCT soldier in the contingent who was known quite interestingly as "Hard Cracker" described to the Anglo-African newspaper the action just after rising from a "nice nap". Then, an order came for the regiment to move forward with "six days rations in knapsacks, and seventy rounds of ammunition" (203):

> ...It would be impossible to describe the wild enthusiasm of the men when they received this order [...] Well, we got ready, and, turning our backs upon our old camp ground, we thought [,] who would live to return [?]
> We marched to Williamsburg, and encamped that night upon the battle-field rendered famous by the victory of Union troops over the rebel Gen. Magruder [during McClellan's Peninsula Campaign]. The night was intensely cold, and orders came that no fires should be made [...] We left Williamsburg at 11 o'clock

a.m., marching to New Kent Court House, a distance of 33 miles, arriving at 1 ½ o'clock a.m., and, I'll assure you, we slept without rocking. Every one felt that we would have a fight before halting, and it would have done your heart good to look down that dark line and noted that stubborn determination to do or die.

We started for Bolton Bridge [i.e., Bottom's Bridge] on the Chickahominy River. We marched to within four miles of the Bridge, and meeting our cavalry, all returned, sadly disappointed I'll assure you. (ibid.)

Union commanders quickly set about to hatch another plan that would prove to be foolhardy. The plan essentially was to have four thousand troops quickly penetrate Richmond and then separate, where "one group would enter the city from the west while the main body pushed north." This "idea was promoted by a flamboyant, egotistical cavalry division commander by the name of Judson Kilpatrick, and then given a big boost by the lurid stories of the suffering told by recent escapees from Richmond's Libby Prison." President Lincoln, usually quite savvy with respect to military missions, fell for the plan and summoned Kilpatrick to Washington for a personal briefing. "Kilpatrick's operation required a cooperative diversion by Butler's men on the Peninsula, which meant that black troops would once more be marching to Richmond. With Lincoln's backing – and despite opposition from the commander of the Army of the Potomac – the Kilpatrick Raid was set in motion" (203-204).

By then the 22ⁿᵈ USCT, which also hailed from Camp William Penn, joined their comrades near Yorktown, according to Trudeau. That regiment's surgeon, James Otis Moore, recollected that by 5:30 p.m., the soldiers were marching to Richmond in pitch blackness and rain. Lieutenant J. H. Goulding of the 6ᵗʰ USCT described the ensuing evening as getting "dark very early and soon it was black – invisible holes wet our feet; if we tried to get out of the mud a little, invisible trees and stumps ran right into us." Lieutenant Joseph J. Scroggs of the 5ᵗʰ USCT recalled that the evening had been "one of the worst nights I ever experienced. We passed through Williamsburg shortly after dark. The citizens kept well within doors. Afraid of the 'nigger' I suppose" (204).

About two thousand infantry backed up by one thousand cavalry soon pushed towards the New Kent Court House. "Here, according to Lieutenant Goulding, after 'catching […] a few minutes sleep, and leaving those who were worn out, we pushed on again, and marched 18 miles further to Baltimore Crossroads, only 16 miles from Richmond.'" The soldiers were likely very thankful to stop and get a bit more sleep. "By now, according to Surgeon Moore of the 22ⁿᵈ USCT, the 'real intent of our hard marching […] disclosed itself.'" There was the realization that the men were to serve as a diversion, surmised Trudeau, that would allow General Kilpatrick's forces at the rear of Lee's Army to infiltrate Richmond and cause plenty of damage (204-205):

It was on the morning of March 3 that Butler's cooperative force met up with the main body of Kilpatrick's expedition. Wrote Lieutenant Scroggs, "Our brigade was drawn up in close column along the roadside to await his coming. We didn't have long to wait." William H. Thomas, a sergeant in the 5ᵗʰ USCT, was among the first to greet the exhausted troopers, with whom he "had a pleasant shaking of the hands." "Some were bare headed," related Lieutenant Goulding of the 6ᵗʰ, 'some with slouched grey hats picked up on the way, some with shawls wrapped around them, and one I saw with a very gaily trimmed lady's hat, the ribbons streaming in the wind behind him […] The weary nodding riders passed at length, and we guarded their rear back to Yorktown." (205)

The initiative was an outright failure on all accounts. "Kilpatrick's raid was at once a military failure and a political disaster. Neither element of his two-pronged advance penetrated Richmond's defenses, and on the body of the officer commanding the smaller force, the Rebels found orders targeting Jefferson Davis for assassination." However, federal authorities would not confirm the reports, even denying them, giving the Confederates a great public relations victory. "Although the Federal high command vehemently denied that these were official instructions, Confederate newspapers nonetheless had a field day with the information" (ibid.). However, in the midst of the setbacks, at least one positive element was not overlooked, as Trudeau noted:

Lieutenant Robert N. Verplanck of the 6th USCT summed up the participation of the black regiments in two letters written soon after the expedition ended. "We had very hard marching & some little skirmishing […] The army of the Potomac

has at last seen colored troops & has received them very well," he declared on March 7. Six days later, he was rather more somber in his assessment: "We have had the toughest kind of time in the mud, rain & dark, did nothing & lost two men from our company who are prisoners in Richmond." (ibid.)

Nevertheless, an even more important priority had been set by General Ulysses S. Grant, now commander of all Union forces. He was determined to crush General Lee's Army of Northern Virginia. Grant planned to use the Union's Army of the Potomac and General

Captain Robert Burns Beath commanded Company A of the 6th USCT, destined to be one of the most active units from Camp William Penn. *Courtesy of the U. S. Army Military History Institute.*

Butler's Army of the James, which consisted of the 3ʳᵈ Division of the 18ᵗʰ Army Corps, "an all-colored unit commanded by Major General Edward W. Hinks." The Division was "composed of two brigades. In charge of the 2ⁿᵈ Brigade was Colonel Samuel A. Duncan. To this brigade belonged the 4ᵗʰ, 5ᵗʰ, and 6ᵗʰ colored regiments (Montgomery 1961, 165)":

> While Butler's ultimate objective was Richmond, which Grant supposed he would reach by moving up the south side of the James, it was necessary for him first to cut out certain communication lines to the south of the Confederate capital. One of these was the Richmond and Petersburg Railroad. If severed, reinforcement of Richmond from the south would be rendered extremely difficult. For nearly two weeks Butler made what Grant described as an ineffective thrust to cut this railroad. At the time of this attack McMurray complained that the Negro troops at City Point were not once called into action. Perhaps Butler did not consider them battle-worthy. That he did not order them to attack the almost defenseless city of Petersburg displeased Grant and raised some doubt about the capacity of the commander of the Army of the James. (165-166)

It wasn't long before Butler lost the advantage because his troops were "hermetically sealed," according to Grant. On May 10ᵗʰ, the Confederates' General P.G.T. Beauregard and his Rebel troops, noted Montgomery, "threw up a strong line of earthworks between the Richmond and Petersburg Railroad and that portion of the Army of the James that occupied Bermuda Hundred" (166).

In the interim, Duncan's brigade of black troops, including the 6ᵗʰ, were still languishing at City Point. Yet, the soldiers by mid-May were ordered about "six miles up the Appomattox River to Spring Hill, about five miles below Petersburg." The black soldiers "set a picket and threw out cavalry videttes toward the city." They quickly built a "small but strong earthwork, later known as Redoubt Converse" in order to "protect the pontoon bridge" nearby. And after "the fortifications were completed, the 6ᵗʰ Regiment was left in charge of this nearest outpost to Petersburg" (ibid.).

The 6ᵗʰ's soldiers, especially those who had slave ties to the area, had to be anxious and anticipating the moment they could take and march into the city, since they were so physically close to it. "The city's church spires and public buildings were in plain view, but between the city and the 6ᵗʰ were the Rebel defenders. However, except for the probing of small patrols, the defenders caused little trouble for Ames's men during their four weeks' stay near Petersburg." According to Montgomery, McMurray reported that "these skirmishes were the first fighting the 6ᵗʰ experienced." And the men, by virtually all accounts, did quite well, except for one soldier, Private Alphonso Cherry (166-167):

> While on picket duty Cherry fell back in good order only to meet his company commander. He explained that his usefulness "out there" had ended when he shot away his ramrod. McMurray told him to return to the camp, get another gun, and report back to his post. Instead of following orders, Cherry fell back all the way to Norfolk. Six months later McMurray found him with a regiment of colored cavalry and persuaded the delinquent soldier to return to his old company. (167)

Even in the midst of war, Union forces sometimes fraternized with Confederate families whose sons and fathers were on battlefields near and far. Montgomery pointed out:

> McMurray and other officers of the 6th found their way into some of their homes. Often they sat in living rooms and chatted with Virginians whose sons or brothers were serving with the Confederate forces. Close as these families were to the Union lines, they could nevertheless get letters from relatives in Lee's army by way of Richmond and Petersburg. McMurray records that his last visit to one of these homes was unceremoniously ended by approaching Confederate horsemen. (ibid.)

Although about nine months had gone by since the 6th was organized, the regiment "had little more to its credit" than the recent skirmishing, as well as "marching and throwing up a few earthworks." That was despite the fact that the unit "was now fairly well trained in company, regimental, and brigade drill, but as a fighting unit its capacity was still unknown" (167-168).

Meanwhile, there were certainly non-combat issues that continued to agitate the black soldiers of the 6th, including lower pay, according to a 6th USCT soldier who wrote the *Christian Recorder*:

> We have showed ourselves fully capable of the trust reposed in us; yet, notwithstanding, we are paid only seven dollars per month, and no bounty is allowed to any of the colored troops called into service in 1863. Are they not as good soldiers as those enlisted in 1864? We all wish and fervently pray the Government to take our case into consideration. Place the white soldiers now in the field in the situation of the black soldiers in the field, and, when the word is given: 'March!' no doubt they will say that there is another division of soldiers which is getting the price of their blood, and we are not. Why do ye call on us? Are they better than we? Have we become a burden to the country, that we should be treated thus? God forbid that such treachery should exist!

The writer, indeed, focused on his precise economic gripes while using his own children and wife as suffering examples:

> We were conscripted and enlisted under the stipulation of thirteen dollars per month and $102 bounty. Our families – hundreds, nay, thousands, of helpless women and children – are this day suffering for the natural means of subsistence, whose husbands and fathers have responded to the country's call. It would be better for Congress to call us instantly out of the field of action, and give us a chance of making our living in the best manner we can, than to cruelly perish and starve so many innocent and defenceless inhabitants of this once bright and sunny land of the brave. I am a private in the ranks of the many thousands of Union soldiers that hold the firelock in their hands in their country's defence, and I have not the pleasure that pertains to a soldier, because I have a large family of helpless children depending on me for their support; but, alas! I despair of the

means of support for them. Our families can go on the commonwealth for their support. I would ask the world, where is the wealth to keep them when there is not as much as will pay the black soldier more than seven dollars per month and no bounty. Yet he is a man, and must be retained in the field to cope with the common hated adversary of the nation. Oh, men, look at this common act of unprincipled treatment the black man must labor under! Do one thing or the other – send us home, or give us justice. We ask no elevation further than our rights as men and natives of their country. Our wives and children are as near and as dear to black men, as the white men's are to them.

I speak to the Senate of the United States to look at their former promise in 1863; that the black soldier who would take up arms to help put down the rebellion, should be treated the same as the white soldier. Now we are in the field, and seven dollars is [not] enough for us: a sum not adequate to keep us in tobacco at the price we pay for the same here. There should be but one of two things to do – pay us full wages and bounty, or else send us home. I am a private in the Sixth United States Colored Regiment, raised at Chelton Hill, Pa., but name UNKNOWN.[22]

The wives of such soldiers had to try and seek employment at home, often finding it exceptionally hard due to the double-edged sword of racism and sexism. In Philadelphia they were even excluded from the Schuylkill Arsenal, which prepared various materials and necessities for Union forces during the war:

The allegedly racist hiring practice at the Schuylkill Arsenal in Philadelphia was protested by black women of the region. Military policy at this time provided for the employment, where possible, of a dependent whose relative had either died or been wounded in the service. Black women were apparently rejected in their bid for positions at the arsenal. In November 1863, aggrieved African American women protested their exclusion from jobs for which they qualified through the blood sacrifice of their loved ones in the Union army. (Johnson 1999, 82)

However plenty of action was on the horizon, so the 6th USCT had to pull together, despite external pressures, such as inequitable pay and the dire circumstances of the black recruits' families, in order to survive and possibly return home.

Meanwhile, stationed in Yorktown, Sgt. Thomas Hawkins of the 6th "befriended a man who could sympathize with his duties and responsibilities – Christian A. Fleetwood, Sergeant-Major of the 4th

Christian Fleetwood, of the 4th USCT, earned the Medal of Honor for his military prowess at New Market Heights or Chapin's Farm on September 29, 1864, along with his friends, sergeants Alexander Kelly and Thomas Hawkins of the 6th USCT from Camp William Penn. *Courtesy of the Library of Congress.*

USCI which was brigaded with the 6th. Both men would be heavily involved in Duncan's Assault at New Market Heights" (Price 2010). Most notably, the duo would earn the Medal of Honor for their valor at New Market Heights.

They would be part of a brigade that, on June 14, 1864, "prepared for a coordinated attack on enemy fortifications outside of Petersburg." In fact, past "attempts on the city had been halfhearted and timid, although at one time Butler had been ordered to take the city with bayonet, if necessary. Now the preparations for an impending assault were evident." That "black brigade, comprised of the 4th, 5th, 6th, and 22nd Colored Troops, totaled about 2,200 able-bodied fighting men that morning. They were accompanied by several white regiments, including the 5th Massachusetts Cavalry, Holman's brigade of 1,300 officers and men, Angel's battery of the 136th, and Choate's black battery of the 111th. The force totaled 3,747 men" (Claxton, Puls 2006, 134-135).

With the Confederates "firing on them from Baylor's Farm about a mile in the distance, near the swampy area around Perkinson's Saw Mill," the black brigade "waited as the 5th Massachusetts Cavalry, which was composed of new recruits, awkwardly moved into line" (135). The 6th and the other black USCT units waited patiently:

> In the early morning light, Fleetwood, [Charles] Veal, Hawkins, Kelly, [Powhatan] Beaty, and the others could see a gauntlet of obstacles. The rebels had bunkered down behind quickly made rifle pits on a crest of a hill about a thousand yards away. The first six hundred yards consisted of a densely wood area; the remainder was across an open field in full view of the hill where the rebels waited securely entrenched.
>
> Even raw recruits appreciated the danger. The Confederates would have a chance to fire on them as they fought their way through a tangle of underbrush in the woods. A turnpike ran through the woods and a railroad line intersected it. These obstacles would tend to delay the advance and cause breaks in the lines even before they confronted the enemy. Furthermore, the floor of the woods, marshy and strewn with fallen timbers, was covered with a dense thicket of vines and bushes that reached twenty feet high. (135)

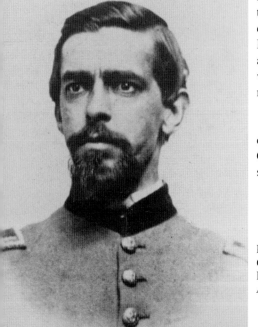

The moment of truth had come for the 6th and others in the companion black regiments, wrote Claxton and Puls. The war was now staring them straight in the eyes:

First Lt. John B. Johnson was in Company D of the 6th USCT and likely saw action at Virginia's Baylor's Farm and Perkinson's Sawmill. *Courtesy of the U. S. Army Military History Institute.*

For many in the black regiments [...] this would be their first real combat experience, their moment of truth. As McMurray put it, "We had considerable experience in marching, some in throwing up earthworks, and were fairly well trained in company regimental, and brigade drill, but in fighting we were novices. But now we were at the turning point, and from this time forward, we were destined to experience our full share of vicissitudes of war." (136)

And then Hell's moment came, with another Camp William Penn regiment, the 22ⁿᵈ, joining in the fury:

> The brigade was formed in front of the woods. General Hinks explained to the men that their mission was to march through the brush and take the enemy fortifications. Colonel Conine and the 5ᵗʰ were on the right. The 22ⁿᵈ, under Colonel Joseph B. Kiddoo, was on the right center; the 4ᵗʰ, under Colonel Rogers, was at the left center; and the 6ᵗʰ, under Colonel Ames, was on the left. Orders were issued to each regimental commander, who passed them to the troops. The first line was to open a heavy fire on the enemy upon reaching the farther skirt of the woods and reestablish the battle line as quickly as possible after passing through the series of obstacles. Then they would wait for an order to charge.
>
> As the men began to move forward toward the wooded area, the enemy's battery opened a furious shelling of the dense brush, inflicting considerable damage. Trees splintered and men fell under the relentless fire. Wounded men screamed in pain as a hailstorm of enemy fire ripped through the ranks. The wood and swamp and creek proved difficult obstacles to cross. Still, the men pushed on, fighting through the six hundred yards of brush. The rebels bore down with cannon fire, heavy artillery, and muskets along the whole line. The 4ᵗʰ Regiment with Fleetwood, [Alfred B.] Hilton, and [Charles] Veal was the first to reach the open field. In the excitement, the center companies cheered in adrenaline-induced excitement and charged up the hill without forming their lines. [...]
>
> Captain King was killed and Captains Mendall and Parrington and Lieutenant Bringham were wounded. Brigham's injury proved fatal. One hundred fifty men out of six hundred from the 4ᵗʰ were killed. Fleetwood saw men fall around him. (136-137)

Next to enter through Hell's doors would be the 6ᵗʰ black regiment of Camp William Penn, according to Claxton and Puls:

> The 6ᵗʰ Regiment with Hawkins and Kelly moved quickly through the trees and brush. But in the early morning darkness they overlapped and became entangled with the 4ᵗʰ. On reaching the edge of the woods the 6ᵗʰ was hit by fire from the left. The men prepared for a charge, but the brigade's line was too torn up to make an immediate advance.
>
> Yet the right side of the line took advantage of the diversion of fire to the left and formed a regular battle line. Colonel Kiddo waited for orders from his 22ⁿᵈ Colored Infantry to charge. He was concerned that the rough terrain would

prevent an order to advance from reaching him, or that his regiment would not be found. He couldn't remain stationary because the rebel guns had begun shelling his troops. So he lined his men up for the advance. [Sergeant Milton M.] Holland and others from the 5th U.S. Colored Infantry were also in the line of enemy fire.

"We were then in the open field, halted, where we kept up a brisk fire on the skirmish line until the regiments could get through the swamps and form in order again," Holland noted. "All this while the enemy poured a galling fire of musketry, grape and canister into ranks slaying many. The order was given to forward the skirmish line one-hundred paces, this being done we halted, keeping up our fire along the line."

Just then, the men saw a curious sight, a rebel soldier riding a white horse while yelling loudly to exhort his men. He drew the attention of the whole Union division. "It was that brave and daring but strange personage that rides with charger," Holland noted. "We could see him plainly riding up and down the rebel lines, could hear him shouting from the top of his voice to stand, that they had only niggers to contend with." The rider seemed oblivious to the danger from the Federal muskets. "This peculiar personage seems possessed with supernatural talent," Holland thought. "He would sometimes ride his horse with almost lightning speed, up and down his lines amid the most terrific fire of shot and shell. But when the command was given to us 'Charge bayonets! Forward double quick!' the black column rushed forward, raising the battle yell, and in a few moments more we mounted the rebel parapets."

At 8 a.m., Hinks gave the order to charge. Milton and members of the 5th and 22nd Colored Troops raced up the rising ground, yelling loudly as they came, and flooded the rebel works. The enemy had fled, abandoning a twelve-pounder gun. Black soldiers from the 22nd immediately turned it around and fired on the retreating rebels. "To our great surprise, we found that the boasted Southern chivalry had fled. They coud not see the nigger part as the man on the white horse presented it," Holland sneered. (138-139)

Indeed, by July 1864 Hawkins and Fleetwood (who joined in August 1863 the 4th at the same age as Hawkins, age 23, in Baltimore, Maryland, where Fleetwood was born on July 21, 1841) were certainly fraternizing and likely close friends, according to Fleetwood's diary (Fleetwood, diary, nationalhumanitiescenter.org 2007).

And they likely shared the terrible news of an unidentified 6th Regiment soldier drowning, according to the diary entry of Wednesday, July 31st: "Reports &c. throughout the day. Sent out Cottin & Hamilton to recover body of 6th Regt. man drowned on Sunday Regt. Mustered for pay by Major. No letters busy as usual all day [...] Weather fine" (ibid.).

Apparently, following Grant's unsuccessful June 3rd attack at Cold Harbor, "he decided to move around Lee's right flank, cross the James River, and strike Petersburg from Bermuda Hundred." And by June 15th the overall commander of Union forces, "Grant himself had arrived at Bermuda Hundred where almost 50,000 troops were preparing to cross the Appomattox River for the projected attack." Then, as the morning sun rose on the 15th, the 18th Corps, led by Major General William F. Smith, "previously detached from the

Army of the James to assist at Cold Harbor," started to move forward. And that's when the 6ᵗʰ began to cross the Appomattox at Point of the Rocks via the pontoon bridge that it "had been protecting." As Smith's soldiers passed, the "6ᵗʰ followed immediately, joining some nine regiments of a colored division under General Hinks" (Montgomery 1961, 168).

The stage was set for more conflict, wrote Montgomery:

> Smith's corps, consisting of his own and Hinks' division, numbered at least 12,000 men. Hinks' division of about 5,000 was composed of three brigades. Of these, Duncan's 2ⁿᵈ, consisting of the 4ᵗʰ, 5ᵗʰ, 6ᵗʰ, and 22ⁿᵈ regiments, totaled in the neighborhood of 2,200. Hinks took his men along the main road. Smith moved his division of over 6,000 to the right of the road, so as to face the Petersburg defenses near the Appomattox River. By 10:00 a.m. the corps was before the city's works, Smith having the advantage of a position in a wood and Hinks being protected

Blacks were often delegated the most grisly jobs during the Civil War, including here on the battlegrounds of Cold Harbor, Virginia, collecting human remains. *Courtesy of the Library of Congress.*

by a slight rise in the ground between himself and the Rebel line. Opposing the bluecoats was a thin band of troops numbering about 2,200. Until late in the day the corps' action consisted of several minor, though sharp skirmishes, those involving the 2nd Brigade occurring at Baylor's Farm. In one of them McMurray's company had several men killed and wounded. For the most part, however, Rebel fire was ineffective in the area of the 6th Regiment's movements. (168)

Indeed, the situation was just heating up, because as the sun began to sink below the horizon, "Smith ordered the long-awaited attack." The commander's "own division of white troops" were "immediately to the right of the colored division" and "moved off first." Hinks' black regiments followed, with the 6th Regiment taking the lead. Also participating, according to Montgomery, were elements of Major General Ambrose E. Burnside's 9th Corps and Major General Winfield Scott Hancock's 2nd Corps, just arriving from Bermuda Hundred:

Crossing a slash that had been burned over, Ames's men moved through a line of abattis in front of a ditch which protected this battery. By sundown the ditch was full of men, who had been pressing hard against a work they believed to be well manned. Not a shot had been fired at the colored troops since they had started forward. As they began to climb out of the ditch, McMurray felt sure that as fast as a Negro soldier put his head above the level of the parapet it would be

blown off. He fully expected every officer and man of his own regiment to meet death while trying to get out of that ditch. This, however, did not happen. Climbing into the battery, they found it deserted, the last Confederate gone, save a handsome youth in his late teens. He was dead. McMurray helped the Negroes bury him "as tenderly as though he had been a Union soldier." Thus at the very climax of the 6th Regiment's first trial under battle conditions not a shot was fired, not a man was killed, but, in the words of McMurray, "some were nearly scared to death." (168-169)

First Lieutenant Nathaniel Hubbard was in Company B of the 6th USCT. *Courtesy of the U. S. Army Military History Institute.*

Both the Confederate and Union forces, including the 6ᵗʰ, dug in, with the Rebels fortifying Petersburg even more, Montgomery observed. "Twelve hours earlier, McMurray observed, Smith could have marched into Petersburg at will. Now Grant's whole army could not force its way in" (170).

Meanwhile, McMurray began to monitor reports from white Union soldiers about the fierceness of the Confederate forces before them, many of them veterans of the battles of the Wilderness and Cold Harbor. "By midnight all the Negro soldiers were ensconced with their regiments and McMurray settled down for the rest of the night in Battery No. 9," with the black troops soon moved to the rear away from the "heavy fighting of June 16-18" (ibid.). Indeed:

> By noon of June 16 Smith's division and the corps of Hancock and Burnside, 60,000 strong, confronted the new Confederate line. Beauregard was now defending with about 14,000 men. Late in the afternoon an assault was begun on the Confederate line. It opened on Smith's left and extended along the front occupied by three corps of the Army of the Potomac (by this time Major General Gouverneur K. Warren's corps had arrived). The fighting continued, with some interruptions, into the night of June 17, when about midnight Burnside was driven back from an advanced position he had gained. On June 18 the final blow was struck. It was no more successful than the earlier ones had been. (170-171)

Although apprehensive, McMurray and the 6ᵗʰ were ready to get into the heavy fighting:

> For McMurray and the men of the 6ᵗʰ Regiment the three days after June 15 were filled with anxiety. The roar of cannon, the crash of muskets, and the yells of men up ahead attested only to hard fighting. The wounded and the stragglers who passed by on their way to the rear brought little good news to the Negroes, who were denied the chance to continue in the battle they had helped to open. McMurray himself was disgusted with the treatment accorded these troops. In his words, Grant had not yet learned "that black men were just as good fighters as white men." (171)

After the "unsuccessful effort" of Federal forces to take Petersburg, the black regiments returned "to the front line of works." It was, in fact, throughout "these six weeks Ames's men, and it would seem the other colored regiments as well, would spend three days in the rifle pits and three in camp." In fact, the 6ᵗʰ "occupied the position in the line where it crossed the road leading from Petersburg to City Point. When McMurray and his men were in the pits, there was scarcely a day that they did not suffer at least one casualty" (ibid.).

And there was duty that all troops considered gruesome and incredibly unpleasant, Montgomery noted:

> A number of dead and wounded had been left behind, the Rebels refusing permission to bury the dead. On a dark night about ten days later, McMurray was sent out with a burial detail. Shortly after 10:00 p.m. the cornfield was reached. In

the darkness it was often impossible to distinguish a dead soldier from a section of a corn row. Decomposition added to the difficulty and repugnance of the task. When a body was found a hole would be dug beside it, the body rolled into the hole and then covered. This assignment McMurray characterized "as possibly the saddest experience of my service in the army." (171-172)

By July 30th, though, they were relieved to participate in the mine explosion melee. Apparently, during the afternoon of July 29th, the 6th Regiment, as part of Duncan's brigade, "moved left to the place in line held by Burnside's corps." The opposing forces were a mere 500 feet apart, perhaps even less. Incredibly, extending from "a ravine located behind this point in the Federal line a mine slightly over 500 feet in length had been run to and under the Confederate works as far as a small fort which stood in Elliott's Salient." The "mine" consisted of a humongous 8,000 pounds of explosive powder. Then "a fuse was laid from the powder to the mine's mouth in the ravine, and one of Burnside's divisions alerted to lead the assault after the explosion." During the resulting confusion Union forces hoped to reach higher ground called Cemetery Hill, just "to the right of the doomed fort. To reach and hold this height, Union commanders believed, would assure the fall of Petersburg" (172).

The spectacle of what McMurray and his black troops witnessed, and experienced with the likes of the 43rd USCT of Camp William Penn was surreal:

> After much delay and confusion, the explosion finally took place a few minutes before 5:00 a.m. on July 30. With his eyes fixed on the fort at the moment of the blast, McMurray observed it moving slowly at first and then suddenly lead up to a height of 150 feet, "breaking into fragments of timber, stone, broken gun carriages, muskets, tents, and black and mutilated bodies, all falling back quickly with a dull, sullen sound." Two hundred men were killed by the explosion and the Confederate line was opened by a hole 170 feet long, 60 feet wide, and 30 feet deep. Although the Rebels were completely taken by surprise, Burnside was unable to reach his objective. Instead, columns of Negro and white troops ordered through the opening floundered in the crater, easy prey for enemy fire. Watching this struggle, McMurray thought the best fighting was done by Burnside's black division. Like all others, it, too, was hurled back into the crater by Confederate fire. (172)

Denied a full opportunity to participate in the Petersburg campaign, McMurray believed "himself and his Negroes cheated when they were moved to the rear during the night of June 15-16" (173). Indeed, Montgomery wrote, more than a few commanders sometimes seemed recalcitrant about the idea of blacks participating in combat, with others ambivalent. Regardless, there were some who began to believe in the black soldiers' combat acumen, Montgomery noted:

> Hinks and Duncan, however, did record their impressions, and both wrote as if they believed the colored trooper had at last vindicated himself. Hinks asserted that the performance of June 15 afforded conclusive proof "that colored men

when properly officered and drilled, will not only make soldiers, but the best soldiers of the line." In a lengthy report of his brigade's activities of that day Duncan admitted that his "troops were all untried in battle, and by many it was still a problem whether the negro would fight." But in his judgment the events of June 15 justified "the most sanguine expectations for the future." On this day he reported that he had witnessed skirmishers push forward "with boldness" and lines advance "firmly"; he had seen the Negro assault "with gallantry" after enduring "with fortitude" hours of inaction under heavy fire; and finally, he remembered the colored trooper as bearing "heroically" the wounds of battle. (173-174)

Several days following the upsetting episode at Petersburg, Dutch Gap was the next destination for the 6ᵗʰ USCT. It was about fifteen miles south of Richmond, "at the neck of one of the numerous bends in the James River. The distance across the neck was slightly over 500 feet; around the bend it was almost five miles." (174) The Rebels, meanwhile, had built or placed many obstructions to discourage a Union naval assault. Nevertheless, General Butler desired that a canal be constructed to dissect the neck, allowing the Federal navy to get closer to Richmond and within shelling range. The 6ᵗʰ USCT was assigned to the task, according to Montgomery:

> The 6ᵗʰ Regiment encamped on the river bank near what was to become the lower opening of the canal. Brigade headquarters were established across the James in the direction of City Point. From August 10, when ground was broken, until September 28 the regiment had a daily force of 100 men working in the canal. They quickly came under the fire of Confederate mortars located up the river. For protection, hiding places called "bomb-proofs" were dug in the sides of the canal. Watchmen warned the workers of approaching shells by yelling "holes." McMurray, who did not share Butler's view of the protective value of the bomb-proofs, complained that workers often found it impossible to reach the shelters; few days passed without casualties. To convey the wounded to the hospital across the river, a small boat was always standing by. McMurray visited the hospital once and was impressed with the pile of legs and arms in the rear of the amputation tent. (ibid.)

Meanwhile, as a testament to Butler's ingratiating feelings about black troopers, the general began to utilize Confederate prisoners for building the canal alongside the African American soldiers in retaliation for USCT soldiers being forced to "work on Rebel fortifications." In fact, for "four or five days they were kept at work, scampering with the Negro soldiers to the shelters when shell warnings were given. McMurray did not recall that a single Confederate had been killed or wounded while working in the ditch." Then, after Butler learned the Rebels had stopped using captured black soldiers for such jobs, they "were taken out of the canal" (175).

Soon to catch a bird's eye view of such activities was the black Civil War correspondent for *The Philadelphia Press*, 30-year-old Thomas Morris Chester, destined to become a defining moment in the annals of journalism and African American history. Chester, in fact, was well prepared for the job, even perhaps over-qualified, since he had started and edited his own newspaper in Liberia, *The Star of Liberia*. Born in Harrisburg, PA, on May 11, 1834, to George and Jane Marie Chester, a former Virginia slave, Thomas was the fourth of 12 children, with seven surviving to adulthood. His relatively privileged upbringing by parents who owned a restaurant and catering business allowed him to receive a very good education at the Allegheny Institute, near Pittsburgh, which became Avery College. He undoubtedly was impressed by his father, George, who died before he became mature, but not sooner than learning his dad was the sole agent for William Lloyd Garrison's *Liberator* newspaper in Harrisburg. Chester's zest for learning, combined with being influenced by such black leaders as Martin Delaney in Pittsburgh, set him on the path to embrace blacks' immigration to Africa's Liberia, as well as become a lifelong scholar, educator, politician, military officer, attorney, and pioneering black journalist dedicated to covering the tribulations and triumphs of African American Civil War soldiers (Blackett 1989, 4-5):

> *The Press* and other major dailies had shown little interest in the activities of black troops prior to 1864. There were a few scattered brief reports, but no sustained coverage of black contributions to the war effort. This was left almost exclusively to two black weeklies, the Anglo-American, published in New York, and the *Christian Recorder*. Chester was commissioned in August, 1864, and for the next eight months sent the Press the most exhaustive accounts of black troop activity around Petersburg and the Confederate capital. The war had wrought significant changes in the image of newspaper correspondents as the public hankered for news from the front. No longer were they just busybodies prying into people's private lives, they had become, with the unexpected length of the war and the new technology that speeded up the transmission of news, the most reliable sources of information about developments on the battlefield. (39)

Then, just two days before the New Market Heights battle, Fleetwood wrote in his Tuesday, September 27, 1864, entry:

> Reports &c. Crossed River with Hawkins. Stopped to See Miller 22d Com Hd. Qrs. Returned with Hawkins [...] After dinner wrote to M [...] Details Formed Guard and picket. Super At Hawkins till 10 P.M [...] retired [...] Awaked at 11 ½ to Hd Qrs [...] Got out the Regt and after much tribulations and several unsuccessful attempts to catch a nap we embarked.

He continued the next day:

> WEDNESDAY 28 on board a gunboat and debarked at Jones Landing. Marched up to works Bivouacked at Deep Bottom... Dined and supd with 5. U.S.C.T. [...] Trimonthly Report made out [...] slept with Kelly [possibly the other Medal of Honor recipient of the 6th, Sgt. Alexander Kelly], Arnold, & Hawkins [...] Letters came from Bradford & Est. & Cootus with carte [...] Stirred up Regt. And, Knap[s]acks C.G.E. [...] packed away Coffe boiled and [...].

And then finally came the battle day of September 29, 1864, when Fleetwood briefly described his own heroism and others saving their regiments' colors (including members of the 6th USCT) during battle:

> Moved out & on Charged with the 6th at daylight and got used up [...] Saved colors. Remnants of the two gathered and Maneuvering under Col Ames of 6th U.S.C.T. Marching in line & flank all day saw Gen. Grant & Staff both Birneys [brother generals] and other 'Stars' Retired at night. Stacked arms & moved three times [...] (Fleetwood, diary, nationalhumanitiescenter.org 2007)

A day earlier, on September 28th the 6th USCT was on the move again with Duncan's brigade, soon to be engaged in their most stringent combat test of the war at a place called New Market Heights, Virginia. And in the vicinity was Chester, the black Civil War correspondent. If McMurray had known what was coming, he surmised afterwards, his own courage and stamina would have been quite suspect:

> On September 28 Duncan's brigade was ordered to prepare itself with rations for three days and to leave behind all men unfit for a heavy march. Before dark the men were aboard a steamer heading for Deep Bottom, approximately five miles downstream from the 6th's Dutch Gap camp. About midnight the men were put ashore. Before sunrise they were marching toward the Rebel entrenchments at the foot of New Market Heights, less than two miles from Fort Harrison. Fort Harrison was Ord's objective. Had he known what was in store for him and his company during the three hours after the march began, McMurray philosophized that he would have been totally unfit for duty. "In mercy and kindness," he explained, "I was allowed to see only what each moment revealed, and seeing that and only that, I went forward, trying to do the best I could, and hoping for the best results." (Montgomery 1961, 175-176)

As the brigade left the river bank for a two-mile march to the Confederate works, they first "marched by flank, then it formed in line of battle, with the 6th slightly to the left and McMurray's Company D near the center of the regiment." Perhaps moments later, as "the men emerged from a wood into an open field on the top of a hill," the sun's rays lit up the panorama and they "saw the Rebel pickets falling back to their lines, turning occasionally to shoot at the black soldiers coming out of the wood." The 6th and Union forces advanced, standing "within 200 feet of the Confederate riflemen, awaiting the order to go forward." Others were in "a strong line" of Rebels in pits in the midst of much debris (176):

> Picking a path through the debris in front of the enemy line was risky work. At every step the Negroes were under heavy fire. There was little chance to retaliate. Indeed, at times muskets were absolute hindrances. As he continued to go forward, McMurray noticed that the ranks were getting thinner. Seeing fewer and fewer of the thirty men he had started with, he wondered if any had turned

back. He passed his first sergeant, who had taken a bullet in his leg; he came upon Emanual Patterson, who had been shot in the abdomen "so that all his bowels all gushed out." On he pressed, urging his men forward and passing others of his company, some dead and some wounded. About halfway through the slash, the captain's life was saved, when a color guard who preceded him through a small opening between the trunk of a fallen tree and its stump was killed instantly by a shot through the breast. (176-177)

The worst parts of the battle, though, were yet to come:

Finally, McMurray broke through the slash into a small open space before the enemy's rifle pits. There for the first time since the assault had begun he met Colonel Ames. The two officers held a hasty conference and decided to fall back with what remained of the regiment. Ames urged the captain to get the men back quickly and stressed the importance of keeping them well in hand. With their backs to the enemy, the Negro troops proved helpless in the tangled mass of debris and bodies through which they had to return. Once back in the open field, each company officer began the work of collecting his men so that the regiment might be re-formed. For McMurray this proved a discouraging task. Of Company D's thirty men who had plunged into the slash less than an hour earlier, only three had survived. Twelve had been killed and fifteen wounded. The company's first lieutenant had also been wounded. Over eighty-five per cent of its men had been lost. (177)

Although the overall regimental losses were proportionately lighter, that toll was also quite terrible. Noted Montgomery, "The regiment's losses were proportionately less, but nonetheless heavy: 3 officers and 39 men killed, 11 officers and 150 men wounded, and 7 missing – a total of 210 out of 367." In fact, McMurray noted that during that forty-minute engagement his group had accrued the greatest losses of any such charge of a company in the Union Army during the war (ibid.).

And on Friday, September 30th, the day after the initial phase of the terrible New Market Heights clash, Fleetwood noted that skirmishes were still ongoing:

We spent the remainder of the darkness with the usual diversions of moving […] Recd [Received] in morning 193 recruits […] Drilled a squad in morning […] Rebels charged our line three times […] repulsed. Lying in ravine. One man killed. Moved in eve. Threw up entrenchments to protect flanks position. First nights sleep since 27th […]. Weather changed to the bad. (Fleetwood, diary, nationalhumanitiescenter.org 2007)

Next followed the grisly and sad task of locating bodies, as well as learning about how the Rebels had treated the black soldiers' remains:

The regimental formation completed, McMurray joined some officers of the 6ᵗʰ in search of dead bodies. All was now quiet before the enemy entrenchments. The Rebels had fallen back, having lost Fort Harrison; but before leaving they had gone over the battlefield and taken everything they wanted. Muskets had been gathered up, shoes taken from dead men's feet, pockets turned inside out, and cartridge boxes and haversacks carried away. Partly stripped bodies of Negro soldiers, 12 of them from his own company, lying among stumps and trees was hardly a sight to inspire McMurray to glorify war. On the other hand, whatever doubts of the Negro's fighting qualities he may have clung to at sunrise had been dispelled by mid-afternoon. (Montgomery 1961, 177-178)

And despite the deprivations, the black troops had helped to take valuable Union ground as Confederate forces prepared for a counter-attack to retake Fort Harrison. "Near the point where the attack was expected Major General George J. Stannard's brigade of Vermont troops was placed," ready for the Rebels' action. Stannard's troops "were armed with 'sixteen shooters' – rifles holding sixteen bullets which could be fired without reloading. To the right of the New Englanders was Ames's 6ᵗʰ Regiment" (179). The question was, would the extra firepower be enough to help cover Ames and his men?

Once the assaulting columns were formed and all was in readiness for the attack, the Confederates opened on the Union lines with about forty guns. During the cannonading additional regiments of defenders were hurried into their places. Shortly after the artillery fire ceased, rebel columns, five brigades of them, emerged from the oak trees. McMurray saw the enemy as "a mighty, resistless, human machine." Knowing that the men in the advancing columns were his sworn foes, bent on killing him and all the defenders of the newly captured Fort Harrison, he yet admired them as they came on with the "steadiness of a great machine, and the determination of death. At this moment the captain, whose company had been almost entirely wiped out a few hours earlier, felt that he was witnessing an exhibition of 'bravery scarcely excelled." (ibid.)

Already the assaulting Rebel force was within 175 feet of McMurray's men:

Then suddenly came the "infernal rebel yell" as the advancing men increased their pace to almost a run. Now the men in the ditch opened a murderous fire and for a few minutes the roar of musketry, the Rebel yell, and the shouting of bluecoats was deafening. On came the Confederates until they were within forty or fifty feet of McMurray and his comrades of the 6ᵗʰ. When they could take no more, the assailants turned about and ran back at full speed. For some reason Union fire abruptly stopped, and the victorious defenders watched what was left of the solid mass of assaulters that had so recently come out of the oak grove vanish at the place of its birth. The men of the 6ᵗʰ would have experienced a "savage satisfaction" had they been assured that the 2,000 Confederate casualties were exacted from the same units that had eviscerated their regiment earlier in the day. (179-180)

The tremendous episode took a mighty toll on the regiment and McMurray's company, as well as the mental health of McMurray. Montgomery noted that following the battle he became delirious about what "had been the bloodiest day of the war for Ames's men (180)":

> As it ended, McMurray was sad and gloomy. He recalled that less than a year before he had left Camp Penn with some 90 men. Of this force, only three were now present for duty. Since sunrise a third of the original group, about the number he had taken into action at New Market Heights, had been killed and wounded. As he ate his supper these frightening experiences kept haunting him. Afterwards a feeling of oppression seized him. Breathing became difficult. For relief he left his hut and spent a good portion of the night walking around it. But there was no relief; instead he became "wild and crazy." In a state of complete nervous exhaustion, he was taken to the corps hospital. There he remained for ten days, consuming a liberal allowance of quinine which "toned" him up. (ibid.)

McMurray's experience at New Market Heights was just one side of the story. Several of his men would earn the prestigious Medal of Honor for their actions, including the white officer Lieutenant Nathan H. Edgerton, as well as First Sergeant Alexander Kelly and Sergeant-Major Thomas R. Hawkins, both African Americans and two of the fourteen blacks in Union forces to receive the honor in that horrific battle. The Camp William Penn contingent was largely recognized for its efforts to save the regimental colors under extraordinary fire.

The trio was part of the 6th Regiment's wave, consisting of more than 350 soldiers to rush into torrents of lethal Confederate bullets at Chaffin's Farm in Virginia, also known as the Battle of New Market Heights, on the damp and cool morning of September 29, 1864. Fog engulfed the ghostly combat zone, severely limiting visibility. Approximately 60 percent of the regiment's men would perish in the clash (Scott, *Black Soldiers in Blue*, 1999):

> That morning, the 6th had rushed toward a line of Rebel fortifications manned by the hardened veterans of Colonel Frederick M. Bass' Texas brigade. Dozens of Edgerton's comrades had been hit and had fallen, including most members of the color guard, when Lieutenant Frederick Meyer of Company B seized the colors and a bullet slammed through his heart and killed him. Meyer, however, maintained a death grip on the staff. (ibid.)

That's when Edgerton grabbed the colors and moved forward before realizing that he too had been seriously wounded (ibid.).

Lt. Edgerton was apparently raised as a Quaker in Ohio and taught to be a pacifist. "When the war broke out in 1861 he refused to join and it was not until Robert E. Lee's invasion of Pennsylvania during the Gettysburg Campaign that he saw the necessity of military service." Rising to the rank of lieutenant by late 1863, Edgerton, by the time of the battle of New Market Heights in late September 1864, was also the regimental adjutant, "and as such he rode behind the men of the 6th as they prepared to seize the New Market

Line. (Price, *Profile in Courage* 2010)" Here's Edgerton's extraordinary account of his experiences during the battle:

As Adjutant of the regiment I received and transmitted to the Company Commanders on the evening of Sept. 28, 1864 order to equip their men for immediate action, and be ready to form line at daybreak the following morning [...] We went forward about a mile without encountering the enemy; then our skirmishers came upon their pickets and lively firing began. The enemy, however, gave way almost immediately, falling back upon their reserves, and again on to their main line. Our skirmishers pursued so rapidly that we had to go at a double-quick to keep at proper supporting distance, and we were close upon their heels when they reached the earthworks at Chappin's Farm. These we charged at once, believing the whole corps was at our backs to support us as we had supported our skirmishers, as we had been told would be the case. The earthwork immediately in front of us was strengthened by an abatis extending along its entire face. This had in front of it a sluggish stream with marshy banks and mossy bottom about four yards wide. Just the left of our regiment, the enemy's earthwork ran at right angle to the front we were charging and enabled him to give us an enfilading fire as we moved forward, which was terribly effective. At the edge of the stream, I jumped from my horse and threw the reins to the orderly, for I was sure the horse would be unable to get across owing to the marshy nature of the ground. The reins had hardly left my hand when the horse went down, shot dead from the opposite bank. When I got over the stream, I found a level space of ground thickly covered with our dead and wounded. Among these I saw Lieutenant Meyers lying upon the flag, dead, but still holding it. I took it from him and pushed forward to bring the colors to their proper place. All at once I went down, but jumped up immediately and tried to raise the flag, for I thought I had fallen over the dewberry vines which grew thickly there, but finding it did not come, I looked down, after trying again, to see why I could not lift it, and found my [...] hand was covered in blood, and

perfectly powerless, and the flag staff lying in two pieces. I sheathed my sword, took the flag with its broken staff and reached the abatis. Colonel John W. Ames was there, and about a corporal's guard of men, others soon appeared out of the powder smoke, which was so dense that we could see only a few feet ahead of us. After waiting a few moments to see how many we could muster, the Colonel said: "We

Lieutenant Nathan Edgerton was a white officer of the 6ᵗʰ USCT who earned the Medal of Honor at the Battle of New Market Heights or Chapin's Farm, Virginia. *Courtesy of the Library of Congress.*

must have more help, boys, before we try that. Fall back.' When we got beyond the stream and out of the cloud smoke, we could begin to see how terribly we had been cut to pieces. We lost more than every other man, and fourteen out of the eighteen officers with which we had begun the fight. (Price, *Profile in Courage* 2010)

As Edgerton began to stagger violently, "Sergeant Alexander Kelly of Company F grabbed the flag and carried it from the field […]. Under similar conditions that day, Sgt. Maj. Thomas Hawkins of Company C also retrieved the flag" (Scott, *Black Soldiers in Blue*, 1999). Despite the combat honors, the harrowing event and resulting injuries would impact each of the warriors for the rest of their lives.

Following the battle, Edgerton received surgical treatment for his arm that was miraculously saved at the Chesapeake Officer's Hospital. And by November 1864 Edgerton apparently returned to Philadelphia, where he received honors during a parade and celebration near the headquarters of the United States Colored Troops with other USCT soldiers and mostly black citizens commemorating the "abolition of slavery in the State of Maryland."[23]

The event of the day took place last evening – or, rather, the festivity culminated in a grand demonstration at the headquarters of the Supervisory Committee for Colored Troops, on Chestnut street, above Twelfth. The building, with its immense transparency when fully illuminated, gave the entire structure a magical appearance – gay, attractive and eminently patriotic. In the midst of the glare of red fire, reflecting upon ten thousand upturned faces, the waving of flags, and other ensigns of patriotism, the musical notes of the band, a meeting was improvised by Mr. Thomas Webster. An address was delivered by Mr. Thomas N. Coleman, though suffering from the effects of a blow that he received from a sneaking Copperhead assassin on Monday night. He was loudly cheered, and he thanked God, as a Marylander, that the bright sun of liberty now illumines his native State.

Mr. Coleman was followed by Mr. Trimble, of Tennessee, Hon. Wm. D. Kelley, Captain N.H. Edgerton, of Chester country [*sic*], recently promoted by the indomitable General Butler for gallant conduct. The Captain was wounded in a recent battle. He was followed by Wm. H. Maurice, who recited the poetry, "No Slave Beneath the Starry Flag." Major Dehring and other gentlemen made patriotic speeches, and the greatest enthusiasm prevailed. [24]

The spectacle of the celebration had to be awe inspiring for onlookers and participants at the event, which was accentuated with the latest high technology accoutrements, according to a November 4, 1864, report that started with the Court of Appeals in Maryland upholding the governor's Constitutional changes that made it a free state in William Lloyd Garrison's *The Liberator*, based in Boston:

The whole front of the building, 1210 Chestnut street, will be covered with designs emblematic of emancipation and progress, pointed by judicious selections from the writings of Washington, Jefferson, Henry, and Jackson, and adorned with well executed portraits of Abraham Lincoln, Grant, Sherman, Sheridan, Farragut, and other military and naval heroes, the whole to be framed and draped with flags and evergreens. Surmounting all will be in gas jets, 'God save the Republic.' Music and colored fires will lend their attractions to the symbolical designs. A salute of 200 guns will be fired by companies of U.S. Colored Troops from Camp William Penn, under the command of Col. Lewis [*sic*] Wagner, during the day. It bids fair to be a most worthy commemoration of the greatest moral victory of the age. We earnestly hope the clergy may open the churches, and give expression to the religious sentiment of the people on this glorious triumph of Liberty, Justice, and Progress in Maryland.[25]

After the war, remarkably Edgerton "launched a successful career as a scientist and inventor, even helping introduce electric power to the Commonwealth of Pennsylvania." Yet, it would take several decades for Edgerton to be recognized for his valor during the battle. "On March 22, 1898 he was informed that his valor on that day had earned him the Congressional Medal of Honor. Edgerton wore his medal proudly until he passed away on October 27, 1932" (Price, *Profile in Courage* 2010).

Edgerton's official citation reads: "Took up the flag after 3 color bearers had been shot down and bore it forward, though himself wounded." ("Lieutenant/Adjutant EDGERTON, NATHAN H., U.S. ARMY," 2011)

Sergeant-Major Thomas R. Hawkins, born in 1840 in Cincinnati, Ohio, enlisted August 3, 1863, apparently for a three-year term at Camp William Penn "as a substitute for a man named Passmore Henry. He was assigned to Company C of the 6ᵗʰ USCI after enlisting" (Price, *Profile in Courage* 2010).

In fact, at only about age 23, "Hawkins must have impressed the white officers of the 6ᵗʰ because he was promoted to Sergeant-Major of the entire 6ᵗʰ USCT regiment just 19 days after enlisting." They would travel to Yorktown, Virginia, performing various duties until the spring thaw of 1864. (ibid.)

Meanwhile, it's likely that Hawkins was in great agony after suffering three very serious injuries during the Battle of New Market Heights, despite receiving a very severe wound earlier on June 15, 1864, while attacking Petersburg as part of the USCT's Hinks' Colored Division. It was caused by "a bullet that struck him near the elbow," actually breaking his arm. "He would be hospitalized for eight weeks and [...] rejoin his regiment at Dutch Gap on August 13ᵗʰ." (ibid.)

Less than two months later, Hawkins likely would not have expected to be near death from three fresh bullet wounds. In fact, the combined injuries that Hawkins incurred during the assault on New Market Heights on September 29, 1864, were much more serious than his Petersburg wound. The initial charge that autumn day was led by Hawkins' 6ᵗʰ and Fleetwood's 4ᵗʰ regiments:

The 6ᵗʰ USCI, along with the 4ᵗʰ, comprised the first wave that went into action around 5:30 in the morning. As the 6ᵗʰ was subjected to severe musket and artillery fire, the color guards of both regiments took severe casualties and Hawkins was credited with rescuing the banner of the 6th before withdrawing with the rest of Duncan's Brigade. When the dead, wounded, and missing for the first assault were tallied, it was learned that the 6th sustained 57% casualties – and once again Sergeant-Major Hawkins was among them, having been wounded in the arm, hip, and foot. Hawkins' friend Christian Fleetwood later wrote that "his recovery from these fearful wounds was deemed hopeless." As it turned out, Hawkins did survive – although he was so badly crippled (the regimental surgeon estimated that he was two-thirds disabled) that he was given a disability discharge on May 20, 1865. (Price, *Profile in Courage* 2010)

Incredibly, Hawkins was not immediately considered for the Medal of Honor, despite his friend, Fleetwood, being awarded the medal on April 6, 1865, with 11 other black USCT soldiers who fought in the battle:

> After the war, Hawkins petitioned Major General Joseph B. Kiddoo about the possibility of being awarded the Medal of Honor. With Kiddoo's urging, the War Department approved the award. On February 8, 1870 a proud Hawkins was hand-delivered his Medal of Honor. Twenty days later, Hawkins died of consumption at the age of 29, survived by his wife and young son. He is buried in Harmony Memorial Park in Landover, MD. Hawkins' official Medal of Honor citation simply reads: 'Rescue of regimental colors.' (ibid.)

Just two days after Hawkins' passing away his dear friend, Christian Fleetwood, noted that "his death leaves a void in the hearts of his associates that will never be filled by another." (ibid.).

The recipient of an impressive education likely provided by a rich sugar merchant (John C. Brunes and his wife), Fleetwood before the war had traveled to Liberia and Sierra Leone, as well as attended the Ashmun Institute in Oxford, Pennsylvania, which later became Lincoln University. He also published one of the first black newspapers in the South, the *Lyceum Observer* of Baltimore. So before and following the war, Fleetwood

possessed the academic skills and background that many of his compatriots did not possess, allowing for a measure of success as he aged:

> After the war Fleetwood married [Sara Iredell] and worked for several agencies of

Sergeant-Major Thomas Hawkins of the 6th USCT saved the regimental colors at the Battle of New Market Heights in Virginia, but had lasting injuries that led to his premature death following the war. *Courtesy of the Library of Congress.*

the federal government in Washington, DC. He also directed the choirs of several churches in the city and helped organize its first black National Guard units. In 1895 he delivered an address, later published as *The Negro As a Soldier*, for the Negro Congress at the Cotton States and International Exposition in Atlanta, Georgia […]. In 1914, Fleetwood died in Washington, DC, at age 74. (Fleetwood, diary nationalhumantitiescenter.org 2007)

Remarkably, the third soldier to earn the Medal of Honor for valor during the Battle of New Market Heights, First Sergeant Alexander Kelly of the 6th USCT, was also about age 23 when he enlisted at Camp William Penn in August 1863, similar to Fleetwood (of the 4th USCT) and Hawkins of the 6th Regiment:

Kelly was born on April 5, 1840 in Saltsburg, Conemaugh Township of Indiana County, Pennsylvania. Despite scarce records regarding Kelly's parentage, service and census data indicate that he was "mulatto" and with "light skin," perhaps indicating mixed ancestry […]. When Kelly became a "substitute volunteer" for his drafted brother Joseph in August 1863, he too had been working as a coal miner. At age 23, Kelly – standing just over 5 feet – joined the 6th USCT of Camp William Penn, located in Chelton Hills. (Scott, *Alexander Kelly: From the coal mines to the front lines* 2011)

After traveling to Virginia with the regiment to Fortress Monroe and Yorktown, Kelly, of Company F, had been promoted to first sergeant after the 6th helped to gain ground at Petersburg, as well as "by August, they moved to fortification duty at Dutch Gap on the James River, enduring rebel mortars and polluted river water. Many became sick or died." (ibid.)

During the fateful battle of New Market Heights, Kelly's Medal of Honor citation, presented April 6, 1865, notes he "gallantly seized the colors," as well as "rallied the men at a time of confusion and a place of great danger." (ibid.)

After being mustered out of the Army on September 20, 1865, in Wilmington, NC, a year after the Battle of New Market Heights or Chaffin's Farm, Kelly "received a monthly pension of $8 that eventually rose to $12, records indicate. Kelly has been described as having "permanent marks" that "included a hole in his cheek, a lump between his eyes on his forehead and a scar on his back." (ibid.)

And despite an education that was certainly inferior to Fleetwood's, Kelly was able to work and find a life mate:

The next year [1866] Kelly married, and with his wife, Victoria, birthed a child, William, and adopted homeless children. Living in Coutlersville, Pa., Kelly and his son were later employed as coal miners. By 1892, Kelly and Victoria moved to Pittsburgh's East End before she died in 1898. After 1900, Kelly worked as a stable watchman. His son taught music. Kelly also joined the Colonel Robert G. Shaw GAR, Post 206 before dying on June 19, 1907 […]. Kelly was buried inconspicuously at St. Peter's Cemetery on Lemington Ave. in Pittsburgh next to his wife Victoria. Today, however, a Medal of Honor grave memorial notes his remarkable military service. (ibid.)

"Roots" of the Rev. Jeremiah Asher

Following the horrors of New Market Heights, in the Spring of 1865 the 6th would move on to Wilmington, NC, where it's virtually certain that Kelly knew of and likely associated with the 6th Regiment's chaplain, the Rev. Jeremiah Asher. Tragically, the good reverend would soon languish in a local bed at the residence of the Days (the black North Carolina family with ties to the local African American Baptist church), far from his wife and children, struggling against a debilitating disease, likely malaria or typhoid.

Asher would have been held in very high esteem by the local community and soldiers like Kelly, especially since the preacher had actually tried to nurse many of them back to health after they were afflicted with the deadly malady. In the end, the preacher had jeopardized his own health in order to save his young soldierly flock.

So it's clear that the Rev. Jeremiah Asher's prominence in Philadelphia certainly helped his stature among the black soldiers in Wilmington, NC, and in the black community there, according to "Arnold," the USCT soldier who penned the letter to the Philadelphia-based *Christian Recorder* editor Elisha Weaver in March 1865. Indeed, Asher had apparently accompanied the chaplain of the 4th USCT, Rev. W.H. Hunter, a former slave in those parts, to a church gathering on Sunday, March 5, 1865, scheduled for 3 p.m. at the Old Bethel African Methodist Episcopal Church:

> Accompanied by the Rev. Jeremiah Asher, Chaplain 6th [U.S.C.T.], Mr. Hunter entered. Robed in his army uniform, that manly form failed, I am sure, to please the eye of one or two Secesh Gents, who came, not to hear him preach, but to see "what was going to be done by the Negroes, and how they Negroes were going to act." […]. The

Sergeant Alexander Kelly was a Pennsylvania coal miner of short stature, but mighty tall in courage, earning the Medal of Honor at the Battle of New Market Heights in Virginia. *Courtesy of the Library of Congress.*

hymn chosen was "Sing unto the Lord a new song." I thought, as did others, that it was the best singing we ever heard. The text was from Psalms, "Sing unto Lord a new song, for he hath done marvelous things: with his right arm he hath gotten him the victory." Eloquence never flowed so freely as on that day; few in the church could say their eyes were dry. Mr. Hunter himself was born a slave on this very soil, sixteen years previously he left the state a slave. But now he comes to the land of his birth an officer in the United States Army. Was not that congregation of citizens proud of him? Yes! They are, they will never cease to remember him. How can they? He worked day and night for them. He had interviews with General Schofield and with General Terry, when finally he showed the letter he received from the former, informing the colored people that they should be protected while worshipping God according to the dictates of their own conscience and the loyalty to the Government of the United States, and, that they might choose whom they desired to preach to them the gospel. Mr. Hunter has thus turned over to the amE. Church of the United States the largest Methodist congregation of any city that has been in the confederacy. (Redkey 1992, 166)

And most interesting, a member of Old Bethel apparently included Thomas Day, according to Arnold's letter, among blacks who seemed to be adamant "Yankee" sympathizers, even risking their lives to harbor some:

Among the acquaintances I made are several who have friends and relatives in the North. Mr. and Mrs. James Golly, Mrs. James Sampson, Joseph Nichols, John H. Brown, Jas Scull, Mr. and Mrs. Wm. Mosely, whose hospitality I enjoyed, Mr. and Mrs. R. Lowry, Mr. and Mrs. James Price, are some of the most prominent. There are many mechanics here, Mr. Thomas Day, Mr. Hostler, Mr. J. Brown, and a host of others. The people are generally refined and well informed. Union to the bone, liberal and modest. Almost or I may say all of the colored people have been engaged in the business of hiding Yankee prisoners. Almost every house in the city occupied by colored people has done this favor for our prisoners. (Redkey, *A Grand Army* 1992)

It is very likely that the same Thomas Day listed above is whose family the Reverend Jeremiah Asher spent his final days with, reminiscing about his grandfather's fateful Africa-to-America sojourn that had so much impacted Jeremiah's own life path. Asher, perhaps, could envision the very moment his grandfather Gad was captured by pursuing slavers in the Guinea wilderness more than a century earlier:

Having been left by his elder brother, he was soon overtaken by the pursuers, who seized their victim and gagged him to prevent his giving an alarm. He was ordered to be quiet, for they were going to take him home; but he was conveyed to the sea, where a slaver was in waiting to receive stolen men, women and children. They arrived therein the dusk of the evening, and saw a large number of others who had been captured in a similar manner, but none that he could recognize. (Asher 1850, 17)

And although it was probably very easy to trick a four-year-old toddler into believing his captors were taking him home to mother, young Gad, due to "his youth, and having no relative or companion on board," was "in a great degree exempt from the horrors and hardships of the Middle Passage," according to Asher's narrative:

> He indeed became quite a favourite of both officers and sailors, who each in their turn endeavored to console him, by telling him they were going to take him home. Of the particulars of the voyage he had little recollection, neither as to the time of sailing, or length of the passage, or the dangers of the sea, but remembered full well he never saw his parents or brother, more. Thus he was suddenly snatched away from all that could be dearest to one of his age, in life. (16-17)

The ship arrived in "due time" with "her cargo safe" in Guildford, Connecticut, according to Jeremiah. "The news of her arrival having heralded in the town, the farmers and others from many parts gathered to attend the sale of the newly-imported negroes." However, the ship's carpenter, "Titus Bishop of Guildford," was "pleased with the apparent brightness and promising appearance of this youth, bought him for £40, current money with the merchant, took him on his back, carried him to his house, treated him with great kindness, and became remarkably fond of him" (17-18).

In fact, Asher noted that the "term of service" for his Grandfather Gad was 43 years, "and doubtless pleasant a one as the peculiar institution is capable of imparting" (18).

However, the origin of the name Gad Asher had not been determined, with Jeremiah writing "he [Gad] was quite at a loss to know" (18).

Regardless, Gad Asher "faithfully" served his master for about 40 years when the American Revolution erupted in 1776. He had to be about 45 years old, pushing towards 50.

Gad's master, Bishop, apparently was quite eligible to be drafted. "At the time referred to, perhaps every able-bodied white man between the ages of eighteen and forty was drafted to go to the war or furnish a substitute," Jeremiah noted. "Among the rest, Mr. Bishop was notified to leave the comforts of home for a field campaign" (ibid.). But, that was not to come to fruition:

> At this time of trouble, he had only to promise Gad his freedom, and he was all right again. This he delayed not to do, but sought an early opportunity to confirm the contract, that when the war should be ended he should be free. Elated with the thought of freedom, though it was from one of the best of masters, the hardships of a seven years' war was borne without fatigue. In view of a fact like this, who will contend the African prefers slavery to freedom, even under its most favourable aspect, or in its mildest form. (19)

Gad Asher bravely "fought in a number of battles, and among others, the memorable one of Bunker Hill, near Boston," his grandson, Jeremiah, wrote. Gad persevered "through the intense heat, and inhaling the dense smoke of gunpowder, and exposure to the dew of heaven by night, he took a severe cold, which settled in his eyes, and deprived him of his sight, which was never restored to him again" (ibid.).

Yet, obviously, it's more likely that the blindness was caused by the concussions of explosions or even the exploding gunpowder of weapons, including cannon.

With black soldiers consisting of about 5 percent of the Americans at Bunker Hill, according to the National Park Service, an estimated 440 Americans were killed or wounded at Bunker Hill, as well as about 1,150 British suffering the same fate during clashes that included bayonets, rifles and artillery. Among the approximately three dozen blacks serving with Gad Asher at Bunker Hill was the free black Salem Poor of Andover, Massachusetts, cited by officers for outstanding service during the battle (*The American Revolution: Lighting Freedom's Flame* 2008). Despite General George Washington's initial reluctance to use black soldiers, various sources indicate that approximately 5,000 blacks ultimately served in the Revolutionary War, with slaves such as Gad Asher being permitted to fight in 1777, when Washington's white forces were seriously depleted.

After the war, Gad Asher "now returned home, but his master refused to grant him freedom without a compensation for the original forty pounds, the amount he first paid for him," Jeremiah explained in his life narrative. "This after a term of near forty years' service, seven of it spent in the defence of a country which denied the right of citizenship both to himself and all his posterity." Gad, though, had no choice but to comply, "principally upon the consideration, that his large family of children would be free," including Gad's father, Reuel, born about 1785, as America won its independence from Britain. (Asher 1850, 20)

Jeremiah pointed out that "they were as free before as they could be afterwards, for my grandmother was free, so his master could have no claim to them whatever: for it is the universal practice among slave-dealers and breeders, for the children to follow the destiny of the mother, whether she be bond or free." However Gad was not aware of the provision, so was "induced to yield to this unrighteous demand of his master." (ibid.)

Fortunately, Gad received "a compensation for his service from the commencement of the war" by the U.S. government in the amount of "ninety-six dollars a year, or about nineteen pounds as long as he lived." (ibid.) Grandfather Gad was eventually able to purchase his freedom, as well as his children's, all girls, with the exception of Jeremiah's father, Reuel:

> He soon removed from the neighbourhood of his master to the town of North Brandford, where he purchased a small plantation and settled down upon it for the remainder of his days. He united with the Independent Church in that place, and I believe was a consistent member of it for nearly half a century, as when he died, he was nearly quite one hundred years of age. (ibid.)

Gad's son and Jeremiah's father, Reuel, was "apprenticed to the trade of a shoe and leather dealer, about eight miles distant from home, who agreed to give him an education, and to instruct him thoroughly in the knowledge" of the enterprise. Reuel was just six years old, and was to serve as an apprentice for 15 years. The unidentified "gentleman" shoemaker was "wealthy" and "influential" according to Asher, as well as operated a "large farm" (21).

Only permitted to return home once a year, Reuel was then "scrupulously examined by his blind father, and [...] mother, who vainly believed he was making the most rapid strides up the hill of science – and compared with their own attainments, his, no doubt, were considered by them surprising." Reuel was required to work summers on the man's farm, "and in the winter was chiefly employed in mending shoes, and waiting upon the other workmen." (21).

Following the apprenticeship, Asher's father started business by picking up the shoes of customers from their homes and fixing them. Next he opened up his own shop. However, Reuel was forced to extend a huge amount of credit to his mostly white customers, most never repaying the black shoemaker. He inevitably had to sell his business "at a ruinous rate, in order to satisfy his creditors" (23).

Asher continued: "This was a shock from which he never recovered, and has since been able to do little or nothing more than provide for the wants of a numerous and dependent family" (ibid.).

Yet, Asher believed that his father could have salvaged his business if it was not for his immense frustration spawned by the racism:

> Had he made an assignment and continued his business, he might have been able to have satisfied his creditors, and to have made provision for his family. But such is the feeling against a coloured man, if his pecuniary matters get deranged, which all business-men, owing to the fluctuation of trade are likely to be more or less effected by, he is at once considered dishonest, unless he immediately surrenders every thing he possesses to satisfy the demand of his creditors, even though his family should go without bread. (24)

Despite his black ethnicity, Asher was allowed to attend the same school as white children in North Brandford. Yet by 1850, when his autobiography was published, Asher believed that blacks were no longer able to attend the public school there (ibid.). "The slave states, of course, make no provision for the instruction of free coloured children, and to teach a slave to read the Bible is regarded in some of the states a crime, which is punishable either by banishment or imprisonment" (25).

Asher described himself as a very quick learner, and within five years, "considered at the head of the first class." At one point he "was represented to my father as being the best scholar in the school," but his dad was advised that "it would be useless for him to send me longer [...] to make a minister or a lawyer of me; otherwise he had better take me out of school, and bind me out to some good master, and then I would be good for something." (ibid.)

However, Reuel at first refused to send Jeremiah down the same road he had gone. "But he had resolved, after what he had experienced during his own apprenticeship, that he would never bind out one of his children, though I believe he did apprentice my brother, who was some twelve years younger than myself" (26). But it wasn't long before Asher was hired out by his father during the summer for "six cents per day." By age 12 "my father considered by education complete, and here my winter's schooling terminated" (26).

Asher was consequently "hired out by the month" on a farm until near the age of 17, when he moved to nearby Hartford via the suggestion of "a relative" to serve as "a servant and coachman" to "the family of the Honorable H. L. Ellsworth, where I continued for four years, when he failed in business, and I was under the necessity of seeking employment elsewhere" at about age 21 (20).

And that's when he met his future wife, "Miss Abigail Stewart, of Glastonbury," and "changed my situation in life" by a "contracted marriage," acknowledging that "although we were both very young we have never since regretted the step." They apparently began to live under the same roof in 1833, a year later being "blessed with a fine little daughter, which was named after its mother, and lived to be nine months old, when God took her to himself." The loss was devastating, causing the couple to ponder "God's grace, or a knowledge of an interest in his saving mercy. This was indeed a severe chastisement, more than we could bear. Our hopes were all blighted" (27).

A short time after the couple was offered employment at the residence of Thomas S. Williams, chief justice of the State of Connecticut. They lived and worked with the family for about four years "when my wife became afflicted apparently with a rheumatic affection in her right arm, which seemed to bid defiance to all medical treatment," Asher said, further noting:

> It was exceedingly painful both night and day for about six months, and it was thought by her medical attendant that the limb would have to be amputated; other advice however being called in, it was finally decided that this would not be necessary, or indeed of any service, for the complaint was declared to be a white swelling, and incurable. (ibid.)

His wife apparently began to board "with a family in the city," presumably in Hartford, "where she continued until our second child was born, a fine boy" (ibid.). However, tragedy would strike yet again:

> When about five months old, he had the [w]hooping cough very severely, so much so, as to occasion fits, which became more frequent, and at last never ceased to have been successively until he ceased to breathe. I was sent for in haste, and arrived just in time to take the dear little fellow in my arms, and saw him breathe his last. This I could bear without a murmur. "The Lord gave," I was enabled to say, "and the Lord hath taken away, blessed be the name of the Lord." (27-28)

The death of the second child really caused Asher to contemplate his religious conviction, prompting him to delve into and reminisce about his profound relationship with Gad Asher, his beloved grandfather:

> The earliest impressions of my wretched state and condition by nature were experienced when I was quite a youth, perhaps not more than five years of age, my poor grandfather, as I have already said, was blind. It became my employment, as the only grandson, to lead him about, and attend him almost constantly, and as he was a member of the Independent or Congregational Chapel, the only dissenting place of worship in the town, I used to accompany him to the meetings. (28)

And during a particularly moving service at a parishioner's house, Jeremiah was struck by the words of the presiding minister, a Mr. Smith:

> 1 Peter iv. 18, "If the righteous scarcely be saved, where shall the ungodly and sinner appear." This was the first text of Scripture that I am aware ever affected me. A very solemn feeling came over me, which I had never experienced before. The next day I was with my grandfather in his field burning the stalks of corn, and preparing the ground for a new crop. We used to gather a cart-load or two in a place, and when thoroughly dry set fire to them. He took occasion to represent to me by this fire the torment of wicked in hell, mentioned its duration, &c., and the certainty of every one going there whose heart was not renewed by Divine grace. (28-29)

It was at that moment, three decades before the Civil War, when Jeremiah Asher says he truly realized the grace and greatness of God Almighty.

Over the next thirty years, Asher had become a seasoned preacher and black activist vehemently opposed to slavery, making his pastoral mark in Rhode Island, Connecticut, Washington, DC and Philadelphia. Further, the preacher was well connected within the abolitionist community in more than a few eastern seaboard cities with Black Baptist and African Methodist Episcopal churches. And he probably participated in elements of the Underground Railroad throughout the region, as well as assisted in the recruitment of black soldiers via Shiloh Baptist Church, where he rose to become a revered pastor.

And then he had valiantly volunteered to leave his family to provide guidance to the young and brave souls desiring to liberate their black brethren and America from the manacles of slavery. But in a sad twist of fate, the savior seemed to have become the sacrificial lamb.

Although the Rev. Asher struggled desperately to recover from his devastating illness just after the tragic war, McMurray certainly did rebound from his mental breakdown 10 months earlier, remaining with his men "bivouacked near Fort Harrison from September 29 until December 18" (Montgomery 1961, 180). Indeed, the regiment received a new complement of men, raising its muscle up to 400, "the approximate strength of the regiment before the action at New Market Heights," with each of the ten companies having about forty troopers (180-181).

Asher undoubtedly helped to arrange with the local Christian Commission religious services for new black recruits, likely keeping in mind the soldiers who had survived the bloody conflicts, such as Kelly and even the severely injured Hawkins. Furthermore, the white officer, McMurray, was clearly interested in the services:

> Anxious to provide religious services for colored troops, the Commission erected a tent near the 6th's quarters. The commander of Company D went to the tent one evening to see how the services were conducted. It was full of soldiers before whom stood a handsome young man on a platform that reached across one end of the tent. After some singing and praying, the young man explained that

the meeting was especially for the Negroes. Eager to make them feel at home, he invited some to join him on the platform and expressed the hope that they be prompt about it. In a few minutes stalwart colored soldiers, entirely at home at such a meeting, filled the platform and took over the meeting "under a full head of steam." (181)

Meanwhile, questions began to rise about the efficacy of Butler's decision to order a second charge of the "Heights" beyond Fort Harrison, especially since the primary jewel – the fort – had been held:

> Why did Butler order the assault? His own explanation was that there had been a "great purpose" back of this decision. In fact, there would seem to have been two purposes. First, he was looking for a chance to prove that Negroes would fight, so as to end the uneasiness of white soldiers who in the future might be flanked by them. The colored soldier, he believed, had not been given sufficient opportunity to prove his valor. This had been McMurray's view after the retirement of Duncan's brigade before Petersburg on June 15. Also, Butler was determined to prove false the cry that Negroes were making no real sacrifices in behalf of their own freedom. It was his judgment, and one shared by both Ames and McMurray, that the Army of the James looked upon a Negro regiment after September 29 "as the safest flanking regiment that could be put in line." (181-182)

Most telling, according to Montgomery, Butler issued a strongly worded general order commending the black troops for their action at New Market Heights:

> In the charge on the enemy's works by the colored division of the Eighteenth Corps at Spring Hill, New Market – better men were never better led, better officers never led better men. With hardly an exception officers of colored troops have justified the care with which they have been selected. A few more such gallant charges and to command colored troops will be the post of honor in the American armies. The colored soldiers by coolness, steadiness, and determined courage and dash have silenced every cavil of the doubters of their soldierly capacity, and drawn tokens of admiration from their enemies. (182)

Asher, McMurray, and their comrades must have been particularly moved when they learned Butler had focused on their valor in particular, as Montgomery noted:

> The order continued by singling out for special mention many individual regiments, among them the 6th, and by authorizing the inscription on their regimental flags of "Petersburg" and "New Market Heights" for gallantry on June 15 and September 29 respectively. For individual acts of bravery at New Market Heights, Butler had a medal struck. Copied after the one Queen Victoria gave to her distinguished private soldiers of the Crimean War, it was awarded to nearly 200 Negroes. (ibid.)

But the combat certainly was not over. Thomas Morris Chester, the black Civil War correspondent for *The Philadelphia Press*, recorded a particularly tragic and gruesome incident as the 6th and other black regiments, including the 36th and 38th, in a report transmitted from "HEADQUARTERS IN THE FIELD," and "BEFORE RICHMOND, NOV. 27, 1864":

> Day before yesterday the programme was a little varied from the customary routine. Instead of the enemy beginning, our batteries near the Howlett House took the initiative, giving to him a specimen of our artillery practice. In a short time a shell, containing Greek fire, was thrown into a house which the enemy used as a picket post, which, exploding, immediately wrapt the building in flames. This seemed to exasperate the rebels. For almost immediately his batteries in the vicinity of the "grave yard" opened upon a picket post, which was at this place, with crushing and fatal effect. Three shells passed through the house, doing it fearful damage, and killing John Richmons, Co. F, 6th U.S.C.T., and Andrew Newbern, Co. G, 36th U.S.C.C., and wounding Silas Hollis, 38th U.S.C.T., severely in the left hand. The bodies of Richmond and Newbern were torn to pieces and scattered in every direction for sixty yards around. Quivering pieces of flesh indicated the locality of the frightful scene, while fragments of the hearts and intestines were hanging upon the branches of the neighboring trees. These men died at their post, and their bodies, or as much of them as could be collected together, received Christian burial on the spot where they fell in defence of the Union. (Blackett 1989, 197)

Overall the bravery of the 6th and other black regiments was commendable, according to most observers, including Chester, the African American *Press* correspondent, acknowledging the 6th USCT in an October 5, 1864, report:

> When the smoke of a battle has partially cleared away, and the thinned ranks of brave men are closed up by the surviving heroes, we can form a fair idea of the bearing of those under fire, and how they acquitted themselves. In the onward to Richmond move of the [September] 29th ult., the 4th United States Colored Troops, raised in Maryland, and the 6th United States Colored Troops, from Pennsylvania, gained for themselves undying laurels for their steady and unflinching courage displayed in attacking the rebels at great disadvantage. (139)

Chester, a bit later in his October 23, 1864, report, wrote about the tattered flags of the black regiments being sure evidence of their immense bravery: "Many of their colors gave evidences of having passed through the fiery ordeal of battles," the black correspondent wrote. "The flags of the 6th U.S.C.T. are in mere strips, and form a glorious record of this brave regiment" (168).

As 1864 wound down, Union commanders had their eyes on "one great port of entry" that "remained in the Confederacy" – Wilmington, North Carolina, resting on the bank of Cape Fear River. "Some twenty miles upstream, its seaward access was protected by formidable Fort Fisher near the tip of Federal Point Peninsula, formed by the Carolina coast and the Cape Fear River running south from the city" (Montgomery 1961, 182).

Chester wrote in a December 26, 1864, dispatch about the importance of Wilmington, NC, for the South, as well as Northern troops set on occupying the city:

> Wilmington is guarded by Nature, and by Nature's anger on the broad sea – howling winds, terrific storms, gigantic ocean waves. Situated thirty-five miles up the Cape Fear river, nearly forty miles from the ocean, it has been, since the closing of the ports of Savannah and Charleston, the principal if not the only port of entry to the Confederacy [...] Millions on millions of dollars' worth of all the material required in war, and all the articles that go to make up domestic comfort and happiness, have come into that river in ship after ship, defying our best efforts to prevent them. We have made many captures, to be sure. Our vigilant blockading fleet, that has cruised around in the very waters where blue dreariness surges, and stretches out before me as I write, made many captures, and brought the dreams of many a rebel financier and spectulator to grief. But through vessel after vessel lowered its stars and bars before our stars and stripes, and went North a prize, still they bore but a small portion to the numbers that stole in when skies were overclouded and stars were dim, and brought more life-blood to swell out the withered arteries of the Confederacy. The Government has always been well aware of the value of this port to the rebels. But the immense drain of the war, the thousand and one duties it had to perform on the long frontier of the rebellion facing the loyal States, have prevented any marked attention being paid the grim Cerberi who frown fiercely over there on those low sand-banks which skirt the heaving waters, and are black with close-growing pine trees. This expedition was at last organized to attack, and, if possible, crumble the proud rebel city. (203-204)

Yet before entering Wilmington, the 6ᵗʰ faced more combat and losses:

> On the 19ᵗʰ of January, 1865, the Sixth participated in a sharp encounter at Sugar Loaf Hill, North Carolina, where Captain Newton J. Hotchkiss was mortally wounded, dying two days after, and considerable loss in killed and wounded was sustained. On the 11ᵗʰ of February, during a sharp contest on the skirmish line, Daniel K. Healy was severely wounded, and Lieutenant Edward Field, commanding Company A, was killed. Upon the death of Lieutenant Field, the direction devolved on Sergeant Richard Carter, (colored,) who commanded with great skill and courage, until the company was relieved. (Bates 1871, 975)

Meanwhile, McMurray was given a special assignment, just before he'd join in the taking of Wilmington, NC:

> He was now placed in charge of some 200 of the brigade's men declared unfit for duty. Shaken up by their late sea voyage, they were to be given a month-

long rest [...] By mid-January of 1865 Union forces were preparing to move up Federal Point Peninsula toward Wilmington. Early in February McMurray and his "invalids" rejoined their regiments, then occupying a line across the peninsula about two miles north of the fort. Here in what was literally a swamp the brigade built many corduroy roads to enable movement from one part of the line to another. (Montgomery 1961, 183)

Union and Confederate forces made several clashes before the Rebels moved up the peninsula, but not without taking detestable action, Montgomery wrote:

A short distance north of the Union works Major General Robert F. Hoke with almost 3,000 Confederates had thrown up a defensive line. Extending across the peninsula, it paralleled Terry's. Early in February Major General John M. Schofield's 23rd Army Corps joined Terry's 10th Army Corps. Both were attached to General W.T. Sherman's forces during the campaign in North Carolina. After Schofield's arrival, Union troops south of Wilmington numbered approximately 20,000. The last of several encounters with Hoke occurred on February 20. Retiring up the peninsula afterwards, the Confederate commander put the torch to much property. (183-84)

McMurray seemed astounded when he set eyes on the city:

Saddened to find the wharves and storage buildings along the river front a smoldering ruin, McMurray recalled that not a man, woman, child, or dog was to be seen in any direction. He believed the city's funereal mien infected the soldiers, who soberly marched over its streets, stooping now and then to pick up some tobacco that had eluded the flames, and finally halted north of it in an open field near the Wilmington and Weldon Railroad. (184)

Soon after, McMurray's 6th Regiment and others of the brigade triumphantly entered Wilmington, where many began to get ill, leading to the demise of their spiritual and physical healer, the Reverend Asher, their beloved chaplain.

And in spite of getting briefly demoted and even locked up for a short period due to the bogus or trite charges of a commanding officer concerning a miscommunication incident about following orders, Montgomery said McMurray rose to the post of "District Inspector" and held it until the war's end. (ibid.)

Meanwhile, as his health seriously deteriorated, it was in late July 1865 when the Reverend Jeremiah Asher's psyche likely drifted to those old days of his salvation in Connecticut, his dear grandfather, Gad, and certainly his beloved wife and children, as the Day family and others struggled to save his precious life. And he likely thought plenty about the souls of his Shiloh Baptist Church members back in Philadelphia.

The 6th's regimental surgeon, Leeman Barnes, had mercifully received approval on July 21, 1865, for his recommendation to allow Rev. Asher to move to "a change of location" in order "to prevent loss of life." Tragically, less than a week "later, however, the gravely ill Asher succumbed to the effects of Typhoid fever [or malaria] at Wilmington, North

Carolina. In determining the cause of death it was concluded that he died, in part, from 'Over exertion while attention to his duties'" (Johnson 1999, 90-91).

His was a life that epitomized the stupendous struggles of many of the black soldiers in the 6ᵗʰ USCT and other Camp William Penn regiments. And Rev. Asher likely realized the irony of his grandfather giving so much for the country's freedom in the original conflict, the Revolutionary War, making it destiny for Jeremiah himself to move on to the "Old Ship of Zion" and his grandfather Gad's heavenly embrace.

In Philadelphia, *The Christian Recorder* marked Asher's July 27, 1865, death in a July 30, 1865, obituary:

> Rev. Jeremiah Asher, Chaplain of the 6ᵗʰ USCT was attacked by a bilious disease a few weeks ago. At first it was thought by many that he was not dangerously ill. He died on the 27ᵗʰ of July, 1865. Bro. Asher was a noble man, and in every way proved himself a worthy minister and a Christian and none who formed his acquaintance could help but love him. He fell at his post, and leaves a dear wife and family [...] Bro. Asher was well cared for while lingering in his afflictions. The ever hospitable Mr. and Mrs. Day took him into their own home during his illness. Wilmington, North Carolina. (Heist, "Afrigeneas Military Research Forum Archive," 2005)

Still, even to the very end Asher had to be proud of his regiment's actions during the war: "The regiment participated in all the movements of the division in North Carolina, until the final surrender of the rebel forces, when it was ordered to duty at Wilmington, and remained there until its muster out of service on the 20ᵗʰ of September" (Bates 1871, 945).

4

The 8th United States Colored Troops
A most terrific shower of musketry

The slave Nelson Davis, AKA Nelson Charles, likely ran away from his Elizabeth City, North Carolina, owner "during or before 1861" and made it to Oneida County, New York, for about two years before traveling to Pennsylvania and joining the Eighth USCT on September 10, 1863, at Camp William Penn. The future and second husband of the great Underground Railroad matriarch Harriet Tubman would "valiantly" fight with the Eighth, which suffered the greatest losses of any USCT regiment of the war (Larson 2004, 239).

Yet, it's very likely that Private Charles or Davis was among the very motivated and excited new black troops, years before he'd marry one of the most well known and celebrated women in American history.

Lieutenant Oliver W. Norton, an officer of the 8th USCT, which was formed next at Camp William Penn in September 1863, noted the incredible enthusiasm of such fresh recruits – many of them runaway slaves just like Nelson – shortly after he traveled to a recruiting post in Delaware during late 1863 after the 6th USCT departed for war:

> "Our camp was thronged with visitors, and darkies who wanted to enlist," he wrote to his sister on January 4. "There are hundreds of them, mostly slaves, here now, anxiously waiting for the recruiting officer." Norton was profoundly moved when many spontaneously began to sing "Rally round the flag." "Cool as I am I found myself getting excited as I heard their songs this afternoon and saw the electrifying effect on the crowds of slaves," he recalled. (Trudeau 1998, 126)

Such recruitment in Delaware was made possible because "on October 3, 1863, the War Department issued General Orders no. 329 authorizing the recruitment of 'colored troops' in the border slave states," according to historian Johnson:

> That directive was extended to Delaware on October 26. Within months, Delaware's recruiting system was operating as it began the process of mustering

Black men at Wilmington, Myrna, and Georgetown. Nearly one thousand Black recruits in Delaware, joined the Union army in this fashion. Two recruiting campaigns were conducted in Delaware by soldiers from Camp William Penn. The first expedition, which occurred in December, 1863, was cut short when the Eighth regiment received its marching orders. A follow-up campaign by soldiers of the Twenty-fifth regiment was carried out in January, 1864. On both occasions the soldiers were warmly greeted by free and enslaved farm workers. (Johnson 1999, 86)

The primary commanders of the 8th USCT were Colonel Charles W. Fribley, formerly a captain of the 8th Pennsylvania; Lieutenant Colonel Nelson B. Bartram, previously of the 70th New York; and Major Loren Burritt, most recently of the 56th Pennsylvania. (Gayley, *8th United States Colored Regiment* 2011)

Apparently Lieutenant Norton must have accompanied Burritt during the excursion south to Delaware to recruit new black troops: "In December, Major Burritt, with three companies A, F, and D, proceeded to the State of Delaware, for the purpose of obtaining recruits. At Wilmington and Seaford, these troops were handsomely received by the citizens, and a number of recruits were obtained." (ibid)

Regardless, political and social tensions were fanned, as racists became quite concerned about the growing number of black manpower leaving the farms, which relied on their labor. "A stiff reception, however, came from pro-slavery, secessionist sympathizers," according to Johnson, because "the loyal slave states […] feared what blacks in uniform might do, and objected to proposals for raising Negro regiments." Meanwhile, however, "Republicans and loyalist factions among Democrats armed themselves and vowed to keep the border state in the Union and to allow the enlistment of black residents." The state was set for a distasteful conflict. "Hard line Democrats controlling the state treasury made sure that bounties were never offered to black recruits in Delaware." In fact, as an illustration of the hostilities, by "late January a brief report on the Eighth regiment's work in Delaware was published in the *Philadelphia Inquirer*," according to Johnson: "About fifty colored men from Delaware came to Head-quarters having been mustered at Wilmington. Nearly all these men are slaves who have left their masters […] One of the party had been handcuffed for ten days by his master to keep him from going off with the soldiers […] The master also came to camp but was quickly halted by the guards" (Johnson 1999, 87).

Colonel Charles W. Fribley of the 8th USCT was killed at the Battle of Olustee in Florida and honored in Philadelphia by his widow and others during a concert and tribute to the lost warrior. *Courtesy of the U. S. Army Military History Institute.*

Indeed, according to Johnson, the recruitment tensions reached the offices of Delaware's governor, as well as the U.S. Secretary of War Stanton. The Republican governor Cannon wrote the secretary about "the affect that the [black] soldiers were having on the African American community," and knocking down the pillars of slavery, noting, "The Battalion of the 8th Regt. U.S. Colored Troops [...] was commencing to do good service in the work of enlisting colored men. Many slaves belonging to disloyal persons signifies [sic] their willingness to enlist and the negroes generally were favorably impressed by the good appearance, drill and behavior of the soldiers." In fact, "Cannon understood the revolutionary potential of strong black support for enlistment. A concerted effort to enlist enslaved and healthy male laborers between the ages of eighteen and forty-five years would deprive slaveowners of their most valued workers of this gender." Hence, Cannon desired to maximize the exposure of the black troops, adding, "I deem it very important that this work should continue. I therefore respectfully request that you will order a squad of (say) sixteen men commanded by a Lieutenant to proceed immediately from Camp William Penn by railway to [Seaford], Delaware to return on foot through this state to Wilmington and from there by rail-way to camp. Twenty or twenty-five days would be ample time for this march" (Johnson 1999, 87-88).

Remarkably, Stanton issued an order that complied with Cannon's request:

> Cannon's letter was given careful consideration by Stanton who soon issued the War Department's Special Orders number 30. Extract 10 of Stanton's directive closely followed Cannon's suggestions. On February 13, 1864, [Stanton's] order, in the form of Regimental Orders number eleven, was conveyed to the rank and file of the Twenty-fifth Infantry. [Stanton's] directive called for a detachment to leave Camp William Penn for Delaware "at 8' o'clock tomorrow [...]. The Quartermaster's Department will furnish the necessary transportation." Another week would pass, however, before the squad was ready to be transported to [Seaford]. When the troopers were ready, the commander of Camp William Penn, as the following note supports, arranged transportation through the Assistant Adjutant General in Philadelphia. "I have the honor to ask for transportation for eighty two [...] men from City Line to Phil. via North Penn RR enroute for Delaware by Special Order no. 30, Extract 10 dated Jan. 20, 1864, War Department, Washington, D.C." (88-89)

During the interim, back at Camp William Penn, Commander Wagner held down the proverbial fort, dealing with such issues as medical care for the 8th soldiers, as well as payment and bounties. Much of his time, undoubtedly, was spent conferring with superiors in Washington about such matters, according to the following correspondence that Wagner received from Major Lewis Foster, based in Washington, who was not shy about setting firm policy parameters:

War Department,
Adjutant General's Office
Washington, D.C., October 21, 1863

Lieut. Col. Louis Wagner
88th Regt. Pa. Vols
Comdg Camp Wm Penn
Philadelphia, Pa.

Sir,

I have the honor to acknowledge the receipt of your letter of the 18th instant, informing the Department of the muster into service of Company "E" 8th U.S. Colored Troops.

I am directed to inform you that any enlisted men sent home on a Surgeon's Certificate must report to the nearest "Military Commander," as provided [by] General Orders No. 1, 5, War Department, 1862, and such men have no business at Camp William Penn.

You are not a "Military Commander," according to the meaning of said order, and have no authority to discharge enlisted men from service.

Hospital Stewards are not appointed by the War Department for Volunteer regiments. Should a Hospital Steward not be assigned to the regiment by the Surgeon General of the Army, an enlisted man may be appointed to that position by the Colonel of the regiment when its organization has been completed.

In the case of drafted men who were not paid the full minimum and bounty before leaving the rendezvous, a remark should be entered on the Muster for pay rolls in each case, to the effect that the bounty and premium is due.

It is respectfully requested that hereafter your official communications relate to one subject only.

The other subjects mentioned in your letter will receive prompt attention.

I have the honor to be

Very Respectfully
Your Obd't Servant
Lew Foster
Asst. Adjt Gen'l Vols. [1]

Meanwhile, the recruits kept pouring through the facility's gates, even from such locales as New York. The following correspondence indicates that some recruits, after reporting to Riker's Island, where the 20th and 26th USCT regiments of New York would soon be raised, were transferred to Camp William Penn. The first letter, from Gen. N.J. Jackson, was sent to Commander Wagner:

Head Quarters Draft Rendezvous
Rikers Island N.Y.H.
October 27th, 1863.

Colonel

I have the honor to state that there are now, Eighty five (coloreds) Drafted men and substitutes at this post.
I respectfully request that you give me instructions in regards to the assignment of them.

I am, Colonel

Very Respectfully
Your Ob'dt Serv'vt
N. J. Jackson
Brig. Genl Vol. Comdg. [2]

The second note indicates that the New York contingent would be assigned to Camp William Penn, a development that likely pleased Col. Wagner:

War Department, A.G.O.
Nov. 2nd, 1863

Official copy respectfully referred to Lt. Col. Louis Wagner, 88th Regt. Penna. Vols. Comdg. Camp William Penn, Philadelphia Pa. who is informed that instructions have been issued directing these men to be sent to Camp William Penn; they will accordingly be received and assigned to the 8th Regt. U.S. Colored Troops.

By order:

Lew Foster
Asst. Adjt. Gen. Vols. [3]

William P. Woodlin, a musician who'd join Company G of the 8th, "enrolled in the Army at Syracuse, New York, in August 1863 at the age of 21," according to his memoirs, which can be found at www.gilderlehrman.org and are entitled "Diary of a Black Soldier," at The Gilder Lehrman Institute of American History. Woodlin wrote the very revealing

123-page diary that focuses on the likes of the black troops' lower pay compared to whites, as well as entries that "deal with travel, weather, food, and the mail" and other matters.

Indeed, Woodlin provides details of life at Camp William Penn in the following journal entries, opening with a November 18, 1863 "General review of troops here by Gen. Casey." Then he continues the November entries:

> 26. Thanksgiving day. A present of $100 made to the Reg which was laid out in apples, pies & coffee. Speeches by Gov. Cannon of Del. A gentle[man] from [England] and some others.
> 27. went over to the Barracks to carry a flag pole, the whole Reg'.
> 28. A very heavy rain and a cold one followed by a cold snap of 3 days.

Then, apparently, the weather began to improve by December 2ⁿᵈ, according to Woodlin, "which is just beginning to ease up this the 2ⁿᵈ day of Dec. tow[a]rd evening."

It was about this time that the 8ᵗʰ USCT got a bit of national notoriety when several of its members appeared at a Boston anti-slavery convention, helping the likes of abolitionists and women's rights advocates Lucretia Mott, Frederick Douglass, Robert Purvis, Susan B. Anthony, John Greenleaf Whittier, Abby Kelley Foster, and Lucy Stone mark the Thirtieth Anniversary of the American Anti-Slavery Society in Boston. Hosted by William Lloyd Garrison, the great publisher and radical abolitionist, his newspaper, the *Liberator*, described: "The gathering of people – members and strangers – seemed at times too large for [the] Concert Hall to hold the multitude. It was a strange meeting; not a stone was thrown; not a hiss heard: not an egg cracked: and yet it was a meeting of Radical Abolitionists!"[4]

In the midst of Arthur Tappan, the well known abolitionist, reading letters of tribute, representatives of the Eighth made a grand appearance:

> During the reading, a company of Living Epistles, in the shape of a squad of black soldiers, consisting of sergeants and corporals of the 8ᵗʰ United States colored regiment stationed at Camp William Penn, entered the house, and amid boisterous cheers took seats of honor upon the platform. Mr. Garrison gave them welcome in a few sublime words, touching all hearts. These men, dressed in the United States uniform, and expecting soon to march to the field of bloody battle against the same institution of slavery for whose peaceful overthrow this society has labored – were living witnesses [of] how great a progress the good cause has made in thirty years.[5]

And just as impressive, the commander of Camp William Penn, Louis Wagner, addressed the audience containing a blockbuster group of nationally-renowned abolitionists:

> [Rev. Henry Ward Beecher] was followed by Susan B. Anthony, Charles C. Burleigh, Stephen S. Foster, Aaron M. Powell, Abby Kelly Foster, Lucy Stone, (who, after her long silence, spoke as naturally as if she had never lost a day's practice,) Mrs. Frances D. Gage, Col. Lewis [sic] Wagner, commander of the colored troops on the platform, Oliver Johnson, editor of the Anti-Slavery Standard, and several others whose names escape my pen in this hurried writing.

The closing session, which was densely crowded by a brilliant audience, filling every square inch of sitting or standing room – was addressed by Robert Purvis, Theodore Tilton, Senator Wilson, Frederick Douglass, Anna Dickinson, and William Lloyd Garrison.[6]

Woodlin, the brass musician, then described the 8th USCT's activities for December that would be followed by the regiment's departure after an amazingly brief training period. His language is blunt, describing incidents that were sometimes unbecoming, but indicative of life at such Civil War facilities, including those composed of white troops. And it's clear that Woodlin is a respected vocalist, since he indicates that he regularly sang during evening camaraderie sessions:

Dec. 5th. We have had Battalion drill for the past two days under our two Field officers. On the third there was a great row in Camp from there being [...] a little liquor brought in. On the fourth one of our Corps had his stripes ripped off for leaving the ranks without leave.

6th Sunday cold but we had an inspection which was hard to endure. In the afternoon we had meeting where I sung again as usual.

7th We did not drill much to day, but in the evening there was a great row, from a drunken man being struck by an officer with his sword. One of our men

knocked the Capt. Down; two were sent to the guard house from this [incident].

8th We struck tents and moved over to our winter quarters, with our own Reg [...]

9th No drill to day but dress Parade at night, at which the Court Martials were read off [...]

10th No drill, but the Brass Instruments having Come I was taken in for one of them. It is still very cold and our stoves have not come yet, though they are up in the Schoolroom.

11th A very cold day, went over to the schoolroom and practiced on our instruments, in the evening we had an entertainment at the

Lieutenant Oliver Norton of the 8th USCT wrote a detailed diary of the regiment's activities and also served as its quartermaster. *Courtesy of the U. S. Army Military History Institute.*

Meeting house of pictures shown through a Lantern, by means of an Oxhydrogen Blow Pipe; a very good selection.

In the interim, recruiting efforts at the start of 1864 continued – even in the state of Delaware – with a detachment of the 8ᵗʰ, including Lt. Oliver Norton, who had been wounded at Gaines' Mill, Virginia, during a June 27, 1862, clash. He apparently was commissioned to the rank of lieutenant in the Eighth on November 10, 1863. Following the war, in 1903 he wrote the book *Army Letters, 1861-1865*, that provided vivid details of the 8ᵗʰ's activities, including the entry below concerning the Delaware Governor Cannon's enthusiasm for recruiting black troops:

> *Seaford. Del., Jan. 4, 1864.*
>
> Dear Sister L.: –
>
> We came by boat from Philadelphia to Wilmington. New Year's day our whole detachment was feasted in the town hall at the same time with the First Delaware Volunteers, home on furlough. We had good times there.
>
> On the 2d we came down on the cars to Seaford, one hundred and thirty-three miles south of Wilmington. I saw Governor Cannon in Wilmington and had quite a talk with him. He is enthusiastic on the subject of negro soldiers.
>
> Arrived here at dark, found a man at the depot waiting, who offered us quarters in a negro church and a school house and all were comfortable.
>
> Sunday morning I got my tents up from the cars and we pitched a camp in one of the most beautiful pine groves I ever saw. Our camp was thronged with visitors, and darkies who wanted to enlist. There are hundreds of them, mostly slaves, here now, anxiously waiting for the recruiting officer. The boys are singing –
>
> Rally round the ting, boys, rally once again,
> Shouting the battle cry of freedom.
> Down with the traitor, up with the star, etc.
>
> They sing with the heart, and the earnestness they put into the words is startling. Cool as I am I found myself getting excited as I heard their songs this afternoon and saw the electrifying effect on the crowds of slaves.
>
> The officers here are lions. I am afraid I'm guilty of putting on a little style. Not with the men of the regiment, though. I was shaved by a woman this morning. (Norton 1903, 196)

During his next correspondence, Norton would report an anticipated, but what had to be a very emotional development:

Seaford, Del., Jan. 9, 1864.

Dear Sister L.: –

I have just time to-night to write you some important news. Important so far as you and I are concerned. An orderly arrived in camp to-night with a dispatch from the Secretary of War ordering the detachment to return to Camp Wm. Penn, and the United States Colored Troops will proceed as soon as practicable to Hilton Head, South Carolina. We shall be off next week.

There is joy in camp to-night over the news. I hardly know whether to like it or not. On some accounts I shall. Almost any place is preferable to Virginia. I shall be far away from home and friends. Letters will be like angels' visits, few and far between. But bid me God speed, L. Far or near, my heart will be with thee. Don't write till I send my address. (196-197)

Not even 10 days into the New Year, rumors began to circulate concerning the regiment possibly leaving campgrounds for the South, despite Woodlin seeming excited and pleased about a dress parade and new "Zouave" outfits. That was regardless of his obvious concern for the band's weapons being taken from them, as well as an apparent freak accident that sent a rifle round "over our heads":

[January] 9th [1864] The news came that we were to move to South Carolina soon.

10th We were all on inspection nearly all day; the Col said that we were to give up our guns, who belonged to the band.

11th We did not play at all as the members were nearly all gone. Shank among the rest. Whiskey held high sway here all day. At night some 100 new recruits came in, with a semblance of a Band with them; and a poor one at that.

12th We were called up and dressed up in our Zouave Suit today, and played for Dress Parade. We also got our leggings; and gave up our guns, who belong to the band. We did not have very good success.

13th We practiced to'day out in the road, and played a dress parade again. Sold vest for 10 cts. To C. Cog and Rece'd it back agan [sic].

14th We went out in the road to practice. Twice to day; a ball whizzed over our heads, which made quite a sensation amongst us.

15th We played for guard mounting this morning and stopped.

16th We rec'd orders to pack up this morning at roll call to be ready to move at a moments warning. Fell in at 10 a.m. and the start was put off until ½ past 1 p.m. When the whole Reg was formed in line, and march out in review before the 22nd. Band playing Yankee Doddle. Paraded through Front & across Walnut Strs and took the carr[ier]s for New York where we arrived at about 9 a.m.

Lieutenant Norton wrote his sister about the regiment's departure:

St. Lawrence Hotel, Philadelphia, Jan. 17, 1864.

Dear Sister L.: –

The regiment started for the sunny south last night, leaving me behind. I shall go to New York before I go and I would like to see you once more first, but it would require too liberal construction of my orders to find any business in Chautauqua. I am left to settle my business as quartermaster and to take command of a squad of men not yet reported to the regiment.

So, sadly, the regiment's training term was shockingly short, a development that would not soon bode well for many of the men during the devastating Battle of Olustee in the swamps of northern Florida when they faced hardened Confederate troops. And instead of heading directly south, as Norton and Woodlin reported, the regiment departed Camp William Penn on January 16, 1864, for New York with Woodlin soon to follow. Reporter James R. W. Leonard of the *Anglo-African* newspaper, observed:

The 8ᵗʰ Regiment, U.S. Colored Troops, from Camp Wm. Penn, Philadelphia, arrived in this city on Sunday last [January 17], and marched through Broadway to the foot of Canal Street, where transports lay waiting to convey them to Hilton Head, their place of destination. A full brass band […] together with a complete fife and drum corps, created in all the wildest enthusiasm, and occasioned many pious feet to stray from the sanctuary, whilst they kept step to the inspiriting Yankee Doodle. (Trudeau 1998, 126)

Woodlin jotted down in his January 17ᵗʰ diary entry: "Paraded through Cort & Broadway down Canall Strs to the wharf where we shipped at night on board the [ships] City of Bath & the Promethius [sic]." It's likely that Woodlin was transported by the *Prometheus*, since he'd soon complain of rough seas and seasickness, problems that were not encountered by earlier departing *City of Bath*.

And despite the officers' and soldiers' immense pride as they paraded through the streets of New York City, the regimental surgeon, Dr. A.P. Heichold, made observations that portended of trouble down the road, noted Trudeau. That was even as he "tramped to the tune of John Brown" (126).

The men appeared keenly alive to the importance of the hour. Bitter experience had taught many of them the value of good government, and the wisdom of making known the power of the iron black arm of this nation. Prominent amongst this class, we noticed Mr. Charles Jackson, now Orderly Sergeant, who was beaten and thrown overboard for dead during the July [1863] riots [in New York]. His keen eye and compressed lips afforded a warning to "nigger killers."

As the vessel did not, as expected, head out on Sunday, I availed myself of the invitation extended by Sergeants Chas. Jackson and John C. Chambers, to visit their men on Monday morning. This visit afforded an opportunity of observing the material commanding.

Col. Fribley, a small wiry man, is a gentleman of culture and has the undivided attachment of his men [...]. The [white] officers seemed proud of the men, as they justly might be, for a nobler band of patriots never carried a gun. But one incident occurred which we had cause to regret. On Sunday, whilst the men were in line on Canal street, Noah Smith, a young private of Co. F, having been clandestinely furnished with whiskey by some of the bystanders, became ungovernable and in a fit of drunken rage, shot the first sergeant of his Co., Sergt. Duty [...]. At last accounts he was doing well. I saw the sullen and indifferent. "Bind his hands behind him," said the Lieutenant. "Don't be afraid of hurting him!" During the whole operation he never moved a muscle – he seemed hardened past all hope [...]. "We must have strict discipline," said Orderly. "Examples, severe examples must be made in such cases or none of us would be safe." The regiment, which numbered 800, was conveyed in two transports, and as they left the dock they rent the air with cheer after cheer to each other and their numerous friends upon the dock. The drums beat, fifes screamed, and lastly the boys broke out amidst waving of hats and handkerchiefs, "We're off for Charleston early in the morning." (126-127)

However, on the 18th there was a delay due to the weather, according to Woodlin's entry that day: "Sailed at 10 & 11 a.m. but the fog prevented our leaving the bay at all."

Nevertheless, the proud 8th departed the New York port on the transporting ships *City of Bath* and *Prometheus*, as Woodlin also mentioned, headed for South Carolina's

Hilton Head as ordered. "The City of Bath made a speedy passage, but the Prometheus was tossed about by adverse weather, and was compelled to put in at Fortress Monroe, delaying its arrival at its destination for two days (*8th United States Colored Regiment* 2011)."

The weather pattern seemed to continue on the 19th, after the ship began to head south and Woodlin wrote, "Started again from Sandy Hook [likely New Jersey] in the morning, met rough weather all day...."

As a matter of fact, the rough seas certainly did not agree with him, compounded by a greasy breakfast, according to his January 20th entry: "Still rough weather had to go into the hold to sleep, was a little sea sick from fat bacon."

Colonel Charles W. Fribley's body was not returned by Rebel forces, despite his wife eventually receiving his personal belongings from a Confederate general who criticized Fribley for commanding black troops. *Courtesy of the U. S. Army Military History Institute.*

The weather apparently began to improve on January 21ˢᵗ, with Woodlin noting, "The first pleasant day we had we got our horns out and practiced; also passed Roanoke Island & Hatteras in the evening slept on deck at night."

And by January 23ʳᵈ the regiment was almost ready to disembark: "Passed Charleston at about 9 a.m., an occasional gun fired; and saw smoke rising from various points."

Then finally, on January 24ᵗʰ came their landfall: "Landed at Hilton [Head] at 9 a.m. formed in line and march outside of the entrenchments and encamped."

And by several accounts, the regiment was visually very impressive once it reached the South and was assigned to "Howell's Brigade of Seymour's Division." In fact, on February 4ᵗʰ "the division was reviewed by General Gilmore, in command of the Department, the regiment eliciting much commendation by its good soldierly appearance." (*8ᵗʰ United States Colored Regiment* 2011)."

Even the mighty 54ᵗʰ Massachusetts, with a magnificent national reputation due to its heroic efforts at the battle for Fort Wagner on July 18, 1863, was impressed with the 8ᵗʰ's veneer after it arrived in the South Carolina Sea Island area in late January 1864, just two days before being reviewed by General Gilmore:

> On February 2, it was given a cool once-over by a veteran of the Fort Wagner assault and a member of the now-famous 54ᵗʰ Regiment Massachusetts Infantry (colored). "Some say that the 54ᵗʰ has a rival," wrote Corporal James Henry Gooding. "The 8ᵗʰ U.S. regiment is indeed a splendid organization, and I may add that no regiment in the department can boast of a more healthy-looking, martial-bearing body of men; although in the manual of arms the old 54ᵗʰ can't be beat." (Trudeau 1998, 127)

And by February 5ᵗʰ the regiment, part of 7,000 soldiers commanded by General Truman Seymour, departed for Florida, arriving in the evening at Jacksonville on the 7ᵗʰ" (Bates 1871, 965).

Not far from the St. John's River, the brigade began marching as the sun rose the following day, reaching an "encampment of rebels from which they had just fled, abandoning, in their haste, a quantity of stores and several pieces of artillery." And then three companies of the Eighth that were commanded by Captain (George) Wagner (brother of Camp William Penn's Commander Louis Wagner) "made a descent *on* Finnegan's Depot, on the Tallahasse Railroad, capturing a quantity of stores, and one prisoner" (965).

However, next was more mundane, but strenuous work for the regiment, including "guarding and repairing railroad bridges," before the Eighth, the Seventh New Hampshire, and Seventh Connecticut "were united in a brigade" under the command of Colonel Hawley of the Seventh Connecticut. (ibid)

Woodlin and his fellow soldiers were likely very excited about the prospect of encountering the Rebels, with the warrior-musician reporting on February 19ᵗʰ: "We marched this morning about 9 a.m. from Baldwinsville by way of the R.R. Saw Gen. Seymour in the morning before we started. Reached a station called Barbers Plantation. After passing two Turpentine distillery's [sic] and halting about ½ hour for dinner, we also passed an earthwork in process of erosion to guard a long tressel-work [sic]."

Little did the men of the Eighth know that these developments set the stage for a debacle:

> The enemy was known to be posted at Lake City, under General Finnegan, and against this post General Seymour determined to lead so much of his force as could be spared from garrison duty in his rear. Finnegan, discovering a disposition of the Union commander to advance upon him, determined not to await an attack at Lake City but to advance some fifteen miles to meet it at a point near Olustee, where he took a strong position, with his forces formed on a swamp extending southward from Ocean Pond, his centre protected by the swamp, his right resting on an earth-work shielded by rifle-pits, and his left posted on a slight elevation, sheltered by pines, and guarded by cavalry. Unaware of this advance and new disposition of the enemy's troops, Seymour, who was at Barbour's early on the morning of the 20th, began to move. A march of a few hours, brought the column to Sanderson's, a distance of twelve miles. After a brief rest, the march was resumed, and at two p. m., a body of the enemy's cavalry was encountered, which quickly gave way. The artillery moved upon the road, and was flanked upon either side by a column of infantry. When nearing Olustee, and while proceeding quietly along without any expectation of meeting the foe, the head of the column was suddenly fired into by the enemy, from his strong lines in his well chosen position. The cavalry, and the Seventh Connecticut, which was armed with Spencer rifles, were thrown forward as skirmishers, but soon found that they could make little impression. Hawley's Brigade was in advance, Barton's and Montgomery's following at short intervals. Hamilton's Battery was quickly brought into position, but in that dead level could get no commanding ground. Without awaiting the arrival of the rest of his force, Seymour put the Seventh New Hampshire in position on the right of the road, and the Eighth Colored upon the left, and pushed them at once into action. (966)

The Eighth, sadly, was ill prepared for the battle:

> The Eighth, though scarcely a month from camp, and with hardly any skill in handling a musket, boldly advanced in face of a withering fire from the enemy's strong and well chosen lines. Hamilton's guns thundered in its rear, adding to the terrors, and in some instances to the dangers of its position; but still it stood firm. For three-quarters of an hour, the action raged with unabated fury, these raw troops maintaining their ground without the least shelter, with a courage worthy of veterans. Several color-bearers were shot down, and many officers fell; but it preserved an unflinching front. At this juncture, the enemy, whose lines greatly overreached the Union front, charged upon the unprotected left flank of the Eighth, threatening its capture. (ibid.)

General Seymour ordered a hasty retreat as his men returned heavy fire. The commander, despite the attempted help of Barton's and Montgomery's forces, was also forced to "retire," even losing valuable artillery (966).

Woodlin described the harrowing episode from a soldiers' point of view this way in his diary entry of February 20:

> We rec'd our rations last evening and got underway about ½ past 6 a.m. at a quick step on the left of the division, passed Sanders Station about 11 a.m., about 12 m: {as near as could be learned} from B's Plantation; we had a very rapid as well as fatiguing march; passed through a'deal turpentine forest. After this halt we were ordered forward, & soon could hear the roar of Canon & the rattle of Musketry ahead of us, we were hurried up to the line of battle at the double quick and our Reg was place in the center and rec'd the hottest fire that was given; The Col. fell [...] the Major wounded [...] a Capt, & several lieutenants. The band and Drum Core [*sic*] went up to the front ahead of the Cavalry and were exposed to a very hot fire: for a while when we fell back to the R.R. until we were in danger of being taken by a flank movement of the Rebs: we got away however and had another station for a while: when we were again move a mile farther from the battle field, which was in the front of Lake City. We built some fires there, & were halted by the Division Dr. for a while after which we moved on until we reached the station. We left in the morning [illegible] [...] below the scene of action nearly worn out with fatigue & cold. We reached there about 1 a.m. that night and stayed until daylight.

In a letter of February 23, 1864, to his friend, Edward M. Davis, the leasor of the land on which Camp William Penn rose and the son-in-law of the anti-slavery abolitionist Lucretia Mott, the Surgeon of the Eighth USCT, A.P. Heichhold, described the action from his special vantage point as the brigade's chief medical officer:

> We left Baldwin, at the junction of the Jacksonville and Tallahassee, and Fernandina and Cedar Keys railroads, about twenty miles west of Jacksonville, on Friday, the twentieth; marched westward eleven miles, and bivouacked for the night at Barber's Ford, on the St. Mary's River. The bugle sounded the reveille before daylight, and, after taking breakfast, we took up the line of march westward. Our march for ten miles to Sanderson Station was uninterrupted, but about four miles further west our advance drove in the enemy's pickets, keeping up a continuous skirmish with them for about four miles, when the Seventh Connecticut, who were in the advance, deployed as skirmishers, fell in with the [enemy's] force in a swamp, strengthened still further with rifle-pits. Here they were met with cannon and musketry. The Seventh were armed with Spencer rifles, which fire eight times without loading, with which they played dreadful havoc with the enemy. They were then ordered to take one of four pieces of artillery the enemy had, but were unsuccessful. They held their ground nobly, as long as their sixty rounds of ammunition lasted, which was perhaps three quarters of an hour, but were retiring just as the main body of our army came up. The Eighth colored marched on the railroad, came up first, and filed to the right, when they were soon met with a most terrific shower of musketry and shell. General T. Seymour

now came up, and pointing in front toward the railroad, said to Colonel Fribley, commander of the Eighth, "Take your regiment in there" – a place which was sufficiently hot to make veterans tremble, and yet we were to enter it with men who had never heard the sound of a cannon. Colonel Fribley ordered the regiment, by company, into line, double-quick march; but, before it was fairly in line, the men commenced dropping like leaves in autumn. Still, on they went, without faltering or murmuring, until they came within two hundred yards of the enemy, when the struggle for life and death commenced. Here they stood for two hours and a half, under one of the most terrible fires I ever witnessed; and here, on the field of Olustee, was decided whether the colored man had the courage to stand without shelter, and risk the dangers of the battle-field; and when I tell you that they stood with a fire in front, on their flank, and in their rear, for two hours and a half, without flinching, and when I tell you the number of dead and wounded, I have no doubt as to the verdict of every man who has gratitude for the defenders of his country, white or black.

Colonel Fribley, seeing that it was impossible to hold the position, passed along the lines to tell the officers to fire and fall back gradually, and was shot before he reached the end. He was shot in the chest, told the men to carry him to the rear, and expired in a very few minutes. Major Burritt took command, but was also wounded in a short time. At this time Captain Hamilton's battery became endangered, and he cried out to our men for God's sake to save his battery. Our United States flag, after three sergeants had forfeited their lives by bearing it during the fight, was planted on the battery by [...] Lieutenant Elijah Lewis, and the men rallied around it, but the guns had been jammed up so indiscriminately, and so close to the enemy's lines, that the gunners were shot down as fast as they made their appearance; and the horses, whilst they were wheeling the pieces into position, shared the same fate. They were compelled to leave the battery [...] The battery fell into the enemy's hands. During the excitement Captain Bailey took command, and brought out the regiment in good order. Sergeant Taylor, company D, who carried the battle-flag, had his right hand nearly shot [off], but grasped the colors with the left hand, and brought it out.

I took my position along the railroad, and had the wounded brought there, and while busily engaged a volley was poured into us. About a dozen of cavalry were preparing to make a charge on us, but disappeared as the Fifty-fourth Massachusetts advanced out of the woods […] and had it not been for the Fifty-fourth, which advanced in splendid order, they would undoubtedly have taken us all prisoners. The Seventh New-Hampshire was posted on both sides of the wagon road, and broke, but rallied in a short time, and did splendid execution. The line was probably one mile long, and all along the fighting was terrific.

Our artillery, where it could be worked, made dreadful havoc on the enemy, whilst the enemy did us but very little injury with his, with the exception of one gun, a sixty-four pound swivel, fixed on a truck-car on the railroad, which fired grape and canister. On the whole, their [artillery] was very harmless, but their musketry [fearsome]. We were informed in the morning that they [had] some ten thousand men, and four guns, while we had less than six thousand, but eighteen guns. The troops all fought bravely; the First North Carolina (colored) did nobly. I saw at an early stage of the fight that we would be whipped, and I went round among our wounded and told them, as many as could get away, to start for Barter, and then started the ambulance crowded full. The day and the field being lost to us, we started on the retreat, and reached our old quarters yesterday. We were compelled to leave a few of our men behind, and they fell into the hands of the enemy. It could not be helped; I had but one ambulance to a regiment, and the railroad was useless, because we had no locomotive. However, we got some horse-cars to within eighteen miles of the field, which aided us greatly. How the rebels have disposed of the colored men who fell into their hands we have not heard yet; but we hope that the fear of retaliation, if not the dictates of humanity, will cause them to reconsider their threat of outlawry. If not, it must act accordingly. Our men are neither discouraged nor dismayed, but ready for another fight […].

We should have at least two hundred men immediately. Will the committee not make an effet [effort] to send them to us? I have no doubt but [that] the War Department would allow it. Please do your best for us. If it could be done, we would [like] two flanking companies of one hundred men each, armed with Spencer rifles. I think they are just the thing for bushwhacking. You [...] tell the committee that we look to them as guardians, and therefore hope they will do all for us they can, and do it quickly. Your friend, A. P. Heichhold, Surgeon Eighth U.S.C.T. (Moore 1865, 417)

Lieutenant Norton reported very similar tragic circumstances to his sister:

Jacksonville, Fla., Monday, Feb. 29, 1864.

Dear Sister L.: –

You will probably see accounts of the battle of Olustee, or Ocean Pond, in the papers. I have ordered a copy of the Brookville Republican, containing a letter from Dr. Heichhold, descriptive of the battle, sent to you, but I will give you some of my own ideas about it, too; you always express a preference for them, you know.

Well, the morning of Saturday, the 20th, found us at Barber's Ford on the St. Mary's river ready to march and loaded down with ten days' rations. Our force consisted of the One hundred-fifteenth, Forty-seventh and Forty-eighth New York Regiments, Seventh New Hampshire and Seventh Connecticut (repeating rifles), Fifty-fourth Massachusetts (colored) of Fort Wagner memory, the First North Carolina Colored and the Eighth, twenty pieces of artillery, one battalion cavalry and the Fortieth Massachusetts (mounted infantry).

We started marching in three columns, artillery in the road, flanked by the infantry on either side. After marching twelve miles we halted near a few desolate houses called Sanders and while resting heard a few musket shots in advance.

We supposed our cavalry had met a few of the enemy's pickets. Their force was supposed to be at Lake City, twelve miles distant, so we moved on up the railroad. The skirmishing increased as we marched, but we paid little attention to it. Pretty soon the boom of a gun startled us a little, but not much, as we knew our flying artillery was ahead, but they boomed again and again and it began to look like a brush. An aide came dashing through the woods to us and the order was – "double quick, march!" We turned into the woods and ran in the direction of the firing for half a mile, when the head of the column reached our batteries. The presiding genius, General Seymour, said: "Put your regiment in, Colonel Fribley," and left.

Military men say it takes veteran troops to maneuver under fire, but our regiment with knapsacks on and unloaded pieces, after a run of half a mile, formed a line under the most destructive fire I ever knew. We were not more than two hundred yards from the enemy, concealed in pits and behind trees, and what did the regiment do? At first they were stunned, bewildered, and knew not what to do. They curled to the ground, and as men fell around them they seemed terribly scared, but gradually they recovered their senses and commenced firing. And here was the great trouble – they could not use their arms to advantage. We have had very little practice in firing, and, though they could stand and be killed, they could not kill a concealed enemy fast enough to satisfy my feelings.

After seeing his men murdered as long as flesh and blood could endure it, Colonel Fribley ordered the regiment to fall back – slowly, firing as they went. As the men fell back they gathered in groups like frightened sheep, and it was almost impossible to keep them from doing so. Into these groups the rebels poured the deadliest fire, almost every bullet hitting some one. Color bearer after color bearer was shot down and the colors seized by another. Behind us was a battery that was wretchedly managed. They had but little ammunition, but after firing that, they made no effort to get away with their pieces, but busied themselves in trying to keep us in front of them. Lieutenant Lewis seized the colors and planted them by a gun and tried to rally his men round them, but forgetting them for the moment, they were left there, and the battery was captured and our colors with it.

Colonel Fribley was killed soon after his order to fall back, and Major Burritt had both legs broken. We were without a commander, and every officer was doing his best to do something, he knew not what exactly. There was no leader. Seymour might better have been in his grave than there. Many will blame Lieutenant Lewis that the colors were lost. I do not think he can be blamed. Brave to rashness, he cannot be accused of cowardice, but man cannot think of too many things.

Some things in this story look strange. Officers should know exactly what to do, you may say. Certainly, but it is a damper on that duty when there is a certainty on the mind that the commander does not know. When, with eight or ten regiments ready, you see only two or three fighting, and feel you are getting whipped from your general's incompetency, it is hard to be soldierly.

I saw from the commencement of our retreat that the day was lost, but I confess to you that I was in doubt whether I ought to stay and see my men shot down or take them to the rear. Soldierly feelings triumphed, but at what a cost!

Captain Dickey was shot early in the fight and the command of the company devolved on me. He was not seriously wounded, a ball through the face.

Captain Wagner was standing by me when he fell, pierced by three balls. I seized him and dragged him back a few rods and two of his men then took him to the rear. I carried his sword through the fight. Several times I was on the point of throwing it away, thinking he must be dead, but I saved it and had the pleasure of giving it to him and hearing that he is likely to recover.

Of twenty-two officers that went into the fight, but two escaped without marks. Such accurate firing I never saw before. I was under the impression all the time that an inferior force was whipping us, but the deadly aim of their rifles told the story.

Well, you are wanting to know how I came off, no doubt. With my usual narrow escapes, but escapes. My hat has five bullet holes in it. Don't start very much at that – they were all made by one bullet. You know the dent in the top of it. Well, the ball went through the rim first and then through the top in this way. My hat was cocked up on one side so that it went through in that way and just drew the blood on my scalp. Of course a quarter of an inch lower would have broken my skull, but it was too high. Another ball cut away a corner of my haversack and one struck my scabbard. The only wonder is I was not killed, and the wonder grows with each succeeding fight, and this is the fifteenth or sixteenth, Yorktown, Hanover, Gaines' Mill, Charles City, Malvern, Bull Run, Antietam, Shepherdstown Ford, Fredericksburg, Richards Ford, Chancellorsville, Loudon Valley, Gettysburg, Manassas Gap, Rappahannock Station and Olustee, to say nothing of the shelling at Harrison's Landing or the skirmish at Ely's Ford. Had any one told me when I enlisted that I should have to pass through so many I am afraid it would have daunted me. How many more?

Company K went into the fight with fifty-five enlisted men and two officers. It came out with twenty-three men and one officer. Of these but two men were not marked. That speaks volumes for the bravery of negroes. Several of these twenty-three were quite badly cut, but they are present with the company. Ten were killed and four reported missing, though there is little doubt they are killed, too.

A flag of truce from the enemy brought the news that prisoners, black and white, were treated alike. I hope it is so, for I have sworn never to take a prisoner if my men left there were murdered.

This is the first letter I have written since the fight, and it is to you, my best beloved sister. It is written in haste, in a press of business, but you will excuse mistakes and my inattention to the matter of your own letter. You may pray for me – I need that, and do write to me as often as you find time. (Norton 1903, 197-201)

Indeed, the event was so traumatic and monumental to Norton that he also wrote his father:

Jacksonville, Fla., Tuesday, March 1, 1864.

Dear Father: –

On the 20th we fought our first battle at Olustee, or Ocean Pond, as some call it. They might as well call any other place in these pine woods some high sounding name, for this country is all alike. Since leaving Jacksonville I have not seen five hundred acres of cleared land in a journey of forty-five miles to the west. The country is covered with scattered pines, most of them blazed for turpentine. The ground between the trees is covered with a dense growth of coarse grass and palmetto shrubs. At intervals there are swamps, not deep, but broad and wet. Once in about ten miles is a small collection of dilapidated looking houses on the Florida railroad, and the people – the most abject, stupid, miserable objects.

I have ordered a copy of the Brookville Republican containing an account of the battle by Dr. Heichhold, to be sent to you, because I have not time to write it myself. I have not yet seen it, but I presume it will be correct, as the doctor had better opportunities for learning the facts than I had.

I shall give you more particularly my own ideas of the performance of our own men. I want to be true and I cannot endorse all that has been said of them. First, I think no battle was ever more wretchedly fought. I was going to say planned, but there was no plan. No new regiment ever went into their first fight in more unfavorable circumstances. Second, no braver men ever faced an enemy. To have made these men fight well, I would have halted them out of range of the firing, formed my line, unslung knapsacks, got my cartridge boxes ready, and loaded. Then I would have moved it up to the support of a regiment already engaged. I would have had them lie down and let the balls and shells whistle over them till they got a little used to it. Then I would have moved them to the front, told them to get as close to the ground as they could and go in.

Just the other thing was done. We were double-quicked for half a mile, came under fire by the flank, formed line with empty pieces under fire, and, before the men had loaded, many of them were shot down. They behaved as any one acquainted with them would have expected. They were stunned, bewildered, and, as the balls came hissing past or crashing through heads, arms and legs, they curled to the ground like frightened sheep in a hailstorm. The officers finally got them to firing, and they recovered their senses somewhat. But here was the great difficulty – they did not know how to shoot with effect.

Our regiment has been drilled too much for dress parade and too little for the field. They can march well, but they cannot shoot rapidly or with effect. Some of them can, but the greater part cannot. Colonel Fribley had applied time and again for permission to practice his regiment in target firing, and been always refused. When we were flanked, flesh and blood could stand it no longer, and Colonel Fribley, without orders, gave the command to fall back slowly, firing as we went.

He fell, shot through the heart, very soon after that. Where was our general and where was his force? Coming up in the rear, and as they arrived, they were put in, one regiment at a time, and whipped by detail.

It is no use for me to express my feelings in regard to the matter. If there is a second lieutenant in our regiment who couldn't plan and execute a better battle, I would vote to dismiss him for incompetency.

The correspondent of the Tribune who was present said he dared not write a true history of the affair here, but he should do it in New York, and it would be published.

You may judge of the severity of the fight by this: Of fifty-five men in Company K who went into the fight but two came out untouched by balls. Of twenty-two officers engaged but two were untouched. I got a ball in my hat that made five holes and just drew blood on my head. Another took off the corner of my haversack.

Colonel Fribley was shot through the heart. Major Burritt, gallant fellow, had both legs broken. Captain [George] Wagner fell pierced with three balls, but got off, and I hear is in a fair way to recovery. (Norton 1903, 201-203)

Woodlin, as well as his compatriots, who were new to such battlefield activities, were greatly impacted emotionally by the regiment's casualties:

The loss in the Eighth was very severe. Two officers and forty-nine men were killed, nine officers and one hundred and eighty men were wounded, and sixty-three missing, all of whom, it was subsequently ascertained, were wounded and left on the field. Colonel Fribley and Lieutenant Thomas J. Goldsborough were killed; Major Burritt, Captain Wagner, and Lieutenants Seth Lewis and George Warrington, were among the officers wounded. The color company went into action with forty-eight enlisted men, and lost in killed and wounded all but six. (Bates 1871, 966)

Historian Dudley Taylor Cornish described the battle and its outcome just as powerfully with similar battle results:

In the battle of Olustee, or Ocean Pond, 50 miles west of Jacksonville, Florida, on February 20, 1864, three Negro and six white regiments (plus smaller artillery and cavalry units) were defeated by Confederate troops after a stubborn fight. Colonel Joseph R. Hawley, commanding a brigade consisting of the 7ᵗʰ Connecticut, 7ᵗʰ New Hampshire, and 8ᵗʰ U.S. Colored Troops, wrote afterward: "Colonel Fribley's black men met the enemy at short range. They had reported to me only two or three days before; I was afterward told that they had never had a day's practice in loading and firing. Old troops, finding themselves so greatly over-matched, would have run a little and re-formed – with or without orders." The 8ᵗʰ U.S. Colored was a new regiment; its men had never been in action before. They "stood to be killed or wounded – losing more than three hundred out of five hundred and fifty." Of the eight infantry regiments involved at Olustee, Fribley's command suffered the highest number of men killed on the field, 48. The regiment was second only to the hard-hit 47th New York Volunteers in total casualties: 310 killed, wounded, or missing in the 8th; 313 in the 47th New York. Total Union casualties at Olustee were 1,861. (Cornish 1987, 267-268)

In fact, Cornish noted that the Rebels actually stripped Colonel Fribley's body, "angry at white officers who commanded black troops" (Blackett 1989, 149). And there was quite a stir, with Fribley's wife in the midst, concerning the body that was never retrieved; although her husband's "personal belongings" were returned with the assistance of a defiant Rebel officer (224):

> Colonel C. W. Fribley of the 8th U.S. Colored Troops was left dead on the field after the battle of Olustee, Florida, in February. Following an exchange of letters between Brigadier General Thomas Seymoure, commanding Union forces at Jacksonville, and General William Gardner, C.S.A., through which Seymour attempted to recover Fribley's body or at least some of his personal belongings for his widow, Gardner wrote, "I have the honor to forward through you to the widow of the late Colonel Fribley, an ambrotype, supposed to be the one referred to in the memorandum accompanying your communication" of February 25. "Traces have also been discovered," Gardner continued, "as his watch, a letter from his wife to himself, and his diary, and steps have been taken to recover possession of them. If successful, the two former articles will be forwarded." Then the Conferate general made his personal position clear: "That I may not be misunderstood, it is due to myself to state that no sympathy with the fate of any officer commanding negro troops, but compassion for a widow in grief, has induced these efforts to recover for her relics which she must naturally value." (ibid.)

A special program in Philadelphia was held to commemorate Fribley, with his wife paying homage there among the city's elite abolitionists and African American citizens. Indeed, a song was composed for the event, entitled "Hymn of the Freedman," with the sheet music cover highlighted with those words and the phrase, "RESPECTFULLY DEDICATED TO MRS. COL. CHAS. W. FRIBLEY." Beneath those words was placed a brilliant lithograph, created by P.S. Duval & Son of Philadelphia, of Fribley holding a battle sword and sporting a commander's brim cocked to the side, as well as eight black soldiers (on this book's cover) of the regiment standing proudly in front of Camp William Penn tents, the U.S. flag and the Chelten Hills panorama of idyllic hills and bright blue skies (Boker 1864). The words to the song were composed by the co-founder of the Union League of Philadelphia, George H. Boker, a well known Philadelphia poet, playwright, director and diplomat. Following the war, "President Ulysses S. Grant appointed him Ambassador to the Ottoman Empire in 1871 and in 1875, to Russia" (*Directors & Members* 2008). And the tune was composed by "A Contraband," who was unidentified, accompanying Boker's moving and strident words: "Surely God him-self has risen over all the wakened world;

burst the darkness of the prison, in-to hell the shakles hurled: For we hear a mighty rattle fill the valleys and the hills, As the freedmen march to battle as the God of freedom wills. Then rally, rally, rally round the flag of liberty; we are men at last and soldiers, we are free, are free, are free" (Boker 1864).

"They had advanced in the morning, arriving at a little after midnight, having in the meantime, marched forty miles, and fought a severe battle" (Bates 1871, 966). Yet, with just several hours of rest, the men made it back to Jacksonville, "where breastworks were thrown up, and preparations made for holding the place" since the Confederates had followed, perhaps intending to attack (966-967).

By April 17ᵗʰ the Eighth was under the new command of Captain Bailey and was commanded to St. John's Bluff, participating in fortifying and watching over the nearby stream to deter Rebels from "planting torpedoes." Yet by June, and under yet still another new temporary commander, Major Mayer, the Eighth "participated in numerous raids into the surrounding country, destroying a portion of the Cedar Keys Railroad, and taking some of the enemy's ammunition" (967).

Meanwhile, Sergeant-Major Rufus Sibb Jones of the 8ᵗʰ USCT penned an April 16, 1864, letter to Rev. Elisha Weaver, editor and publisher of *The Christian Recorder* in Philadelphia, from the battle front. The correspondence described the regiment's escapades, including a regimental dog, apparently wounded in battle, which many of the men had taken a liking to. Most notable, the regiment's strength was still greatly depleted following the Olustee debacle:

> My last letter, dated March 24ᵗʰ, was written on the premises of Mrs. Fort, on the bank of the beautiful river St. John's. The camp was just beginning to look handsome, when the 8ᵗʰ was ordered to exchange camps with the 7ᵗʰ Conn., one of the regiments with which the 8ᵗʰ was brigaded. The 8ᵗʰ having suffered in the late battle of Olustee, and their strength being hereby greatly diminished, were not considered sufficiently strong to hold as important a position, though strong enough to perform the labor of intrenching, fortifying, and beautifying that point. Details for fatigue were very heavy, and the work pushed forward with rapidity, for the first eight or ten days after encamping there. The exchange of camps was reluctantly made by the men of both regiments; having just completed their camps to suit their eccentric tastes. The exchange, on the part of the 8ᵗʰ, was rather profitable than otherwise, as to convenience of water facilities. Water in the camp of the 7ᵗʰ Conn., is obtained with little or no labor. Barrels had been sunk at the front of nearly all the company streets. These improvements were appreciated by the 8ᵗʰ, with the exception of the view of the St. John's river. Soldiers, as well as farmers, have their signs, and can tell pretty truthfully when the moving camp day comes, though they do not use the horn; but the preparing and decorating of a camp, are signs that orders for moving will soon follow, and no one is surprised when the order comes. Although such irregularities occur, the soldier is not reluctant in trying to make another camp to please him as well as the one he left behind.[7]

The writer then describes important deployments, including soldiers in his brigade and other Camp William Penn regiments:

I have just learned that three regiments are embarking on board of transports, to join the army of the Potomac. The 7th Conn., 7th New Hampshire, (with which the 8th has been brigaded,) and 40th Mass. Mounted Infantry, leaving this department almost to the colored troops. Colored regiments are, the 1st N.C., 54th Mass., 55th Mass., 2d S.C., 7th Wis., organized at Baltimore, Md., 3d U.S.C.T., (first regiment organized at [Camp] Wm. Penn, Pa.,) and 8th Regt., U.S.C.T. Company F, of the 3d, have been detached as artillerists, and garrison "Fort Sammons, on the extreme left." Co K, of the 3d, also garrison a fort on the right of the line of intrenchments. Some of the troops of which I speak, have been sent to Pilatka, and other different points, to perform garrison duty. Co. D, of the 8th, has been ordered to St. John's Bluff, some ten miles down St. John's river, to do garrison duty. It is intimated that the 8th will soon be ordered to Yellow Bluff, on the St. John's.[8]

And of particular interest, the status of the regiment's prisoners and other black soldiers captured by the Rebels at Olustee was obviously on Jones' mind:

The rebel Gen. Patten Anderson, commanding the rebel forces in Florida, has furnished the commanding General of the federal forces, at this place, with a list of names of those taken prisoners at the battle of "Olustee." It may possibly be that they will be treated as prisoners of war; yet it is uncertain what disposition will be made of the colored troops in their possession, eventually. It is hoped that the authorities at Washington will give special attention to the selection of officers to command the colored regiments. Such officers as Isaiah E. Richardson, Adjutant of the 8th, and 1st Lieut. Elijah Lewis, possess qualities, as officers of colored soldiers, I truly admire. These officers are kind and respectful to those whom they command, and feel interested in the welfare of the colored soldier; and at the same time, demand that respect which is due to an officer. These good qualities are appreciated by the men; and if the promotion of these officers were in the power of the men of the regiment, they would soon occupy the most prominent positions in the regiment.[9]

And then there were such serious matters as medical treatment and hospitals, as well as the prevalence of alligators and the absence of pay:

The sick and wounded colored troops of this department, in the hospital at Jacksonville, are treated with the utmost attention and kindness. Hospital No. 5, occupied by the colored troops, is pleasantly located. The building, probably, once belonged to one of the prominent citizens of Jacksonville, from the appearance of the construction of it, and the beautiful shade-trees, and flowers with which it is surrounded. It must be humiliating to those who once lived in style, and owned slaves, to see their property, and that of others, occupied as hospitals by negro soldiers from the North. It often happens here, that the mistress and servant eat together in sutler stores. I have seen beautiful bouquets, here, in the month of March. Florida, for pleasantness of climate, and beauty of country, is almost a "Paradise." With the exception of the prospective crop of the Alligator family, and flourishing condition of the reptile kingdom, I should prefer making Florida as my future home. The part of the State which I have seen, with a little capital and labor, on the yankee system, could be greatly improved; and in a short time, make it an enviable State.[10]

Even more discouraging was that the regiment had not, for the past nine months, received its payment for services rendered:

It seems the farther South the 8ᵗʰ advances, the farther "pay-day" gets away from it. Just think of the colored troops not receiving any pay for nine months! Every vessel which lands at Jacksonville, from the North, is expected to bring the Paymaster; but I have begun to think none has been sent; and that the privilege of fighting and getting killed, is the only pay given. The 54ᵗʰ Mass. has had one of their sergeants recently promoted to 2d Lieutenancy, on recommendation of Col. E.N. Hallowell, of the 54ᵗʰ, (now acting Brig. General of the 3d Brigade, composed of the 54ᵗʰ, 55ᵗʰ, Mass., and 8ᵗʰ U.S.C.T.,) and by Gov. Andrew, of Massachusetts; and no doubt the appointment of one of "African descent," to that position, will create a little flutter among those officers (of the 54ᵗʰ, and other regiments,) who are not favorable to promoting black soldiers. The Government probably places some estimate of value on the services and patriotism of the nearly organized army, which it has put into the field to combat slave catchers.[11]

However, very confounding to Sergeant-Major Jones was the practice of Rebel forces being released as prisoners to operate businesses in Jacksonville:

The freedom given to the rebels in Jacksonville, who were taken prisoners by the federal forces on the advance to the front, and sent to Jacksonville, really surprises me. It seems that they can obtain permission to open stores, restaurants, and engage in business generally, in preference to citizens from the North. In appearance, one would think that all the rebels about Jacksonville were millers, (by occupation,) going or returning from their meals. The clothing worn by them is of a grayish color, and made after the fashion of tights, showing that cloth is scarce, or too many men for the supply of cloth.[12]

And before closing out his letter, Jones pays tribute to the regiment's band and, remarkably, but jovially, to the regimental mascot of sorts, a feisty canine named Lion:

Captain Anderson, (the instructor of the band) of Philadelphia, is with the regiment, and gives the band his undivided attention; having already taught it some twenty pieces of music. The band is highly prized by the regiment, being the only one belonging to a colored regiment, except the 55ᵗʰ Mass., in the department. "Lion," the old white dog, which has been with the 8ᵗʰ ever since its organization, (at Camp "Wm. Penn," Pa.,) is with it yet, and has no objection to being among black soldiers. He was in many battles in the army of the Virginia previous to enlisting in the 8th, and lastly took part in the battle of "Olustee," and was wounded in the fore-leg, from the effects of which he has not recovered, but is ready to march at any moment the regiment is; if going on board of a vessel, he is the first one on board. He is a soldier, and has no respect for citizens who may visit the camp; and does not hesitate to bite. He attends "Dress parade," and usually lies in front of the band, having some musical taste, and shows that he has not been brought up a savage. RUFUS SIBB JONES, Serg't Maj. 8th U.S.C.T. Jacksonville, Fla., April 16th, 1864.[13]

Still trying to rebound from the terrible Olustee episode, the Eighth rejoined General William Birney's Brigade and was ordered to Virginia, joining General Butler's men on August 12th at Deep Bottom. "As the regiment went into position, the enemy opened upon it from his heavy guns at Fort Darling, wounding eight or ten men" (Bates 1871, 967).

By that evening Woodlin reported that he had marched with members of his brigade back to the Petersburg area, in "Virginia dust, which is terrible indeed. Water was very scarce and the evening was enlivened by the bombardment of Petersburg."

And the bombing, which seemed to worry Woodlin quite a bit, would not let up for a good spell, according to the next series of the soldier's August entries:

13th The morning was ushered in by the Monitors shelling the woods. Things very uncertain about our future destiny. The Guns soon opened on us and some 8 or 9 shells were thrown in on our camp before we could get out of the way our Srgt. Major was wounded and several in the 7 U.S.C.T. We fell back about half a mile and left our dress clothes and knapsacks and moved in height marching order. We started about 11 p.m. and moved across the river on a pontoon bridge and haversacks for the night. Sunrise was ushered in by sharp skirmishing.

14th We fell back and started on a new line. Our Reg was left in the entrenchment. Our Brigade is composed of the 7th U.S.C.T. 8, 9, & 29 Conn Vol. We are not allowed to leave camp, about 5 p.m. We were ordered out about a mile & a half where the 7 & 9 made a charge the 8 being disappointed in finding any thing but riffle pits [sic]. We lost no men out of our crowd. We fell back about 10 p.m. to the breast works and lay all night without any trouble.

15th Still quiet in our front, but the remainder of the Brigade was moved over to the right on Strawberry plain with Hancock's corps who are to attack the Rebs who are at Malvern Hill today. Our Dr has gone over there to attend to his duties. He is Brigade Surgeon.

16th The fight still continues & the report is that Malvern Hill is taken. We are pitching tents at present. Two small tents are up for the Comd Officers. Everything moves about as usual in camp. One man was drounded [sic] this morning by the cramp. We are going to have the sick here after today and quite a detachment of other Regts are in here. We moved out at night and forced the skirmish line out a little. Had some 8 men wounded. 5 men of us went down the skirmish line under fire. The Regt. moved back about 10 p.m.

17ᵗʰ The 2ⁿᵈ Brigade moved in to our camp comprising the 97ᵗʰ Penn, 76ᵗʰ Penn & another Reg. Just at night we had rations issued and marched under heavy rain shower over the Bontown Bridge & another to the right about 4 miles. We halted for the night and were alarmed by heavy picket firing most of the night.

18ᵗʰ We marched up to the front about a mile to some breast works where we lay all day expecting an attack which came just at sundown on the extreme right. Heavy but soon change to the center where it was very fierce. Our Regt stood their ground loosing but 3 men wounded. The 9ᵗʰ drove them back and Charged on them. It then broke out with extreme fierceness on the left like a continued roar of musketry. The Artillery then opened and drove them back the forces then fell back and entrenchments on another line farther back.

However the Eighth, on August 25ᵗʰ, was back on the move again, traversing the James River "and went into position upon the Petersburg front, where it was kept on active duty" (Bates 1871, 967). And in between the fighting, the men were blessed to hear the music of Woodlin and his musician compatriots, according to a September 5, 1864, report of the *Press* correspondent Thomas Morris Chestnut:

The colored bands attached to the 22ⁿᵈ and 8ᵗʰ U.S.C.T. were discoursing excellent music yesterday evening til dark. The band of the 8ᵗʰ, under the instruction of Captain Joseph Anderson, the leader of Frank Johnson's famous band, has progressed to an efficiency in music which has endeared it to the officers and men of that excellent regiment, and is calculated to surpass in correct playing any of the similar institutions which have had their existence in this rebellion. Captain Anderson is still instructing them, though they can execute, to the satisfaction of competent judges, some forty pieces of scientific music. He will probably visit Philadelphia in a day or two, from which city he has been absent since the 8ᵗʰ Regiment left Camp Penn, about nine months ago. (Blackett 1989, 121-122)

Then, on September 9ᵗʰ, "Major Burritt, who was still suffering from the wound received at Olustee, returned and assumed command, and was promoted to Lieutenant Colonel, in place of Lieutenant Colonel Bartram." Bartram was chosen to be Colonel of the Twentieth Colored with "Major Mayer returning to his place in the Seventh, and Captain [George] Wagner being promoted to Major" (Bates 1871, 967).

Sadly, though, after just several weeks, "Colonel Burritt's wound again opening, he was sent to the hospital, and was subsequently, by order of the War Department, put in command of the recruiting rendezvous at Newport News, the command devolving on Major Wagner" (ibid.).

By September 13ᵗʰ the 8ᵗʰ USCT and Woodlin were eyeballing Petersburg and could see "a large portion" of the Appomattox River valley, areas that would prove crucial in the war's climax. This included the taking of Petersburg after a long siege: "Things were quiet here near night when there was a fierce fire of pickets and an occasional shell," Woodlin wrote in his September 13ᵗʰ entry. "I went up on the heights in rear of our Camp & had a splendid view of Petersburg's environs and surrounding country, which included a large portion of the Appomattox River valley; the real town itself I could not see much of though I saw 5 steeples of churches or some other Public buildings & a lookout."

And the clearest indication that the 8th and other regiments of the brigade were knocking on the door of the town came with these words: "Our lines are very closely pushed up to the confines of [Petersburg] there appear to be some very fine buildings there of brick; the Heights make it look very picturesque worthy of a painter's pencil. Fort Clifton is reported silenced. We could see it in the distance. A relief came from the batteries in front today."

Still, in the midst of anticipating the taking of Petersburg, from the 14th through 26th of September there was some tragedy, war action, and even a reunion of sorts, with at least three regiments from Camp William Penn (the 43rd, 45th and 127th) of the Chelten Hills, PA, facility:

14th A fierce fire of musketry was kept up all night and about 10 a.m. this morning a fierce cannon [...] was commenced and kept up for about 2 hours; a No of men being wounded from our Brigade one shell rooted into our trenches being spend [...] and one struck 2 rods to the right of us against a tree. About as brisk a fire as we have had since we have been here.

15th All quiet today, but our Reg't was Policing their camp & forming a line of Battle & drawing rations; Col. Howell died this morning from injuries rec'd from falling or being thrown from his horse. We also had a Reg'tmental inspection under our New maj. formerly Capt. Wagoner & an aid of Col Shaws. A great many flying reports in camp just now of various kinds [...].

16th We practiced this morning. I got a letter from home last night. There was a little firing at noon and a little more in the afternoon. 3 of our men were wounded in the trenches by pieces of shell. One went over our camp [...] howling. I went over into the second Divis. The first Brigade has three bands. 169, 115 N.Y. & 4 N.H. the first & last being consolidated in the next brigade there are only one, the 48th N.Y. formerly of 24 pieces now, of 16 as 7 of the men's times are out the next brigade has one. The 3rd N.Y. 10 piece had a splendid view of Petersburg from another point. Crossed the R.R. near where the Rebs had had two Batteries planted of three guns I should judge [...] we are now putting up a 16-gun batter to the right of the R.R. going towards P. with the express purpose of paying the respects of 14 of 15 of them to [Petersburg] and the remainder to fort Clifton. Also a mortar Battery farther down expressly for Clifton. We saw the battery, which throws over to us so spiteful, the new battery, which we have building over, received her guns again last night. (*Diary of a Black Soldier* 2009-2012)

Woodlin, in fact, was probably delighted to ascertain the activities of another Camp William Penn Regiment, the 22nd USCT, as well as recognizing the importance of Union forces winning in the Shenandoah Valley:

17th All quiet this morning. A few shots fired for trial of guns or some such idea, but no harm done I had some papers come last evening. The 22nd is under marching orders.

18ᵗʰ the 22ⁿᵈ left about 9 a.m. for the purpose of going to [Deep] Bottom. I wrote to Capt Anderson & to J. I went out on [...] the Picket line last night our folks are putting up a tremendous sight of guns out there, and fixing guards against Calvalry.

19ᵗʰ A man was [shot] [...] accidentally this morning in Co. D. of our Regt while in Camp cleaning guns & c. by a member of Co A. The Batteries played briskly this afternoon one shell coming down and striking the Hd. Qe'r Tent after bounding 3 times.

20ᵗʰ A brisk fire kept up during the afternoon by two batteries on our side. Some of them came very close to our camp. Went over my head struck the ground near the Sergt Major's & Capt. Steward but did [...] not injure them. Our Regt was ordered out again on picket on the left. During the night firing was kept up at long intervals & in the morning about Sunrise a Salute was fired from nearly every battery along our line in commemoration of Sheridan's victory in the Shenandoah Valley. (*Diary of a Black Soldier* 2009-2012)

And the musician also seemed disappointed when he and his fellow musicians could not practice, but was uplifted by the sighting of General Birney and his son:

21ˢᵗ We did not play this morning as the salute was fired and the shells came straight down to where we generally play one striking the Bombproof & another striking so close that it glanced over. one struck the Serg. Major's tent or bombproof. We practiced this forenoon, two men killed out of the 29ᵗʰ. Reg't Conn. Vol. [...] last night on fatigue Gen Birney rode through camp today with a portion of his staff and a little boy which I suppose was his son [...].

22ⁿᵈ The Gen was through Camp again today. another man shot through the head by sharpshooter {G. Miner} Co. G. I rec'd a letter & my folio from my Br. Last night. 'A just suits. A No of the Officers rec'd their promotions at night Lieut. Col to Col. 3 Lieuts to Capts. Burrows, Richardson, Lewis, Camp of C. to 1ˢᵗ Lieut. & c.

23ʳᵈ There was a grand Salute fired this morning from all the Batteries. The Petersburg express starting [...] in honor of Sheridan's victory in the Shenandoah Valley. Occasional firing all day. Weather cold & damp, nothing stirring.

24ᵗʰ Another salute was fired this morning for some victory I could not tell [...] Raining all day. Rec'd marching orders this afternoon, we prepared at dark and about 11 p.m. we were relieved by the 2ⁿᵈ Corps. The 11ᵗʰ, 126ᵗʰ, 37 N.Y. Regts forming the Brigade which relieved us. We marched about two miles back near the City Point R.R. where we formed for Division Organization. The 45ᵗʰ U.S.C.T. joining us on the next day [...].

25ᵗʰ The Camp was laid out in the Old Style Cos, Strs, Pioneer Corps, Drum & Band on the right of the Regt. The new officers assumed their places today. Lieut. Shefflin as Ajut. Lieut. Richardson, Capt. Co. C, Lewis Co, F. Burrows, Co. B. The 127 will join us soon. The [...] Regts were ordered out on a Dress Parade in the evening The Band played down the entire line & played the Brigade off the

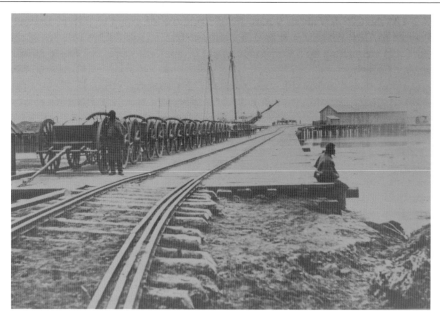

The City Point wharf and railroad were heavily relied upon by Union forces as a rendezvous center that received many of the Camp William Penn regiments. *Courtesy of the U. S. Army Military History Institute.*

African Americans, including soldiers from Camp William Penn, were often assigned to unload vessels at the City Point wharf. *Courtesy of the U. S. Army Military History Institute.*

City Point Hospital received many injured, but mostly sick soldiers suffering from diseases. More than a few Camp William Penn soldiers spent their last hours on earth at such facilities. *Courtesy of the U. S. Army Military History Institute.*

General Rufus Ingalls was the chief quartermaster assigned at City Point, responsible for distributing massive amounts of equipment, ammunition and weapons, some destined for Camp William Penn regiments. *Courtesy of the U. S. Army Military History Institute.*

field; it was a fine night; there was but one white Regt present that the 37th N.Y. 100 day men, they were formed on the extreme left of the whole Brigade & the 45th U.S.C.T. next then came the 29th Conn., vol [...] 9th U.S.C.T., 8th & 7th on the extreme right. It was the longest march, which we have had & play at the same time.

26th We were ordered out to Brigade guard Mount this morning; the whole Brigade was inspected by Cos, three at a time. Everything is being reduced to order now., Sergt. Major delivers all our mail to us now; the Officers have Co drill & rigid drill too, everyone has to come to time now. Brigade Dress Parade again in the evening. The 37th N.Y. went home this afternoon & the boys got a lot of rations over there, which they left behind. Our [absent] player came back also well again or nearly so, so we are full again as a band [...]. (*Diary of a Black Soldier* 2009-2012)

By the end of the summer, as September wound down, Woodlin and "the Tenth Corps, to which the regiment belonged, crossed the James, and in connection with the Eighteenth Corps, advanced upon the enemy's works at Chapin's Farm, and the New Market Road." This is where the Eighth's comrades, the 6th USCT, would perform heroically, with several earning the Medal of Honor. "An attack was made early on the morning of the 29th, by the Eighteenth Corps, supported by the Tenth, and a long line of works was carried, and sixteen pieces of artillery and three hundred and fifty prisoners were captured." Later that day, General Birney assigned the Eighth with the Seventh and Ninth USCT units to charge "a bastioned fort in his front." In fact, the "Ninth was first led to the charge, and after a resolute movement was forced to retire, having suffered severely" (Bates 1871, 967).

However, that did not deter the Eighth from trying:

The Eighth was next put in. It numbered only about two hundred men; but deploying eight companies as skirmishers, Major Wagner promptly moved to the assault, and gained a position within one hundred yards of the enemy's works, where the men commenced pouring in a steady fire, effectually driving the rebel gunners from their pieces. For several hours, and until the troops on its left were withdrawn, this position was held, the regiment not being in sufficient strength to carry the fort. Seeing the flank of the regiment exposed, the enemy immediately charged; but Major Wagner delivered a counter charge, breaking the hostile line, and thus saving his entire regiment from capture. At dark, it was relieved, and with the division fell back to the line of works captured in the morning. (ibid.)

Although the casualties could have been greater if not for the fierceness of the Eighth, it still lost 12 men with more than 60 wounded. "Captains Cooper and Richardson, and Lieutenants Seth Lewis and Charles C. Cone, were among the severely wounded, the latter mortally" (ibid.).

Soon after, according to Bates, "while the troops were busy reversing the breastworks," the Rebels attacked. The Eighth rushed to "the threatened point" and helped to repel the Confederates, "sustaining some loss" (967-968).

The Eighth was back on the road again early on October 13th and assigned to a thick wooded area adjacent to Darbytown Road, Bates noted. "The enemy's skirmishers were encountered, and after sharp fighting were driven from three successive lines where they had taken shelter back to their main line (968)." And that day, in the afternoon, the men were finally relieved by other troops. Yet there were valuable losses. "It entered the engagement with one hundred and fifty men, and lost seven killed, thirty wounded and one missing. Captains Alexander G. Dickey, Elijah Lewis, and Electus A. Pratt, were among the severely wounded, Captain Dickey mortally, and Captain Pratt with the loss of an arm" (ibid.).

Thomas Chester Morris, the writer for *The Philadelphia Press*, reported in an October 14, 1864, dispatch: "Among the killed is Capt. A.G. Dickey, 8th U.S.C.T. He belonged to Lewistown, Pa., where he is well known as a gentleman, while here he was highly appreciated as an excellent and brave officer" (Blackett 1989, 149).

More promotions were in store, including Commander Louis Wagner's brother, George Wagner, promoted from major to lieutenant colonel of the "Ninth Regiment, and Lieutenant Colonel Burritt, owing to his wounds, being still unfit for duty in the field […]." And the Eighth acquired a new commander, Lieutenant Colonel Samuel C. Armstrong, who had been promoted to colonel (Bates 1871, 968).

The Eighth's service, indeed, would soon climax with it being, according to *The Philadelphia Press* correspondent Chester, "involved in the final assault on Petersburg and was the first infantry regiment to enter the city after its fall, followed by the 45th, 41st and 127th," all regiments from Camp William Penn (Blackett 1989, 120):

> When the spring campaign opened, the regiment crossed the James and participated in the operations which resulted in the fall of Petersburg, and was among the foremost to enter the city. Soon after the surrender of Lee, it returned to Petersburg, and thence proceeded by sea to Texas. Upon its arrival there, it was stationed at Ringgold Barracks, on the Rio Grande, and beyond the usual camp duty, and an occasional expedition to settle Indian troubles, was little employed. The Mexican (Liberal) troops were quartered on the opposite side of the river, and between the officers of the two encampments, an intimacy sprang up, which resulted in a free interchange of social hospitalities. On the 10th of October, the regiment started on the homeward march, and proceeding via Santiago, New Orleans, and New York, arrived at Philadelphia on the 3d of December, and on the 12th, was mustered out of service. It was worthy of note, that of all the colored regiments in the United States service, this one, as shown by the official army register, lost in battle, more officers and men than any other. (Bates 1871, 968)

5

The 22ⁿᵈ United States Colored Troops
Phase of hellfire baptism

With one of the fiercest combat records of the 11 regiments raised at Camp William Penn, the 22ⁿᵈ USCT suffered heavy losses in 1864 at Petersburg and the Battle of New Market Heights in Virginia. The regiment would also get to march in the assassination procession of President Abraham Lincoln, as well as help to capture his killers.

The 22ⁿᵈ USCT was organized in January 1864 at Camp William Penn and led by Colonel Joseph B. Kiddoo, Lieutenant Colonel Nathan P. Goff, and Major John B. Cook. And those officers, for the most part, were quite experienced. "The majority of the field and line officers had previously served in other regiments, Colonel Kiddoo having been

The 22ⁿᵈ USCT of Camp William Penn saw plenty of action at Petersburg, but like other black regiments, was often assigned to dig trenches and other heavy manual labor as they waited to participate in combat. *Courtesy of the U. S. Army Military History Institute.*

promoted from Sergeant of the Sixty-third Pennsylvania to Lieutenant Colonel, and Colonel of the One Hundred and Thirty Seventh, and subsequently appointed Major of the Sixth Colored, whence he was selected to lead this regiment" (Bates 1871, 991).

Yet, many of the black enlisted men had New Jersey or Garden State ties, according to archival records at the New Jersey State Archives and the following letter found at the National Archives Regional Center in Philadelphia:

> War Department,
> ADJUTANT GENERAL'S OFFICE
> Washington, D.C.
>
> Dec. 29ᵗʰ 1863.
>
> Colonel James B. Fry,
> Provost Marshal General, U.S.
> War Department
> Washington, D.C.
>
> Colonel,
>
> By direction of the Secretary of War, you will please instruct the Officers of your Department in the State of New Jersey, to enlist into the service of the United States for three years or during the War, all suitable colored men who may offer themselves for enlistment.
>
> Persons offering themselves as recruits should be informed by the Recruiting Officer that they will receive ten dollars per month, and one ration, three dollars of which monthly pay may be in clothing.
>
> The recruits will be sent as soon after enlistment as practicable, to the 22ⁿᵈ Regiment U.S. Col'd Troops now organizing at Camp William Penn, near Philadelphia, Pa.
>
> Very Respectfully
> Your Obdt Servant
> Signed, E.D. Townsend
> Assist Adjt General
>
> Official copy respectfully furnished Commanding Officer Camp William Penn near Philadelphia, Pa. for his information.
> Lew Foster Assist Adjl Genl[1]

The Salem, New Jersey, resident William H. Warner joined the 22nd Regiment's Company A on December 7, 1863. He quickly rose to the rank of sergeant and subsequently to quartermaster sergeant (Scott 2008, 74).

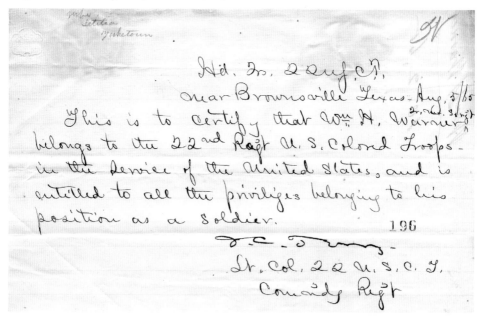

This document requests that Private William H. Warner of the 22nd USCT Regiment's Company H receive due benefits and "privileges" as a federal soldier. *Courtesy of the New Jersey State Archives.*

Cornelius Wharton, a private in Company A of the 22nd USCT, held certification entitling his family to receive "relief," often translating to monetary and other support. *Courtesy of the New Jersey State Archives.*

Captain Jacob F. Force commanded Company H of the 22ⁿᵈ USCT. *Courtesy of the U. S. Army Military History Institute.*

Meanwhile, Private Cornelius Wharton of Newark, New Jersey, also joined Company A, and was actually "married with three children during the war." Apparently in an effort to get a pension following the hostilities, when his "wife and children were living in Newark," Wharton's commanding officer, Captain Albert James, signed a certificate in May 1864 that verified the soldier's service in the 22ⁿᵈ USCT. "The document noted that Wharton's family was 'dependent upon him for support' and 'entitled to proper relief'" (Scott 2008, 75).

Private Henry Jackson of the 22ⁿᵈ USCT valued his bounty certificate that provided monetary support for his family. *Courtesy of the New Jersey State Archives.*

Although this black soldier is unidentified, he represents the marital status of many Camp William Penn soldiers, with wives and children needing the military incomes that were virtually always much less than their white counterparts. *Courtesy of the Library of Congress.*

Private George Collick's mustering-in certificate was very valuable to prove his eligibility for a pension following the war, due to his service in the 22nd USCT. *Courtesy of the New Jersey State Archives.*

Private James H. Jenkins of the 22ⁿᵈ USCT was mustered in at the end of the year 1863. *Courtesy of the New Jersey State Archives.*

Then there was Henry Jackson, again in Company A and a resident of Newark, who was mustered in during early 1865 and served about a half-year when he requested a bounty to help support his unnamed wife, according to a certificate originating from the "Head Quarters 22ⁿᵈ Regiment, U.S.C.T." The document read: "This is to certify, that Henry Jackson has been enrolled and mustered in Company 'A' 22ⁿᵈ Regiment, U.S. Col'd Troops and has been duly inspected and mustered into service of the United States; and that the said Henry Jackson having a family consisting of Wife living in Newark, N.J. dependent upon him for support, is entitled to the State Bounty for his said family" (ibid.).

Other New Jersey residents included George Collick of Camden, who mustered into Company F of the 22ⁿᵈ as a private on December 29, 1863, as well as Charles S. Bowles of Cape May, also a private, who joined Company K. (78) In addition, Mercer County resident "Pvt. James H. Jenkins was mustered into Company C of the 22ⁿᵈ USCT at Camp William Penn on December 21, 1863" (81).

However, certainly not all of the soldiers were residents of New Jersey:

> Pvt. John Davis, born in Kent County, Delaware, joined the 22ⁿᵈ USCT's Company G and lived in New Jersey's Camden County. Mustered in at age 26, his stature was small and complexion "dark." Similar to many USCT soldiers, he was classified as a laborer at first but likely saw action as the war heated up […].
>
> George W. Keyes, a private in Company F of the 22ⁿᵈ USCT, was a member of GAR Post 139 in Scranton following the Civil War. Keyes likely saw action in Virginia, including at the Battle of New Market Heights or Chaffin's Farm on September 29, 1864. (77)

George Keyes, a private in the 22nd USCT, survived the war and served in a Grand Army of the Republic chapter after moving back to Scranton, Pennsylvania. *Courtesy of the Library of Congress.*

Meanwhile, the training of white officers at Philadelphia's Free Military School at 1210 Chestnut Street picked up as the 22nd filled its ranks with the earlier regiments already on duty or headed there:

The Third, Sixth and Eighth Infantry Regiments of United States Colored Troops had completed training at Camp William Penn on the fringe of Montgomery County at Chelten Hill. The Twenty-second Regiment was nearly filled to capacity when, on December 29, 1863, the doors of the school at 1210 Chestnut Street were opened to the first thirty applicants [...] The institution would operate on a six-day week and the applicants, when accepted, would have the opportunity for practical experience in commanding the troops in training Camp William Penn. (Binder 1950, 281-291)

By early February 1864, Pvt. Keyes and the 22nd were "ordered to the front, and proceeded to join the Army of the James, under command of General Butler" (Bates 1871, 991):

The regiment got its first "marching orders" in early February, 1863. On February 6, Col. Wagner informed Maj. Foster that the Twenty-second would be ready to pull out as soon as transportation could be arranged. Anticipation mounted as the departure date approached. On February 10, the *Philadelphia Inquirer* newspaper published the expected parade route by which the regiment would march to their sailing vessel: "They will arrive in the city at Berks Street Station, North Pennsylvania Railroad, at ten o'clock this morning, march down Second to Arch, out Arch to Broad, down Broad to Chestnut, down Chestnut to Third, down Third to Lombard, down Lombard to Second, down to foot of Washington street where they will embark on the steamer Gov. Chase." (Johnson 1999, 160)

The fanfare surrounding the regiment's departure, according to historian Johnson, was covered quite aptly by the *Inquirer*:

The twenty-second Regiment United States Colored Troops, under command of Colonel J.B. Kiddoo, left Camp William Penn, yesterday morning, and arrived in the city about noon. The men looked admirably well, and were fully armed and equipped. After marching through a number of our streets they countermarched at Twelfth and Chestnut streets, and were reviewed by Major-General Meade at this point. A large number of the friends of the colored soldiers were present at Washington street wharf, to see them embark on board the steamer Governor Chase. After the soldiers and officers had been provided for at the refreshment saloons, the crowd were invited to "help themselves," which they did. About two thousand persons were on the ground and in a very short time the tables were cleared of what the soldiers left. The officers and men were much pleased with their reception, and left in the steamer with many thanks to the citizens of Philadelphia, and three cheers for the Union Volunteer and the Cooper Shop Refreshments Saloons. (160-161)

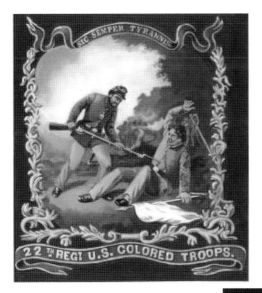

This image, designed by the artist David Bustill Bowser, was revolutionary during the Civil War period, because it depicts a black soldier killing a white man – in this case, a Rebel soldier. Previously, such a depiction under other circumstances would have been certainly censored. *Courtesy of the Library of Congress.*

The reverse of the 22ⁿᵈ USCT's flag highlights the American bald eagle, noting that a group of Philadelphians likely financed the regimental colors. *Courtesy of the Library of Congress.*

According to researcher Johnson, the 22nd USCT had at least several men missing from the ship, likely angered that they had not received their promised bounties:

> As the steamer Chase left port several men stayed behind in the city and were classified as deserters. Within days, many of the AWOL soldiers were captured by the authorities. But not everyone missing from roll call aboard the Governor Chase were simply men of bad character. Absence, for some, represented legitimate protest against the army's refusal to pay bounties to the [black] troops. Corporal Obidiah Telford and Sergeant Edward Stone were two such soldiers who stayed home because they hadn't received bounty payments. In subsequent disciplinary actions each man testified that his absence was a protest against the army's failure to make such payments. Charges against both men were finally dropped and both went on to become "excellent soldiers" who were killed on September 29, 1864, at the battle of Chapin's Farm, Virginia. (160-161)

After reaching the South, the 22nd USCT "went into camp near Yorktown, where it was drilled and disciplined, until the opening of the spring campaign, when it was assigned for duty to the Third Brigade, First Division of the Eighteenth Corps" (Bates 1871, 991):

> By March, 1864, Yorktown, Virginia was the command point from which the regiment engaged rebel troops. The men were now settled in and operating as part of the famed "Hinks' Colored Division" to which the Sixth Regiment also belonged. On one of their earliest missions they attempted to confront the Rebels by sailing up the Mattapony river in a convoy guarded by Navy gunboats to a place called Sheppard's Landing. Upon arriving in heavy rain they took up predetermined positions in order to "intercept and capture" rebel parties which were being flushed out of hiding by several hundred Union Cavalry. However, the engagement lacked coordination in its execution. The rebels evaded this trap when the pursuing cavalry acted prematurely by giving chase to the enemy before the Twenty-second had commanded strategic positions on the rebels' route of retreat. (162)

But it wasn't long before the 22nd would get its initial combat experience. That's because the regiment was assigned to "Wilson's Wharf, on the north side of the James River, where it was put to constructing an earth-work for the protection of the supply transports on their way up the river" (Bates 1871, 991). The ensuing combat, precipitated by a "hellfire" Rebel attack, would surely test the 22nd's resolve:

> A few weeks later, however, a significant phase of hellfire baptism took place for the Twenty-second. At that time, the activity was centered along the James River at a place called Wilson's Wharf. There, three-thousand Confederate Cavalry attacked the first brigade of Hinks' Division on May 20. As an element of the First Brigade, the Twenty-second's initial trial by fire had now reached its peak. The fire-fight lasted all Friday afternoon – "from 2 till 6 p.m." one report exclaims. The geographical terrain, considered important for transmitting intelligence, was

captured from the South in this encounter […] [The] Twenty-second's gallantry under fire does not come until the following day in its defense of Fort Powhatan. Col. Kiddoo complimented the abilities of his sentries as they fought off a daring mid-day attack: "I have the honor to report that the enemy's Cavalry, about 100 strong, made a demonstration upon my pickets yesterday at noon. The pickets held them in check until the infantry was formed and the artillerymen got to their guns […]. The pickets behaved most creditably, one man standing his post, and after firing and loading three times, fenced with a rebel officer till he disabled the officer, and received a stroke across the face with a saber." (Johnson 1999, 162-163)

With the men likely anticipating that more combat was imminent, the regiment "was sent to the south side of the river, in the neighborhood of Fort Powhattan, where it was again employed in constructing works, and preparing for the crossing of the Army of the Potomac, on its arrival from the Wilderness campaign." And that's when the "enemy's cavalry from Richmond attacked at this point, but after a spirited engagement, was handsomely repulsed by the 22nd" (Bates 1871, 991).

The superior commanders were very impressed with the 22nd's recent action, despite the forthcoming tragic execution of two of the regiment's black soldiers who were captured by the Rebels:

> On Saturday evening, May 21, 1864, General Edward W. Hinks' high level of confidence in the Twenty-second's fighting ability was implicitly expressed as he discussed the previous day's defense of Fort Powhatan. In a message to General Benjamin F. Butler Hinks wrote: "All quiet here. No enemy in sight. A few shots from our guns entirely scattered them […]" Colonel Kiddoo is the right man in the right place, and sufficient for any affair that is likely to occur here. But the assault did result in the Rebel capture of two soldiers from the regiment. Taken to Petersburg they were executed as seditious criminals. In a counter-measure, Hinks sought permission from General Butler to execute "all the prisoners captured from Gen. Fitzhugh Lee, at Wilson's Wharf […] in retaliation for the number of the soldiers of

Private Benjamin Furguson of the 22nd USCT's Company C died before the end of the war in January 1864. *Courtesy of Kristopher H. Scott.*

JAN 6 1864

the Twenty-second Regiment [...]" However, Butler displayed no zeal for this kind of equal treatment. He wired back to Hinks: "Nothing will be done tonight. Telegraphed you at length." But the idea of retaliation was almost certainly [...] on the minds of the black rank and file. Whether they knew of Hinks' request, however, is unknown. Nonetheless, the absence of a positive response to the murders may have been one more indication of how tlittle the humanity of black soldiers meant to white Northerners when weighed against the lives of Southern enemies who were also white. (Johnson 1999, 164)

Next the 22nd would lead the charge, despite "fearful" losses, on Petersburg just after General Baldy Smith returned on June 15th "from his march to Cold Harbor, where he had gone for the reinforcement of Grant," allowing the 22nd and "his corps to the attack of the rebel entrenchments before Petersburg":

> The Twenty-second headed the charge in this assault, and captured six of the seven guns taken by the division, and two of the four forts. The victory was gained, however, at a fearful cost to the regiment. Its loss was one officer, Lieutenant Emery Fisher, and seventeen men killed, and five officers and one hundred and thirty-eight men wounded, and one missing. Lieutenant Colonel Goff was among the severely wounded. Its conduct on this occasion was warmly commended at corps and army headquarters. (Bates 1871, 991)

With its reputation surely soaring, the 22nd found itself participating with the 6th USCT of Camp William Penn in "the assault upon the enemy's strong works at Chapin's Farm, on the 29th of September" (ibid.). The soldiers and officers fought heroically:

In 1864, Sergeant Edward Richardson, a sergeant and color bearer for the Twenty-second Colored Infantry Regiment, fought in Civil War battles as part of the "Hinks' Colored Division." Through his actions at

Sergeant Edward Richardson and his wife Fannie Surges settled in South Jersey and had 10 children. He was lauded for his courage as the color bearer of the 22nd USCT, fighting in some of the heaviest combat of the war. He became a respected businessman and civic leader. *Courtesy of the U.S. Army Military History Institute.*

New Market Heights and Petersburg he symbolized what Christian Fleetwood called "the bravest and the best." For distinctively bearing aloft his regiment's banner, Richardson, of Company "A," was awarded the Butler Medal for Valor. (Johnson 1999, 159)

Although "it delivered a most daring and impetuous charge," the 22ⁿᵈ "was repulsed, suffering a loss of eleven men killed, two officers and two men wounded, and eight missing." Major Cook, "who led the regiment," was very badly wounded (Bates 1871, 991).

Yet the 22ⁿᵈ's travails were not over:

Petersburg was located just twenty-one miles to the south of Richmond and as Grant's noose tightening siege took effect, casualties mounted as the Twenty-second's encounters with desperate Rebel units intensified. Between June, 1864 and April, 1865, the battles of Chaffin's Farm, New Market Heights, Dutch Gap, and Fair Oaks became etched in the memories of these men and their officers. Seventy-two of their number lay down their lives with weapons drawn and more then twice that number were killed by disease. In the most extensive discussion of this regiment, Frederick Binder has written: "the 22ⁿᵈ formed a part of the attacking force which [...] assailed Fort Harrison near Chaffin's Farm [...] New Heights and Chaffin's Farm were successful assaults in spite of heavy casualties among the Negro troops [...]. The colored regiments gained a medal and much needed glory [...]." (Johnson 1999, 165)

However, by the end of October 1864, the ferocious regiment bravely endured "heavy slaughter" during a massive assault engineered by General Grant:

On the 27ᵗʰ of October, Grant inaugurated a general movement along his entire lines, reaching out on his left to Hatcher's Run and Armstrong's Mill, while upon the right, General Butler demonstrated in force, and the Eighteenth Corps moved upon the Richmond defenses on the Charles City and Williamsburg roads. The Twenty-second led the column on the latter, and at a point near the old Fair Oaks Battle-ground, charged on the rebel intrenched position with great steadiness and courage, but was again repulsed with heavy slaughter. (Bates 1871, 991-992)

This time, however, while leading the charge, Colonel Kiddoo "was severely wounded and Captain William B. Clark was killed. The entire loss in killed and wounded, exceeded one hundred." Incredibly, following the combat, "all three of its field officers were in hospital at Fortress Monroe together, for wounds received in separate engagements" (ibid.).

The 22ⁿᵈ certainly endured defeat at Fair Oaks, Johnson wrote, according to historian Frederick Binder (author of the 1952 article "Pennsylvania Negro Regiments in the Civil War" in the *Journal of Negro History*), partially based on bogus orders, according to the observations of Colonel G. Draper, commander of the Third Division, Eighteenth Army Corps, noting that "The Twenty-second was thrown in to disorder, either because the command of Colonel Holman was not properly repeated, or because it was not understood by the regiment," remarked the colonel. "Captain James states that Colonel Kiddoo [...]

said to him 'Captain turn to the left and go on' [...] Lieutenant-Colonel Terry states that he heard no such order to change direction [...]. Instead being halted for the formation of the line, the regiment allowed to charge as it was, and therefore accomplished nothing." (Johnson 1999, 166)

Johnson indicates that *The Philadelphia Press* newspaper dispatches of the war's only black correspondent for a major metropolitan newspaper, Thomas Morris Chester, "provide a perspective from the view point of a remote observer [...]. Of that Thursday battle in 'heavy rain' he wrote the following: 'Col. Holman was wounded in the thigh [...] the brave Kiddoo fell, badly wounded in the back with a piece of shell. To the credit of this excellent regiment it must be said that, notwithstanding they saw their officers carried off the field, and with no one to command them, they still rushed forward until they had caputured the enemy's fort and works, the only victory of the kind gained by our forces during the day,'" Johnson notes, quoting Chester. "'Just as our colored troops had captured the rebel lines they received orders to fall back and the right flank [...] Such is the record of the colored troops under colonels Holman and Kiddoo, who were sent only to demonstrate against the enemy's line, but it would not be satisfied until it was captured at the point of the bayonet'" (166-167).

However, following that initial report, Chester likely received information that gave him another perspective concerning the battle and the 22nd's participation:

Three days later Chester relayed a different account of the engagement to the Press. In this version he pointed out that, indeed, something unusual had occurred at Fair Oaks: "The line of the battle being formed, the 22nd marched towards the enemy's works, which were nearly a mile distant, and within five hundred yards the rebels opened a galling fire [...] a charge was ordered, but unfortunately a dense woods through which it was obliged to pass, seriously deranged the line, and the troops came out in such a state of confusion as to be in no condition for an assault [...] Here a charge was ordered [...] within about ten yards of the rebel flags on the breastworks [...] a severe fire caused the line to waver. Even this would not have happened if a number of new recruits, who unfortunately had been sent to this regiment without drill, went into this, their first engagement, had not given way in much confusion. The regiment fell back about three hundred yards and reformed the line, preparatory to charging the woods again, when Major Weinmann reported a heavy body of rebels massing in the right of the 22nd, which was deemed sufficient to countermand the order for another assault. The officers and men, mortified at the conduct of the new recruits, and regretting the absence of supports, fell back in good order, bringing off their wounded with them." (Johnson 1999, 167)

And then there were charges that the 22nd's commander, Colonel Kiddoo, "was drunk when he led his men into battle at Fair Oaks," according to Johnson (168), extracting the following statement from the Army's Official Records:

Early in the morning of October 26 our regiment left its place in the trenches and bivouacked a short distance in the rear. During this day Colonel Kiddoo was not with the regiment. Late in the afternoon he approached, in undress, a group of officers of the Twenty-second [...] sitting around a campfire, asking, "what regiment is this?" And "Where are my headquarters?" [...] Kiddoo did not know where he was nor recognize his inferior officers. This peculiar state of mind appeared to continue during the next day, reaching its climax in the charge late in the afternoon, which ended so disgracefully.

We beg leave to state that our complaint against Colonel Kiddoo is based upon that most disgraceful route the Twenty-second U.S. Colored Troops sustained on the evening of the 27ᵗʰ ultimo [...] we, from our subordinate standpoint can ascribe our failure only to Colonel Kiddoo's management, the cause of which, we are impressed, was his being under the influence of liquor [...]. The regiment was put through a number of strange and harassing maneuvers and evolutions solely by Colonel Kiddoo's orders [...] we failed in taking the enemy's works through our colonel's mismanagement; and the most charitable conclusion we can come to is, that, being under the influence of liquor, what he gained in courage as the day wore on and evening set in to all appearances he certainly lost in at an increased ratio in judgment and discretion. (Johnson 1999, 168)

Furthermore, Johnson said, exacerbating problems following the battle were likely issues concerning poor medical treatment and increased tensions between the regiment's black soldiers and some of its white officers:

Just weeks before the debacle at Fair Oaks, Major J. B. Carr wrote to headquarters of the Third Division, Tenth Army Corps seeking medical help for the Twenty-second (the regiment was temporarily attached to the Tenth Army at the time). Carr complained of there being "quite a number of sick and [...] no surgeon or medical officer available [...]" for the regiment. Before the end of September, however, the Twenty-second was reassigned to the First Brigade, Third Division, Eighteenth Arm. In this same period, signs of increasing tension between the officers and men can be found among the sources. In one dispatch sent from the field on October 23, 1864, the case of Lieutenant J.B. McMurdy is mentioned by Thomas Morris Chester as an example of Colonel Holman's intention, as division commander, to prevent the abuse of "any man, whether be he white or black." According to Chester, McMurdy was charged for "unwarrantable treatment to a colored sergeant [...]" The particular abuse visited upon the sergeant has yet to be discovered by this writer, but its occurrence was undoubtedly tucked away in the minds of rank and file African American soldiers as another overt reminder of Northern racism in Union army facilities. (169)

Overall, Chester must have had a favorable impression of the 22ⁿᵈ USCT, at least based on his *Philadelphia Press* dispatch of February 15, 1865, acknowledging that "the 22d U.S.C.T., who, under Colonel Kiddoo, achieved a name and a fame in front of Petersburg on the 15ᵗʰ of June, and at New Market Heights on the 29ᵗʰ of September. This regiment, regarded as among the best in the service, was recruited in Philadelphia, and the people of Pennsylvania may justly feel proud of its record." (Blackett 1989, 261-262)

In fact, McMurdy was apparently dismissed from his command and replaced by Lieutenant Colonel Abial G. Chamberlain as October came to an end in 1864. However, "like McMurdy, his treatment of rank and file in the brigade drew the attention of divisional headquarters. A week after McMurdy's dismissal Chamberlain apparently felt the need to punish the brigade under the guise of instilling discipline into already battle-hardened troops" by mandating excessive drilling. This led to his replacement by Colonel Elias Wright of the Tenth U.S. Colored Troops, because Wright's superiors believed his actions would lead to protests and even mutinous behavior (Johnson 1999, 170).

However, it seems as one such problem was solved, even more formidable ones arose for the black soldiers:

> In December, 1864, most black regiments operating in the Virginia, Maryland, and North Carolina region were consolidated into the Twenty-fifth Army Corps. Placed in command of the Twenty-fifth Army was Major General Godfrey Weitzel, "who earlier had refused to serve with black troops." In 1862, while serving in Southern Louisiana, Weitzel rejected the idea of arming fugitive African Americans who had voluntarily joined up with his forces. How the Twenty-fifth's rank and file might fare under Weitzel's direction was not a comforting thought given his earlier views on the subject of black enlistment. Weitzel claimed: "I cannot command these negro regiments. The commanding general knows well my private opinions on the subject. What I stated to him privately [...] I see before my very eyes. Since the arrival of the negro regiments, symptoms of servile insurrection are becoming apparent. I could not, without breaking [my] brigade all up, put a force in every part of this district to keep down such an insurrection. I cannot assume command of such a force, and thus be responsible for its conduct. I have no confidence in the organization. Its moral effect in this community [...] is terrible. It is heart rending." (171)

The question that historians have grappled with, according to Johnson, is: Was General Weitzel a converted racist when he took command of the brigade? Johnson has serious doubts:

> The sources do not support a positive transformation for the general. For example, despite fairly strong evidence that Kiddoo's drunkenness caused the rout at Fair Oaks, Weitzel, nonetheless, supported the colonel unequivocally. Responding to questions about the matter he wrote: "forwarded because orders compel me to. I think all this unwarranted and prompted by malice somewhere. I consider Colonel Kiddoo the finest gentleman and officer in my Third Division." (171-172)

Yet, the regiment would carry on until reaching the capital of the Confederacy, Richmond, VA. "Upon the fall of Richmond on the 3d of April, 1865, this regiment was among the first of General Weitzel's troops to enter the city, and rendered important service in extinguishing the flames which were then raging." That experience must have been quite

Above: Black refugees in Richmond, following the entrance of such Camp William Penn regiments as the 22ⁿᵈ USCT, were ecstatic that they were finally liberated, despite the horrible destruction. *Courtesy of the Library of Congress.* Below: The Exchange Bank in Richmond was completely destroyed during the evacuation of the Rebel forces and entrance of the Union army, including regiments from Camp William Penn. *Courtesy of the U.S. Army Military History Institute.*

rewarding for those who had once worn the manacles of slavery that were unmistakably shattered in the heart of Rebel territory (Bates 1871, 991-992).

According to Chester, the black correspondent, the 22nd and other regiments in a brigade directly commanded by General Draper were definitely the first to enter Richmond, despite other Union commanders trying to take the credit: "To Gen. Draper belongs the credit of having the first organization enter the city, and none are better acquainted with this fact than the officers of the division who are claiming the undeserved honor. Gen. Draper's brigade is composed of the 22d, 36th, 38th, and 118th U.S. colored troops, the 36th being the first to enter Richmond" (Blackett 1998, 303).

Meanwhile, as the South "stood in solid military defeat," black groups, some even armed, resisted perceived racism from southerners and northern occupiers, according to Johnson. "Evidence suggests that bold efforts like these were attempts to build independent, maroon-type societies. Union authorities at the highest levels grew concerned enough to discuss the matter after African Americans from both the North and South were found in the camps of these black revolutionaries" consisting of some black troops, thus coming to the attention of General Grant. "On April 17, General Grant was apprised by General George Gordon Mead of the alarming situation," motivating them to send cavalry forces after the so-called marauders (Johnson 1990, 172).

Just days before he would be cut down by an assassin's bullet, President Abraham Lincoln perhaps experienced his most profound moments as commander-in-chief when he entered the vanquished Confederate capitol, Richmond – an event likely witnessed by some members of the 22nd USCT and other Camp William Penn regiments. Chester, the black reporter for the *Press*, vividly captured the moments in an April 6, 1865, dispatch:

> The great event after the capture of the city was the arrival of President Lincoln in it. He came up to Rocket's wharf in one of Admiral Porter's vessels of war, and, with a file of sailors for a guard of honor, he walked up to Jeff Davis' house, the headquarters of General Weitzel. As soon as he landed the news sped, as if upon the wings of lightning, that "Old Abe," for it was treason in the city to give him a more respectful address, had come. Some of the negroes, feeling themselves free to act like men, shouted that the President had arrived. This name having always been applied to Jeff, the inhabitants, coupling it with the prevailing rumor that he had been captured, reported that the arch-traitor was being brought into the city. As the people pressed near they cried "Hang him!" "Hang him!" "Show him no quarter!" and other similar expressions, which indicated their sentiments as to what should be his fate. But when they learned that it was President Lincoln their joy knew no bounds. By the time he reached General Weitzel's headquarters, thousands of persons had followed him to catch a sight of the Chief Magistrate of the United States. When he ascended the steps he faced the crowd and bowed his thanks for the prolonged exultation which was going up from the great concourse. The people seemed inspired by this acknowledgement, and with renewed vigor shouted louder and louder, until it seemed as if the echoes would reach the abode of those patriot spirits who had died without witnessing the sight. (Blackett 1989, 294-295)

The black inhabitants of Richmond were beyond ecstatic, according to Chester:

> It must be confessed that those who participated in this informal reception of the President were mainly negroes. There were many whites in the crowd, but they were lost in the great concourse of American citizens of African descent. Those who lived in the finest houses either stood motionless upon their steps or merely peeped through the window-blinds, with a very few exceptions. The Secesh-inhabitants still have some hope for their tumbling cause. (296)

However, the rebounding of Confederate forces certainly was not possible. For even the notorious slave pens were taken by pro-Union forces, including the blacks held in bondage there, as well as the abysmal prisons now held by United States Colored Troops to imprison the criminal Rebels. Chester, noted Blackett, seemed very moved by ex-slaves who didn't seem to at first comprehend their long-sought liberation:

> I visited [...] several of the slave jails, where men, women, and children were confined, or herded, for the examination of purchasers. The jailors were in all cases slaves, and had been left in undisputed possession of the buildings. The owners, as soon as they were aware that we were coming, opened wide the doors and told the confined inmates they were free. The poor souls could not realize it until they saw the union army. Even then they thought it must be a pleasant dream, but when they saw Abraham Lincoln they were satisfied that their freedom was perpetual. One enthusiastic old negro woman exclaimed: "I know that I am free, for I have seen Father Abraham and felt him." (296-297)

Indeed, as Lee ordered the evacuation of Richmond, Hell's fires erupted in many parts of the city, probably set by the retreating Rebels and those under their influence, Chester noted:

> Gen. Lee ordered the evacuation of the city at an hour known to the remaining leaders of the rebellion, when Gens. Ewell and [John Cabell] Breckinridge [Confederate Secretary of War and former 1860 Democratic presidential candidate before seccession], and others absconded, leaving orders with menials, robbers, and plunderers, kept together during the war by the "cohesive power

President Abraham Lincoln received a jubilant welcome from Richmond's African Americans when he visited following the Union's taking of that Confederate capital. A few even dropped to the ground upon setting eyes on the president. *Courtesy of the Library of Congress.*

of public plunder," to apply the torch to the different tobacco warehouses, public buildings, arsenals, stores, flour mills, powder magazines, and every important place of deposit. A south wind prevailed, and flames spread with devastating effect. The offices of the newspapers, whose columns have been charged with the foulest viturperation against our Government, were on fire; two of them have been reduced to ashes, another one injured beyond repair, while the remaining two are not much damaged. Every bank which had emitted the spurious notes of the rebels was consumed to ruins. Churches no longer gave audience to empty prayers, but burst forth in furious flames. Magazines exploded, killing the poor inhabitants. In short, Secession was burnt out, and the city purified as far as fire could accomplish it. (Blackett 1989, 297)

Union soldiers, including those of Camp William Penn, such as the 22nd, were involved "with the citizens to stay the progress of the fire, and at last succeeded," Chester wrote, "but not until all the business part of the town was destroyed" (297-298). But the prisons, where many of the USCT prisoners, such as those from the 8th USCT after the Battle of Olustee, had suffered unimaginable torture and death, were saved to hold the Confederate traitors, as Chester observed firsthand in his April 6, 1865, dispatch:

> The Hotel de Libby is now doing a rushing business in the way of accommodating a class of persons who have not heretofore patronized that establishment. It is being rapidly filled with rebel soldiers, detectives, spies, robbers, and every grade of infamy in the calendar of crime. The stars and stripes now wave gracefully over it, and traitors look through the same bars behind which loyal men were so long confined. (298)

And recommending "swift" punishment for Rebels who seemed to be intransigent or guilty of horrendous crimes during the war, Chester clearly reveled about situations that allowed black soldiers – in some cases former slaves – to retaliate against the Confederate captives being held in the very facilities where Union forces had been imprisoned under horrendous conditions:

> A large squad of rebels, being escorted through the streets yesterday by colored guards, came to a halt in front of Libby, when one of them observed his former slave pacing up and down the line with genuine martial bearing. Stepping a little out of ranks he said: "Hallo, Jack, is that you!" The negro guard looked at him with blank astonishment, not unmingled with disdain, for the familiarity of the address. The rebel captive, determined upon being recognized, said, entreatingly, "Why, Jack, don't you know me!" "Yes, I know you very well," was the sullen reply, "and if you don't fall back into that line I will give you this bayonet," at the same time bringing his musket to the position of a charge. This, of course, terminated all attempts at familiarity. (304-305)

Head Quarters,
Department of Pennsylvania,
Philadelphia, Pa., April 20, 1865.

Special Orders,
No. 90.

Extract:

9 — All United States Troops in the vicinity of Philadelphia, not required for duty at their respective Posts, will report to Brig. Genl. C. S. Ferry U. S. Vols, Comdg. District of Philadelphia, for the purpose of participating in the funeral obsequies of the late President of the United States, Abraham Lincoln, on the arrival of his remains in this City, at 6.00. P.M, on the 22d inst,

By Command of Major General Cadwalader.

Comdg. Officers
Camp Wm Penn

Jno. L. Schultz
Assistant Adjutant General.

Camp William Penn soldiers were given an order to participate in the funeral of President Abraham Lincoln, according to this official correspondence sent to commanders at the facility. *Courtesy of the National Archives, Mid-Atlantic Region, Philadelphia.*

President Abraham Lincoln sat in this chair at the Ford's Theater when he was shot by John Wilkes Booth on Good Friday, April 14, 1865. Camp William Penn Regiments helped to track his killers. *Courtesy of the U.S. Army Military History Institute.*

Indeed, a few regiments from Camp William Penn, even the likes of the ex-slave who refused to be cozy with his former owner, joined in the pursuit of Lee:

> By April 9 Lee's forces were virtually cornered. Five Camp William Penn regiments at Appomattox Court House "were there to witness the surrender of Lee's army to General Grant," including the 8th, 41st, 43rd, 45th and 127th, according to data of the African American Civil War Memorial in Washington. (*Camp William Penn* 2011)

But soon the devastating news of Lincoln's assassination came.

Incredibly, the 22nd USCT would play a major role in his funeral, with camp authorities receiving a letter requesting that Camp William Penn soldiers participate in Lincoln's funeral. "As plans for the funeral ceremonies were being made in Washington, an order was sent to Major General Weitzel in Richmond, directing him to provide a black regiment for the occasion. According to its unit history, Weitzel chose the 22nd on 'account of its excellent discipline and good soldierly qualities.' The men received their orders at 5:00 p.m. on April 17 and within an hour were marching toward City Point, finally reaching it just after midnight," surely proud, but somber about the terrible tragedy. "At 4:00 a.m. on April 18, they boarded a river transport, which landed them in Washington around noon the next day" and made history (Trudeau 1998, 434):

> On April 20, the 22nd USCT took position on Pennsylvania Avenue near Sixth Street, in front of the Metropolitan Hotel. There the black soldiers waited until the long funeral cortege that had left the White House on its way to the Capital drew near. "As the head of the column approached where the 22nd was standing 'at rest,'" wrote a reporter, "the band struck up a dirge, and the regiment immediately moved forward, thereby becoming the head of the procession."

Johns Wilkes Booth was a Confederate sympathizer and well known actor when he killed the president with a single shot to the back of his head. *Courtesy of the Library of Congress.*

Another correspondent thought the men "appeared to be under the very best discipline, and displayed admirable skill in their various exercises." (434)

And then the 22ⁿᵈ made even more history, Trudeau wrote, with the 45ᵗʰ and other Camp William Penn regiments surely taking notice:

Two days after performing this ceremonial duty, the 22ⁿᵈ joined the hunt for John Wilkes Booth. Between April 23 and 27, the black soldiers moved through portions of southern Maryland, often in widely dispersed skirmishing order. Seven miles from Bryantown when they learned of Booth's capture, the men were soon headed back to Petersburg. (ibid.)

The 22ⁿᵈ USCT ventured into swampland searching for the president's assassins with other Union forces. *Courtesy of the Library of Congress.*

On May 6th a black soldier, Sergeant John C. Brock of the 43rd USCT, set down his thoughts on Lincoln's death:

> Thank God! [He] was permitted to see the fruits of his toil, to see the work he had persevered in so nobly, and arduously, well nigh completed, before he received the summons [...]. He still lives in the hearts of the thousands, yea, millions of those whom he by his love of justice, liberty, and his well known belief in the right of man, redeemed from the curse of slavery, [...] thousands of whom are now in the ranks of the armies of the Union, hurling avenging justice on those who were the cause of this foul rebellion, and whose sworn purpose was to perpetuate human bondage. (434)

Johnson noted that the 22nd too would be chosen to help find the president's assassins: "Soon thereafter a detachment [from the 22nd USCT] searched the Maryland swamplands for John Wilkes Booth and his cohorts" (Johnson 1999, 173).

Remarkably, the search for Lincoln's killers was coordinated by Lafayette C. Baker, "chief detective of the U.S. Marshals and founder of the U.S. Secret Service, who actually mentioned the 22nd USCT in "an account of the hunt" for the assassins: "The military forces [departed] to pursue the fugitives were seven hundred men of the Eighth Illinois

Lincoln's killers were hanged following the pursuit of Union forces, including the 22nd USCT of Camp William Penn. *Courtesy of the Library of Congress.*

Cavalry, six hundred men of the Twenty-second Colored Troops and one hundred men of the Sixteenth New York. These swept the swamps by detachments, the mass of them dismounted with cavalry at the belts of clearings, interspersed with detectives at frequent in the rear" (173-174).

And yet, instead of immediately returning to Philadelphia following its remarkable service, in May the regiment rejoined the corps, and with it proceeded by sea to Texas, where it was assigned to duty upon the Rio Grande.

Some historians assert that white nervousness about so many black men carrying weapons led to the government policy of sending many of the USCT regiments to the "southern border" or Texas, to avoid the possibility of them participating in an armed rebellion.

> As black soldiers sought to consolidate the Union victory by insuring the enfranchisement of black people their militant actions exposed the bogus reconstruction policies of the newly installed administration of President Andrew Johnson. On April 29, 1865 Grant was informed by the Twenty-fifth Army Corps' commander that antagonisms with black troops had reached a dangerous stage. Major General Henry W. Halleck's message was alarmist and revealed the sexual paranoia [that] underlay the racism of many white men: [The] "want of discipline and good officers in the Twenty-fifth Corps renders it a very improper force for the preservation of order in this department. A number of cases of atrocious rape by these men have already occurred [...] influence on the colored population is also reported to be had. I therefore hope you will remove it to garrison forts or for service on the Southern coast." (Johnson 1999, 174)

The following letter, sent to Commander Wagner and found at the National Archives Regional Center in Philadelphia, indicates that there was an organized effort to send black troops to the southwest, with some likely joining units that would become "Buffalo" soldiers following the war:

> War Department
> Adjutant General's Office
> Washington Oct. 7ᵗʰ 1864
>
> Lieut. Col Louis Wagner
> 88ᵗʰ Pa. Vols.
> Comd'g Camp William Penn
> Philadelphia, Pa.
>
> Sir,
>
> I am directed to instruct you to select from the unassigned recruits, arriving at Camp William Penn, one hundred of the most active and intelligent, (men who can read and write) with a view to their assignment to colored regiments in the South West, and appointment as non-commissioned officers, and for detail as

clerks. When the number above mentioned has been selected, Lt. Col. Wagner will inform this office of the fact.

It must be understood that the foregoing does not authorize the transfer of any men who have been, or may be hereafter, assigned before their arrival at Camp William Penn.

Very Respectfully,
Your Obdt Servant
Lew Foster
Asst Adjt Genl Vols.[2]

Johnson explained that, from the viewpoint of "military planners, the defeat of the Confederacy rendered USCT units expendable in the emerging struggle between social classes of the postbellum South." The significant number of black soldiers "demonstrating an allegiance to their liberated people in the South" was enough to alarm the white power structure, observing that "abuses from white officials were not being tolerated and a growing sense of power could be observed among the civilian and military African American population." Johnson asserts that the new "form of black militancy intensified in the Twenty-fifth Army Corps and the men of the Twenty-second Regiment were at its epicenter" (Johnson 1999, 175).

One government report, according to Johnson, in the *War of the Rebellion: Official Records of the Union and Confederate Armies*, U.S. War Department (Ser. 1, vol. 46, pt. 3, 1148), says such soldiers of the 22nd USCT were certainly pushing the limit:

Many complaints are made at this headquarters of depredations committed by soldiers of the Twenty-Fifth Army Corps, consisting principally in the destruction of buildings and the exciting of the colored people to acts of outrage against the persons and property of white citizens. It is asserted that the buildings are destroyed that the boards and timbers may be used to build huts and quarters for the soldiers, and the bricks of chimneys are carried off, probably for the same purpose. Colored soldiers are represented as having straggled about advising negroes not to work on the farms, where they are employed, and been told by the soldiers that if they had not arms to use against their former masters that they (the soldiers) would furnish them. Such acts must create discord and discontent, and should be stopped at once. (ibid.)

The 22nd finally "returned to Philadelphia in October, where, on the 16th, it was mustered out of service" (Bates 1871, 991-992).

However, official government records of the Adjutant General's Office indicate that the 22nd USCT sacrificed mightily to save the Union, including more than a few from Company F. The loss of blood or life is exemplified by the likes of James Dunwood, 19 years old, who was "killed in action" before Petersburg on July 15, 1864. Enlisted at Pittsburgh on December 23, 1863, Dunwood, described with a "black" complexion, hair and eyes, had worked as a machinist before the war. Charles Moore, 24, a farmer from East

Windsor, New Jersey, was "wounded in action" at Chapin's Farm in Virginia on September 30, 1864. Committed to serve for three years, he was discharged on May 26, 1865, due to an undisclosed "disability." John Sullivan, 21, was enlisted by the commander of Camp William Penn, Louis Wagner, for a three-year term before being "wounded in action before Petersburg" during the mid-summer of 1864. He was discharged on November 23, 1864. Then there was laborer Charles Williams, 35 years old, from "U.P. Neck," New Jersey, also enlisted by Commander Wagner for three years and "wounded in action at Fair Oaks, VA" on October 27, 1864. John Triplett, age 47, From Franklin County, Virginia, was a farmer, and enlisted on December 23, 1863, for a three-year term before being "wounded in trenches before Petersburg" on June 28, 1864.[3]

Following the war Sgt. Richardson, the "ex-slave and native of Cecil County Maryland," had 10 children with his wife, Fannie Sturges. The couple, married in 1886, was hailed as "respected citizens of South Jersey" and encouraged their children to successfully pursue college educations. This must have been especially rewarding to Richardson, since he "learned to read and write after running away to a family (the Lippincotts) that would allow him to study" when many slaves were brutalized for seeking such knowledge. "Although his mother had left him as a child via the Underground Railroad, Richardson's determination, intelligence, and enterprise allowed him to accrue wealth and property. He also became an accomplished musician and member of the local school board in Woodstown, New Jersey" (Scott 2008, 79).

6

The 25th United States Colored Troops
'Disease had run its course'

Direct orders from President Abraham Lincoln and trying fiercely to save the sinking ship that carried them to war were important early highlights of the 25th USCT of Camp William Penn, perhaps the most popularly photographed regiment of Camp William Penn.

Its Library of Congress image appears as a complete regiment on the campgrounds of Camp William Penn in full dress uniforms, likely shot in the winter of 1864, with the facility's U.S. flag flying high on a pole in the winter skies above an array of wooden structures and tents. And an image of the 25th USCT, possibly Company C, according to Temple University Civil War scholar Andrew Waskie, was adopted into a very colorful lithograph poster to recruit black soldiers, also featuring the U.S. flag and a drummer boy.

UNITED STATES SOLDIERS AT CAMP "WILLIAM PENN" PHILADELPHIA, PA.

"Rally Round the Flag, boys! Rally once again,
Shouting the battle cry of FREEDOM!"

This color lithograph, produced by Duval & Son, of the 25th USCT of Camp William Penn was developed from an original photograph of the soldiers and a white officer. At least one neo-Confederate group inaccurately claims these soldiers were actually fighting for the Rebels. *Courtesy of the Library Company of Philadelphia.*

Note the identical facial features in this original image of 25th USCT members that match those in the lithograph developed by Duval & Son. *Courtesy of Dr. James Spina.*

Indeed, as the regiment organized, flag maker David Bowser also worked on the 25th's regimental colors:

> The flag which the regiment carried, was painted by a colored man in Philadelphia. It represented a Freedman in the foreground, the shackles of his bondage having just fallen from his ankles, in the act of stepping forward eagerly to receive the musket and uniform of his country's defenders which the Goddess of Liberty is presenting to him. (Bates 1871, 1027)

The 25th USCT, organized in February 1864 at Camp William Penn, hailed mostly from Pennsylvania and New Jersey. Commanding the group were field officers Colonel Gustavus A. Scroggs, Lieutenant Colonel Frederick L. Hitchcock, and Major James W. H. Reisinger. (ibid.)

Colonel Frederick L. Hitchcock commanded the 25th USCT when they traveled to New Orleans and other southern locales. *Courtesy of the U. S. Army Military History Institute.*

Abbott A. Shattock, a lieutenant who helped to command Company C of the 25th USCT, likely was appointed via the special school to train white officers for commanding Camp William Penn regiments. *Courtesy of the U. S. Army Military History Institute.*

William H. Brown of Newark, New Jersey, was mustered into Company A of the 25th United States Colored Troops as a sergeant for a three-year term on what was likely a cold day on January 12, 1864. Obviously impressing the commanding officers, his mustering-in certificate, requesting a bounty, and on file at the New Jersey State Archives, says:

> This is to certify, that Sergt. Wm H. Brown has been enrolled 12th Jan. 1864 in Company "A," Regiment, U.S. Col, d Inft. And has been duly inspected and mustered into service of the United States; and that the said Sergt. Wm H. Brown having a family consisting of a Wife and three children living in Newark, N.J. dependent upon him for support, is entitled to State Bounty for his said family. Dated Fort Barrancas, [Florida], May 4th 1865. (Scott 2008, 87)

Meanwhile, some of the men were even mustered in by Colonel Wagner himself, including Private Thomas Crawford on January 20, 1864, about a week after Sergeant

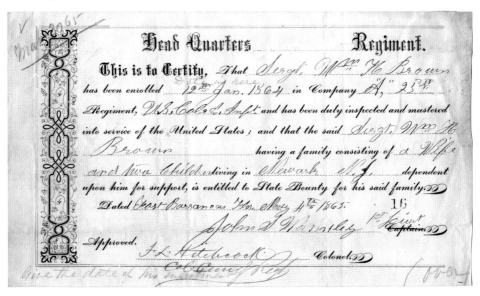

Sergeant William H. Brown, like other soldiers of his 25th USCT, very much valued this family support certificate granting financial and other benefits. *Courtesy of the New Jersey State Archives.*

Captain Chester H. Greenleaf had command duties with Company F of the 25ᵗʰ USCT. *Courtesy of the U. S. Army Military History Institute.*

Brown joined the ranks. Private Crawford, however, was assigned to Company D, and at some point likely lived in Salem, New Jersey (Scott 2008, 77).

Six days later (January 26ᵗʰ) Edward Bruno, from Bucks County, Pennsylvania, also joined the 25ᵗʰ as a private, according to a certification letter of May 22, 1865, and authored by his company commander, Captain Chester A. Greenleaf, himself mustered in on February 3, 1864 (108): "This certifies that Edward Bruno of Bucks County State of Pennsylvania is a Private of Company F 25ᵗʰ U.S.C.I. was mustered into the service of the United States at Trenton State of New Jersey by Capt. Woolsey on the Twenty-sixth day of January 1865 to serve for three years during the war" (88).

Bounty certificates were relished by the black soldiers, such as Theodore Kennedy of the 25ᵗʰ USCT, especially since a number of such warriors had difficulty receiving bounties as well as pensions following the war. *Courtesy of the New Jersey State Archives.*

Other 25th USCT enlistees included Pvt. George B. Andrews, joining the federal army on January 29, 1864, as well as Julius C. Allen, mustered in at the very end of the year on January 30, 1864, as a corporal in Company E, an indication that his commanding officers were impressed with his leadership acumen (ibid.).

Interestingly, "Colonel Scroggs was ordered by the President to proceed with his regiment to Indianola, Texas, and there recruit three other regiments from among the freedmen, which should with his own, constitute a brigade, of which he was to be appointed Brigadier General." Scroggs embarked "with the right wing of the regiment on the 15th of March, for New Orleans, on the steamer *Suwanee*, with orders to report to General Banks." However, during a fierce "storm off Hatteras, the steamer sprung a leak. The water rose to within a foot of the fires, although the ship's pumps were in active operation. The men were put to work with buckets, and after thirty-six hours of the most strenuous and incessant exertions to keep her afloat, she was brought into the harbor of Beaufort, North Carolina, where she was abandoned" (Bates 1871, 1026).

The 25th then switched commanders, reporting to General Wessels "at a time when the enemy was closely pressing the siege of Little Washington, and it was immediately ordered into the defenses." After "the emergency had passed," the 25th continued "to its destination, arriving about the 1st of May." Meanwhile, "the left wing, under command of Lieutenant Colonel Hitchcock," traveled to New Orleans, encamping at Carrolton, "a few miles above the city." It arrived at New Orleans "during the progress of the Red River campaign, which having ended in disaster, so modified the situation of affairs, that General Banks, who was in command of the department, refused to allow the regiment to go forward to Indianola" (ibid.).

A shakeup, according to Bates, in the 25th command hierarchy was imminent: "Colonel Scroggs, thereupon resigned, and Lieutenant Colonel Hitchcock was promoted to succeed him," while "Major Reisinger [was promoted] to Lieutenant Colonel, and Captain Boudren to Major." The regiment was quickly sent to Barrancas, Florida, "where it relieved the

Seventh Maine, and was charged with garrison duty" (ibid.).

However, the re-shuffling of the officers gave Hitchcock a very important and impressive command post:

Colonel Hitchcock, with six companies, was ordered with regimental

Lt. Colonel J.W.H. Reisinger and the 25th USCT served in Barrancas, Florida, where several other Camp William Penn regiments were assigned. *Courtesy of the U. S. Army Military History Institute.*

Major Thomas Boudren of the 25ᵗʰ USCT appears to be determined and resolved, certainly characteristics needed to command the troops. *Courtesy of the U. S. Army Military History Institute.*

headquarters to the command of the post of Barrancas Barracks, including Fort Barrancas, and the adjoining fortifications, where his men were drilled in infantry and heavy artillery service, in both of which they became proficient. Lieutenant Colonel Reisinger, with four companies, was detached, and placed in command of Fort Pickens, commanding the entrance to Pensacola Harbor. (ibid.)

At the start of the Mobile campaign, initiated January 1865, the 25ᵗʰ USCT was "ordered to report to General [William A.] Pile, for immediate service in the field, it being the purpose of the Government to organize an entire division of colored troops" (Bates, 1026). The regiment briefly associated with "the 'Old New Orleans First,' composed principally of Creoles of wealth and standing." (1027)

Some of the group's activities, often on diverse paths, as most companies likely suffered substantial illness that led to deaths, were described in a January 24, 1865, letter written by Nathan Flood, the orderly sergeant of Company K:

> For the Christian Recorder. LETTER FROM 25ᵗʰ U.S.C.T.
> Camp near Barrancas, Fla., Jan. 24ᵗʰ, 1865.
> MR. EDITOR: - I have come to the conclusion that I would try my hand for the first time, to address you a few lines for your columns. It would be a hard task for me to undertake to give you the full account of the 25ᵗʰ U.S.C. Infantry, for it is separated in so many different parts. My company (K) the most unlucky company of the regiment, has not been with the regiment since last May. We have been doing picket duty ever since we have been separated; it is the smallest company in the regiment. When we left camp William Penn, Phila., it numbered 90 men, but sickness has reduced it to 65. After we were separated from the regiment, we were removed to Gunboat Point, an out post on the picket line; there the men were very sickly and died very fast, they not being used to the climate, which was the occasion of so much sickness. A few days after we had removed to Gunboat Point one of the members of my company came to my tent, and told me that his mess mate was dying. I went, and found him dead, sitting up in his bed. Perhaps some of the friends of your city are acquainted with the old gentleman, (Spencer

Bolden), and was said to be an old citizen of Philadelphia. Several have died in that way.[1]

And although there were some health improvements, and the soldiers were able to build wooden barracks, the writer and his fellow soldiers were very concerned about the absence of pay, despite being thankful for having sensitive and laudatory officers:

> But since our company has been withdrawn from Gunboat Point the health of the men is much better: out of 65 men we have 63 for duty. We have been living in our tents ever since we have been out, and in wet weather it is very disagreeable. Since we have been at this camp the company has been separated; one platoon has been ordered to a picket post called Bragg's Bridge, one mile and a half distant, under command of our 2d Lieutenant J.W. Adams, in charge of two pieces of artillery. After the company was separated, Lieut. Adams got permission from the commanding officer of the District to go up the Bayou in search of lumber. He took a squad of fifteen men, went eight miles up the Bayou, destroyed a saw-mill which belonged to the rebels, brought a large quantity of lumber, and built very comfortable barracks. All that bothers us now is the non-appearance of the man that carries the greenbacks (the pay-master). He has not been with us for nine months, but we lie in hopes. Mr. Editor, I am not ashamed to say that we have the best officers that ever left Pennsylvania in command of colored troops. We have a noble chaplain; he takes a great interest in teaching the men to read. The men have prayer-meetings twice a week. We have never been in any engagement yet, but we are ready and willing at any time that we are called upon. We came here to fight for liberty and right, and we intend to follow the old flag as long as there is a man left to hold it up to the breeze of heaven. Mr. Editor, as this is my first attempt, you will please excuse all errors and imperfections.
> Respectfully yours,
> NATHAN FLOOD, Orderly Sergt. Co. K, 25th U.S.C. Inf.[2]

However, "before arrangements had been perfected for taking the field, the enemy threatened a counter movement against Pensacola, and it became necessary to strengthen the defenses, and put the forts in a condition to withstand the siege." Likely to the men's dissatisfaction, officers "deemed [it] inexpedient to relieve the Twenty-fifth," believing it to be "a regiment inexperienced and undrilled in garrison duty, and hence it did not take part in the active operations in the field, which were soon after inaugurated" (Bates 1871, 1027). And adding insult to injury, many of the men again became very ill, despite the many medical advances during the Civil War:

> During the spring and summer of 1865, the men suffered terribly from scurvy, about one hundred and fifty dying, and as many more being disabled for life. The mortality at one time amounted to from four to six daily. This was the result of want of proper food [...] Urgent appeals were made by the officers in command; but not until the disease had run its course, were these appeals answered. (ibid.)

One of the soldiers who likely suffered from the effects of the scurvy the rest of his life following the war was Pvt. Perry Hall of Company C. "During the summer of 1865, scurvy struck and more than 150 died, with many suffering lifetime illness as a result." A modern descendant (Cicero Green) of Hall's living in the same neighborhood where Camp William Penn was located says Hall suffered "from physical problems due to his service" (Scott 2008, 93).

Private Jacob S. Johnson of the 25ᵗʰ USCT, stationed at Fort Pickens in Florida, wrote to the editor of *The Christian Recorder* about the situation (including general morale, religious and educational activities, as well as insufficient diets), despite the 25ᵗʰ's efforts to remain upbeat, in a letter dated November 7, 1864:

> MR. EDITOR: – Sir: – Allow me again, through the medium of your paper, to call your attention to a few things which I would wish to relate to our friends at home, relative to our regiment. We are at Fort Pickens, Florida, one of the greatest forts our country, or I might say, this country ever produced. Yet I have one fault to find with it, and that is, its scarcity of vegetable diet. Scurvy has been amongst our ranks since our embarkation from Philadelphia, and many a stout heart has yielded to its influence, and passed to that bourne from whence no traveler ever returned. Yet the boys keep up buoyant spirits. Thinking it might be interesting to you, as well as the numerous readers of the Recorder, to know something concerning our condition, I submit the following for your and their perusal. For the last few weeks there has been an awakening among my brother soldiers, to their spiritual as well as to their temporal affairs; and on last Sabbath the Sacraments of Baptism and the Lord's Supper was administered to some 14 or 15 of our regiment. My earnest desire is, and shall ever be, that they may "Gird on the whole armor of faith, and fight the good fight, looking unto Jesus, the author and finisher of our faith." We have also a school of an average of 60 to 80 scholars, in reading, writing, arithmetic, and geography, and also a Bible class. All these things tend to make our sojourn out here tolerably comfortable.[3]

However, there was really something that dramatically hurt the men's morale, Johnson wrote – the absence of pay:

> Yet there is one thing lacking, and that is, our pay. We want, that in order to make comfortable those that are near and dear to us, and those we have sworn to love, cherish, and protect. Likewise, we are willing to suffer privations, endure hardship, and combat with the enemy, but when we sit down to meditate, 'tis hard; it almost drives one to do things contrary to law and military discipline, to think your partners relying on you for support, happiness and comforts, with probably one or two children to look to them for maintenance and support. Now, Mr. Editor, I ask in the name of justice, can you blame the soldiers of the 25ᵗʰ regiment for being discontented? Reasons says, no. Why are we not paid? Why are we promised and promised time and again, and yet receive no pay? Are we not worthy of it? The Scriptures say, "The laborer is worthy of his hire." They

tell us we shall wander from house to house begging their daily sustenance? Or, when driven from place, they shall seek the alms house for refuge? Justice echoes shame on such dilatoriness; and your humble servant says, Give us our just and honest dues; 'tis all we ask and all we want. Now, Mr. Editor, I will close, hoping you will insert in your paper such passages of this document as may be of interest to you and to the friends of the 25th U.S.C.T. I cheerfully subscribe myself your humble servant, JACOB S. JOHNSON, Co. H, 25th U.S. Col'd Infantry. P.S. In behalf of the regiment, I will tender our best wishes to Colonel Wagner, Camp William Penn, [Chelten] Hill, Philadelphia.[4]

The regiment served until December. It was then ordered to Philadelphia, and on December 6th at Camp Cadwálader the 25th was mustered out of service (Bates 1871, 1027).

The regimental flag, however, was presented to a group that helped to organize Camp William Penn and raise funds for its establishment and operation:

> After the return of the regiment to Philadelphia, and at the close of its last parade through the streets of that city, this flag was presented by Colonel Hitchcock, to the Union League Association of Philadelphia, George H. Boker, Esq., the poet, receiving it on behalf of the League, and responding to the language of the Colonel in an eloquent and impressive manner. (ibid.)

Although the 25th did not have as stellar a combat record as other regiments from Camp William Penn, its commanding officer still gave it reasonable adulation:

> In regard to the character of the Twenty-fifth, Colonel Hitchcock says: "I desire to bear testimony to the *esprit du corps*, and general efficiency of the organization as a regiment, to the competency and general good character of its officers, to the soldierly bearing, fidelity to duty, and patriotism of its men. Having seen active service in the Army of the Potomac, prior to my connection with the Twenty-fifth, I can speak with some degree of assurance. After a proper time had been devoted to its drill, I never for a moment doubted what would be its conduct under fire. It would have done its full duty beyond question. An opportunity to prove this the Government never afforded, and the men always felt this a grievance." (ibid.)

7

The 32nd United States Colored Troops
'A feeling of despair'

Most of the 32nd USCT was raised in Pennsylvania, as well as from several neighboring states, and received not much more than a month of training before embarking on quite an eventful journey by ship to South Carolina with Confederate prisoners of war.[1] Organized at Camp William Penn in March 1864, the regiment would depart the facility on April 23, 1864, about a year before the war would end and President Abraham Lincoln's assassination (Bates 1871, 1047).

Consisting of field officers that included Colonel George W. Baird, Lieutenant Edward C. Geary, and Major Benjamin W. Thompson, the "regiment was ordered to duty in the Department of the South" (ibid.) and boarded the steamship *Continental* for South Carolina's Sea Islands.[2]

But after boarding the steamship *Continental* "for the seat of war," the crew picked up very interesting, if not unwelcome guests, according to a soldier identified as B.W. via his letter to the editor of *The Christian Recorder*, the Rev. Elisha Weaver:

> We left Camp William Penn April 23d, and embarked on board the steamship Continental, for the seat of war. We went down the river to Fort Delaware, and took on board two hundred and eighty prisoners (white,) of the Union Army, which made the ship very uncomfortable, making, in all, fifteen hundred souls on board, which crowded us so, that we had not enough room to lie down. During the passage, we lost one man overboard. He was sea-sick and was leaning over the side to cast up his accounts, and lost his balance.[3]

Serving under the Union's "Department of the South" after arriving at Hilton Head on the 27th of April, the 32nd "was here assigned to a brigade of colored troops, commanded by Colonel Bailey, in which it was associated with the First Michigan, and Ninth United States, and was posted beyond the intrenchments, where it was engaged in drill, guard, and fatigue duty." The regiment was later sent to Folly and Morris islands, "where it participated in

This *Harper's Weekly* image shows a white officer training a black recruit in the use of a mine rifle, despite some regiments clearly not being properly trained, likely due to racial problems. *Courtesy of the Library of Congress.*

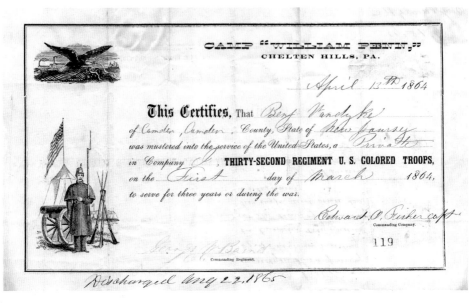

Private Benjamin Vandyke's muster certificate was part of the ticket that would allow him to collect various benefits, as well as a pension following his departure from the Army and the 32nd USCT. *Courtesy of the New Jersey State Archives.*

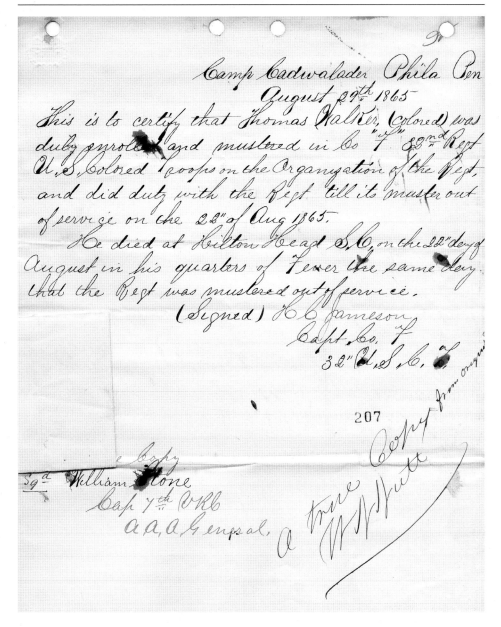

Private Thomas Walker of Company F of the 32ⁿᵈ USCT died at Hilton Head, South Carolina, of a fever in the heat of the summer – the very day the regiment was mustered out: August 22, 1865. *Courtesy of the New Jersey State Archives.*

the operations against Charleston; but returned again to Hilton Head in November."[4] And although B.W. did not discuss the fate of the Rebel prisoners that his regiment traveled with via steamship, he noted that the 32nd "arrived at Sea Brook, eight miles up the creek, west of Hilton Head," and set up camp, soon to endure deadly and unhealthy conditions:

> We staid there one week. We had nothing to eat but oysters and five hard tacks a day, that we picked up along the shore. As usual, after we had fixed our camp so nicely, orders came for us to strike tents, and march, which was promptly executed. We marched back to Hilton Head, and took the steamer Cosmopolitan, and reported at Folly Island, and marched to Morris Island, where we are still in camp, near Fort Shaw. We encamped on the old hospital ground, where they buried all their dead. We had to dig wells in the graveyard, and drink the water off the putrid bodies, and it is killing our men. The health of the men, in general, is as well as can be expected. We have lost ten men since our departure, and, among the brave hearts was that of Jesse Dexter, the Quartermaster-Sergeant, who leaves a wife and child behind to mourn his loss.[5]

And similar to the Massachusetts 54th black regiment that had served on Morris Island so valiantly during the assault on Fort Wagner about a year earlier, the 32nd would not generally accept its lower wages of $7, compared to the white troops' $10 and $13, as a form of protest. However, regimental officers apparently retaliated:

> The paymaster made us a visit, and offered us seven dollars a month, which all of the men refused, except a few in the left wing, who sneaked up at night and signed the pay-roll; but the majority of the men would sooner stay their time out and do without the seven dollars. Our officers seem very much put out, and beg the men to take it. They said, that the next day we would get all that is coming to us, and said: "Boys, we think that you had better take the money." But we told them that it was a big thing on ice, but we could not see it; and, after the officers found out that the men would not take the seven dollars, they began to treat the men like dogs. The least thing that the men would do, they were bucked and gagged, and put on knap-sack-drill, and made to stand in the hot, broiling sun for four hours at a stretch; in consequence of which, a few of the men got sun-struck.[6]

The warrior writer even charged the officers with cowardice:

> We have drills and dress-parades and battalion-drills, which none of our officers know anything about. When they are ordered by a command, they do not know how to do it. One night we went on picket duty. Every thing went on well all through the night, and in the morning, when the pickets were taken off, the rebels began to shell and cross-fire. Our brave officers sent the men on ahead, and they staid behind, because they were afraid of the rebels' shells; and, when they came down to camp, they were under arrest for their cowardice. The officer in command told them that they had not as much heart as their men had, and that the regiment would be better drilled if they had the officers to command them, but

they had not an officer in the regiment that they knew his business and knew how to do his duty, and that the regiment was hardly worth the rations that they drew.[7]

There were multiple complaints concerning the slow issuance of equipment and uniforms, specifically for the drum corps. Furthermore, the writer certainly was not pleased with the medical supplies, and used cutting sarcasm to criticize the regiment's physician, making a very serious charge that he was capable of intentionally killing black soldiers:

> And there is our drum-corps, that we brought with us from Philadelphia. They have not got their uniforms yet, and they are the worst corps on the island. They are laughed and sneered at by all the other regiments. We know that it is not the fault of the drum-major. It is the fault of the commanding officers. The General says, that, if we were to go to field with such officers as we now have, we would all get cut to pieces, and that there is no use of taking us into action until our officers have learned a little more. Mr. Editor, it looks hard that a party of men should treat colored men in this way. There is our gentlemanly doctor. He is a nice man, indeed. He has not got any medicine fit to give the men. If they get very sick in their quarters the doctor will order them to be brought to the hospital, where they will not be more than twenty-four hours before they are dead. That is the way the men are served. Dr. White growls and snaps at the men as if they were dogs, and he says, if the men are not fit for duty, send them to him, and he will soon get them out of the way. And he does put them out of the way, for he says, it is no harm to kill a nigger.[8]

The soldier then released a barrage of complaints, summarizing his case, and even venturing to identify a black officer that he charged with reneging on a promise not to accept lower pay:

> When the regiment first encamped here, we were treated more like soldiers; but as soon as we refused to take seven dollars a month, they commenced to treat us like dogs. Before the Paymaster came around, there was not anything like bucking and gagging; but as soon as we refused to take the pay, they commenced. They even bucked and gagged a boy because he happened to not have the seat of his pants sewed up on inspection. It was impossible for him to sew them up, as he had no money to buy a needle and thread with. Now, Mr. Editor, don't you think this is bad treatment for a Pennsylvania regiment to get? I think it is ridiculous and a shame before God and man. There was not a camp that left Camp William Penn with such a set of officers as the Thirty-second United States Colored Troops. Look at the Forty-third Regiment United States Colored Troops, which was raised after we were. They have been brigaded, and are now acting as rear-guard over the baggage-train of the Army of the Potomac, whilst we are not fit for any thing but to do all of the picket duty and drudgery work on the island; and we don't get our rations as we ought to. All the rations that are condemned, by the white troops, are sent to our regiment. You ought to see the hard tack that we have to eat. They are mouldy and musty and full of worms, and not fit for a dog to eat, and the rice and

beans and peas are musty and the salt horse (the salt beef, I mean,) is so salt, that, after it is cooked, we can't eat it. Some days the men are sent on fatigue in the hot sun, and when they come home to dinner, there is nothing to eat but rotten hard tack and flat coffee, without sugar in it. Now, Mr. Editor, if this is not killing men, I don't know what is [...]. Please insert this in *the Christian Recorder*, so that it will be seen. Please rectify all mistakes, and send several copies to the thirty-second Regiment U.S.C.T. No more at present.

B.W. 32nd Reg. U.S.C.T.[9]

Noah Andre Trudeau, in his book *Like Men of War: Black Troops in the Civil War 1862-1865*, reported that *The Christian Recorder* was consistently concerned with the issue of lower pay when it printed an earlier letter authored by another disgruntled soldier of the 32nd USCT:

> The divisiveness of the pay issue was made clear in another letter, written on August 9 to the *Christian Recorder* by a member of the 32nd USCT, then stationed at Morris Island: "We were mustered in for pay at Hilton Head, and were not offered it till we came to Morris Island, but prior to it were told on company drill that we should prepare ourselves for being paid on a day specified by the colonel, and should come out in good shape on the day that pay would be offered, and we had better take that offer, which would be seven dollars per month, – not that it was any interest to him at all, for he would get his pay if we did not, and to take it, as we could not do any better, – the Government allowed no more for colored troops, and there would be no more appropriated for us. A feeling of despair passed over the whole regiment. There were but few to sign the pay rolls and those who did a great many of us tried to influence to the contrary, but to no purpose; they, through ignorance, informed the Captain of it, to which he said, if he heard any one say aught against any one that would take, or had taken their pay, he would have him severely punished for it [...]. They try to perpetuate our inferiority, and keep us where we are. This regiment came out just as manfully as any other regiment now in the field; there was no compulsion in our rear at all; we came to have a more legal claim to equality – we responded to the call unhesitatingly, – when we were asked to attend the rally for the preservation of the country, we did not falter, but came up with the expectation that we would be treated accordingly, – though, sad to say, we have been disappointed to some extent in it." (Trudeau 1998, 253-254)

As November came to a close, "General Foster, in command of the Department, was directed by General Halleck to make a demonstration in the direction of Pocotaligo, for the purpose of diverting attention from General for this purpose, and with these, ascending the Broad River in transports Sherman's front, who was now approaching the sea." However, "Foster could spare but five thousand troops to Boyd's Neck," hence landing and "hurried forward a force under General J. P. Hatch, to break the Charleston and Savannah Railroad. The Thirty-second was in Hatch's command" (Bates 1871, 1047).

Then, during "the morning of the 30th, Hatch encountered a rebel force under command of General Gustavus W. Smith, at Honey Hill, three miles from Grahamsville, in a commanding position behind breast-works. Hatch immediately attacked, and though pushing his advance with obstinacy and bravery, he was compelled to fall back, sustaining heavy losses. The Thirty-second had nine killed and forty-two wounded. Lieutenant Robert D. Winters received a mortal wound, and died on the 22d of December" (1047-1048).

Earlier that morning the 32ⁿᵈ had been "marching near the rear," but "was halted in column so the troops up ahead could be sorted out." After its service on Hilton Head and the "Morris Island trenches" the regiment's commander, "Colonel George W. Baird, was listening to the firing when Captain William C. Manning of Potter's staff reined up before him." The 32ⁿᵈ, led by Baird, was asked to charge up the causeway and eliminate the guns (Trudeau 1998, 322).

According to Baird, "The order was promptly obeyed; the advance of the double quick was necessarily by the flank along the causeway enfiladed by the two pieces of artillery […]. Owing, probably, to the shortness of the range the missiles flew just over the heads of those of us who were at the head of the column, but they told with deadly effect at the center and towards the rear," the commander recalled. "Here the regiment lost […] a large number of enlisted men killed or wounded. The enemy's artillery was thus driven away and our line advanced" (322).

However, Trudeau wrote, as the Confederates pulled back they torched the "open fields on either side of the road," hampering the Federals' progress. As some were ordered to try and extinguish the flames, about a half-hour was lost, allowing the Rebels to bring in reinforcements. That's when many of the Union soldiers, in an effort to get off of the road, became stuck in the thick vegetation lining the route. "As Potter's men came around a sharp turn in the road, they were immediately exposed to fire from the crest of Honey Hill, and had to go scurrying for cover; in response, their commander began to orient his brigade into some semblance of a line of battle, directing the men to file off to the left of the road form, and then gingerly feel their way toward the enemy" (323).

The 32ⁿᵈ arrived in the middle of the action. "By the time the 32ⁿᵈ USCT arrived," said Colonel Baird, the "sound of heavy musketry firing in front was our guide, and spent balls indicated that the infantry of the enemy had been developed." A rough woods road led off toward the northeast, and the 32ⁿᵈ used this to extend itself before moving into line on the right of the 25ᵗʰ Ohio, which Baird found to be "hotly engaged with the enemy." Baird's soldiers "were blocked by a morass ringed with thick undergrowth that made further advance impossible, but just beyond it, he could see an 'abrupt rise of ground covered with an earth work.'" The 32ⁿᵈ sought cover and pulled their triggers (323-324). Still, things did not bode well for the regiment, according to Trudeau:

> The movement of the 32ⁿᵈ was part of a doomed effort on Hatch's part to press the enemy along a broad front. According to the *New York Times* reporter, "As our men advanced they were met by a concentrated fire of musketry from the rifle-pits and the lower part of the fort, and the woods, while from the parapet of the fort they were being mowed down by continuous charges of grape and canister." (324)

Even the Confederates, who won that battle, were surprised about the amount of grisly harm done to the Federals, Trudeau noted:

> The Confederates who ventured from their earthworks the next morning were appalled by the raw violence done by their firepower. The bodies of the soldiers from the 55th Massachusetts (Colored) and the 35th USCT "lay five deep as dead as mackerel," observed one of the Rebel gunners. A reporter who had arrived from Savannah "counted some sixty or seventy bodies in a space of about an acre, heads shot off, and others completely disemboweled." All the Southerners on the scene were convinced that the black troops had been purposely put in front of the white ones; from their racially biased point of view, no other explanation was possible. (330)

Although the Confederate casualty losses were estimated to be only between 150 and 200 men, Union forces counted many more at 750, including more than 60 from the 32nd USCT and 138 soldiers of the 25th Ohio, the unit suffering the heaviest Union losses (330-331).

And there were other grave developments, including clashes near the Coosawhatchie River, as the year 1864 ended. "Lieutenant Colonel Geary was severely wounded, by which he was incapacitated from further duty." Still, commanders were undeterred. "Intent on the purpose of his expedition, Foster sent a force under General E. E. Potter, across the Coosawhatchie to Deveaux Neck, where, on the 6th of December, he seized a position commanding the railroad, which he began to fortify. Early on the following morning, the enemy approached stealthily and attacked, thinking to surprise the Union forces." That's when this "attack fell mainly on the right wing of the division, the Thirty-second holding the extreme right of the line, Company A, standing upon the right of the regiment, receiving the first shock. The regiment was taken unawares, but rallied manfully and repulsed the attack, the position being held without further molestation until General Sherman, in triumph, entered Savannah." However, "Companies A, F, and D, sustained the severest losses. The loss in the regiment was nine killed, thirty-nine wounded, and one missing. Captains Robert W. C. Farnsworth, George M. Templeton, and Augustus A. Woodward were among the wounded, the latter mortally" (Bates 1871, 1047-1048).

It seems, though, that despite some relief of combat intensity, the 32nd still had quite a lot to deal with as the war climaxed. "On the 14th of February, General Potter moved with his command for a diversion in favor of General Schimmelfennig, who was operating against Charleston. Landing on James Island, Potter charged and drove the enemy from his works. In this engagement Colonel Baird was wounded, and the regiment sustained, besides, considerable loss." Then, on the morning of February 15th, "Potter re-embarked his troops, and proceeding to Bull's Bay, landed under fire of the gun-boats, at a point on the coast fifteen miles north-east of Charleston, with the design of cutting off the retreat of the enemy from that city, but arrived too late to effect the purpose." The regiment spent a couple of days "scouring the country, following the enemy along the railroad towards Cheraw, to the crossing of the Santee. Potter then marched down and entered the city on the evening of the 18th, the day of the surrender," Bates wrote, a time that had to be quite exhilarating and rewarding for the black soldiers, many of them ex-slaves (1048).

Obviously aware of the 32ⁿᵈ's combat readiness, the government's plans for the regiment were certainly not over. "At the beginning of April, it was discovered that the enemy was moving his naval stores, and other property of the rebel government inland. General Potter was sent with his division to intercept them. Landing at Georgetown, on the Winyaw Bay, he marched to Florence, thence to Manchester Junction, and thence to Camden, the terminus of the railroad. Returning again to Manchester, he there came upon the trains, capturing twenty locomotives, and two hundred cars heavily laden with naval and military stores. In this expedition," Bates said, "the Thirty-second was kept upon the march, skirmishing almost daily, for nearly three weeks, participating in brisk engagements at Sumpterville, and at three other points along the Wateree, between Camden and Statesboro" (ibid.). The 32ⁿᵈ rode the towering crest of the war as it cruised back down towards sea level with startling, but greatly extraordinary results: "At two o'clock on the afternoon of the 9ᵗʰ, after having had a running fight during all the earlier part of the day, the joyful intelligence was received by flag of truce, of the surrender of Lee" (ibid.).

Yet soon "the joy was turned to mourning, by the sad news of the assassination of President Lincoln" (ibid.), Bates wrote. And with that terrible and foreboding news, it had to be clear to most of the men that, despite the hard-fought victories on the battlefield, other clashes were eminent on other social battlefronts.

Regardless, it was nearly time to go home: "After the cessation of hostilities, the regiment performed garrison duty at Charleston, Beaufort, and Hilton Head. About the middle of August, it was relieved from, duty, and returned to Philadelphia, where, on the 22d, it was mustered out of service" (ibid.), according to Bates.

8

The 41ˢᵗ United States Colored Troops
We did not falter

Destined to help corner General Lee's army near Appomattox, Virginia, and for combat in that state and Maryland, the 41ˢᵗ USCT was organized at Camp William Penn in the autumn of 1864, with most of the men hailing from Pennsylvania. The black recruits, in general, seemed to highly respect the officers, including Colonel Llewellyn F. Haskell, Lieutenant Colonel Lewis L. Weld, and Major Alpheus H. Cheney (Bates 1871, 1066).

And among those African American recruits was an ex-slave, William J. Simmons, who joined the 41ˢᵗ at just 15 years old, destined to become a university president and nationally-known Baptist preacher (Logan, Winston 1982, 556).

Meanwhile, the backgrounds of Simmons' line officers were not too much unlike their white company commanders, including First Lt. Benjamin Franklin of companies G and I, who was an alumnus of Washington and Jefferson College in Washington, Pennsylvania:

> He came from Virginia with his father's family to Cross Creek, Pa. His father was a farmer, and an elder in the Presbyterian Church […]. Ben was carefully raised, his mother being also a sincere and devoted Christian, whose prayers were constantly that her boy might be led into the gospel ministry. She died before she had the pleasure of seeing the answer to her supplications […] His college course was marked by quiet, persistent study, and free from all the follies which are so common in college days. He was modest and conscientious […]. He began his theological training immediately after leaving college. In 1862 his Hebrew Bible was laid aside for the Springfield musket. He enlisted, and was made Orderly Sergeant in Co. "K," 140th Penn'a. Vols. For two years he was one of the bravest, quietest, most conscientious and faithful soldiers in this crack regiment of veterans. For a long time he not only did the onerous work of first sergeant, but really commanded the company whilst his superior officers were detailed to other duties. He was a slender, delicate looking soldier, but he never flinched in the fight. He was promoted to First Lieutenant Co. "G,' 41st U.S.C.T.,

and was afterward placed in command of Co. "I," of the same regiment. He was never wounded, though he was always in the front, and participated in the battles of Chancellorsville, Gettysburg, Bristow Station, Deep Bottom, Reams Station, Petersburg, and many other smaller engagements. He was on the advanced line at the surrender of General Lee, after which he was ordered with his regiment to the Rio Grande border. (*The Annual of Washington and Jefferson College* 1884, 171-172)

Many of the soldiers of the 41ˢᵗ USCT hailed from Pennsylvania and nearby eastern-board states, but also came from other locales, often working as laborers before joining the unit. For instance Isaac Johnson, a native of Anne Arundel County in Maryland, was born about 1829. A laborer before the war, he was drafted at the end of the war in April 1865, joining Company B of the regiment. While in Edinburg, Texas, where the regiment was deployed with other USCT regiments as the war ended, Johnson moved on to Company G before being discharged on December 10, 1865. Meanwhile, born in New York about 1835, Jacob V. Saddler also worked as a laborer "before he joined Company A of the 41ˢᵗ USCT in Morristown, Pennsylvania on September 5, 1864. Saddler became First Sergeant on October 14, 1864 and Sergeant Major in January 1865." He was discharged in September 1865. Gabriel Boyer, a Pennsylvanian from Chester County, was born about 1845, and found work too as a laborer before joining Company C "in West Chester, Pennsylvania on September 12, 1864." Unfortunately medical "records indicate that Boyer arrived at Point of Rocks Hospital in Virginia in early February 1865 and died on March 4 from 'acute dysentery.'" And although Joseph E. Turner was born in Cuba about 1844, likely a slave, he was also a laborer before joining Company F of the regiment on September 22, 1864.

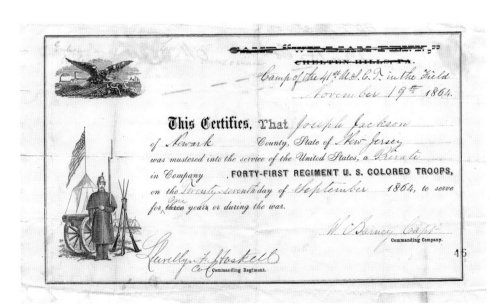

Private Joseph Jackson of the 41ˢᵗ USCT was mustered in September 27, 1864. *Courtesy of the New Jersey State Archives.*

However, he was a "substitute for David Wilson in Newark, New Jersey" before being promoted to sergeant after transferring to Company B. He was discharged on December 10, 1865, in Brownsville, Texas. (*Pennsylvania Grand Review* 2007-2010)

On October 13th, after about six to eight weeks of training, the 41st, consisting of six full companies, was "ordered to join the Army of the James, and proceeded to Deep Bottom, where, for a few days, they performed guard duty, and then moved up to the front in rear of Fort Burnham" (Bates 1871, 1066).

In a March 25, 1865, letter to the *Christian Recorder's* editor, Rev. Elisha Weaver, Private William H. Fray of Company D described his first experiences at Camp William Penn, as well as his regiment's departure and then early field service in Virginia:

MR. EDITOR: – I have come to the conclusion to try my hand, for the first time, in penning a few lines for your columns respecting the 41st U.S.C.T. Infantry. We left Camp William Penn on the 13th of October. We received our marching orders on the 12th of October. We were then marched to Shoemakertown, and there took the cars, arriving in Philadelphia, at Berk street Station, at 10 o'clock. We marched down Second street to Prime, and down Prime to the Refreshment Saloon, where we halted, stacked arms, unslung knapsacks, and walked around a few minutes, until we were ordered to fall into ranks, and marched into the Saloon, where the table was set, and we went to work. After we had enjoyed a very good dinner, the word of command was given, when we fell into line, slung knapsacks, and marched up Prime street to the Depot, and there halted. It was then about half-past four o'clock. We then got on the cars and pushed off for Baltimore. The boys were as merry as you please. We arrived in Baltimore about half-past 12 o'clock, and then marched down to the Soldiers' Rest, where we stacked arms, unslung knapsacks, and lay down until the next morning, when the drum sounded, and we fell in for roll call. The boys were in high spirits. We then fell in line, and marched across Pratt street to the Soldiers' Rendezvous, where we took breakfast, and then marched back again.[1]

Meanwhile, it's likely that Fray and his comrades felt more than a tinge of apprehension as they prepared to board the steamer *Wenona* for a trip to the southern war zone. Spotting the destruction of the war along the way was probably even less comforting; yet, Private Fray noted that the morale of the soldiers anticipating action was quite high:

At 7 o'clock we were ordered to sling knapsacks, and marched to the landing, where we embarked on a large transport steamer called the *Wenona*, for Fortress Monroe. We lay there until 3 o'clock, when we pushed off on our long journey, arriving at Fortress Monroe at about 7 o'clock on Friday morning, the 14th. We anchored off old Point Comfort awaiting orders, until 11 o'clock, when we raised anchor and proceeded up the James River, another long journey, when we saw some of the ruins of this war. On Saturday night, the 15th, we anchored at Bermuda Hundred, and on Sabbath morning, the 16th, we again raised anchor – and at about 9 o'clock on Sabbath morning we landed at Gen. Butler's Headquarters. They were then fighting so hard at the Dutch Gap Canal, that we were obliged to turn back to Deep Bottom, where we anchored alongside of a large hospital boat. We lay on board of her for about four hours, and were then ordered ashore. We passed through the boat referred to. We then marched up the hill, where Major Wells ordered us to pitch our tents. The boys are in as good spirits as ever. We had not been there long before myself and Corp. John Woods were detailed out for Provost Marshall duty, and while going about for four days, our regiment received marching orders to go to the front. We had then to return to our regiment. We then struck tents for the first time, and started for the front. It was very warm and dusty, with no air stirring. We again pitched our tents in the woods; and we had been there but a few days, when we were ordered to strike tents and pile knapsacks; and at daylight that morning we commenced our march. We marched about three-quarters of a mile, halted, and laid there for two days, without any shelter over us.[2]

A couple of weeks later, on October 27ᵗʰ, the 41ˢᵗ "took part in a reconnaissance [*sic*] in force on the right of the Army of the James, in the vicinity of the Darbytown Road, and had one, a Sergeant, wounded," (Bates 1871, 1066) during operations designed to confuse the enemy: "This movement was undertaken as a diversion in favor of Hancock, who was moving upon the Boydton Plank Road, on the extreme left of the Army of the Potomac. The command soon after went into camp on Chapin's Farm, where it was engaged in drill and picket duty, and where it was joined by the remaining companies" (ibid.).

Near Darbytown the 41ˢᵗ would reunite with other Camp William Penn regiments. "Black troops marched with both the Tenth and Eighteenth corps. The two brigades in the Tenth," including "Colonel Shaw's, consisting of the 7ᵗʰ, 9ᵗʰ, 41ˢᵗ and 127ᵗʰ," the latter two originating at Camp William Penn, as well as the 8ᵗʰ and 45ᵗʰ USCT, also from the Chelten Hills' camp, approached "the enemy lines near the Kell House, south of the Darbytown Road" (Trudeau 1998, 305).

The Union forces apparently pushed back entrenched Rebels before they were relieved by the 7ᵗʰ USCT. Several Confederate soldiers were captured and "many" were "killed and wounded" (305-306).

During related skirmishes near Williamsburg Road, another Camp William Penn regiment, "the 22ⁿᵈ, tangled up in underbrush and raked by flank fire," began to retreat. "Colonel Holman was hit, as was the commander of the 22ⁿᵈ, Colonel Joseph B. Kiddoo," who was seriously wounded. Still, men such as Sergeant John Loveday of the 22ⁿᵈ were valiant. Although "severely wounded" in the leg, he continued towards the enemy's position. And Corporal Nathan Stanton, also of the 22ⁿᵈ, continued to carry the regimental colors, despite being "shot through the hand" (307).

Regardless, starting "the 1st of January, 1865, the [41ˢᵗ USCT] regiment moved to the vicinity of Fort Durham, exchanging camps with the One Hundred and Seventeenth Colored, where it continued in drill and picket duty" (Bates 1871, 1066).

Indeed, with winter now upon the regiment commanders believed it was prudent to prepare suitable quarters. The weather would get so adverse that Private Fray reported the men one morning rising from the frigid earth with hair "white with frost!":

We then returned again – and the next thing on the programme was to go to work and build our winter huts. We completed our task, and then moved into them, and remained there for about a month, and again we were ordered to take four days' rations and strike tents. The orders came about noon, and we were to move at 8 o'clock. So you may know that we had a very short notice. It was on the 4th of December. We halted that night, and were obliged to lie on the bare ground. In the morning, when we arose, our heads were white with frost! We were all again ordered to go to work and build quarters. We got them done; and every morning at about 5 o'clock, we had to fall out to the breastworks, and then stand under arms until 6 o'clock. We lay there until the 1st day of January, and then moved back to the rear again, where we now remain.[3]

Despite losing almost a half-dozen men, Fray reported that his company was physically and mentally in very good shape. He even had very kind words for several officers:

Our regiment is very healthy; at least, my Company is. We have lost but five men. We mustered ninety-three men last month; we have lost five men since we left Camp Wm. Penn. We have very kind and nice non-commissioned officers. Crawford Hardy, our Orderly, and 2d Sergeant Howard Allmond, have proved themselves capable of honoring their office. Third Sergeant J.B. Fray, and Fourth Sergeant John Hood, are both very nice men, and attentive to their duties. Our Orderly Sergeant, Crawford Hardy, is one of the heroes of Morris Island; he received a severe wound there. Our Colonel, [Llewellyn] F. Haskel, is gentlemanly, yet firm. He is a native of New Jersey. Adjutant Babcock, formerly our First-Lieutenant, is, or was of our Company. He is a very fine man, and a gentleman of education and talent. Our Second-Lieutenant, A.K. Kepner, is indeed a splendid young man, and possessed of a free and generous spirit. Our Captain, Frederick A. Allmond, is a noble and dashing fellow. Indeed all of our officers are highly respected and much spoken of throughout the entire regiment as model commanders. I shall now come to a close, hoping that these lines may be inserted for the encouragement of your subscribers in the 41st Regt., and wishing that your paper may circulate throughout the whole army. I hope these few lines may prove of interest to your readers. I am, sir, your obed't servant, WM. H. FRAY, Private Co. D, 41st U.S.C.T.[4]

More action was sure to come, because on March 27th, "in connection with the Twenty-fourth Corps, under command of General Ord, to the Second Division of which it now belonged," the 41st USCT "moved to join the Army of the Potomac, arriving at Hatcher's Run on the 29th." The unit was "immediately ordered upon the front, where it threw up breastworks and skirmished with the enemy" (Bates 1871, 1066).

Next there would be fighting at Petersburg, when on April 2nd one soldier was killed "and eight wounded." Nonetheless, in what had to be a very rewarding assignment, the 41st that evening joined in pursuit of the Rebel army that was moving towards Appomattox, "following the line of the South Side Railroad. The pursuit was pushed with little interruption until the regiment reached Appomattox Court House, where, on the 9th, while upon the skirmish line, Captain John W. Falconer was mortally wounded, dying on the 23d." After witnessing the historic surrender that day, "the regiment encamped in the neighborhood of Appomattox, where it remained until the 11th, and then moved back to Petersburg" (1066), wrote Bates.

However, shockingly bad news regarding President Lincoln would rattle the black troops to their nucleus:

> The men of the 41ˢᵗ USCT, who only days before had occupied Richmond, were settled South of Petersburg on the afternoon of April 15 when they learned of President Abraham Lincoln's assassination. "This cast a gloom over our camp," remembered a regimental officer, "and one could see and hear the grief of those poor colored men over his tragic end." (Trudeau 1998, 433)

And similar to other Camp William Penn regiments, following the surrender, the 41ˢᵗ was ordered to the Texas frontier:

> On the 25th of May, it embarked at City Point, for Texas, arriving at the Island of Brazos de Santiago, early in June. After remaining here a few days, it proceeded to Edinburg, where it was employed in guard and provost duty. On the 30th of September it was consolidated into a battalion of four companies. These were mustered out of service at Brownsville, on the 10th of November, and returning to Philadelphia, were paid and disbanded on the 14th of December. As only the muster-out rolls of these companies were returned to the Adjutant General's office, the men whose names are borne upon them are, alone, accounted for. (Bates 1871, 1066)

Upon his return back to Pennsylvania, First Lieutenant Benjamin Franklin was said to be "proud" of his military service and became very involved in a variety of activities:

> He certainly has reason to feel proud of his military record in the Federal army during the rebellion, as well as that in the army of the Lord since those days of blood and fire. When his soldier service was ended he re-entered the Western Theological Seminary and graduated in 1867. He, without delay, went to Missouri. Having been licensed by the Presbytery of Washington in 1862, he was ordained and installed in charge of the church at Deep Water, Mo. He afterwards established Butler Academy, in that State, which is now a first-class institution, with 125 students and property valued at $20,000. Many of his students have done and are doing him honor in the learned professions. He delivered several public addresses while in charge of this academy, which were published, and were highly valued by the people. For the past two years he has been pastor of the Presbyterian Church at Lyons, Kansas, and is doing a good work [...]. In 1870 he was married to Miss Mersie J. Austin, of Deep Water, Mo., a granddaughter of Rev. Amasa Jones, who was a distinguished missionary among the Osage Indians. Eight children have been born to them, five of whom are now living. He has had much sickness and many afflictions in his family, still his heart is buoyant and his hands full of

work [...]. He is [...] Clerk of his Presbytery, and has much labor to perform in the organization of new churches, and other duties incident to the extended fields of a frontier missionary pastor. His church is self-sustaining, and well organized for Christian effort [...]. He served the Washington Literary Society in the contest of 1859 [just before the war] as original orator, against J. D. Kerr, of the Union Society, and whilst Ben was speaking the floor gave way. You may know who deserved the prize, when he could literally bring the house down in that manner. (*The Annual of Washington and Jefferson College* 1884, 171-172)

William J. Simmons, a black veteran of the 41st USCT, became active as a church leader and then a preacher in Lexington, Kentucky, following the war. He eventually rose to become a prominent publisher, biographer and college president, remarkable accomplishments for an ex-slave.

Simmons experienced much adventure and hardship as a child, born June 26, 1849, in Charleston, SC, into slavery. Both his parents, Edward and Esther Simmons, were slaves. However, when "still a young child his mother fled with him and her two other children to the North" to seek refuge, quite possibly via the Underground Railroad network of William Still, Harriet Tubman, and Chelten Hills' Lucretia Mott. "In order to evade slave catchers they lived successively in Philadelphia, Roxbury, Mass., and Chester, Pa., before finally settling in Bordentown, N.J." Fortunately, his "uncle, Alexander Tardieu, helped to support the family during these years and personally provided the children with their basic education." At the tender age of 12, Simmons was apprenticed to a white dentist and became able "enough to treat several of his employer's patients" (Logan, Winston 1982, 556).

However, after being rejected "in an attempt to enroll in a dental school in Philadelphia," Simmons enlisted at just age 15 in the Union Army's 41st USCT. "During his year of military service he participated in several engagements in the vicinity of Petersburg, Va., and was present at Appomattox when Lee surrendered to Grant in April 1865." (ibid.) Following the war, Simmons was determined to get a superior education:

> Upon returning to civilian life he resumed his occupation as a dentist's assistant. A turning point in his life came, however, when he joined a white Baptist church in Bordentown [New Jersey] and subsequently decided to become a minister. Encouraged and assisted by members of the church to continue his education, he first attended Madison (later Colgate) University and then Rochester University, in New York State. Forced by difficulties with his eyes to leave the latter institution after his first year, he enrolled in Howard University in Washington, D.C., in 1871 and graduated two years later with his B.A. degree; in 1881 he received an M.A. degree. (ibid.)

While at Howard University, Simmons taught at a couple of public schools, soon "becoming the principal of Hillsdale Public School." For a brief time he taught in Arkansas, then returned to teach at Hillsdale in Washington. And soon marriage was on the horizon:

On Aug. 25, 1874, he married Josephine A. Silence of Washington, who bore him seven children. After the marriage the Simmonses moved to Florida where they lived for the next five years. After unsuccessfully trying his hand at land investments and growing oranges, Simmons returned to teaching, serving as the principal of Howard Academy. He also became an ordained minister, pastured a small church, and held such public offices as deputy county clerk and county commissioner. About 1877 the family returned to Washington where Simmons again taught school until 1879 before going to Lexington, Ky. (ibid.)

Becoming pastor of the First Baptist Church in Kentucky, Simmons also "accepted the presidency of a failing black Baptist College, the Normal and Theological Institution in Louisville," which evolved into the State University of Kentucky at Louisville after he 'revived' the institution. Starting in 1883, Simmons also edited the *American Baptist*. His position as a college president and editor gave him twin platforms from which to promote his views and himself within Kentucky and nationally." Simmons was also prominent in other areas, such as rising "to chair of the executive committee of the State Convention of Colored Men of Kentucky, an organization that fought for the interests of African Americans." Furthermore, Simmons "used American Baptist to organize the American National Baptist Convention in 1886 and become the organization's first president. (The American National Baptist Convention was an important forerunner of the National Baptist Convention, U.S.A., and the first major umbrella organization for black Baptists in the United States)" (Shaffer 2004, 91).

In addition to his church and religious activities, Simmons was very active in political circles, stressing a clear independence:

> Although he campaigned in Florida in 1876 for Rutherford B. Hayes, the Republican candidate for president, Simmons was politically independent. In subsequent years he admonished Negro voters against becoming "a slave to party." He advised them to support instead only those candidates and political factions on the state and local levels who were willing to promote their interests. An outspoken critic of Jim Crow practices in general, he singled out for special condemnation the mistreatment of Negroes in southern courts and their exclusion from state and municipal jobs. (Logan, Winston 1982, 556)

Yet, Simmons' claim to "posterity" was "as the author of the biographical dictionary *Men of Mark: Eminent Progressive, and Rising* (1887), most of whom were born in slavery." He aimed "to counter the growing tendency within white academic and lay circles to portray the Negro as inherently inferior," seeking to "show both friends and oppressors of Negroes that they had survived the ordeal of slavery with 'their spirituality and love of offspring' undiminished and 'that the Negro race is still alive, and must possess more intellectual vigor than any other section of the human family.'" Simmons was especially interested in motivating young blacks to seek higher education. (ibid.)

However, Simmons' death by a heart attack, ironically at just age 41 (the number of his regiment), probably hampered him from reaching even greater prominence (Shaffer 2004, 91). He exemplified more than a few of the black warriors and officers from Camp William Penn determined to lead meaningful and productive lives after witnessing the horrors of war as America struggled to emerge from a pro-slavery society.

9

The 43rd United States Colored Troops
These redeemed sons of Africa

    With most hailing from Pennsylvania, soldiers of the 43rd USCT organized during the spring of 1864, and would participate in some of the war's heaviest fighting at the Battle of the Crater in Virginia, as well as experience and witness there atrocious war crimes of Rebel forces against black troops, including mass murder.

Brigadier General Edward Ferrero (in the field with staff) commanded a brigade of black soldiers consisting of several Camp William Penn regiments, including those at the Battle of Crater in Virginia, where members of the 43rd USCT were involved in very intense combat. *Courtesy of the Library of Congress.*

Commanded by Colonel Stephen B. Yeoman, other top officers of the 43rd were Lieutenant Colonel H. Seymour Hall and Major Horace Bumstead (Bates 1871, 1081), the future president of Atlanta College (today Clark Atlanta University) and responsible for hiring the preeminent black scholar W.E.B. DuBois there as a researcher and professor following the war.

In fact, the 43rd was soon destined to become part of Brigadier General Edward Ferrero's Ninth Corps campaign from the Rapidan River to the James River from May 1 through June 12, 1864, despite Annapolis, Maryland, being designated the brigade's "assembly point" on March 14th:

> The far-flung black division taking shape under Brigadier General Edward Ferrero consisted of five full regiments and a sixth partial one. Three of the five (the 19th, 30th, and 39th USCT) had been recruited in Maryland; the fourth (27th USCT) came from Ohio, and the fifth (43rd USCT) from Pennsylvania. Joining these was a detachment from the 30th Regiment Connecticut Infantry (Colored). (Trudeau 1998, 206)

Just seven companies full when ordered to Annapolis that April, the 43rd "marched into Philadelphia, boarded a vessel bound for Baltimore, and from there sailed to the assembly point," likely anticipating action:

> "We moved off the boat," Sergeant John C. Brock told the readers of Philadelphia's Christian Recorder, "and we found ourselves on the soil of a state which was once under the despotic sway of slavery, but which we soon hope shall never more allow human bondage to prevail on its borders. After we reached the town, we took up the line of march for our camp, which is about four miles from town. We found the road, as we went out, lined with tents and soldiers, all of which cheered us as we passed. When we got to our camping ground, we found a great many colored troops there." (207)

On April 18, 1864, six companies of the 43rd, "the only ones then organized, were ordered, under command of Lieutenant Colonel Hall, to Annapolis, Maryland, where

Apparently General Ferrero had a close-knit staff, evident by this image of them proudly posing on these stairs together. *Courtesy of the Library of Congress.*

they were assigned to the First Brigade, Fourth Division, of the Ninth Corps." Several days later, "the corps moved for the front, and in its march through Washington, these colored troops attracted special attention," since they were to be assigned to the prestigious Army of the Potomac (Bates 1871, 1081).

In Washington, they would soon be scrutinized under the probing eyes of two of the greatest Americans in U.S. history, the President of the United States, Abraham Lincoln, and a future literary icon, Walt Whitman, in Washington, DC:

> When the Ninth Corps was at last ready to join the Army of the Potomac near Brandy Station, Virginia, it was decided that the men would parade through Washington en route. Captain Rogall noted that the troops that left Annapolis on April 24 [1864] endured a "long hard march, raining, sleeping in wet, nothing to eat." Nevertheless, on the morning of April 26, the Ninth Corps was encamped on the outskirts of Washington, where the men scraped the mud from their uniforms, shined their buttons, blacked their shoes, and polished their weapons.
>
> The corps formed up at about 11:00 a.m. to begin a slow march down New York Avenue toward the heart of the city. The dense columns pressed on until they reached Fourteenth Street, where a halt was called to allow the long procession to close up. Then the men made the turn south to march past Willard's Hotel. Waiting on a second floor balcony to review the troops was a small crowd of notables, including the sideburned Burnside and President Abraham Lincoln. (Trudeau 1998, 207)

It was an incredible, almost surrealistic moment, since these were actually "the first black troops that Lincoln had ever formally reviewed" (ibid.), wrote Trudeau. The nationwide press did not miss out on such a tremendous historic development:

> Charles Coffin, a reporter for the *Boston Journal*, described the moment as one of "sublime spectacle." "Accoutered, as we were, with a full complement of clothing, etc., and the day being very warm, the march from outside the city until across Long Bridge, without a stop and with cadenced step, was very trying," recalled Captain James H. Rickard of the 19th USCT, "but not a man left the ranks until the bridge was passed."

Walt Whitman, the great American poet, watched the 43rd USCT on parade in Washington, DC. *Courtesy of the Library of Congress.*

Standing across from Willard's was a newspaperman turned hospital attendant named Walt Whitman. The forty-four-year-old poet had come down to watch the procession in hopes of seeing his brother, George, in the 51st New York. Lincoln was not wearing a hat, and Whitman thought it odd for the President to have his head uncovered as the black regiments marched below. (207-208)

However, the president certainly noted the splendiferous giddiness of the black troops as they marched by, expressing their utter delight with unanticipated and boisterous admiration for the so-called "Great Emancipator." The moment was electrifying, wrote Trudeau:

> According to Coffin, the President acknowledged the African American soldiers with "dignified kindness and courtesy." But the discipline of only a few weeks was not enough to hold the former slaves in line as they recognized the man who had issued the Emancipation Proclamation. "They swing their caps, clap their hands and shout their joy," Coffin wrote. "Long, loud and jubilant are the rejoicings of these redeemed sons of Africa." (208)

And the 43rd USCT, the last regiment in the glorious parade, was especially impressive, according to its proud commander, Colonel H. Seymour Hall:

> "My regiment was the very last in the corps," recalled Lieutenant Colonel H. Seymour Hall of the 43rd USCT. "The constant battalion drill that I had given them the four weeks that I had been in command, and their excellence in the manual of arms, made them appear like veteran soldiers, and the crowd of spectators gave us loud and prolonged applause." (ibid.)

The *Boston Journal* reporter, Coffin, according to Trudeau, captured the essence of the day, noting he "was not unaware of the irony of "brigades which never have been in battle, for the first time shouldering arms for their country; who till a year ago never had a country, who even now are not American citizens, who are disfranchised – yet they are going out to fight for the flag!" (ibid.) It wouldn't be long before the issue of not having combat experience would become convincingly moot, as the 43rd and other black regiments faced the enemy at nearby Manassas Junction in Virginia:

> At Manassas Junction, the command halted for a few days; but when the army under General Grant, encountered the enemy in the Wilderness, it was hurried forward, to his support, and performed excellent service on that desperately contested field. Lieutenant Charles Wickware [of the 43rd USCT] was severely wounded on the second day of the battle, losing an arm. (Bates 1871, 1081)

Although Bates noted that Wickware would survive his terrible injury and be mustered out following the war on October 20, 1865, with the rest of his company (1087), rest was not on the immediate horizon for the brigade and other regiments of the Ninth Corps. Next, they'd play a "supporting role" in early May when the Army of the Potomac engaged

General Robert E. Lee's Army of Northern Virginia just west of Fredericksburg. They were part of the "first Brigade, led by Colonel Joshua K. Sigfried," consisting of the 27ᵗʰ, 30ᵗʰ, and 39ᵗʰ (Trudeau 1998, 209). In fact, Lieutenant George H. Walcott of the 30ᵗʰ USCT described the activities:

> We left Manassas Junction, May 4; marched until one o'clock that night; started again next morning, and marched until nine at night; halted until two o'clock [that morning] [...], then formed again. Crossed Germanna Ford [entering the Wilderness] at eight o'clock a.m. Friday, 6ᵗʰ. Immediately upon crossing were ordered to quickly reinforce [Maj.] Gen. [John] Sedgwick (Sixth Corps), who was hard pressed. We marched up lively, the men singing. It was a frightfully hot march through the woods. It amounted to nothing but to tire us out, for we were ordered back again to the ford. We halted until eleven o'clock at night, when orders came to advance. Passed the entire Sixth Corps; marched up a hill, and formed line of battle [...]. About five o'clock [A.M.] the "Rebs" opened on us, and such a roar of artillery, peals of musketry, and bursting of shells cannot be imagined by one who has not heard it. This battle lasted half an hour. Gen. Grant sat before his tent, smoking a cigar, as though nothing unusual was transpiring. There were troops enough in front of us, and we lay still all the while, and did not fire a gun. After the battle we were ordered [to move east] to Chancellorsville. (ibid.)

The Army of the Potomac then began moving toward the Spotsylvania Court House on the evening of May 7ᵗʰ, according to Trudeau. "In entering the Wilderness, U.S. Grant severed nearly all communication and supply lines through Brandy Station, so Meade's army controlled only the land it actually occupied" (210-211). However, as the so-called front moved forward and away from the Rapidan River, "the rear was left vulnerable to hit-and-run attacks; responsibility for defending this quarter was given to Brigadier General Fererro's two black brigades," including the 43ʳᵈ USCT, "augmented by three white cavalry regiments." The black units, noted Trudeau, for the first time in that campaign, would see "combat action" not far from the "Alrich Farm, southeast of Chancellorsville" (211).

The next series of engagements seemed to be just warm-ups for a debacle on the horizon. But before that, the black regiments would get a good taste of Confederate aggression. And the Rebels would certainly feel the responding vigor of the black regiments, including at Piney Branch Church on May 15ᵗʰ and then Chancellorsville, primarily involving the 23ʳᵈ USCT. The 30ᵗʰ USCT then engaged Rebels on May 19ᵗʰ, "a few miles west of Salem Church, outside Fredericksburg." By virtually all accounts, Trudeau said, the soldiers fought very bravely and won praise from officers and soldiers in the field (ibid.). Five days later the brigades were on the march again:

> The Federal army commenced marching south from Spotsylvania beginning on May 20 [1864]. Lee's men countered in a series of engagements along the North Anna River from May 23 to May 26, and then the sidestepping continued, leading to some large-scale fighting at Cold Harbor, Virginia, on June 1 and 3. Ironically, even as the daily toll of this bloody combat began to drain the morale

and fighting ability of Grant's white soldiers, his black troops were finding increased validation for their participation. Writing to the *Christian Recorder* from Hanover, Virginia, Sergeant John C. Brock of the 43rd USCT explained: "We have been instrumental in liberating some five hundred of our sisters and brothers from the accursed yoke of human bondage [...]. As several of them remarked to me, it seemed to them like heaven, so greatly did they realize the difference between slavery and freedom [...].

The slaves tell us that they have been praying for these blessed days for a long time, but now their eyes witness their salvation from that dreadful calamity, slavery, and, what was more than they expected, by their own brethren in arms. What a glorious prospect it is to behold this glorious Army of black men as they march with martial tread over the sacred soil of Virginia!" (ibid.)

A reporter for the *Philadelphia Press* asserted that the African American soldiers "in the Overland Campaign 'were invariably selected to bring up the rear of the Army of the Potomac, because of their known disinclination for straggling.' Yet a glance through the Regimental Order Book of the 43rd USCT suggests that the black regiments may have been no better or worse in this regard than their white counterparts." Still, Trudeau wrote, Colonel Sigfried's headquarters issued orders on May 24th "exhorting his to ensure that the 'troops in their commands do not straggle on the march,' while on May 26, Brigadier General Ferrero railed against the 'frequent acts of vandalism [...] perpetuated by stragglers and followers of this army.'" (213)

The 43rd's six companies, during the Wilderness campaign, "moved with the Ninth Corps, and proved by their steadiness and intrepidity their title to trust." By June 6, 1864, company G of the 43rd, "which had been recruited at Camp William Penn, joined the battalion at the front," and then was assigned to "fatigue duty, in erecting fortifications and covered ways, under an almost constant fire of the enemy" (Bates 1871, 1081).

James H. Harden, who started off as a private with the 43rd USCT, described the regiment's assignments and his promotions in a letter to *The Christian Recorder* dated December 17, 1864:

> For the Christian Recorder. LETTER FROM THE FRONT.
> Camp between Richmond and Petersburg, Va., December 3d, 1864.
> MR. EDITOR: – I seat myself, for the first time, to write a few lines to be published in your paper. I, having enlisted as a private in the 43rd Regiment, U.S.C.T., on the 14th day of March last, was promoted to 2d Sergeant of Co. C, of which the Rev. John R.V. Morgan is the Orderly Sergeant. I held that position until the 1st of April, when I was appointed Quarter-master Sergeant of the regiment, which position I still hold. I remained at Camp William Penn until the 11th of July, when three companies of the 43d, and part of the 45th regiment [the next group to be organized at Camp William Penn] were ordered to Baltimore, to drive the rebels from the railroad between Baltimore and Washington. After arriving at Baltimore, we were ordered to Washington; from thence to Camp Casey, on the other side of the river, opposite Washington. We remained there until the 1st of

August, when the three companies, namely, H, I, and K, left for City Point, Va. We arrived there on the 3d, and marched to the front of Petersburg, and remained there until the morning of the 26th of last month, (November,) when we struck tents and marched across the Appomattox river, near Bermuda Hundred, where we are now encamped. We are constantly under the fire of the enemy, who shell our camp nearly every day. There has been some few wounded in our regiment, since we have been here, but no one killed as far as I can ascertain. There was one poor fellow soldier, belonging to the 23d regiment, which is in our brigade, struck in the head by a bullet, which caused his death. The next morning, I saw some four or five men of his company digging a grave, and I inquired after him, and was told that he was dead, and that he was to be buried there. After the grave was finished, his body was borne by some of his comrades to its resting place, and laid in the grave. His clothing formed his shroud, and his blanket the coffin. The chaplain then made some few remarks, and prayed over the grave where the remains were laid, after which he was covered with the earth by some of his comrades.[1]

Harden, obviously quite sensitive about his wounded comrades and the deaths of others in various regiments, probably was quite worried about the day when his own regiment would receive casualties. He vividly describes his own close call:

The same day, another man of the same regiment [23rd USCT] was struck by a shell, which [s]hattered his thigh to pieces. Another man was struck by a shell, which cut him in two. How will their families and friends [feel], when they receive the sad tidings of their husbands, fathers, brothers, or sons, or whatever relation they may be, who have fallen in behalf of our glorious Union, and their fellow comrades in the South? I had a very narrow escape myself, the other day. Commissary Sergeant John C. Brock and myself were standing together, and had just finished issuing rations, when a shell came hissing over us and bursted. We started and ran a few yards, and I fell to the ground, and the pieces flew all around us. One piece struck an old log, which was lying on the ground where we were standing, and glanced off and cut through the cooks' tent, striking a glass bottle, smashing it, and then struck the upright pole that holds the tent up, which stopped its progress. I thank God that he has spared my life so far, and still hope to see the city of brotherly love once more [...]. Your obedient servant, JAMES H. HARDEN, Quarter-master Sergeant of the 43rd Regiment, U.S.C.T. – P.S. – People having friends here, will direct letters – 43d Regiment U.S.C.T., Gen. Ferrero's Division of Colored Troops, Bermuda Hundred, Va.[2]

Before long, the 43rd and other black regiments were on the front at Petersburg and involved in intense manual labor:

The work was particularly hard for the black soldiers of Brigadier General Edward Ferrero's Ninth Corps division. "We have been marching for the last two weeks from one part to another along the front," Sergeant John C. Brock of the 43rd USCT wrote on July 16, [1864].

Engaged in picket and fatigue duty. Our division has built two immense forts […]. Sometimes they were in the trenches, in very dangerous places, the bullets whistling over and among our troops all day and all night long, while the men were engaged in digging […]. But notwithstanding all these dangers, the boys shoulder their shovels and picks merrily every day, and go out front to the trenches, ready and willing to do every thing in their power that will lead to the capture and overthrow of the rebel stronghold. (Trudeau 1998, 229)

The location was near "a Confederate strongpoint known as Elliott's Salient." Primarily utilizing the manpower of the black regiments, Union troops "dug in and soon established a line of earthworks not four hundred feet from the Rebel defenses – closer together than any other points in the Union and Confederate trenches." But the Confederate position seemed to be impregnable, to the degree that Union forces began to contrive a very peculiar plan. "It happened that the soldiers in the first Federal unit assigned to duty there, the 48th Pennsylvania, had been recruited among the coal miners of Schuylkill County, and the man commanding the regiment, Lieutenant Colonel Henry Pleasants, was a mining engineer in civilian life." According to Trudeau, the bizarre "idea of tunneling under the enemy's fort and blowing it up seems to have occurred simultaneously to the rank and file of the 48th and to several key officers in the regiment's brigade and division" (229-230). Oddly enough, the plan soon began to take shape.

After all, despite the sheer bodacious risk, if the plan worked, it would have been a spectacular success and "promised glittering possibilities" that might lead to the shelling of Petersburg. The nearby "Jerusalem Plank Road ran along a slight ridge roughly parallel to the line of works and only a few hundred yards behind Elliott's Salient," which was the Confederate stronghold. So, "once Federal troops reached that concourse, a quick march would take them to Cemetery Hill in Blandford, where their cannon would dominate Petersburg and the rear of the Confederate front lines" (230).

Union forces, including the 43rd and other black regiments, earnestly began digging "into the face of a sheltered ravine about a hundred feet behind the Union line." These included soldiers of the 48th, who "slowly gouged their way through the red clay soil." Although Major General Ambrose Burnside very strongly approved of the plan, there was "only lukewarm approval from the man heading the Army of the Potomac, Major General George G. Meade." In fact, Meade's staff even "refused to provide" the "proper tools and measuring instruments" to implement the plan most effectively (ibid.). Still, the plan went forward, according to Trudeau:

Pleasants and his men nonetheless managed to make remarkable progress. A way was found surreptitiously to dispose of the excavated dirt; shoring timbers were produced at an abandoned sawmill reactivated by the regiment; specialized digging tools were improvised or borrowed; and the problem of ventilation within the mine was solved with a simple chimney system that exchanged bad air for good. (230)

Less than a month later, by July 17th the men had dug a tunnel running about 510 feet that reached the Confederate salient. Then the "work was temporarily halted while an examination was undertaken to determine if Confederate countermines posed any danger." Once the threat had been ruled out, the Union forces continued digging, constructing "a pair of lateral galleries" that ran "parallel to the enemy line, each stretching an additional thirty-seven to thirty-eight feet." The Union Pennsylvania coal mining experts then "began to pack these galleries with four tons of gunpowder" (230-231).

General Burnside, contemplating the military execution of the plan, believed that black troops at this point were better suited for the operation, noting that they had performed "very honorably" when assigned to "outposts of the army." His rationale was backed by General Ferrero and "all of his officers," according to Burnside, who'd later testify to a Congressional Committee regarding the explosive conflagration and outright slaughter about to occur (231).

The plan, according to Ferrero's future testimony, was "to make an assault at the moment of the explosion of the mine," advancing "one brigade, which was to be the leading brigade, then divide it in two parts, one portion to go to the right and sweep the enemy's lines in that direction, and the other portion to go down the left and seep the lines in that direction." Another contingent would "march forward in column, and carry the crest of Cemetery Hill" (ibid.).

As initially planned, the 43ʳᵈ USCT of Camp William Penn would be among the first regiments, consisting of African American troops, to lead the assault. That was despite questions concerning if the regiments had been adequately drilled for the endeavor:

> Colonel Joshua K. Sigfried, whose first Brigade (27th, 30th, 39th, and 43ʳᵈ USCT) would lead the attack, recalled that beginning in early July [1864], his men were "daily drilled from two to three hours with a special view of making the assault when the mine should be exploded." His recollection was seconded by statements from officers in three of the brigade's four regiments. Although the commander of the Second Brigade (19th, 23ʳᵈ, 28th, 29th, and 31ˢᵗ USCT), Colonel Henry G. Thomas, likewise avowed that his men "drilled certain movements to be executed in going and occupying the crest," no similar independent confirmation exists for his statement; in fact, Captain R.K. Beecham, in the 23ʳᵈ USCT, would later declare, "I am prepared to say from actual knowledge derived from personal experience with the Fourth Division that the only duty assigned to the said division for more than a month before the battle of the Mine was work upon our trenches and fortifications. The Fourth Division during all that time was drilled especially in the use of pick and shovel, and in no other manner." Against this, however, is the word of an officer in the 19th USCT that his colleagues "had expected we were to lead the assault, and had been for several weeks drilling our men with this idea in view, particular attention being paid to charging." It may be that since the most critical maneuvers would be required only of the First Brigade, Sigfried's men underwent special training, while Thomas's did not; it is also possible that since the movements to be made by Thomas's men were standard ones, the officers who carried out the drills never noticed anything out of the ordinary. (232)

Nevertheless, wrote Trudeau, the Union commanders began to squabble about the initial plans of the black troops leading the attack:

After arguing with Meade, who promised to lay the entire matter before General Grant, Burnside went back to his own headquarters to wait for an answer. By now the time for exploding the gunpowder had been set at 3:30 a.m. July 30, so the clock was ticking. At midday on July 29, Burnside convened the three commanders of his white divisions to go over their roles in the forthcoming attack. Still assuming that his original plan was in effect, he did not summon Brigadier General Ferrero, who already knew what to do. Hardly had Burnside begun the briefing, however, when there was a knock on his tent pole announcing the arrival of General Meade and members of his staff. General Grant had sustained Meade's decision, Burnside was told: the black troops were not to lead the attack. Having dropped that bombshell, Meade and company departed. (ibid.)

Colonel H. Seymour Hall of the 43rd later recalled that the change in plans came as a surprise, and nearly at the last minute. Late on July 29th, he said, his division had already begun to take position "to the left of the entrance to the covered way leading out to our most advanced line in front of the mined salient of the enemy, and with my regiment in advance, formed [...] in readiness to lead the assault." Hall continued: "No hint of change of plans had reached me and General Ferrero does not state when he was informed of it [...]." Apparently, though, others were notified as the deadline approached. "The commander of our other brigade [Thomas] says that he was not informed of any change till near midnight of July 29th, and as his [...] officers were apparently in quiet sleep, they were not aroused to be informed of what would do them no service. I did not know of any change till the morning of July 30th" (235).

However, before that fateful morning, "after dark on July 29, the Ninth Corps troops began to file into their jump-off positions." A division of the Tenth Corps joined "as a reserve." Meanwhile, the white troops of Burnside amassed in the ditches near the "jump-off line, filling the communications passages, or covered ways, leading forward, while the black troops massed on the open hillside below the ruins of the Taylor House, not far from an entranceway to the forward trenches." The darkness was overwhelming. The blackness was punctuated with the flashes of rifles, noted Lieutenant Freeman S. Bowley of the 30th USCT, likely situated not far from the troops of the 43rd USCT. And although bullets could be heard whizzing overhead, the officer said that most of the regiment fell quickly asleep due to exhaustion. Other black soldiers could be seen praying, including Sergeant Joseph H. Payne of the 27th USCT: "Many professors [of religion] appeared to be greatly stirred up [...] while sinners seemed to be deeply touched and aroused to a sense of their danger and duty. Our prayer meeting was short but not without good and lasting impressions being made upon the hearts and minds of many" (235-236).

And the prayers were certainly needed for the calamity about to unfold, as not long before sun-up "on the morning of the 30th of July, Lieutenant Colonel Hall led his command through the covered way, up to the mouth of the mine which had been excavated on the Ninth Corps front, and was that morning to be sprung," with Union forces anxious as ever. "The lot fell to Ledlie's Division to lead in the charge, though General Burnside had selected the Colored Division for that duty, but had been overruled in his choice," (Bates 1871, 1081) surely a great disappointment to many of the black soldiers:

The time appointed for the mine explosion – 3:30 a.m. – came and went. Soon it was 4:00 a.m., then 4:30, and still there was only silence. Near the mine entrance, Lieutenant Colonel Pleasants and his tunnel team waited, the tension mounting sharply until, at about 4:15 a.m., someone volunteered to go in and find out what had happened. He quickly returned to report that all three fuse lines had failed at a splice point only a short distance inside the tunnel. Pleasant's man was joined by a second volunteer, and together they relit the fuse and scrambled back out. By now it was about 4:30 a.m.; at a time officially reckoned as 4:44 a.m., the sputtering flame at last reached the four tons of gunpowder packed in the galleries beneath Elliott's Salient. (Trudeau 1998, 236)

The ensuing raucous was nothing less than catastrophic, even dumbfounding the 43rd's Colonel Hall, wrote Trudeau:

Chaplain Garland H. White, an ex-slave himself, was moving among his flock in the 28th USCT when the explosion went off. "Just at this junction the earth began to shake," he wrote afterward, "as though the hand of God intended a reversal of the laws of nature." Colonel Thomas recalled it was a "dull, heavy thud, not at all startling; it was heavy, smothered sound, not nearly so distinct as a musket shot." The experience was more vivid for Captain Warren H. Hurd of the 23rd USCT, who watched in awe as a "large black cloud […] appeared to

The 43rd USCT would have charged similar to these black soldiers depicted at the Battle of the Crater, where many of those warriors were slaughtered by Rebels after being ambushed in a massive hole in the earth dynamited by Union forces. *Courtesy of the Library of Congress.*

rise out of the ground." Lieutenant Bowley, 30th USCT, remembered first a "jar of the earth under our feet," followed by a "terrible rumbling." Colonel Hall of the 43rd USCT watched in openmouthed astonishment as the cloud "burst into innumerable fragments and fell in a confused inextricable mass of earth, muskets, cannon, men, an awful debris." (236-237)

The explosion site itself was a horrendous marvel: "Where there had lately been a redoubt and trenches holding three hundred men, four cannon, and thirty gunners, there was now only a great smoking cavity, 150 to 200 feet long, sixty feet wide, and some thirty feet deep" (Trudeau 1998, 237). Union forces wasted no time with a follow-up assault:

> Cued by the explosion, 110 Federal cannon and fifty four mortars opened fire along nearly two miles of trench lines. This cannonade, declared Lieutenant Bowley, 'was one of the most terrific of the war.' Captain James Rickard of the 19th USCT was certain that it was this artillery barrage that 'made the ground tremble as by an earthquake,' a shaking that woke up the sound-sleeping Lieutenant Stinson. It all proved too much for Private Miles Keyes of the 28th USCT, or so thought his comrades: [its] these events that they would later attribute [to] Keye's contraction of an 'unsoundness of mind' that would cause him to end his days in a lunatic asylum near Cincinnati. (237-238)

Private Prestley Dorsey, in Co. H of the 43rd and born about 1840 in Howard County, Maryland, remembered the debacle long after the war, according to descendants, and was likely the most memorable of his combat experiences, including the Virginia battles of Hatcher's Run and the Rapidan campaign (Scott 2008, 125). Standing 5 feet, 8 inches, medical records indicate that Dorsey had "hazel eyes, dark hair, a 'yellow' complexion" and a 'scar on outside of left thigh." It's quite possible that he received during the Battle of the Crater the "severe leg injury and was hospitalized at least twice for various ailments before being mustered out October 20, 1865 in Brownsville, Texas." However, before

leaving service, his Dorsey surname was changed due to a "clerical mistake" to Dawson, a surname that modern descendants use today (*Tracing legacy of a black Civil War soldier* 2005).

And Private Christian Morris, another black soldier of the 43rd, probably was afflicted with a lasting injury during the Battle of the Crater, as well as harboring horrible memories. "In addition to being injured, he suffered from scurvy and rheumatic fever," despite during the war marrying his sweetheart Susan Williams on April 12, 1863,

This rare image of Private Christian Morris of the 43rd USCT in full uniform was likely taken during the war. *Courtesy of Lee Carol Cook.*

Christian Morris of the 43rd USCT remembered the horrible Battle of the Crater long after he was mustered out of the war. He apparently contracted scurvy during the war and suffered from rheumatic fever. He married Susan Williams and the couple had 13 children, with only about a half-dozen living to adulthood. One of his sons, Rev. Joseph Edward Morris, became a well known African Methodist Episcopal preacher and trustee of Wilberforce College, founded by the AME Church. *Courtesy of Lee Carol Cook.*

and having "13 children, including five or six who survived to adulthood. One son, Rev. Joseph Edward Morris, born on November 24, 1866, in Highville, Lancaster County, became an AME preacher and trustee of the black AME college, Wilberforce." Morris would remember that battle until his death "on February 19, 1913, of a cerebral hemorrhage at the Soldiers and Sailors Home in Erie, [Pennsylvania] where he is buried in the veterans' cemetery" (Scott 2008, 113).

Private Gabriel Butler retired to Monessen, Pennsylvania, and likely saw plenty of action during the war. It's also probable that Butler marched with his regiment in President Lincoln's second inauguration parade in March 1865 after Lincoln took office for a second time.

Captain Jesse Wilkinson of Company A, despite his combat experience with the 18th Connecticut, must have been awestruck by the incredible blast. He was likely in the thick of things, suffering a bayonet wound in his left arm on July 30th and then surviving a musket

ball wound in his left side days later on August 9th "in the trenches before Petersburg." Officers senior to Wilkinson were also injured, including the commander of the regiment, Col. H. Seymour Hall, who suffered wounds described as serious on July 30th, as well as two of his adjutants, James O'Brien and James W. Steele.[3]

Private Gabriel Butler survived the war, and was apparently quite active while living in Monessen, Pennsylvania. He is dressed as a band leader and living in or visiting an area of town that seems reasonably prosperous. *Courtesy of Lee Carol Cook.*

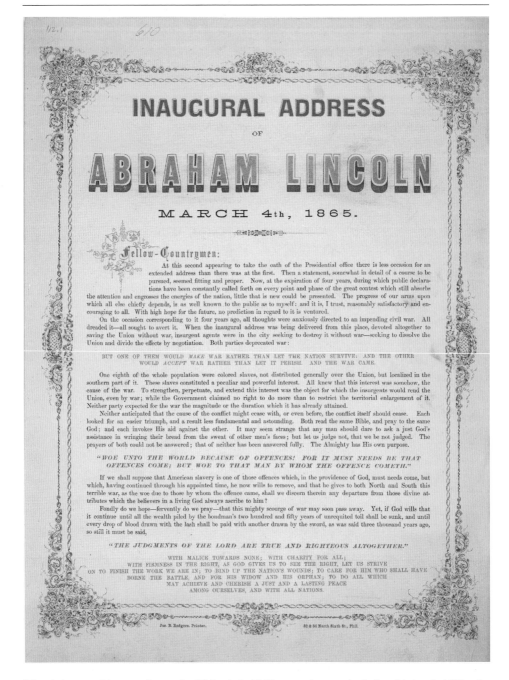

Lincoln's second inaugural speech of March 4, 1865, came just weeks before his tragic killing by John Wilkes Booth, who was in the crowd listening with other conspirators that day. *Courtesy of the Library of Congress.*

One of the officers who seemed to come through the debacle relatively unscathed was Captain John D. Brown, commanding Company B, and who was actually appointed by the office of the Secretary of War, Edwin M. Stanton. Previously serving as a private with the 18th Conn. Infantry Volunteers, he took command of the company just after being mustered in March 18, 1864. Indeed, records indicate that he and his company actually charged the mine area "before Petersburg" on July 30th. The soldiers also skirmished at Hatcher's Run, VA, a few months later, on October 27, 1864.[4]

Meanwhile, the "consternation created by the horrors of the explosion, enabled Ledlie's Division to advance to, and [temporarily] take shelter in the crater, without serious loss." (Bates 1871, 1081) However, that progression would not last long:

> The divisions of Potter and Wilcox were soon ordered up to its support; and finally, when the enemy had fully recovered from his fright, had brought supports to cover the threatened point, and was fully prepared to repel further assaults, the Colored Division was ordered to advance. It was a forlorn hope; but the division moved gallantly forward, in the face of a decimating fire, and passing to the right of the crater, charged towards the crest beyond. Here so deadly was the fire of infantry and artillery which it met, that it was soon swept back in disorder amongst the *debris* of the demolished fort, though it succeeded in bringing in some prisoners, Captain Albert D. Wright, taking, with his own hands, a rebel battle-flag. Little protection was afforded even here, the enemy soon getting the range, and mercilessly slaughtering the helpless victims huddled together. (1081-1082)

The scene and situation was apparently a bit too much for even General Ledlie, especially after he had ordered his two brigades to advance into the withering Confederate bullets:

> About five minutes after the debris stopped raining down, General Ledlie ordered the two brigades of his division to advance, then retired to a nearby aid station for a drink. There he would remain, save for an occasional foray to observe what was happening, for the rest of the battle. Neither of his brigades seems to have been apprised of Burnside's instructions to press toward Cemetery Hill; both stopped in or alongside the great pit, where they began to take cover from the already intense Confederate defensive fire. More men piled in from behind as two other white divisions dutifully pressed forward. Two brigades of Willcox's division tried to adhere to the plan by swinging left around the crater to secure one of the shoulders of the penetration; they enjoyed some success before the increasingly murderous Rebel rifle and cannon fire drove them to ground. When Potter's division went in on the right, it got mixed in with some of Ledlie's men and shot up by the Confederates who tenaciously held the trenches on the flank. (Trudeau 1998, 238)

Meanwhile the black soldiers, including the 43rd, waited for the order to advance as they witnessed wounded white Union soldiers returning, some ushering in terrified captured Rebels. Trudeau noted:

> All of this took perhaps ninety minutes. Back where the black troops were waiting for the order to advance, the soldiers got ready. "The men were ordered to pile their knapsacks, and while doing so we heard the cheers of the second assaulting party, and the brisk musketry fire told us that they were meeting with a desperate resistance," recollected Lieutenant Bowley. Chaplain White was suddenly besieged by individuals asking him to write their loved ones for them and begging him "when pay-day comes, if it ever does come, [to] send what money is due [home].'"
>
> Even as the black troops anxiously prepared to enter the covered way, squads of wounded white Union soldiers and captured Confederates began to stumble back through their ranks. "The latter were terribly frightened at the site [*sic*] of the colored soldiers, and besought their white guards 'not to let the niggers bayonet them,'" noted Lieutenant Bowley. "They could not be pacified, until a colored corporal gave a severely wounded rebel a drink of water from his canteen, and this little act seemed to instantly restore confidence among them." There were some last-minute exhortations by officers to their men, with the colonels commanding the 28th and 29th USCT each vowing to lead their units into Petersburg this day. (238-239)

The black troops then moved gallantly forward, with the awaiting Rebels agitated and determined to destroy as they saw the flag-bearing USCT regiments coming their way. And destroy they did:

> Said Colonel Bates of the 30th, "The appearance of the regimental colors seemed to be the signal for the enemy's batteries, and it was volley after volley of canister and shrapnel they gave us." "Down went our flag," recalled Lieutenant Bowley, "the color-sergeant staining the stars and stripes with his blood. A grape-shot had torn his head in pieces." Behind the 30th, the rest of the brigade spilled into the killing ground – first the 43rd, then the 39th, and finally the 27th USCT. "I will remember the 27th marching in double quick up that approach to the crater and through it, stepping over our dead and wounded,' wrote Captain Matthew R. Mitchell. Captain Albert Rogall of the 27th described the enemy fire 'tearing the ground in our midst." (240)

Yet, despite the above account, the military historian Bates described the black troops with the 43rd USCT in the thick of the action as "fearlessly" trying to advance, regardless of the heart-breaking setbacks. "The Forty-third Colored Troops moved over the lip of the crater and engaged the enemy in close combat, taking two stands of colors and 200 prisoners, for the only Union success of the day" (Quarles 1953, 304):

A charge made upon them by the enemy, was bloodily repulsed; but it was madness to attempt to hold the position, and almost certain destruction to attempt to go back, every inch of the ground being raked by the enemy's concentric fire. Nevertheless, the attempt to retire must be made. By skillful maneouvres [*sic*] along the Union line, the enemy's attention was for a moment attracted from the fatal ground, and taking advantage of this, large numbers escaped. "In this battle," says Chaplain J. M. Mickley, "it would be difficult to enumerate particular cases of great bravery, where all seemed to vie with each other in the brilliancy and gallantry of their achievements." Colored non-commissioned officers fearlessly took the command after their officers had been killed, or borne severely wounded from the field, and led on the attack to the close. As each brave color-bearer was shot down, another, and another would grasp the National emblem, all riddled with balls, and plant it further on the enemy's line. In this terrific engagement, this battalion of the Forty-third had its colors almost entirely cut up by the fire, and the color staffs splintered and broken. (Bates 1871, 1082)

The soldiers and officers of the 43ʳᵈ USCT continued to fight valiantly, according to several accounts, as "horror was piled upon horror" (Trudeau 1998, 246):

Colonel Bates tried to lead his men around to the right of the crater, but Confederate fire pressed the head of his column into the pit. "Push down the line," Bates called out to Captain David E. Proctor, in charge of the leading company. Proctor and his men rushed through and out the other side, where they formed a rough line of battle. Behind them, the 43ʳᵈ USCT also stumbled into the smoking hole, but Lieutenant Colonel Hall saw at once that the mob inside would make it impossible for his unit to follow the 30ᵗʰ. Although the enemy still held trenches close to the right, Hall spotted a partially sheltered route of approach and personally led his men "along the front of the enemy's intrenchments, so close that some of my officers and men were wounded by the bayonets, others burned by the powder flashes of the foe." Once his regiment was aligned, Hall ordered a charge that plunged his black soldiers into hand-to-hand combat. "The men killed numbers of the enemy in spite of the efforts of their officers to restrain them," Hall wrote, "and we took prisoners in these intrenchments." (The colonel himself received a severe wound that would knock him out of action and cost him his right arm.) The 43ʳᵈ linked up with the 30ᵗʰ on the outside slope of the crater, and the two were then joined by the remaining two regiments of the brigade – or rather, what was left of them, following their deadly passage across no-man's-land and through the disorderly crowd in the pit. (240-241)

As terrible as the situation was, Trudeau wrote, the worst was yet to come – the merciless, gruesome slaughter and murder of the black soldiers:

The situation facing these officers and men was a pure nightmare. "The enemy's works on this part of the line was a perfect honeycomb of bomb proofs, trenches, covered ways, sleeping holes, and little alleys running in every direction, and in each hole there appeared one or more rebel soldiers, come ready to "kill the niggers when they came in view and some praying for mercy," said Bates. For the next minutes, the black soldiers were occupied with the grim task of clearing out the nearest network of trenches and holes. (241)

And as the black soldiers began to clear some of the hard-held ground, even pouring into the crater to take on the Rebels, the Confederate forces rebounded and began to encircle most of the ridge above the massive hole now harboring too many USCT soldiers. The Confederate firing was relentless and devastating. "Lieutenant Bowley of the 30th USCT watched in horror as the black battle lines bent under the onslaught, then shattered. 'For a moment the men moved backward, to the left, firing as they retreated; then the enemy charged with a yell, and poured a volley into our very faces. Instantly, the whole body broke, went over the breastworks toward the Union line, or ran down the trenches towards the crater.'" Many of the soldiers simply panicked, according to Trudeau. "This was the end of Ferrero's division as a cohesive fighting force" (243).

And as if matters couldn't get any worse, continued Trudeau, they certainly did:

> By 10:00 a.m., the entire Union breakthrough had been reduced to about a thousand disorganized men, both black and white, now trapped in the crater or next to it. For the moment, the Confederates (whose fierce counterattacks had cost them dearly) lacked sufficient manpower to finish things off, but even as they built up strength for that purpose, they subjected the crater to a pitiless barrage of mortar and artillery shells, while riflemen targeted anyone who showed himself or tried to run back to the Union lines.
>
> Lieutenant Bowley of the 30th USCT was among those who huddled in the crater. He remembered that the "men were dropping thick and fast, most of them shot through the head. Every man that was shot rolled down the steep sides to the bottom, and in places they were piled up four and five deep." During a brief lull in the storm, the desperate Federals built up barricades made of dead bodies. "How we longed for reinforcements," said Captain Hurd of the 23rd USCT. "It did seem too bad [to have] so many thousand of our men within a few hundred yds. of us and no effort made for our relief." (244)

The lack of help would prove to be devastating. That's because by 11 AM all "hope of expanding the assault had dissolved." The ensuing atrocities were almost beyond description and plainly "slaughter," according to John W. Pratt of the 30th USCT: "We say slaughter for we can call it nothing else – nor can any one who was present say truthfully that it was not" (245).

The horrid details were later recalled by Lieutenant Bowley, noted Trudeau:

> The day was fearfully hot; the wounded were crying for water, and the canteens were empty. A few of our troops held a ditch a few feet in front of the crater and were keeping up a brisk fire [...]. The artillery [...] kept up a constant

fire of grape and kept the dirt flying about us. A mortar battery also opened on us, and, after a few shots, they got our range so well that the shells fell directly among us. Many of them did not explode until after they were buried in the earth, and did but little real damage, although the dead men were thrown high in the air; some did not explode at all, but a few burst directly over us, and cut the men down most cruelly. Many of the troops now attempted to make our lines, but, to leave, they had to run up a slope in full view of the enemy, that now surrounded us on three sides; nearly every man who attempted it fell back, riddled with bullets. (ibid.)

Matters got so bad that the white Union forces tragically turned their guns on black comrades, fearing Confederate retribution should they have been caught fighting side-by-side with their darker-hued warriors, Trudeau reported:

> In a bitter proof of the racism prevalent throughout the Union ranks, a new and terrible cruelty was inflicted on the black troops caught in the disaster. "It was believed among the whites that the enemy would give no quarter to negroes, or to the whites taken with them, and so to shut up with blacks in the crater was equal to a doom of death," recalled a New York soldier who was there. "It has been positively asserted that white men bayoneted blacks who fell back into the crater. This was in order to preserve the whites from Confederate vengeance. Men boasted in my presence that blacks had thus been disposed of, particularly when the Confederates came up." (ibid.)

But some Union white officers did admit their leadership of black troops when they were captured, often dooming them to death or tremendous hardships in a Confederate prison. Other white officers "tore off their unit insignias and denied having any association with them" (247).

By 2 p.m. the Rebels gathered "enough troops to storm the crater," a development that would have horrific consequences. Rebel forces shot into the crater at the black troops and white officers desperate for any kind of shelter. Much of the pit's bottom was crimson with white and black blood. Even those blacks taken prisoner were unmercifully executed, often begging for their lives:

> Horror was piled upon horror. Another Rebel never forgot the sight of a black sergeant begging for his life before two Confederate soldiers, one of whom was beating the man with his ramrod, and the other trying to get a shot at him. "The man with the gun fired it at the negro, but did not seem to seriously injure him, as he only clapped his hand to his hip where he appeared to have been shot, and continued to beg for his life. The man with the ramrod continued to strike the negro therewith, whilst the fellow with the gun deliberately reloaded it, placing its muzzle closer against the stomach of the poor negro, fired, at which the latter fell limp and lifeless at the feet of the two Confederates." Another Southerner avowed that all the blacks would have been killed "had it not been for gen. Mahone who beg our men to Spare them." (246)

The few blacks taken prisoner often faced more horrors that ultimately were followed by death in a deplorable and filthy Confederate prison. However a few survived, according to Trudeau, including "Private James Meyers of the 43ʳᵈ USCT, who according to his military records was 'one of the burial party and crossed the lines and was taken prisoner, returned to Co. Apr. 21/65, having been engaged as laborer by Lee's Army up to the surrender'" (249):

> The Confederates' hatred for their black captives was amply demonstrated when the prisoners were paraded through Petersburg on the day after the mine explosion. The officers and men, remembered a lieutenant from the 43ʳᵈ USCT, "were formed in double file, two officers between four 'niggers'[,] and marched through the principal streets of Petersburg much after the style of a circus." "I was in the third file of officers," recalled Freeman S. Bowley, "and as the head of the column reached the streets of Petersburg we were assailed by a volley of abuse from men, women and children that exceeded anything of the kind that I ever heard." The 43ʳᵈ USCT officer said some of this abuse was along the lines of, "See the white and nigger equality soldiers!" and "Yanks and niggers sleep in the same bed!" A few blacks were forced to march with untreated wounds. "In many cases the negroes were hardly able to walk," testified an officer in a Maine regiment, "and in such case we were ordered to support them." (247-248)

The 43ʳᵈ USCT suffered very heavy casualties during the mine debacle. "Its casualties were one officer [Lieutenant James T. Hayman] killed, ten severely wounded, including the gallant Lieutenant Colonel Hall, who sustained the loss of his right arm, and two taken prisoners, and twenty-eight men killed, ninety-four wounded, and twelve missing," Bates' Pennsylvania military statistics indicate: "It was afterwards discovered that the missing were men rendered helpless by reason of severe wounds, and whom the rebels deliberately put to death on the field by bayoneting" (Bates 1871, 1082).

And again, the horrible battle also took its toll on others of the 43ʳᵈ, including line officers and recruits of Company A. First Lt. James Hayman was reportedly "killed in action" on July 30ᵗʰ "before Petersburg," as well as black officers such as Sergeant Horace Adams, 30 years old and described as a "laborer" from Richmond, VA, raising the distinct possibility that he was once a slave. Private Barton Airy, 21 years old, described as having "hazel" eyes and "dark" hair, joined Company A after working as a Teamster in Lancaster, PA. He likely died of wounds at the General Hospital on July 31ˢᵗ. However, his 24-year-old brother Milton, a farmer also hailing from Lancaster who had been promoted to the rank of corporal on March 20, 1864, was just wounded during the July 30ᵗʰ battle and discharged on a surgeon's certificate June 22, 1865. Also surviving wounds at the Battle of the Mine was Company A's Lewis Alexander, a Jefferson Parish, Louisiana, cook who had been promoted to corporal. Later in October he served at Hatcher's Run in Virginia and must have impressed his superiors, since he was promoted to sergeant in August 1865. And then there was the survivor William Bundy of Company B, an 18-year-old who was mustered in March 14, 1864, by the Commander of Camp William Penn, Col. Wagner, and then appointed to the musician corps. Participating in the July 30ᵗʰ assault, he was sent to the hospital for an undisclosed reason on August 8, 1864, returning to duty on February

22, 1865. Company H's Private Asu Augborne, age 24 of Montgomery County, Tennessee, apparently survived the battle too, but was killed in action at Smith's Farm, VA, on October 27, 1864.[5]

There were peculiar incidents too, such as when 23-year-old Sylvester Butcher of Company C, a Germantown, PA, lawyer with presumably an excellent education as a black soldier, shot himself "in the fingers" of his right hand on July 31, 1864, one day after the mine explosion. Meanwhile John Castle of Company E, age 35 and a Maryland laborer, just weeks before Christmas on December 2, 1864, wounded himself as he cleaned his gun at Bermuda Hundred, Virginia, exemplifying the common follies of war.[6]

And there were certainly very heartbreaking incidents. Private Joseph Crossman, a 43-year-old farmer from Greene, Maine, participated in the action at Petersburg and the Battle of the Mine and survived. A few weeks later he was sent to the hospital due to an undisclosed illness, returning to duty on October 26, 1864. And although it seemed that he might survive the terrible war, Crossman was "shot through the heart" during a skirmish near Petersburg on October 27, 1864.[7]

In summary, the military historian Bates noted the brave actions of the 43rd USCT, according to an official report's extract:

> The Forty-third regiment, United States Colored troops, charged over the crest of the crater, and right upon the enemy's works, carrying them, capturing a number of prisoners, a rebel battle-flag, and re-capturing a stand of National colors. Lieutenant Colonel Hall, commanding the Forty-third, lost his right arm, while bravely leading his regiment. "Here, on this, as on many other fields during this war, for the sacred cause of our republican liberties, free institutions, and Union, the blood of the Anglo Saxon and the African mingled very freely [...]." (Bates 1871, 1082)

Following the terrible battle and under the command of Major Bumstead, the future president of Atlanta College (later known as Clark-Atlanta University), the 43rd "for nearly three weeks [...] was industriously employed in fatigue duty, on the fortifications and field works, in which it rendered most efficient service." Next, however, joining "the corps, it marched for the Weldon Railroad, and in the action at that point, on the 19th and 20th of August, and at Poplar Grove Church, on the 29th and 30th of September, it was engaged, but fortunately suffered little loss." During "the battle of Hatcher's Run, on the 27th and 28th of October, it held the position of skirmishers in front of the Ninth Corps, and gallantly assisted in repulsing the repeated charges of the enemy. Two lines of breast-works which served an important purpose in the fight, were constructed in the face of a severe fire, by this regiment, for which it was highly commended." In fact, the 43rd "was the last regiment to leave the field, covering the retiring movement. Its loss in the action was one officer, Lieutenant James Roantree, and seven men killed, four officers and eighteen men wounded, and one taken prisoner." The 43rd was next "sent by a forced march, to the Bermuda front, to assist in re-gaining some ground which had been lost. This was successfully accomplished. Nettled by the triumph of the colored troops, the rebels attempted every stratagem to annoy, and gain some advantage over them, massing men and charging, masking their operations by the most incessant firing, by night and by day, for nearly a month." However, the black soldiers, according to Bates, "everywhere met their assailants with equal courage and daring, preserving an unbroken front, answering shot for shot, holding resolutely their ground, and inflicting great slaughter upon the foe" (1083).

As the last year of the war approached (1865), the "Forty-third was […] assigned to the Third Brigade, First Division of the Twenty-fifth Corps. Colonel Yeoman, soon after his appointment as Colonel of this regiment, had been detailed by order of the War Department, as superintendent of recruiting service at Camp Casey, Virginia, where he remained until near the close of November, when he joined his regiment, and assumed command." It was during "an inspection held by the Inspector General of the corps, this regiment acquitted itself so well in every particular, as to call forth a complimentary general order, in which it was mentioned as the best drilled and disciplined in the command" (ibid.). Yet, the regiment's combat duties certainly were not finished:

> On the 24th of January, 1865, the enemy's gunboats proceeded down the James River, to a point in the bend, just below the upper end of the Dutch Gap Canal, with the design of silencing the Union fleet, and capturing City Point, the base of supply for the entire army. The Forty-third was posted on this occasion, along the river bank, from Cox's Landing to Dutch Gap, and when the enemy's boats came within range, it opened so hot a fire upon them, as to prevent the opening of their port-holes. A detachment was also sent across the canal, which skirmished through Farra's Island, to within a short distance of the Howlett House Battery. Until the fall of the rebel Capital, and the victorious entrance of General Weitzel's command, it was actively employed on the front lines. (ibid.)

Similar to other black regiments, the 43rd's courageous combat did not translate to an order to immediately return home. Indeed, more excitement and substantial risks were in the immediate future:

> After the surrender of Lee, it returned to City Point, and on the 30th of May, embarked with other colored troops, for Texas. Upon its arrival, it was posted on the Rio Grande, opposite

Horace Bumstead, a line officer of the 43rd USCT, was destined to teach after the war, become president of Atlanta University, and then hire a promising young black professor, W.E.B. DuBois. The two were instrumental in launching studies that would lead to the establishment of the civil rights' Niagara Movement and the National Association for the Advancement of Colored People (NAACP). *Courtesy of the U.S. Army Military History Institute.*

the city of Matamoras, Mexico. Early in November, it was ordered north, and returning to New Orleans, embarked on the steamer Merrimac, on the 9th, bound for Philadelphia. The boat had not been long out, before it sprung a leak, and it was only by the almost superhuman exertions of officers and men of this regiment, that it was lighted and kept afloat until it could be run upon the bar, at the mouth of the Mississippi. All on board were saved. "After a gratuitous issue of clothing," says Chaplain Mickley, "by order of General Sheridan, to supply, in part, the loss incident to this perilous trip," it embarked on the steamer Costa Rica, arrived at New York, November 26th and was finally discharged at Philadelphia, November 30th, 1885. Its casualties in the service were, officers killed three, wounded eleven, and three discharged by reason of wounds [with] men killed, died of wounds and disease, three hundred and six, and missing, one hundred and ninety-six. (1083-1084)

Following the war, Major Horace Bumstead returned to his native New England, where his parents had been involved in the anti-slavery abolitionist movement. The son of merchant Josiah Freeman Bumstead and Lucy Douglas Willis Bumstead, Major Bumstead had been very well educated at the Boston Latin School and then Yale College, graduating from that Ivy League institution just before the war in 1863. "He later joined the faculty of Atlanta University and served as their second president from 1888-1907," according to documents at Harvard University where his papers are kept (*Horace Bumstead* 2003).

Even before commanding the 43rd USCT, Bumstead was a Congregationalist minister and educator in New England. After mustering out of the 43rd, he'd join "the faculty of Atlanta University in 1875 as an instructor in Natural Science and in 1880 was appointed Professor of Latin." Then, less than a decade later, from "1886-1887 he was asked to serve as Acting President and continued as the second President of the University serving from 1888-1907." He was apparently a very prolific leader, with "much of Bumstead's efforts focused on fundraising." His efforts led to the "physical campus" being "extended and several new buildings constructed. The curriculum was restructured to include kindergarten, grade school, college prep, and college level courses" (ibid.).

W.E.B. DuBois, the great African American scholar, associated with his boss, Horace Bumstead, a former officer of the 43rd USCT, as well as the great writer and poet James Weldon Johnson, who wrote a poem commending Bumstead's commitment to black rights. *Courtesy of the Library of Congress.*

And, perhaps most notably, he hired a young black professor, W.E.B. DuBois, who had just completed a book while based at the University of Pennsylvania, *The Philadelphia Negro*, an epic sociological study of that city's African Americans that became a pillar for Du Bois who, with the support of Bumstead, later formed the NAACP (National Association for the Advancement of Colored People). A portion of the book, in fact, involves the history of Camp William Penn. Apparently friends with some of the top black intellectuals of the time, Bumstead corresponded with the likes of Du Bois, Charles Chestnut, Booker T. Washington, and James Weldon Johnson. (*Horace Bumstead Records* 2009)

Johnson, a renowned writer and poet, penned these eternal words (published in 1930) about the major and his former teacher, entitled, "To Horace Bumstead," with combat symbolism that must have reminded the old soldier of his 43rd USCT Civil War days:

> Have you been sore discouraged in the fight,
> And even sometimes weighted by the thought
> That those with whom and those for whom you fought
> Lagged far behind, or dared but faintly smite?
> And that the opposing forces in their might
> Of blind inertia rendered as for naught
> All that throughout the long years had been wrought,
> And powerless each blow for Truth and Right?
>
> If so, take new and greater courage then,
> And think no more withouten help you stand;
> For sure as God on his eternal throne
> Sits, mindful of the sinful deed of men,
> The awful Sword of Justice in His hand, –
> You shall not, no, you shall not, fight alone.
> (*To Horace Bumstead* 2010)

10

The 45th United States Colored Troops
'The Rebs gave way'

Destined to become the first black regiment to march in a presidential inauguration (President Lincoln's) and help with other African American units to corner Confederate General Lee's forces, the 45th USCT, was shaped at Camp William Penn in the summer of 1864 during the tail-end of administrative setbacks at the facility. With Wagner still in the commander's seat, officers of the 45th included Colonel Ulysses Doubleday, Lieutenant-Colonel Edward Thorn, and Major James T. Bates (Bates 1871, 1106).

At the end of the 45th USCT's tenure at the facility, as well as the ensuing start of the 127th's formation at the facility, there was an era of "unmistakable decline in the Camp William Penn operations" and then some improvement, according to historian Johnson, followed by its ultimate closing, largely due to the deterioration of operations. They were caused by severe social problems that often revolved around charges of white racism and sometimes classism within the black community – actually problems that had erupted even months earlier.

And that was despite several positive camp developments, including "organization of the music band, Brigade Band Number Two" (Johnson 1999, 98): "Led by bandleader Joseph Costley and featuring the talented Ray brothers of Morristown, New Jersey, Brigade Band Number Two established itself as one possessing 'a very efficient organization of Musicians – who are finely equipped, and have an extensive repertory [sic] of music,'" according to a letter that Commander Wagner wrote to his boss, Brigadier General Robert Foster. "In addition to forming a first class military band, a permanent chaplain, the Reverend Reese Evans, was obtained to minister to an increasing number of sick recruits and officers. An evening school, sponsored by the civilian led Supervisory Committee, was established" (98-99).

However, as administrative matters seemed to improve, the 45th USCT apparently received training simultaneously with the 127th USCT, also based at the facility, according to a September 17, 1864, article in *The Christian Recorder* written by an unidentified correspondent (likely the editor of the paper, the Rev. Elisha Weaver) who actually visited the post store and sutler William Still, renowned as the "father of the Underground Rail Road." The visit came about nine months after "the destruction of William Still's sutler concession, in February, 1864 by members of the Twenty-fifth regiment [that] exposed an antagonistic element of class relations within the black community" (99).

And there had certainly been other problems. Johnson wrote:

> Frustrations for the rank and file were exacerbated the following month [in March 1864] when an influential soldier from Kent county, Delaware named George Wells was shot to death by a guard in the prison compound. Within days a further unraveling of the administration's consolidation effort occurred following the death by disease of another recruit who was left in his warm barracks for more than twenty-four hours. The body was removed for burial only after the threat of unspecified action by the troops and file of the Thirty-second regiment. A strong letter of protest was lodged against the regimental surgeon, Charles M. Wright, whose neglect of the matter permitted the calamity to unfold. By early May 1864, the post commander felt it necessary to make his second request for "a permanent camp guard" to keep order among the ranks. (ibid.)

However, the two regiments, in fact, were exceptionally proud and much more upbeat by mid-September during post ceremonies when they received their colors, again designed by David Bowser:

> On last Thursday, 15th inst., the Forty-fifth and One Hundred and Twenty-seventh regiments U.S.C.T. were the recipients of a couple of flags, presented by the Supervisory Committee for recruiting colored troops. About quarter past two o'clock, the two regiments above named and a part of the One Hundred and forty first U.S.C.T. formed in line, and maneuvered around until they were displayed to all the visitors on the ground. In the mean time we visited the Sutler's Department, under the charge of our well-known and esteemed citizen, Mr. William Still, who treated us in such a manner as to leave a lasting impression of his many good qualities upon us. At four o'clock, General Birney, on behalf of the Supervisory Committee, presented a beautiful ensign to the Forty-fifth U.S.C.T. His remarks were well and enthusiastically received. The flag was received by Major Babe, in a few patriotic remarks, after which cheer after cheer [filled] the air. After this, our well-known lawyer, Charles Gibbons, presented a flag to the One Hundred and Twenty-seventh U.S.C.T. The speech was lustily cheered, and we regret that we can only give one extract. Said he: "The Government that acknowledges black men as soldiers, at the same time recognizes black men as her citizens." This flag was received by Lieutenant-Colonel Given, in a neat speech. At the conclusion, three cheers were given for the Union, for the Supervisory Committee, and the Stars and Stripes. The Regimental Band now discoursed several tunes, much to their credit.[1]

Most of the 45th's men who participated in the flag reception ceremonies were from Pennsylvania "and assembled at Camp William Penn, during the summer of 1864" (Bates

1871, 1106). However, more than a few had reasonable educations and came from outside of the Philadelphia area. For instance, in a December 22, 1864, letter to Rev. Elisha Weaver and *The Christian Recorder*, Private S.H. Smothery of Company C wrote from Camp Casey, "near Washington, D.C.":

> On the 5ᵗʰ of last September, I and twenty other colored men, from Darke and Miami counties, Ohio, and Randolph county, Indiana, were mustered into the service at Urbana, Ohio, for the term of one year. Nearly all of our squad are men of education and intelligence, among whom are Henry L. Spears, Rev. C.P. Clemens, W.H. McCowan, and Aaron Gilibal. We, in company with 348 other men, from Ohio, were brought to this camp, as unassigned recruits, on the 9ᵗʰ of September. We were kept here six weeks before we were assigned to any Regiment, (I mean my squad.) We were finally assigned to Companies A, B, and C, of the 45ᵗʰ United States Colored Troops. The first four companies of the 45ᵗʰ Regiment are stationed here on detached service, to guard this post. The other six companies of the regiment are at the front.[2]

Atmospherically Smothery seemed quite pleased, noting that:

> This is a camp of Rendezvous. Colored recruits are brought here from all parts of the Northern States. They are coming in and going out all the time. When they arrive here they are assigned to regiments, mostly old ones, and sent on to the front. We are very comfortably, and pleasantly situated here. Our barracks, five in number, are large and commodious frame buildings, each capable of accommodating two hundred men. The camp is kept neat and clean, and we have a most beautiful parade ground. Most of our officers are kind and gentlemanly to the men, and seem really to have the cause of their country at heart.[3]

By the time the 45ᵗʰ USCT was organized during the summer of 1864, the barracks and other wooden structures supplanted many of the tents, although some troops still were housed in Sibley tents. *Courtesy of the Historical Society of Pennsylvania.*

Recognizing that many of his compatriots were from southern states, Smothery admired them for their great enterprise, even striving to improve their intellectual capacities and education. Such soldiers took advantage of company schools, with Company C's session starting at "five a.m. and holding until seven." Indeed, he noted that a few of the "men of our Company, who, two months ago, did not know the alphabet, are now spelling readily in words of two syllables, and writing a plain hand."[4]

A good chunk of the 45th's men came from West Virginia and Indiana with Commander Wagner on June 11, 1864, reporting that 40 men and six officers from that state were enrolled into Company A, while 50 were sent to Company B. Furthermore, obviously delighted that such black recruitment would help minimize the number of white men drafted for the war, local West Virginia authorities invited recruiters from Camp William Penn. Wagner requested permission to send a couple commissioned officers and a half dozen "enlisted men of the 45th Regt. USCT into West Virginia on recruiting duty, with permission to have the recruits brought to Philadelphia for muster and credit [...] A committee of citizens are willing to pay all extraordinary expenses if they can receive credit for their wards and township for the men recruited [...]," Wagner wrote. "The men would receive from $225 to $275 bounty, and the government would only be expected to ration the recruiting Party and the recruits. I am satisfied that a considerable number of men would be obtained." (Johnson 1999, 89)

Meanwhile, Smothery said, a couple of religious meetings each week were a tremendous morale booster for the soldiers.[5]

However, before reporting to Fort Casey, where Smothery and the Ohio-Indiana contingent would join, the 45th was assigned to participate in the president's second inauguration parade, the first such black regiment to ever do so for such an auspicious occasion:

> Early in July, and when only four companies were full, the enemy under General Early, advanced into Maryland, and approaching Washington, assumed a threatening attitude. These four companies were, accordingly, hurried away to the Capital, under command of Captain Wilhelm Yon Bechtold, and were assigned to a provisional brigade, commanded by General Casey, in charge of the defenses of the city. By him they were placed on garrison duty at Arlington Heights, where they remained until the middle of March, 1865. They were on duty in the city on the occasion of the second inauguration of President Lincoln, the only colored troops in the procession. (Bates 1871, 1106)

Then, on September 20th, the six original regiments, "under command of Major Bates, proceeded to City Point, where they were assigned to duty in the Tenth Corps, commanded by General Birney, then occupying a position in front of Petersburg." Thomas Morris Chester, the black Civil War correspondent for *The Philadelphia Press*, observed in a September 24, 1864, report: "For several days past colored recruits have been arriving to fill up depleted regiments. The 45th U.S.C.T., from Camp Wm. Penn, arrived at City Point yesterday. It looked as if it was made of good material" (Blackett 1989, 138). However, it wasn't long before they were sent as part of the Tenth Corps "to the north side of the James

River, with which it took part in the engagements of the 29ᵗʰ and 30ᵗʰ of September, and the 1st of October, at Fort Harrison" (ibid.).

The actual movement of troops, however, including the 45ᵗʰ USCT, started the evening of September 28ᵗʰ:

> Throughout the night of September 28, 1864, and well into the next morning, tens of thousands of Union soldiers tramped on dark roads leading north toward the James River. One of the many units on the move was the second battalion of the 45ᵗʰ USCT. 'We left front of Petersburg in the evening at three o'clock and we marched all night till some of the boys gave out and lay down along the road and some throde their things away," recalled John M. Christy of Company H. The snaking files eventually began to converge into two distinct columns, one aimed for a crossing point known as Aiken's landing, and the other following a well-worn trail out Jones Neck to Deep Bottom. (Trudeau 1998, 284)

Part of a force of 26,600 men, the 45ᵗʰ "was moving according to detailed orders from Butler's headquarters that claimed as their primary objective 'to get possession of Richmond.'" If that was not possible, "the Army of the James was to tie down as many Confederate troops as possible in order to prevent them from shifting south to Petersburg,

General Benjamin F. Butler was a reasonably early proponent for recruiting black troops and was well aware of the activities of Camp William Penn regiments. Tiffany medals, named for Butler, were given to 300 USCT soldiers at the commander's request. However, the troops were later told not to wear or display them after Butler was relieved of command duties. *Courtesy of the Library of Congress.*

where the Army of the Potomac was about to launch its own offensive." Butler devised a relatively intricate plan "to level two heavy blows on the strong Rebel defenses protecting Richmond. His left wing, under Major General Edward O.C. Ord, was to attack the Confederate entrenchments running parallel to the Varina Road, even as the entire Tenth Corps, supplemented by a division from the Eighteenth, all under Major General David B. Birney, debouched from the Union-held pocket at Deep Bottom and, in Butler's words, 'endeavor[ed] to carry Newmarket road and the heights adjacent'" (Trudeau 1998, 284-285).

Yet, the black brigades from Camp William Penn, including the 45th and 22nd USCT, would see limited action in this initiative, with the exception of the 6th USCT, part of Colonel A. Duncan's brigade (285-286).

On October 8th the 45th was again under the command of Colonel Doubleday of the Third Division, which was overall commanded by General William Birney (Bates 1871, 1106).

And several days later, on October 13th, the 45th "participated in the action at Darbytown Road, and on the 27th at Charles City Cross Roads. It was soon afterwards placed in winter-quarters, and until the opening of the spring campaign, was engaged in fatigue and picket duty, in front of Fort Harrison" (1106).

Then, remarkably, the 45th would again get to set eyes on the Commander-in-Chief Abraham Lincoln. An extra bonus was being saluted by General Grant, as well as being among the first Union troops to march into Petersburg, despite losses, noted Bates:

> Upon the formation of the Twenty-fifth Corps, it was assigned to the Second Brigade, of the Second Division, and on the 11th of March, Colonel Doubleday was promoted to Brigadier General. The four companies which had been on duty in the defenses of Washington, were, on the 14th of March, 1865, united with the other companies at the front. On the 26th, the corps was reviewed by President Lincoln and General Grant, and on the following day crossed the James, for active duty with the army of the Potomac. With the forces of that army, the regiment participated in the fighting at Hatcher's Run, and in that before Petersburg, on 30th, and 1st and 2d of April, losing in the engagements, one killed and eleven wounded, and entering Petersburg the victorious forces on the 3d. (ibid.)

In fact, about one "week before Richmond's surrender, on the night of March 27, in a movement calling for great secrecy, white and black troops from the Army of the James left their camps near the capital, their destination unknown," including several Camp William Penn regiments, such as the 45th USCT:

> Even as the soldiers marched into the darkness, their encampment fires were kept ablaze, and bandsmen sounded the routine calls. When the men reached the wooden pontoon bridges over the James and Appomattox rivers, they found them "covered with moist straw and compost" to muffle the noise of so many feet.
>
>   "Our march proved to be an all-night one," recalled an officer with the 7th USCT, "and the halts were few and short. The night was very dark, and several

times the road was lost and we had to retrace our steps. When daylight [on March 28] came we found ourselves behind the Petersburg lines." A full division of black troops joined two white divisions in carrying out this maneuver. Commanded by Brigadier General William Birney, the African American division consisted of brigades led by Colonel James Shaw, Jr. (7ᵗʰ, 109ᵗʰ, and 116ᵗʰ USCT), Colonel Ulysses Doubleday (8ᵗʰ, 42ⁿᵈ, 45ᵗʰ, and 127ᵗʰ USCT [all of Camp William Penn]), and Colonel William W. Woodward (29ᵗʰ and 31ˢᵗ USCT). As soon as daylight disclosed something of the size and location of the operation, Woodward became convinced that he and his men "were to take a part in … the last great struggle for the overthrow of Lee's army." (Trudeau 1998, 424-425)

A chaplain of Camp William Penn's 127ᵗʰ USCT, then marching with the 45ᵗʰ, remembered the regiment's travails as part of Birney's black division, when on March 29ᵗʰ "the men 'laid down out of doors with no shelter or fire through a cold rainy night.' Together with the two white divisions accompanying them, the USCT men held the Union line linking the Sixth Corps with the Second below Hatcher's Run." However, combat certainly was not eminent for the majority of the soldiers. "For some black units, this meant combat duty, but for most, a shovel and pick were the assigned weapons. The 116ᵗʰ USCT built a small fort in advance of the main Federal line: [Camp William Penn regiments, including] the 41ˢᵗ USCT scooped rifle pits in the rain; and the 127ᵗʰ USCT sent more than half its strength out on trench-digging duty" (425-426).

However, it wouldn't be long before the black regiments of Camp William Penn, including the 8ᵗʰ, 41ˢᵗ, and 45ᵗʰ USCTs, would enter Petersburg and Richmond, the grand prizes, on the tails of the retreating Rebels:

> During the night of April 2 and into the early morning hours of April 3, Confederate military forces pulled out of Petersburg and Richmond, following a westward course on the northern side of the Appomattox River. All along the Federal lines, soldiers began to ease forward as dawn arrived. Units from the Ninth Corps, entering Petersburg from the east, had U.S. flags flying from the courthouse steeple by 4:30 a.m.
>
> Lieutenant Colonel Oscar E. Pratt of the 7ᵗʰ USCT (Shaw's brigade) led two companies in skirmishing order into the Cockade City at 6:00 a.m., "amidst the joyous acclamations of its sable citizens." The nearby 8ᵗʰ and 41ˢᵗ USCT (Doubleday's brigade) advanced at about the same time. Colonel Samuel C. Armstrong of the 8ᵗʰ noted that his soldiers received a "most cheering and hearty welcome from the colored inhabitants of the city, whom their presence had made free." As the 41ˢᵗ passed through Petersburg's streets, its commander, Colonel Llewellyn F. Haskill, left "guards to protect all inhabited houses, by order of General Birney." After capturing Battery 45, the 127ᵗʰ USCT, too, crossed over the municipal boundary. "The approach of the Union soldiers partook of the spirit of the occasion and marched well through the city. Some recognized acquaintances who marched along and visited us as they went, others burst out in singing a song of which 'Babylon is fallen, Babylon is fallen,' and 'I'm Going to Occupy the Land' was the chorus." (428)

And as the victorious soldiers soaked up the rejoicing, they knew their job was not completely done. Not far down the road was Lee's embattled army, licking its wounds and desperately trying to regroup, according to Trudeau:

> The USCT units had only about three hours in which to savor their victory before being marched out the Cox Road to join in the chase after Lee's retreating army. Their route took them along the South Side Railroad, which now became an important link in Grant's supply chain. It had fallen to Birney's division to secure the first stretch of the route, so one by one, the USCT brigades dropped off the line of march. First to stop was Shaw's brigade, which, after tramping some extra miles thanks to a missed turn, set up near Sutherland Station. The two remaining brigades, Doubleday's and Woodward's, covered the track route as far as Wilson's Station, where they waited while the other Union columns raced to overcome Lee's head start. On April 5, Grant's soldiers successfully block Lee from turning south through Jetersville, forcing him to move farther and farther west. (429-430)

Indeed, mighty rewarding had to be the 45th's pursuit of the leader of the Rebel forces, Robert E. Lee, and his compatriots: "With the corps, it joined in the pursuit of the rebel army, passing through Burkesville, and Farmville, to Appomattox Court House, where it was present at the capitulation on the 9th." (Bates 1871, 1106-1107):

> More than thirty miles passed beneath the feet of the black soldiers as they marched through April 8. By nightfall, they had reached a position near Appomattox Station, where Sheridan's riders had earlier battled with Rebel troops charged with protecting Lee's commissary trains. In the early hours of April 9, the Federal Cavalrymen set up roadblocks across the main routes leading west from the village of Appomattox Court House, where Lee's reduced army was now bivouacked. In a final effort to resume his course toward North Carolina, Lee ordered his infantry to open that route on the morning of April 9. Starting at around 7:00 a.m., Confederate lines of battle moved along the Richmond-Lynchburg Stage Road, shoving Sheridan's horsemen before them. The feisty cavalry commander needed reinforcements to stem this tide, so an urgent call went back for the trailing Yankee infantry to come up on the double-quick. (Trudeau 1998, 431)

Camp William Penn regiments, including the 41st, 45th, and 127th were part of the tightening rope applying the last stranglehold on the army of the Confederacy:

> Foster's white troops (Osborn's brigade) were the first on the scene. Deployed south of the Stage Road, they pushed east as far as the enemy's advanced line of battle before being repulsed and falling back a short distance. Now the rest of the Army of the James began to come onto the field. Foster's other brigades hurried to support Osborn, while Turner's division took station south of Foster. Connecting these divisions were the two black brigades that had reached the battle ground – Doubleday's and Woodward's. Doubleday's three regiments (the 127th USCT was

off guarding ammunition trains), on orders from Sheridan, moved against some Confederate cavalry. "Early we advanced and our skirmish lines met those of the enemy," wrote Colonel Armstrong of the 8th USCT. "We expected a fight – I never felt more like it.... A few bullets whistled around, a few shells passed over." "We rush in, our left in front, a hurrying deployment of two companies of skirmishers," recorded a member of the 41st USCT, "a fine march into a field by the rear rank in our haste." "The rebs gave way," added Armstrong, "all was quiet." (431)

The silence was almost deafening, as just "the occasional crackle of a skirmisher's rifle disrupted the quiet along the Army of the James' front as the men waited for *something* to happen. There was talk of a truce; then "other rumors came" said Colonel Armstrong [of Camp William Penn's 8th USCT], "and finally it was certain that the cruel war was over. The first inkling I had of it was the continuous cheering of troops on our right. Some staff officers galloped up with the news that Lee was making terms of surrender; the firing ceased," Armstrong declared. "It was impossible to realize that the terrible army of Lee was in existence no longer! The truth was stunning (431-432)."

The chaplain of the 127th USCT, Thomas S. Johnson, seemed to speak for all of the Camp William Penn regiments, including the 45th and other black brigades, when he said: "We are a part of the army to which Gen. Lee, the Generalissimo of the C.S.A., has surrendered and have a share in the glory" (432).

Yet, news of President Lincoln's assassination on April 14th had to be devastating for the 45th and other Camp William Penn regiments who pursued his assassins. That's while the 22nd was chosen to participate in Lincoln's funeral procession.

After the president's assassination, the 45th USCT was sent that May "with General Weitzel's forces to Texas, and was stationed at Edinburg, on the Mexican frontier." And on September 8th "it was ordered to Brownsville, where it was mustered out of service on the 4th of November, and returning to Philadelphia, was paid and discharged at Camp Cadwalader, on the 13th of December" (Bates 1871, 1106-1107).

11

The 127th United States Colored Troops
Smiting the reeling rebellion

Thomas Scott Johnson became the chaplain of one of the last regiments to leave Camp William Penn (the 127th USCT) through sheer desire and persistence, as well as via his friendship with an officer at the facility who desired to help a "contraband" slave become a soldier at Camp William Penn. And although the trio were not from the Keystone state, the "regiment was formed from men enlisted and drafted [primarily] in the State of Pennsylvania, to serve one, two, and three years. It was organized at Camp William

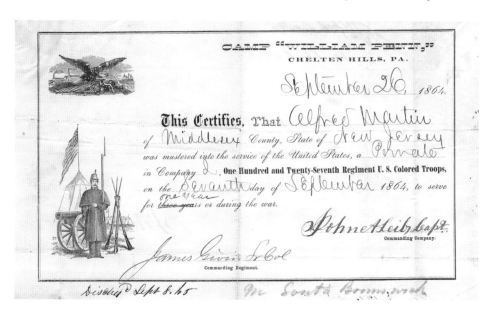

Private Alfred Martin of the 127th USCT was mustered into service on September 27, 1864. *Courtesy of the New Jersey State Archives.*

Penn, during the period extending from the 23d of August, to the 10ᵗʰ of September, 1864" (Bates 1871, 1125). Commanding the regiment was Colonel Benjamin F. Tracy, a Medal-of-Honor recipient and destined to become a famous jurist, as well as the U.S. Secretary of the Navy (Horigan 2002, 80). And before the war's end Tracy would move on to take the commandant's position at the notorious Union prison Elmira, where many Rebels died in horrendous conditions. The 127ᵗʰ's top officers also included Lt. Col. James Givin, as well as Arthur M. Greene and Thomas Young as majors (Bates 1871, 1125).

One of the youngest officers of the 127ᵗʰ's officers corps was the New York City native Charles Lawrence Cooper, who at just age 17 enlisted in 1862 "as a private in Company B of the Seventy-first New York State Militia, taking part in the defense of Washington, D.C., and the Gettysburg campaign." Then, in 1864 Sergeant Cooper, who had been promoted, again ascended to become "commissioned a second lieutenant, serving in Companies A, K, and B of the 127ᵗʰ U.S. Colored Infantry." After serving gallantly and as the Civil War ended, the 21-year-old would marry Flora Green, just 19, in Philadelphia after meeting her at the wedding of a fellow officer at Camp William Penn the previous year (Hooker, Wilson 2003, 253).

The couple's daughter, Florrestine Cooper, would be born in Philadelphia in 1867 and later write about her father's career and their experiences in vivid memoirs, including his promotion to "first lieutenant in the Thirty-ninth Infantry at Ship Island, Mississippi." Eventually marrying and taking on the surname of Hooker, Florrestine's reminisces would focus on her father's 1871 reassignment and duties in the "Tenth U.S. Cavalry, black troops with white officers, later to become known as the Buffalo Soldiers," at first with Company A. They were then "ordered to Fort Sill in the Kiowa and Comanche country, where it [arrived] after a march of 225 miles from Camp Supply" (ibid.).

Hooker's memoirs succinctly capture many aspects of life for such officers and their families, as well as the black Buffalo Soldiers, some from the USCT units of Camp William Penn. They fought in the so-called Indian wars in the southwest that included the Geronimo campaign. And Hooker also reveals the social dynamics of white officers assigned to Camp William Penn when the 127ᵗʰ was raised, such as when her parents first set eyes on each other and later married:

> It was during September 1864 that my mother and a party of girl friends were invited to go to Camp William Penn for the afternoon and dinner. Major Arthur Greene was engaged to be married to my mother's most intimate friend, Ellie Lowry. Leaving his guests to watch dress parade, he hastened up country to purchase a horse. Field officers were mounted.
>
> Camp William Penn held the unique distinction of having been the first place in the United States where black men were enlisted and trained to serve as soldiers of the regular army. Congress had authorized such action and Taggart's "Free Military School for Applicants for Command of Colored Troops" was established in Philadelphia. There men who had served as privates in the white regiments were sifted and selected, then trained for appointments as commissioned officers to serve in regiments of colored men. Among the men who graduated was Second Lieutenant Charles Lawrence Cooper [the author's father].

That September afternoon just before parade was formed, Colonel John Gibbon was standing a short distance from Major Greene's guests. None of the girls was acquainted with him, but he walked over to them. He held a long narrow box in his hand and a dark red silk sash such as officers wear.

"Will one of you young ladies take care of this for me?" the colonel asked. "It is a sword to be presented to a young officer by his former comrades with whom he served as an enlisted man. I have some duties to attend to, but will soon return." Although each of the girls was eager to hold the sword, the officer laid the box containing the sword, then the silk sash, and finally a smaller one which held the shoulder straps for the newly appointed officer, in my mother's lap.

Parade formed and at its close, Colonel Gibbon presented the shoulder straps, sash, and sword to a very much embarrassed, but tall and handsome young officer as a token of esteem and affection from the comrades with whom he had served from the beginning of the war, when he had enlisted at the age of seventeen. Those comrades were proud of the nineteen-year-old soldier who had carried a bullet from the field of Gettysburg, but their gift was a complete surprise to Lieutenant Charles Cooper. (Hooker and Wilson 2003, 20-21)

The young couple would become romantically acquainted, so that during and following the war they would share lives of almost unsurpassed adventures. And it's quite likely that they associated with or knew of Chaplain Thomas Johnson.

Born in Greenville, New York, on February 19, 1839, to Baker and Electa Johnson, Thomas S. Johnson attended New Jersey public schools and the Newton Presbyterial [*sic*] Academy, where his father, Baker Johnson, was the principal, as well as a minister. Yet in 1855, by the time he reached about age 15, Johnson's family moved to Portage, Wisconsin, where his dad became the principal of Portage City Classical Institute (Hartwig 1970, 1).

Apparently Johnson Sr. and his son, Thomas, had a very close relationship. While the father purchased "unbroken" farmland "near Oxford, Wisconsin and moved his family there," he also served as pastor at a town church and "conducted a small private school in his home," even personally providing his son the first two years of a college education. Thomas then "entered the Junior year class at Carroll College, Waukesha, Wisconsin in March of 1859, graduating with the class of 1860," soon to teach at least a year at Blairstown Academy in New Jersey. And before long he'd be faced with making very weighty decisions, including whether to follow his father's footsteps into the ministry, as well as possibly joining Union forces and fighting the Confederates, which included extended family members (ibid.).

It didn't take long for the young Johnson to pursue the ministry. After completing his teaching assignment at Blairstown Academy, "he entered Princeton Theological Seminary and was graduated at the end of the regular three year course" (2). And with hostilities finally reaching a boiling point between the Union and rebellious states, a decision was imminent concerning whether he'd join Union forces, despite his father Baker's ambivalence, Hartwig noted:

Even though Baker Johnson vigorously supported the Union, he was typical of many Americans of this time who did not want their sons to fight because, in many cases, they had to fight against their own relatives. Thomas wrote to a brother commenting: "If I had been home this winter I should have had to go to war." His brother replied that the town of Oxford had held a meeting to discuss levying a tax for a bounty to attract volunteers. The majority of the people were in favor of it and they raised twelve hundred dollars. And he added, "I think the United States will have quite an army if all that are called for go. A great many have volunteered in Wisconsin since the last draft and I don't think they will have to draft only in a small portion of the state. I hope you don't have any trouble about it. I see by the papers that they are paying large bounties in New Jersey." (2-3)

Thomas began to ponder his possible role in supporting the Union. He went to his father for advice, according to Hartwig:

Thomas Johnson asked his father's opinion about becoming a chaplain in one of the New Jersey units in the United States Army. He felt that as long as he was unmarried and had no plans for matrimony he could serve in this capacity. Determined to obtain a chaplaincy, he requested and obtained a recommendation from the colonel of the regiment to which he wished to apply. The colonel's approval became an application which was granted by the governor of the state.

Johnson obtained an introduction to Governor Joel Parker who promised to sign any application that could be presented from the colonel of any of the regiments needing a chaplain. There were at that time only three regiments in New Jersey lacking a chaplain – the 4ᵗʰ, 10ᵗʰ and 12ᵗʰ. Thomas had written to Colonel Ryerson of the 10ᵗʰ but had received no answer. Mr. W.S. Johnson, a friend of the family, suggested that Thomas should go to the Army of the Potomac and contact the proper officers/ "This will cost money and seems to be the only way." The Christian Commission constantly sent out delegates. Johnson believed that under the auspices of the commission,

General Benjamin F. Butler was part of the U.S. House of Representatives following the war, and unsuccessfully campaigned for president in 1884. However, he did earlier ascend to become governor of Massachusetts in 1882. *Courtesy of the Library of Congress.*

he might work his way into the office of the 10th regiment. Another process might have been to become a low salaried teacher at any army post for the Freedmen's Association and thereby have an opportunity to become a chaplain. (3-4)

Despite the obstacles he faced, joining "the army never left Johnson's mind." Letters were sent to friends and relatives asking about any possible way to become a chaplain for the Union. A cousin even "offered to write a letter of recommendation to authorities in Washington, including a member of General Butler's staff" (4-5).

Ultimately, though, unable to land a position as a chaplain, Johnson decided to become a delegate for the Christian Commission, and "on June 1, 1864," noted Hartwig, he "was sent to Fort Monroe, located at the tip of Virginia's peninsula, guarding the mouth of [the] Cheasapeake Bay." He surmised that might be a great pathway to becoming a chaplain, since the Christian Commission's priority was to care for Union soldiers:

  The Christian Commission was an outgrowth of the Sanitary Commission which had been established in 1861 to assure care and comfort for the service men. It originated after the first call for troops was made; measures were taken to supply religious reading matter to all regiments. The Young Men's Christian Association volunteers held prayer meetings and printed a soldier's hymn book. When the armies began to move, some of these volunteers went along at their own expense and continued their work. One of these volunteers was Vincent Colyer who wrote to the National Committee of the Association urging the formation of a Christian Commission to carry on the work that had been started. As a result, the commission was organized on November 14, 1861. Letters of approval were

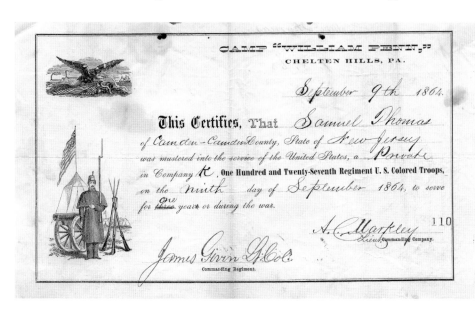

Private Samuel Thomas of the 127th USCT was likely familiar with the regiment's very respected chaplain, Thomas Scott Johnson. *Courtesy of the New Jersey State Archives.*

sent to the United States Christian Commission by President Lincoln and the War Department […]. In its early stages the work of the Commission was limited, but after an appeal to the public in 1862, it was able to equip and send out fourteen delegates as they were called, ten of whom were clergymen. By the end of the year the Commission had sent over four hundred "delegates" to the army and had more than a thousand engaged in work at home. The work of the Commission increased rapidly. They furnished chapel tents and chapel roofs to the armies, established diet kitchens in the hospitals and extended the service called "individual relief." The Commission opened schools for children of colored soldiers and wrote thousands of letters for disabled men in the hospitals. (Hartwig 1970, 7-8)

Meanwhile the regiment's commander, Col. Benjamin F. Tracy, had made quite a name for himself as an attorney in Owego, New York. Marrying Delinda E. Catlin of nearby Nichols in 1851, Tracy was known to be a "devoted husband" and "dedicated father of two daughters and a son," noted Horigan. Sadly, his wife and one of his daughters would die in a tragic Washington, DC fire in 1890, long after the war. However, well before their deaths, as his law career blossomed during the 1850s, Tracy became very politically astute and committed to the Whig Party before gravitating to the Republicans:

> A staunch Whig who opposed both abolitionism and the expansion of slavery, Tracy was elected district attorney of Tioga County in 1853. With the demise of the Whig Party, he became a key figure in the organization of the Republican Party in 1854 in Tioga County, and emerged as the first county chairman of that fledgling political organization in 1856. He actively supported Republican John C. Frémont during the 1856 presidential campaign. As a rising Republican leader in Tioga County, Tracy worked closely with his good friend Thomas Collier Platt – a future Republican powerhouse in New York State.
>
> With the outbreak of the war in April 1861, Tracy entered state politics. Campaigning as a strong Unionist and a supporter of President Lincoln, he was elected to the New York State Assembly in November 1861. It was in the Assembly that Tracy quickly allied himself with a rapidly rising star in the Republican Party – Henry Jarvis Raymond. Raymond at this time was on the verge of emerging as a member of a redoubtable Republican political triumvirate in New York State that included William H. Seward

General John C. Frémont and Col. Benjamin F. Tracy, commander of the 127ᵗʰ USCT, were involved in New York State and even national politics before the war. Frémont commanded Edward M. Davis, Lucretia Mott's son-in-law, near the start of the war. Camp William Penn would be constructed on Davis' land. *Courtesy of the Library of Congress.*

(Lincoln's secretary of state) of Auburn, and the state's domineering practitioner of political power – Thurlow Weed, a man who made his mark in journalism in both Albany and New York City. (Horigan 2002, 78-80)

In 1862, Tracy promptly dropped his political ambitions and joined Union forces "in response to Lincoln's July 1 call for 300,000 volunteers." He was destined to start at a remarkably high rank due to his high society background:

> Since one's socioeconomic status determined one's general prestige, Tracy emerged as commander (with the rank of colonel) of the 109th New York – a regiment that was made up of recruits from Tioga, Broome, and Tompkins Counties. On August 30, 1862, Colonel Tracy and the 109th left Binghamton by train for Elmira and then on to points south. For the next year and a half Tracy's regiment performed the perfunctory task of guarding railroads in the Baltimore and Washington areas. (80-81)

However, according to Horigan, it wasn't long before Tracy would prove his mettle:

> In the spring of 1864 General Grant moved to mount an all-out offensive against Lee's Army of Northern Virginia. In doing so, Grant ordered the majority of units (including Tracy's 109th) in Baltimore and Washington sectors to the front. In early May Tracy and his inexperienced regiment were thrown into battle against tough, seasoned Confederate troops at the battle of the Wilderness. When the 109th faltered, Colonel Tracy took the regimental colors and charged the enemy. His unit quickly followed him into battle. (81)

Tracy's bravery led to him being hospitalized, and he was awarded the Medal of Honor:

> From May 5 through May 12 the 109th engaged the enemy in a series of fierce encounters that eventually took its toll on the courageous Tracy. Suffering from heat prostration and heart problems, he was diagnosed by military doctors on May 14 as no longer capable of enduring the rigors of combat. Responding with courage and valor to the shot and shell of combat, the patriotic Tracy had exhibited exemplary leadership. His brief but harrowing moment of battle over, he now reluctantly returned to his home to regain his health. In June 1895 Tracy would finally be awarded the Medal of Honor "for gallant and distinguished conduct in action at Wilderness, Va., May 6, 1864."
>
> Through the summer months Tracy regained his strength to the point where he was able to rejoin the military in some capacity. On September 7, his health completely restored, he accepted another military assignment – this time as the commanding officer of the 127th U.S. Colored Troops. At about the same time his political ally from his New York Assembly days, the formidable Henry J. Raymond, journeyed to Owego to personally suggest to Tracy that he assume the position of military post commander at Elmira. (81)

At Fort Monroe, Johnson was likely still very busy according to his account book, taking care of a variety of the men's needs – from letter writing to purchasing and providing the likes of milk, ice, paper, berries, beef, squash, chopping knives, and even brooms (Hartwig 1970, 8-9).

Then, one day, a very fortuitous letter arrived for Johnson:

> In early September, Johnson received a letter from a friend, Arthur M. Greene, announcing Greene's appointment as Major in the 127ᵗʰ United States Colored Troops. He further inquired if Johnson could obtain a pass and transportation for his contraband, David, a Negro slave within the lines during the Civil War, whom Greene wanted to send to Camp William Penn at Philadelphia. Greene had no doubt that any number of black boys were available in Philadelphia. Due to David's loyalty, Greene did not want to part with him. David's services warranted ten dollars a month. Personal belongings and information reached Greene. David was "useful and honest" and Greene trusted his horses in David's care. David's arrival was patiently awaited by the Major. (10-11)

In fact Greene, in that letter to Johnson, made him an offer to join him at Camp William Penn:

> I am pleasantly situated here and like it very much. Should be most happy to see you here. We have no chaplain, and in fact very few officers yet. We have nearly 1000 men and ought to have a spiritual advisor. Should you like a chaplaincy if it could be obtained! Nothing would suit me better than to have you here. My men are quite intelligent. Coming mostly from the Northern States. The Lt. Col. Commanding the reg't is an old acquaintance, Jas. Givin. (11)

Johnson must have applied for the position immediately, Hartwig noted. "Less than two months later, Johnson received his appointment as Chaplain of the 127ᵗʰ United States Colored Regiment on November 4, 1864," and would experience for the first time the rigors of serving as a chaplain during war, despite the group's limited combat duties, but participating in several campaigns (ibid.).

That's not to say that matters during this period were always ideal. Undoubtedly, Johnson had to deal with a variety of issues within the camp, as well as the virulent racism that his soldiers dealt with outside of its walls, including morale issues stemming from violent physical attacks on some of the men. One black officer, Sergeant-Major Green, was brutally attacked in late September and received jail time along with his assailants:

> A few days ago, as Sergeant-Major Green, of the One Hundred and Twenty-seventh United States Colored Troops, was quietly passing along South Street, he was assailed by a number of ruffians, without any provocation whatever. We can conceive of no cause for this cowardly assault, but suppose that it was on account of his wearing the uniform of a sergeant-major.
>
> Words fail to express our indignation at this wholly uncalled for assault. We will place it on the same list with outrages of a similar nature. We know that there

is a party of vile miscreants in all our Northern cities, who delight in persecuting colored men; but they will never attack a colored man unless they are in large numbers, and, even then, should he look as though he would defend himself, they stand off at a safe distance and throw stones at him.

Major Green told them to stand back; but they, no doubt, thought themselves fully competent to handle, the (nigger) Sergeant-Major. The Major then pulled his pistol out of his pocket and beat them over the head with the butt end of it. They then tried stones, when he fired, shooting one of the assailants in the leg. The majority of people with whom we have conversed on the subject, regret that the ball did not enter a vital part, and that he did not serve more of them in the same way. However, a police-officer arrested the Sergeant, who, like a man, offered no resistance. We were informed that some of his assailants were also arrested, and had a trial before Alderman Carter, who committed them and the Sergeant.

The wounded man was taken to the William Penn Hospital. On last Wednesday, Sergeant-Major Green was admitted to bail. From all accounts, he should never have been put in prison. We hope that this occurrence will teach these renegades a lesson.[1]

The next step for Johnson was to receive an official ordination, so he applied to the Presbyterian Church, following his father's footsteps, and became ordained on December 7, 1864. A letter from his cousin, Theodore, praised Johnson for his dedication to saving the Union. Theodore patriotically wrote:

I hope you may not be called to any great danger and often think of you way down there, surrounded by so many foes of our country, sacrificing your ordinary comforts and luxuries for the good of those who are battling for our beloved Union. May your life and health be spared to return again soon to rejoice over the downfall of this cruel rebellion, and the reestablishment of National Authority over every inch of the U.S. (Hartwig 1970, 12)

The regiment's departure from Camp William Penn was described in a poignant letter, written by an unidentified correspondent and sent to *The Christian Recorder*, published on October 1, 1864:

The 127th Regiment of United Sates Colored Troops took their departure for the field of battle on last Wednesday. Leaving their late camping ground, known by the name of Camp William Penn, and located the immediate line of the North Pennsylvania Railroad, the regiment arrived in this city in due time and order. They marched down Chestnut street to headquarters with all the precision of veterans, and from thence down either Second or Third Street (we cannot say positively which) to the Union and Cooper Volunteer Refreshment Saloons, where they were regaled most sumptuously with the good things of life. The regiment, all told, numbers one thousand strong, and presented a truly warlike and beautiful appearance as they moved steadily forward with battle-flags flaunting proud defiance, and reflecting bayonets gleaming in the sun. They were headed by a splendid brass band of colored performers, who discoursed some elegant music. We received a very kind and pressing invitation to enter the Union Saloon from several of the gentlemanly managers, thus had a good opportunity of taking a complete survey of the table set and good things prepared for our brave kind-hearted ladies and gentlemen present waited on them with much apparent alacrity and pleasure. They deserve great praise for their zeal. We next repaired to the Cooper Shop Saloon. We did not see Mr. Cooper, but observed an officer standing by the door, who, upon our making ourself known, politely requested us to step inside. Complying with the invitation extended, we entered and took a good view of their accommodations for the dinner man – and we must say that here also everything was served up in the very best style for both officers and men – and that without stint. This Saloon regaled one-half of the regiment, namely, five hundred men. We were much pleased throughout the whole affair. After they had all fared sumptuously, they were marched down to the Washington, Baltimore and Philadelphia Depot, where they took the cars for the seat of war. They are ordered to Fortress Monroe. This is the ninth regiment that has left Camp William Penn, and the tenth is already more than half full.[2]

However, the regiment's combat duties would be limited during the war as the great debacle wound down, despite "arriving at the front" and being "incorporated with the Army of the James" (Bates 1871, 1125). Still, the 127ᵗʰ's experiences provide insight into the many wartime and post-war social, classism and political dynamics that impacted and often haunted African American soldiers.

Nonetheless, the 127ᵗʰ's arrival in Virginia allowed some of the men the immense satisfaction of guarding Rebel soldiers, many of them likely doomed and captured near Richmond, according to an October 21, 1864, report by the correspondent for *The Philadelphia Press*, Thomas Morris Chester:

> The rebel prisoners, who were put to work in retaliation for compelling colored troops captured by the enemy to assist in erecting fortifications around Richmond, are still at Dutch Gap, where the experience which they acquired with the pick and shovel in erecting fortifications, within their lines, is of immense utility in progressing this great enterprise. Officers and men, under a guard of Companies E and F, 127ᵗʰ United States Colored Troops, are required to perform a good day's work. The rebels at times furiously shell the workmen from a mortar battery, which renders it exceedingly unpleasant for the Johnnies, who, though they previously refused before they were aware of their destination, are now clamoring to take the oath of allegiance. Their appeals will have no influence with General Butler; but they will be required to remain, in what will likely prove "the last ditch" to many of them. The prejudice which the rebels have pretended to entertain against negroes seems to be entirely eradicated from these prisoners – for they not only work side by side with the race, but under the superintendence of negro guards, with whose instructions and orders they most cheerfully comply. The rebs have too much good sense to provoke in the least their colored custodians. It was a curious sight to see the proud sons of the F.F.V.'s [First Families of Virginia],

who had been accustomed to command negroes wherever they met them, humbly acknowledging the authority of the blackest of the race. (Blackett 1989, 165)

Hartwig noted that Johnson seemed to be very dedicated about his duties from the very start of his tenure. "In his first monthly report as chaplain from the Field Virginia on December 31st, 1864, Johnson wrote that General Birney of the 2nd Division, 25th Army Corps had issued an order requiring the establishment of schools." That, in fact, was great news for Johnson, given his educational and teaching background. He was especially elated that the chaplains were to be central to organizing such schools. He wrote:

> It is hoped that early in January we may have the Regimental School of the 127th U.S.C.T. in full and successful progress. The 127th is mostly employed now on guard and fatigue duty. We have a fine encampment on the right of Fort Harrison up to the front and just in the rear of the parapet of the 1st line of work. The state of morals of the regiment is fair. (Hartwig 1970, 16)

With matters at the moment decent in the field, Johnson and his men had to also be optimistic about the upcoming second anniversary of the empowering Emancipation Proclamation, a date that was certainly on the minds of their compatriots still training at Camp William Penn. *The Christian Recorder* newspaper marked the occasion, referring to Camp William Penn and commemorations in Philadelphia, most notably at the Banneker Institute, a renowned educational and social institution for black Philadelphians:

> "Proclaim liberty throughout all the land unto all the inhabitants thereof." The second anniversary of the Emancipation Proclamation will be celebrated, under the auspices of the Banneker Institute, on Monday evening, January 2d,

> 1865, in National Hall, Market street, above 12th. Henry Highland Garnet will deliver the Oration. Frederick Douglass, Robert Purvis, Messrs, John W. Simpson, Octavius V. Catto, and several distinguished men of the nation, will address the meeting, either in person or by letter. The exercises will be varied, with Music by the United States Military Post Band, from Camp

Frederick Douglass was still quite busy with abolitionist and recruiting activities as the war climaxed and the 127th prepared for battle. Following the Civil War Douglass aged gracefully, but remarried after his first wife, Anna, died. Controversy was sparked when he took the hand of his white secretary, Helen Pitts. *Courtesy of the Library of Congress.*

William Penn, and by several gentlemen of musical profession, prominent among whom are Messrs. Bowers, Cliff and Lively. Members of Literary Societies of New York, Washington, Baltimore, and neighboring cities, and our own citizens generally, are invited to participate. The doors will be opened at half-past six o'clock. The exercises for the evening will commence at half-past seven o'clock. Tickets, 25 cents – for sale at the office of the Christian Recorder. Decemb. 24 – [unclear].[3]

A follow-up January 7, 1865, article in *The Christian Recorder*, though, indicated that the program went quite well, despite Frederick Douglass not being able to attend the event, providing the chance for an up-and-coming Philadelphia activist and orator to take center stage, Octavius V. Catto. His father, the Rev. William Catto, was an outspoken Philadelphia preacher who had moved his family from the Charleston, SC, area:

> The anniversary celebration of this classical and well-known Institution came off on last Monday night, the 2d instant, according to arrangement, at the National Hall, Market street, above Twelfth. The Hall was completely crowded, at an early hour. Mr. J.C. White, Jr., the worthy and efficient Chairman, called the meeting to order, and opened the exercises for the evening by calling on Rev. Jeremiah Turpin, from Allegheny, who delivered a most beautiful and appropriate prayer. Mr. White [then] arose and addressed the audience with a few potent and pithy remarks, after which the several letters received were read to the audience by Mr. Taylor. Mr. O.V. Catto, one of the teachers connected with the High School (Institute for Colored Youth), delivered a very able address, and one that was a credit to the mind and heart of the speaker. The colored Band from Camp William Penn discoursed some very fine and eloquent music on the occasion. Professor Bassett read letters from Mr. Fred. Douglass and Hon. Charles Sumner, stating the cause of their absence. The renowned orator, Rev. H.H. Garnett, of Washington, D.C., now made his appearance upon the stage, and gave the audience one of his eloquent and soul-stirring speeches. As a man of honor and a speaker of ability, we feel that Mr. Garnett needs no encomium from us. His personal worth and public merits are now wide-spread.[4]

Chaplain Johnson seemed to relish his duties that were honed as a previous delegate of the Christian Commission. In addition to "writing letters to the wives and parents of the men who were on the sick list," he furnished the men with Bibles and even educational books "in the quarters and found

Octavius V. Catto was the quintessential black activist, with his fame rising rapidly during the war. Members of the 127th and earlier Camp William Penn regiments undoubtedly heard the anti-slavery orations of the teacher and administrator at the Institute for Colored Youth. *Courtesy of the Library of Congress.*

the men eager to learn." Many of the men were very highly motivated, helping to build a "schoolhouse and chapel" by carrying "logs on their shoulders for nearly a mile" (Hartwig 1970, 16-17):

> On February 28, 1865, from the field near Fort Harrison, Virginia, Johnson related that the regiment had occupied the new chapel for divine services and there had been at least one religious service in the chapel during the week and two on each Sabbath. He observed that the attendance was good and was appreciated by the religiously minded men of the regiment and that it had a good influence on others. He also stated: "Many of the backsliders and those who have yielded to the temptations of camp life have seen the evil consequences of their course and taken a new stand resolving from henceforth to be not only true and loyal to their country but also to be good soldiers on the crop." (17)

Indeed, Hartwig noted, there were matters that disturbed the chaplain as a Christian leader:

> Profanity and indecent language were common in the company streets. Johnson pointed out in all large communities of men living together, vice and immorality have opportunities to grow. With the help of God and earnest endeavor of the officers and men, he believed this immorality would be repressed. (ibid.)

In the intervening time, the regiment's school seemed to be functioning quite well. It was generally supported by the officers, with most of the black recruits glad to attend. The mission of the school was to help make the soldiers useful American citizens. Several sessions of classes were held daily, excluding Sunday. Johnson remarked:

> The men are all eager to learn and the patience and perseverance they exhibit at their adult age in the elemental branches of an English education is remarkable. Where ever they have an opportunity in the camp – on fatigue, on picket or in the Guard House – they draw from their pocket the treasured book and earnestly study its pages. From the great encouragement that has been given to this enterprise and the success that begins to appear, I confidently expect that every soldier of the regiment not physically disqualified will be able to read and write intelligibly before he leaves service. (18)

However, the regiment, on February 25, 1865, was required to move from "its dry camp" to one that had been abandoned by the 9th USCT, presumably at a damper locale. There, at Hatchers Run, Virginia, adequate sanctuary and school facilities were not available, and there was really no available time to construct them. Johnson wrote in his diary:

> Still I am able to report that the desire for knowledge has not been lost by all, though no regular school was established and many hindrances were in the way of their education – many of the soldiers – both those reared in slavery where learning

is forbidden and those who have rejected all the advantages of free schools in the northern states – have been struggling along with their primers and spelling books and will assuredly have the reward their patience and toil deserves. (19)

Johnson indeed had to resort to enterprise and creativity, holding services outside in the open and attracting a small number of the men. Yet, those men attending the services were often dedicated and enthusiastic. "Johnson had also distributed religious newspapers and books weekly to the men and officers during the month" (ibid.).

In fact, Chaplain Johnson was very impressed with the cleanliness of the new camp, as well as the "soldierly" discipline and sharp drilling. He noted:

> No white soldier ever presented a finer appearance or carried with them a more soldierly bearing than these colored men as they passed in review. With even tread in full shining uniforms, with streaming flags and martial music the sable columns presented a spectacle that is seldom equaled in the military world. (19-20)

Apparently, according to Hartwig, senior commanders must have appreciated the sharp demeanor of the 127ᵗʰ USCT, with even General Grant and the commander-in-chief, President Lincoln, at one point observing them:

> It was reviewed with the division on March 17ᵗʰ by Generals Grant and Ord along with Secretary Stanton and other officials. On March 25ᵗʰ the regiment moved to an unoccupied camp of another unit and on the 26ᵗʰ returned to its position near the base of a signal tower. Johnson stated, "At 4 p.m. the regiment was reviewed by the President so that we made three distinct moves and had a grand review in less than twenty-four hours." (20)

However, it wouldn't be long before the regiment moved again, heading to Aikens Landing, across the James River, and over a peninsula also bounded by the Appomattox River. After resting and camping at City Point and other nearby locales, the regiment established camp on March 29ᵗʰ at Hatcher's Run during heavy rain (21).

The next day the regiment, after so many days of not seeing combat, was anxious to engage the enemy as they prepared for battle just outside Petersburg. They worked furiously during the night on a breastwork that was just before a rebel fortification, remarkably in the cold and rain. However, at that point the regiment still did not get the opportunity to fight, since it was held in "reserve," likely disappointing many of the men (22). Still, Johnson noted his men's qualities, according to Hartwig:

> In the severe marches – exposure and hard labor – continuing night and day with scarcely any intermission this regiment has shown great powers of endurance and courage that never faltered. These colored men have uncomplainingly performed their work as soldiers and laborers – and both their officers and themselves have exerted their utmost power to aid in triumph over the enemies of our country and in smiting the reeling rebellion with victorious blows. (ibid.)

Soon ensued the opportunity for Chaplain Johnson to observe from a unique perch just how ferocious the fighting had been outside of Petersburg and elsewhere, Hartwig noted:

> General Birney, Commander of the Second Division of the Twenty-fifth Corps ordered all of his chaplains to report for duty in the hospital department by April 1, 1865. Johnson reported to Major C.P. Heichhold, Surgeon-in-Chief Second Division, Twenty-fifth Army Corps. There he remained and attended the sick and wounded until he was relieved on April 3 and sent back to the regiment. Although Johnson had been assigned to the hospital department, he never lost track of what the rest of the Union Army was doing. He noted General Sheridan's Calvary aided by the 5th Corps crossed enemy lines to Dinwiddie Court House and proceeded toward Boydtown Plank Road. At that point they moved westward to White Oak Road and on to defeat the enemy at Five Forks taking six thousand prisoners. (23)

The victory at Five Forks prompted General Grant to order an assault on Petersburg. Johnson, again, had a bird's eye view, providing details of the action, as described by Hartwig. "His regiment, with General Birney's division, moved to the rebels' works to find that they had left in great haste and near panic leaving behind tents, camp furniture, and clothing." The 127th followed the fleeing Rebels to Petersburg, just several miles "along the inside of the rebel lines." The action was fierce, Hartwig wrote:

> The 127th Regiment halted with the Brigade opposite battery number forty-four and forty-five of the rebels, who according to Johnson, were sending cannon fire in salvos. Company A of the 127th Regiment advanced as skirmishers. Several men were wounded and one died soon after. The regiment stayed in position all night expecting to charge in the early morning. It was then discovered that the rebels had left their works entirely. Upon finding no enemy to dispute their entrance, the troops marched into the city of Petersburg. (21-22)

Johnson observed:

> The approach of the Union Soldiers was hailed with joy by all the colored population – which were the only people visible in the city – they came out and lined the street – they filled the doors and windows with eager faces – old men took off their hats and thanked "de Lord dat de good time had come"– old matrons bowed their heads reverently as we passed – the young people were delighted that the day – the long expected day of their deliverance had come. The bands of music struck up and played the national airs and it was thrilling to hear the delightful notes of the "Star Spangled Banner" and "Yankee Doodle" in the street of the city which was so lately the home of the traitor and the hotbed of treason. The soldiers partook of the spirit of the occasion and marched finely through the city. Some recognized acquaintances who marched along and visited as they went – others burst out in singing a song of which the chorus is "Babylon is fallen, Babylon is fallen" – "And I'm a going to occupy the land." (25-26)

With the Petersburg campaign now over, costing 75,000 combined casualties, General Lee and his army were on the run. He warned Richmond, the Confederate capital, that federal troops would soon enter the city (26). The 127th joined in the pursuit of Lee as he moved towards Danville, according to Hartwig:

> The 127th regiment of the 2nd Division of the 25 Army corps was an important segment of the Union Troops. It rested at Sutherland's Station preparing for a long march on April 4. On April 5, it halted at Wilson's Station where ambulances awaited to convey the sick and wounded to the long-established hospital there. The regiment traveled on in soaking rains, through mud and swollen rivers. On April 7, it camped on a hill overlooking the town of Farmville. That evening Johnson remarked about General Birney's dismissal as commander of the 2nd Division, 25 Army Corps. He wrote, "A brave and enthusiastic officer of the Colored Soldiers, he held the uniform respect of officers and soldiers and his removal is regretted." Brigadier General Jackson from the artillery service took over command of the 2nd Division, 25 Army Corps, on April 8. The troops under orders of General Sheridan marched nearly forty miles in one day. Johnson asserted that this was probably the greatest march ever made by infantry. (26-27)

The 127th USCT was left to guard multiple artillery wagons as the rest of the 2nd Brigade moved to the battle front. "The Army of Northern Virginia was completely surrounded and demoralized with no escape route possible." And soon a very historic moment came. "A cease fire took place and the articles of capitulation were signed in Appomattox Court House at 5 p.m. that day." Johnson noted that Rebel and Union men rejoiced, with their

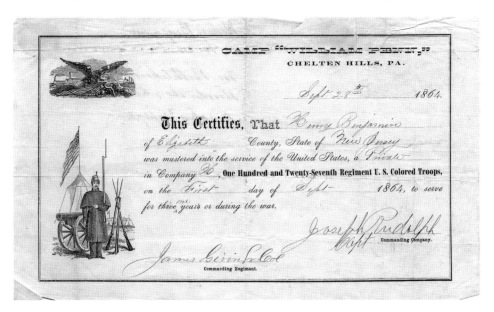

Private Henry Benjamin of the 127th USCT likely witnessed the surrender of Gen. Lee at Appomattox. *Courtesy of the New Jersey State Archives.*

respective bands playing such national favorites as "Yankee Doodle" and "Hail Columbia." Johnson observed:

> Great credit is due to the officers and men of this regiment for the unflinching energy and their heroic endurance of all the suffering of this march. Although the colored men (in the present state of popular feeling) will not receive full credit for their share of the memorable transaction of the 9th April, it is well known that if it were not for the timely presence of Doubledays' Brigade by a tremendous march the day before supporting General Sheridan's Cavalry the enemy would have continued their retreat and General Lee and his whole army escaped. (28)

However, Hartwig noted, sadly with the good news soon came a horrendous revelation, as the 127th and other black regiments returned slowly in rain and mud:

> During the march back the regiment heard the news of Lincoln's assassination. The regiment continued to move until encampment was made with the whole 25 Corps along the Boydtown Plank Road two miles from Petersburg. The 127th was stationed in front of Fort Gregg. On Wednesday, April 26, the day appointed for mourning for President Lincoln, the regiment was drawn up in line of battle at 10 a.m. and the command was given to rest arms. The colors were dropped in mourning and the colonel of the regiment announced the death of the President. All unnecessary work was suspended and the day was spent in prayer and mourning. (ibid.)

If there was any saving grace at all the war was finally over, and it appeared that African Americans were headed towards their long-awaited liberty. And at least for the 127th battle losses were miniscule, with only one soldier killed and several injuries reported (Bates 1871, 1125):

> It was [then] sent with other troops to Texas, after the close of hostilities in the east, and was posted on the Mexican frontier. On the 11th of September, 1865, it was consolidated into a battalion of three companies, and the men and officers whose term of service had expired, were discharged. The battalion was mustered out of service on the 20th October. The muster-out rolls only of the consolidated companies were returned to the office of the Adjutant General, and consequently the records of the men who left the regiment before close of its term, cannot be given. (ibid.)

However, before the war ended the commander of the 127th, Colonel Tracy, would receive a politically motivated transfer that was recommended by his back-home political ally, Henry J. Raymond, with close ties to a very powerful person – President Abraham Lincoln:

> Tracy, apparently after a lengthy discussion with Raymond, then wrote (on September 10) Secretary of War Stanton: "Mr. Raymond supposed it would be

necessary for me to visit Washington in person and handed me the enclosed note to you. Finding upon an examination of the papers that I was ordered to report in writing, I have done so, and only inclose the note [Raymond's letter to Stanton] to you that you may then more vividly recall the circumstances of my appointment and the special duty to which as I understand you intend to assign me."

On September 19 [1864] the War Department stated that Tracy's order (dated September 17) "to repair to Elmira, New York, and relieve Lieutenant-Colonel S. Eastman, U.S. Army, in command of the Draft Rendezvous and the Prisoner's Camp, at that place, is hereby confirmed." The following day Eastman affixed his signature to a post order that officially turned the Elmira command over to Colonel Tracy. (Horigan 2002, 83)

According to the writer/historian Michael Horigan, there was clear evidence that Raymond and Stanton believed that Col. Tracy could be manipulated or forced to comply with their desires regarding the facility's operations. Charged with being too narrow minded with respect to operating the prison and strictly adhering to military conventions, Tracy's command of the prison was characterized with ongoing deprivations to the Rebel prisoners, including starvation and atrocious sanitary conditions. Yet, as long as he remained politically aware and astute to the Federal hierarchy, Tracy did not receive the wrath of his superiors. That was most likely due to the perceived need for Union retaliation against Confederate prisoners based on the reported atrocities committed against imprisoned Yankees at Rebel prisons such as Andersonville and Libby.

Following the war, according to Horigan, Tracy's proverbial ship reached dock in several remarkable ways:

After moving his family from Aplachin to a pleasant residential section of Brooklyn, New York, his postwar career would be launched when President Andrew Johnson appointed him to the position of federal district attorney for the eastern district of New York State. Returning to private practice, Tracy would defend the Reverend Henry Ward Beecher in a famous 1875 adultery trial, which lasted six months and ended in a hung jury. Tracy's distinguished legal career would include a brief term as a judge on the New York State Court of Appeals (the state's highest court) in 1881-82.

In 1889 President Benjamin Harrison would appoint Tracy to the post of secretary of the navy. The new secretary would enthusiastically embrace the idea of a two-ocean navy, and immediately embark upon the construction of a powerful American fleet. Secretary Tracy's initial steps were significant and would come to fruition under President Theodore Roosevelt who sent America's "great white fleet" around the world in 1907.

Following Harrison's presidency, Tracy chaired a commission that drew up the charter for the incorporation of Greater New York City in 1896. In 1897 Tracy ran as the unsuccessful Republican mayoral candidate in New York City, and he remained active in veterans' affairs and (behind the scenes) in politics until his death in August 1915. In 1920 the destroyer USS Benjamin F. Tracy was commissioned in memory of the former secretary of the navy. The Tracy, remaining on active duty through the Second World War, was retired in 1946. (Horigan 2002, 80)

Other 127th Regiment members would move on to illustrious military careers, including Lieutenant Charles Lawrence Cooper, whose daughter, Florrestine Cooper Hooker, noted his career as an officer with the Buffalo Soldiers' 10th and 9th cavalries. Joining Cooper would be some of his black compatriots, opening up a new chapter of intrigue as America solidified its Westward holdings with the muscle of former United States Colored Troops warriors.

12

The 24th United States Colored Troops
'The last to leave'

The 24th United States Colored Troops was the last regiment to leave Camp William Penn, despite its numerical sequence obviously placed before the 127th USCT. And soon the 24th would host a tremendous guest at the facility: the Underground Railroad icon Harriet Tubman. Most of its men were "principally recruited in the eastern section of Pennsylvania."

The 24th USCT's regimental colors were also designed by David Bustill Bowser, almost prophetically predicting the mountaintop themes of an African American leader who would rise less than a century later: Dr. Martin Luther King, Jr. *Courtesy of the Library of Congress.*

The unit was "organized at Camp William Penn, on the 17th of February, 1865, with the following field officers: Orlando Brown, Colonel; James M. Trippe, Lieutenant Colonel; Robert E. Stewart, Major." Most of the commissioned officers were experienced and seasoned (Bates 1871, 1011).

However, although the majority of the rank-and-file soldiers of the 24th regiment hailed from Pennsylvania, others came from a wide range of backgrounds – from former and runaway slaves escaping the South to those from the Caribbean with substantial sailing experience. One soldier even hailed from Cape Verde. And their ages were quite diverse too, with some soldiers joining as mere teenagers and others hitting almost 50 years old when they were mustered into service.[1]

Some were substitutes for whites who were usually well off and could afford to pay for such a service for a black servant or free African American in need of capital. For instance John Jackson, a laborer and 18 years old, of Company C, standing just over five feet, with ebony skin, black hair and eyes, hailed from Chambersburg, PA, and substituted for Alexander Hunter. Likely a free black, he mustered in on March 22, 1865. Eighteen-year-old Simon Caulsberry, described in service records with a "yellow" complexion, "hazel" eyes and "black" skin and hailing from an unidentified Pennsylvania locale, was a substitute for an Issac Ditler, despite evidence of a rugged or hard life. The Company B enlistee had scars on the right forearm and "on the right groin," according to his service records.[2]

Soldiers such as Jackson were likely intrigued by their compatriots who had arrived at Camp William Penn from distant places, including the one-year substitute William Brewster, age 45 and originally from Jamaica, who was old enough to be Jackson's father. Living in nearby Reading, PA, for a while before joining the service, Brewster of Company A was described as five feet, five inches in height with work experience as a steward.[3]

Then there was Brinmonde Willis, a "chairmaker" and native of Boston, MA, who was three inches shy of six feet tall and mustered in on January 11, 1865. Described with "dark" hair, eyes and complexion, Willis likely knew or was familiar with Brewster, since both belonged to Company A. And they were probably able to pick up on the oral accent of John Antonia, a 26-year-old sailor from Toga, Cape de Verde, who enlisted on October 12, 1864, for a term of three years. Antonia's skin, eyes and hair were described as sable, or black.[4]

Indeed, Antonia was not the only islander in the 24th. Robert Battese, 23, was tall, standing just over six feet, and very dark complexioned, with ebony eyes and hair. The "sailor" who was native to the "West Indies" was mustered in with Antonia on October 12, 1864, making it very likely that he was acquainted with the Cape Verdean. And being mustered in two days later, on October 14th, was John Baptist, 22 years old and described as a "laborer" from the "West Indies." Sadly, Baptist apparently died in the post (Camp William Penn) hospital of an undisclosed illness or injury on March 30, 1865. The sailor John Liverpool, 22 years old and of the "West Indies," also met the same fate as his comrade, Baptist, raising the possibility that contagious diseases were still a problem at Camp William Penn despite environmental improvements there. These men too were in Company A. In fact, Alexandria, VA, native Peter N. Matthews, an 18-year-old laborer and in the same company, was just five feet, four inches, and was tragically listed as dying in the post hospital on February 27, 1865, of "typhoid fever".[5]

That's not to say that every ill soldier at Camp William Penn at this point was destined for the grave. Thirty-year-old Lewis F. Moore, a laborer from Mendham, New Jersey, who enlisted on January 17, 1865, apparently became ill or was injured. A medium-height soldier at about five feet, eight inches, with black skin, hair and eyes (although many of the African American soldiers' eye colors were likely actually dark brown), Moore was discharged via a "Surgeon's Certificate of Disability by Order of Maj. Gen. Cadwalader" from Camp William Penn on May 18, 1865.[6]

Although environmental conditions had improved somewhat as the end of the war was finally within sight, there were obvious problems with contaminated drinking water, the usual culprit with respect to typhoid.

Still, it's likely that the morale of the 24th USCT while training was optimistic, especially given recent Union victories as spring approached. Indeed, by April, probably some of the men and officers attended a lecture and concert sponsored by abolitionists featuring the well known speaker and judge, Hon. Wm. D. Kelley, as well as the popular singer the "Black Swan," or Elizabeth Greenfield. Camp William Penn's band provided the supporting music:

> An enormous gathering assembled last night at Concert Hall. The occasion was that of an address by Hon. Wm. D. Kelley to the "Social, Civil and Statistical Society" of Philadelphia. This society, composed of the cultivated and more intelligent portion of the colored people of Philadelphia, has inaugurated a series of meetings, which have been addressed thus far by learned and eloquent men, irrespective of color. This course of lectures has been attended by immense audiences. Frederick Douglass, and other Americans of African descent have addressed the association. Last night, Hon. Wm. D. Kelley, following the example

The 24th USCT, on parade at Camp William Penn, was lectured to by one of the greatest figures in American history: the venerable Harriet Tubman, matriarch of the Underground Railroad, which was quite active in Chelten Hills. *Courtesy of the Library of Congress.*

of other gentlemen, did so, terminating the course. As we have said, the house was packed, though the whites predominated in numbers over the colored people. The band from Camp Wm. Penn gave the music. Their fine brass band of thirty musicians performed with such acceptability that at times the entire audience applauded them. Upon the platform were benevolent Christian gentlemen of both colors, with not a few clergymen, fair and dusky, mingling together as followers of the same Lord, irrespective of complexion, or color of cuticle. Prominent among them was Rev. Stephen Smith, a man of color, who, for thirty years, has been a preacher of the Methodist faith, and who, without shame and without reproach, has amassed a very handsome fortune. Miss Greenfield, known as the Black Swan, sang, accompanying herself upon the piano by way of preliminary.[7]

Organized by a committee headed by William Still, the program, which featured Kelly expounding on the evils of slavery and contradictions of slaveholders, was punctuated with much applause.

Later that month, the high spirits again soared during the 24th's flag presentation ceremonies in front of the State House, where the "Declaration of Independence was adopted," featuring the scintillating speaker and young black leader O.V. Catto. *The Christian Recorder*, in its April 22, 1865, edition, hailed the event as a historic occasion, and a sign that America was beginning to live up to its ideals of universal equal opportunity:

> It was announced in the papers that a regimental flag would be presented to the 24th United States Colored Troops, in front of the State House, on Friday, at noon. In response to the announcement, at the appointed hour, an immense concourse of citizens had assembled in front of that historical building to witness the interesting ceremonies. The troops Lieutenant-Colonel Trippe commanding, followed by various civic organizations, arrived about 12 o'clock, and were brought up in front of the edifice. A meeting was organized by the appointment of Mr. J.C. White, Jr., as President; Messrs. Jos. La Combe; Jos. C. Bustill, Richard Gleves, Clayton Miller, and Chas. Simpson, as Vice-Presidents; and W.H. Minton, Secretary.

After a feeling prayer by Rev. H.H. Garnett of Washington, the President introduced Mr. Catto, in substance as follows:

> "Fellow Citizens and Soldiers – here, under the shadow of Independence Hall, within whose sacred walls the glorious Declaration of Independence was adopted – at the very moment when the gallant Anderson is raising the Stars and Stripes over Fort Sumpter, we have gathered to give a God-speed to the noble men of this regiment, who are going forth to assist in establishing the law and maintaining the integrity of this Government, a regimental flag, gotten up under the auspices of the Banneker Institute, by contributions from the public, will be presented by Mr. O.V. Catto, whom I now introduce."[8]

The paper then described the eloquence of Catto's presentation, noting his profound understanding of American and world history, as well as the contributions of the nearly 200,000 black warriors serving the Union amid fierce opposition from two sides during the Civil War:

> The speaker then paid a tribute to the two hundred thousand blacks, who, in spite of obloquy and the old bane of prejudice, have been nobly fighting our battles, trusting to a redeemed country for the full recognition of their manhoods in the future. He thought that in the plan of reconstruction the votes of the blacks could not be lightly dispensed with. They were the only unqualified friends of the Union in the South. In the impressive language written on this flag, "Let Soldiers in War be Citizens in Peace." The Banks policy may plant the seed of another revolution. Our statesmen will have to take care lest they prove neither so good nor wise under the seductions of mild-eyed peace, as heretofore, amidst the tumults of grim-visaged-war. Merit should also be recognized in the black soldier, and the way opened to his promotion. De Tocqueville prophesied that if ever America underwent Revolution, it would be brought about by the presence of the black race, and that it would result from the inequality of their condition. This has been verified. But there is another side to the picture; and while he thought it was duty to keep these things before the public, there are motives of interest founded on our faith in the nation's honor, to act in this strive. Freedom has rapidly advanced since the firing on Sumter; and since the Genius of Liberty has directed the war, we have gone from victory to victory. Soldiers! Accept this flag on behalf of
> the citizens of Philadelphia. I know too well the mettle of your pasture, that you will not dishonor it. Keep before your eyes the noble deeds of your fellows at Port Hudson, Fort Wagner, and on other historic fields. Desert them not. Accept, Colonel, this flag on behalf of the regiment, and may God bless you and them.
>
> Colonel Trippe, in a very chaste reply accepted the flag, thanking the donors, and assuring them that it should never be dishonored.
>
> At the conclusion, cheers were given for the Union, Abraham Lincoln, Benjamin F. Butler, Colonel Draper, and his black troops, (the first into Richmond,) Colonel Wagner, Col. Trippe, and others.[9]

Harriet Tubman told the soldiers of the 24ᵗʰ USCT about her exploits as a scout and rescuer of enslaved Africans, as well as encouraged them to be brave when they took to the battlefield. *Courtesy of the Library of Congress.*

Yet, the men of the 24th had to be also very elated when a "charismatic black woman strode in front of hundreds of black soldiers at Camp William Penn and delivered a stirring speech" a week later (Scott 1999, 82):

> [Harriet] Tubman was a wanted woman by Confederate authorities. She had made many trips into the Deep South and escorted hundreds of runaway slaves to freedom via the Underground Railroad that extended through Chelten Hills, Pa. There was a $40,000 reward on her head.

Like Frederick Douglass and "many of the Camp William Penn's soldiers, Harriet Tubman was an escaped slave with the scars of slavery on her body. Although she spoke a slave dialect and not standardized English, she greatly inspired the men that day [April 6th, 1865, less than two weeks before Lincoln's April 15 assassination]," noted a *Christian Recorder* article published April 15, 1865 (ibid.).

The correspondence was likely sent directly to the paper's editor, the Rev. Elisha Weaver of the African Methodist Episcopal Church, which now seemed to fully support the recruitment of black soldiers for the war:

> MR. EDITOR: - I beg your indulgence for intruding upon your columns so soon again. As there are so many very interesting incidents occurring, just about this time, in and around Camp Wm. Penn, we think it would be interesting to so many of our brave colored soldiers, who have left this camp and are now on the field of battle, or doing garrison duty in the South, to hear from us through your paper.
>
> On last Saturday evening we had a very entertaining homespun lecture from a colored woman, known as Harriet Tubman. It was the first time we had the pleasure of hearing her. She seems to be very well known to the community at large, as the great Underground Rail Road woman, and has done a good part to many of her fellow creatures, in that direction. During her lecture, which she gave in her own language, she elicited considerable applause from the soldiers of the 24th regiment, U.S.C.T., now at the camp. She gave a thrilling account of her trials in the South, during the past three years, among the contrabands and colored soldiers, and how she had administered to thousands of them, and cared for their numerous necessities. After the lecture, resolutions were passed by the regiment to be published in the Recorder. The lecture was interspersed with several gems of music. Professors Burris and Turner presided at the organ. After a liberal collection for the lecturer, the meeting adjourned.[10]

And as the inspired regiment, the last to leave Camp William Penn, prepared for war, matters at the facility had improved dramatically. In fact, at least since the beginning of the year, citizens throughout the Philadelphia region relished in their optimism, most notably the black community, which continued to raise money for its black warriors via lectures by the likes of Frederick Douglass and musical presentations, including by the "celebrated" "Black Swan":

FRED. DOUGLASS, will deliver the 3d Lecture of the Course before the Social, Civil and Statistical Association of the Colored People of Pennsylvania, on Thursday evening, February 16ᵗʰ, in Concert Hall. Subject, "Equality before the Law." Miss E.T. Greenfield, the celebrated "Black Swan" and the Post. Band from Camp [*sic*] William Penn, will perform on the occasion. Admission, twenty-five cents. For the benefit of freedmen, sick and wounded soldiers, &c. The subsequent lecture will be by Mrs. F.E. Watkins Harper, Monday evening, February 27ᵗʰ; J. Mercer Langston, Esq., Thursday evening, March 9ᵗʰ; and Hon. W.D. Kelley, evening not fixed. Committee – Isaiah C. Wears, U.B. Vidall, J.C. White, Sr., Jonathan C. Gibbs, Stephen Smith, Redman Faucet, William P. Price, Maurice Hall, S.M. Smith, C.H. Bustill, Henry Gordon, J.C. Bustill, WM. STILL, Chairman. Tickets for sale at the office of the *Christian Recorder*.[11]

Several weeks later, soldiers from Camp William Penn and Philadelphia's black community were likely very happy to attend yet another event featuring Harper and the Black Swan, as reported by *The Christian Recorder*'s March 4, 1865, edition:

On Monday night last Mrs. F.E.W. Harper delivered her lecture before a very large and intelligent audience, at the above named hall. The evening's entertainment was opened by the colored Post band from Camp William Penn, who are remarkably proficient in the musical line. Shortly after Mrs. Harper made her appearance, and was welcomed by another stirring air from the band. Miss Greenfield, the celebrated "Black Swan" now took her seat at the piano, and accompanied another young lady, who sang a beautiful piece, in a highly finished style. Mrs. Harper was now introduced to the audience, which, by the way, was one of the largest assembled during this winter's course, by Mr. Wm. Still [...] At the conclusion the band struck up that soul-stirring battle song, "We'll rally round the flag, boys," which excited the audience to the highest pitch of enthusiasm, and called forth continued rounds of applause. Miss Greenfield again took her place at the piano and accompanied her young companion, who executed another piece of music in such a masterly style as to bring out an encore, which was responded to by Miss Greenfield, who sang a very sweet and touching piece of music, accompanying herself upon the piano, after which the audience dispersed to their homes, highly gratified with the evening's entertainment, and feeling that they had indeed enjoyed "a feast of reason and flow of soul."[12]

About the time of the concert, in early March, the 24ᵗʰ Regiment's warriors were also very proud when one of its officers, Lieutenant P.P. Carroll, was presented with a sword for his generally exemplary service to the regiment as described in the April 15, 1865, issue of *The Christian Recorder*. The correspondence is clear evidence that the black soldiers and more than a few of their officers had great rapport with each other, with the recipient of the sword even telling the black soldiers of his dedication to extinguishing slavery:

H'd. Q'rs. Camp William Penn, Chelton Hills, Pa., March 17ᵗʰ, 1865.
MR. EDITOR: – Dear Sir: – I am requested by the members of Company

"D," to inform you of a sword presentation which took place in this camp this afternoon.

The presentation took place immediately after dress parade, 5 p.m. The members of the above named company were paraded by Orderly Sergeant John A. Fauset; after which they were drawn up in line under arms, before the quarters of Lieut. P.P. Carroll, who was the recipient of the present. On appearing on the ground he was received with cheers. The presentation address was delivered by Capt. C.H. Coxe, 24ᵗʰ U.S.C.T., which was very patriotic and well adapted to the occasion. The Captain concluded with some eulogies and complimentary remarks, after which the Lieutenant responded as follows, namely: - "Captain: You have done me quite an honor, and it is needless for me to intimate how sincerely I appreciate the eulogies bestowed upon me in behalf of the soldiers who have contributed to the purchase of a sword, which they desire to present to me as a token of their friendship and esteem. And to you, fellow soldiers, I cannot find words to express my thanks for the kindness exhibited in conferring upon me an unearned and unexpected honor from your hands [...]. Now, soldiers, accept of my thanks, and from this day forward, the seventeenth of March shall bring to my mind two happy recollections, the day of my birth, and the day that I received this handsome sword from Company 'D,' 24ᵗʰ U.S.C.T." After which he received "three hearty cheers."

JOHN A. FAUSET, O. Sergeant.[13]

So morale was strong at that point due to the generally supportive atmosphere and the soldiers, at least some of them. Despite contrary evidence, some seemed even impressed with General Wagner and how the facility was managed, a marked difference from when the fort was first established in the summer of 1863. That's according to a letter sent to the *Recorder*'s editor, the Rev. Elisha Weaver, by a soldier identified as simply "A.B.," despite some concerns about camp conditions and operations:

I enlisted in the service of the United States, on Monday, February 27ᵗʰ, 1865, and, after having a pass for a few days, as the military term is, I was taken to Camp William Penn, where, upon my arrival, I was presented to the Adjutant of the Camp, who, after having my papers properly entered upon their record, consigned me to my place of sleeping and eating, called the barracks. Now, Mr. Editor, after being in camp a few weeks, I must acknowledge myself very agreeably disappointed, (with some few exceptions,) especially with Col. Wagner. My mind having been filled with the many strange stories I had heard of the Colonel, I must acknowledge my utter astonishment at finding so gentlemanly, kind, and Christian a man, and, to my limited knowledge of military tactics, so efficient an officer. The Col. is always to be found attending to the welfare of the soldiers in Camp, both moral and religious, although, I am constrained to say, there are many who contrive to elude his vigilance. With regard to the Camp, Mr. Editor, if you could only spend a week in it, and witness the Colonel, the Adjutant, the officers generally and the regiment, and their manner of operating in military affairs, I think you would pronounce it excellent. We have Divine service every Sabbath afternoon, at half past three o'clock, by a spirited young minister of the Protestant Episcopal Church [likely Rev. Parvin of the nearby St. Paul's Episcopal Church]; we have a Sunday-school which is very well attended by the soldiers who are anxious for knowledge; we have, also, a fine organ in the chapel and an efficient choir, composed of the soldiers, which adds greatly to the services on the Sabbath.[14]

Behind the scenes, though, Wagner apparently had to deal with charges that the camp's operations were far from perfect. His superior officers actively debated whether to actually close Camp William Penn as the war simmered down:

Finally, in the waning months of the war, documentation of the camp's decline was reinforced by leaded correspondence between high ranking officials in the Bureau of Colored Troops. In March, 1865, the camp's worried commander sought confirmation of the War Department's plans for the facility: "I have the honor to state that I have been furnished with an official copy of a letter from you, dated 10ᵗʰ inst. To Bridg. Gen'l James B. Fry, Provost Marshall General, in which you state that 'It is not contemplated to organize any additional Colored regiments at Camp William Penn' […] and would very respectfully ask that if it is intended to discontinue this Post, you notify me immediately, as their [*sic*] are several improvements in process […] which ought in that event to be discontinued as they would entail unnecessary expenses." (Johnson 1999, 102)

Meanwhile, religiously, at least a few of the soldiers also were influenced by the local Quaker doctrines, not so surprising since the mighty Quaker theologian, Lucretia Mott, lived just a stone's throw from the camp near other prominent Friends: "James Thompson of Shoemakertown, Pennsylvania, for example, wrote to a friend about a new-found spiritual development acquired after he began associating with nearby Quaker residents," thoughtfully writing: "You know I used to swear once but now swearing does not trouble me for I have the Good Lord always in my heart and I know that no ill can befall me. I am now nursing our doctor who is at a Quaker's house … these good people teach me to be good" (74).

Despite rumors and reports that the camp might be closing, the 24ᵗʰ had good news to enhance its morale – the fall of Richmond, according to an April 15, 1865, *Christian Recorder* article:

On Monday, about 3 o'clock, when the 24ᵗʰ regiment was drawn up in line for Battalion drill, Col. Wagner received a dispatch that Richmond had fallen, and that the colored troops who had left Camp Wm. Penn, were the first to enter the city. You can imagine, better than I can describe, the scene that followed the reading of the dispatch to the regiment by the Colonel. The vociferous shouts and hurrahs were indescribable. On Tuesday the Post Band was ordered to Jenkintown, and paraded through the town, playing all the national airs, in honor of the great victories of our army.[15]

The elation of pro-Union forces, including the black community, was captured vividly in an April 8, 1865, report in the *Christian Recorder* that also gave great praise to Commander Ulysses S. Grant:

> Steady and ever onward has been the march of the Union army since its command was intrusted to Lieutenant-General Grant, until, at last, that cry is heard, "Richmond is ours!" Not a mere game of chance was that strategical movement by which Lee, that most impenitent traitor, was so beautifully checkmated. It was a problem requiring the most consummate skill for its solution. On the one side was a cool, determined and skillful General, conscious of final victory, and fighting for his country's honor. On the other a desperate and oath-breaking leader, seeking individual renown, even when mindful of the utter hopelessness of his espoused cause.
>
> All honor to Ulysses S. Grant. His name will ever be placed on the list with those of Geo. Washington and Abraham Lincoln. All dishonor to the name of Robert E. Lee – and, as the Press of Tuesday says, "Away with the pretext that this wretched ingrate has any claims to the consideration of the American Government."
>
> To the colored troops, who were the first to enter the doomed city, let all praise be given. History will record the fact that the black man, whose services were at one time refused by the Government, struck the death-blow, and planted the dear old flag where for nearly four years has hung the rebel rag.[16]

A follow-up article in the *Recorder* published April 22, 1865, certainly captured the fanfare, with a handsome and rising black intellectual, Octavius Valentine Catto of Philadelphia, a central figure in the activities:

> On last Friday the colored people of Philadelphia celebrated the capture of Richmond, and the other recent victories of the Union army, by a grand parade. The procession passed through most of the principle streets, and when it reached the State House, a flag was presented to the 24th U.S.C.T. The presentation speech was made by Mr. O.V. Catto.
>
> The Delmonico Assembly, No. 1, formed one of the leading features of the parade. There was quite a profusion of carriages and open barouches along the line, and every one seemed highly pleased with the affair. A squad of sailors, carrying a large American flag, made a fine display. The whole was under the direction of Mr. J.E. Glascow, Sr., assisted by a large number of deputy marshals, among whom were Sergt. Major Green, of the 127th U.S.C.T., and Mr. W.B. Decordover. At a late hour the 24th regiment left the city for Camp Wm. Penn, carrying with them a beautiful flag, the gift of our colored citizens. This regiment contains quite a number of the most intelligent colored men of our city. We trust they will give a good account of themselves.[17]

And for the moment, the soldiers seemed especially impressed with the facility's musicians, specifically the post band and a Renaissance man of sorts identified as "Judge

Ludlow," despite acknowledging activities at the camp that may not have been necessarily Christian-like:

> We have many leisure hours in Camp, which we enjoy as inclination dictates; and there are a few among us who are of that stamp that incline to an indulgence in the minor practices of camp life, but, taken altogether, it is pleasant. Of the second United States brigade post band it can be said, without the least vanity of flattery, that it is made up of the most efficient artists, whose capacity and taste are displayed in performing some of the most difficult compositions in music, is truly remarkable; some of the difficult gems from Verdi, Guonod, Von Weber, &c., are rendered with perfect ease, and they are deserving of great credit for their musical abilities. It would afford me inexpressible pleasure, could I say as much of them in a literary point of view; however, there is an exception among them, one who is full of wit, and has sailed to nearly every port in the world, and to whom it is quite interesting to listen, during our leisure intervals, as he gives us reminiscences of his travels through Asia, Africa, Europe and America, and, in days of yore, would have equaled the king's fool, but, among us he is known as Judge Ludlow.[18]

Apparently conditions at the post hospital had also improved somewhat, with Chelten Hills' residents helping with aiding the ailing soldiers, something that elated the writer:

> The hospital connected with the Camp is handsomely fitted up, and the patients therein are properly cared for under the direction of Surgeon Styer, Dr. Beal, and others whose names I have not yet learned; there is also in the neighborhood, a lady named Mrs. Mears, who gives much of her time and attention to the comforts of the invalids, and also to the Sunday-school. May God bless her and the ladies who assist her; may their paths be crowned with peace, and, when their voyage of life is over, may theirs be joy and happiness above. More anon. A.B. Chelten Hills, Pa. March 29th, 1865.[19]

There was even talk of giving promotions to several of the 24th USCT's black sergeants after much of the regiment departed for Camp Casey, near Washington, DC, according to an apparently official correspondence published by *The Christian Recorder* on June 3, 1865:

> For the Christian Recorder.
>
> LETTER FROM LIEUTENANT-COLONEL TRIPE.
>
> Headquarters Camp Casey, 24th U.S.C.T.,
> May 19th, 1865.
>
> MR. EDITOR: - I TAKE THE LIBERTY OF WRITING A FEW LINES WHICH I CONSIDER WORTH RELATING RELATIVE TO THE YOUNG

MEN ENLISTED IN Philadelphia for the 24th U.S.C.T., and organized at Camp William Penn.

There is Sergeant Stephen F.R. Burdy, Sergeant Simpson, and William H. Rex. All of these named gentlemen have proved themselves to be men and soldiers in every respect by their praiseworthy efforts to elevate their race. I do think it no more than right and proper that these smart and intelligent men should be promoted to a higher office, if a colored army is retained, – and I do most cordially recommend them as being worthy of promotion. They are now engaged in teaching school, and instructing the uneducated; and as for instructions in the manual of arms, there are none to surpass them. They are worthy of the fullest confidence.

Yours respectfully,

LIEUTENANT-COLONEL TRIPPE, Commanding 24th Regt., U.S.C.T.

CHAS. H. POTTER, Acting Adjutant.[20]

In fact, during early May, "the regiment proceeded to Washington, and was placed in Camp Casey, on the Virginia side of the Potomac, opposite the city." Then, on June 1st, the men were sent to Point Lookout, Maryland, where they guarded Confederate prisoners of war. One of those soldiers was Lloyd F.A. Watts, a Gettysburg native who "trained at Camp William Penn in the spring of 1865 as the war wound down. Eventually rising to the rank of sergeant, Watts guarded Confederate prisoners at Point Lookout in Maryland. In a letter to his wife, he noted that there were 'twenty-five thousand [rebel] prisoners here we have to guard. It takes one hundred men for guard duty'" (Scott 2008, 84).

Watts, in fact, would have likely been one of the more compassionate black soldiers guarding the Rebels who had been dedicated to keeping such African Americans in chains,

or even worse. And although he'd proactively demonstrated his black pride throughout life, Watts was under no delusions that he didn't live in a society that was too often pro-racist, even in Gettysburg:

Probably no one worked harder for personal respectability and for collective black dignity in the Civil War-era Gettysburg, though, than Lloyd F.A. Watts. Born in 1835 in Maryland, Watts moved to Pennsylvania as a child and worked as a laborer before the war, helping his

Private Lloyd F. Watts likely heard Harriet Tubman speak at Camp William Penn and later guarded Confederate prisoners at Point Look Out, Maryland. *Courtesy of the Adams County Historical Society.*

family – six brothers and sisters and a widowed mother – stay afloat. Lloyd Watts was an ambitious man. In a notebook, he practiced his penmanship, performed mathematical equations, kept track of debts, and composed short paragraphs about how to be a better person. Swearing, he noted was to be frowned upon. It was "very ungentlemanly" and "cowardly." Every time a man swore, in fact, it revealed his heart to be a "nest of vipers" and "one of them sticks out his head." Novel reading was just as bad. If someone read "high exciting novels on Saturday night till eleven or twelve o'clock," it destroyed the taste for the Bible. He knew; he had tried it "only once" and that was enough. Watts was also a romantic. He wrote ditties about sweet doves and bowers of ladies, and he listed in his journal all the girls "of Col." in the neighborhood. And even though he was dedicated to learning and prayer, he found time for love. In 1861, he married Philena Cameron, the nineteen-year-old daughter of a blacksmith, whose father was prominent in the town's temperance fight and active in the church. (Creighton 2005, 62-63)

So as the war climaxed, it's not surprising that Watts picked up arms with his comrades of color. His principles and growing status in the local black community almost demanded that he enlist. And once he joined the 24ᵗʰ USCT, Watts quickly moved up in rank, likely due to his maturity and dedication. Still, he was clearly upset about his role of guarding the Confederates, perhaps preferring to meet them on the battlefield:

> Lloyd Watts and Randolph Johnston joined Company B of the 24ᵗʰ United States Colored Infantry in early 1865. Within a week of enlisting, Johnston had been appointed first sergeant and Watts sergeant, and they were on their way to soldiering in a wasteland. Point Lookout, Maryland, wrote Watts sarcastically, was a "great looking place." "There is nothing," he said, "but warter [*sic*] as far as your eyes can carry you it is a narrow strip of land ninety miles from Baltimore and there is only one way to get out" (216).

Yet, the newly-anointed black officer had other concerns: Watts predictably "worried that he could not honor Sunday with rest" (ibid.).

Meanwhile, most of the regiment would move towards the Confederate capital, Richmond. "About the middle of July, it was ordered to Richmond, Virginia, and after a delay of two weeks, was assigned to duty in the sub-district of the Roanoke, comprising six counties, with headquarters at Burkesville." Apparently, a number of posts had been "established at each county-seat, where government supplies were distributed to needy inhabitants, and the troops were employed in preserving order." The 24ᵗʰ USCT performed "this duty until near the close of September, when it was ordered to Richmond, and on the 1ˢᵗ of October, was mustered out of service" (Bates 1871, 1011).

Following the war, Private John Merryweather of the 24ᵗʰ Regiment's Company C became a member of GAR Post 139 of Scranton, Pennsylvania. He appears in an image found at the U.S. Army Military History Institute in Carlisle, PA, to be relatively well off, attired in fine clothes, proudly smiling lightly, with a thick mustache and goatee (Scott 2008, 83):

And not long before being discharged, Watts' compatriot, Johnston, struggled with various ailments. "Johnston, whose years of training men to be soldiers now amounted to gang labor and guard duty, lost his health," similar to other warriors in the regiment. "In the summer of 1865," after the terrible war's combat ended, "when his regiment marched to Roanoke, Virginia, for peacekeeping and supply work, he could barely keep up. He suffered increasingly from piles, and by the time they had marched into Virginia, he could no longer drill the company." (Creighton 2005, 216)

However, fortunately Johnston and Watts returned home to Gettysburg, but faced the racist pressures that many black servicemen endured upon returning from the battlefield. Nevertheless, they remained generally cohesive and proactive regarding black rights, despite the rise of such pro-racist groups as the Ku Klux Klan. That was even in Gettysburg, where President Abraham Lincoln had declared the North's positive momentum change following a string of Confederate victories, and labeled the great struggle as a war to end slavery in his timeless Gettysburg address of November 19, 1863. Blacks in Gettysburg faced incomprehensible animosity and hurtful insults, including Watts' brother, a survivor of the Battle of Olustee in Florida:

> Watts and Johnston and Gettysburg's other black soldiers returned home to Pennsylvania borough that was beginning to remake itself as a war memorial. Already historians were engrossed in measuring and studying the battlefield, and the press was extolling Gettysburg's white Union soldiers. The local men of color who had been eager to stem the invasion, and who with other black American soldiers had also worked to win the war, attracted little attention. That did not mean that local black soldiers had been totally ignored. During the war, the borough's Democratic paper had devoted considerable column space to these men. Editors reported that black troops were among the first "to turn tail and run" outside of Petersburg in the summer of 1864 and that engagements in Florida earlier that year were disastrous thanks to African American soldiers. Certainly aware that Gettysburg's own black men were fighting at the Battle of Olustee, the paper had insulted them viciously. "It is now reported," the paper said, "that the Florida disaster is mainly due to the cowardice of the colored troops. We do not know how true this report is, but we are very certain that before the war is over the negro will not be found as brave, enduring, or efficient as the white." At least two black Gettysburg soldiers died fighting at Olustee, and more were wounded. John Watts, Lloyd's brother, had been shot in the shoulder and hospitalized. (Creighton 2005, 216)

Regardless, Watts and other black veterans formed tight-knit groups, including "a branch of a fraternal society called the 'Sons of Good Will.' Johnston was the association's first president, Watts the association's first secretary." The group was involved with "taking care of the sick, honoring the dead with a proper burial place, and celebrating with speeches and festivities Emancipation Day on January 1" (217).

The African American veterans, though, had to bury their deceased in a segregated cemetery, "along Long Lane," where "members bought plots for their families and put in a fence and a gate." The site struggled, since black economic affluence was minimal, often initially resulting in unmarked graves at the Lincoln Cemetery, where Watts and about 30 Camp William Penn warriors are buried today, and highly upsetting at least one unidentified white observer:

> The growing distance between black and white Civil War commemoration did not go unremarked. In 1873, during exercises at one of the black graveyards, a speaker reminded his audience of the meaning of the war. It had been, he said, a fight against "traitors" whose Confederacy had as its "corner stone Involuntary Servitude." Black soldiers had enlisted and fought with "heroic, self-sacrificing spirit" for a country that they hoped would recognize their "Manhood." But what had happened? Here in Gettysburg, while black men and women were now invited to decorate the graves of the white men who died in the Civil War, who honored men of color? The answer was obvious. "The colored people [were] requested to decorate the graves of the colored soldiers." The speaker was horrified. Did not these African American men "fraternize with their white comrades on many well contested fields of carnage and blood?" With this sort of segregation, he wondered, "where is the boasted civilization of America?" He called for flowers on the black soldiers' graves, so that the heroism of these men would not be lost, but rather be "green in our memories" (ibid.).

Johnston and Watts, however, were destined for different paths in life not long after the war, with Watts outliving his compatriot by many years. Illness had finally taken its toll on Johnston, who had nevertheless become quite religious, and would eventually claim the industrious Watts. Wrote Creighton:

> Randolph Johnston, who in 1863 had organized black soldiers to help repel Confederate invaders, left the Borough of Gettysburg in 1867. Shortly after delivering some "spicy remarks" as president of the Sons of Good Will (on an unknown subject), he moved with his wife to Maryland. There he taught school and became increasingly unwell. The piles he had suffered in the Civil War grew worse, and in his early fifties he complained that he could "hardly stand upon my feet." "I am oblige," he wrote in a pension affidavit, "to keep hot bricks to the soles of my feet to get to sleep." Johnston died suddenly in Baltimore in 1901 of a cerebral hemorrhage. He was sixty-one years old. His service to his country, his eagerness to fight invading Confederates, and his private strivings at home and at church barely grazed the public record (ibid.).

Lloyd Watts continued to be very active in the AME Zion Church and was hailed as a church leader, "one of the first black teachers in the borough," as well as "worked on behalf of the Republican Party, and he spoke at ceremonies and town affairs," remaining a proponent of black rights:

> And he served in the battles over Civil War commemoration. As an active veteran, he not only helped the Sons of Good Will honor the work of fellow soldiers, but he campaigned independently to encourage the celebration of Emancipation Day. While many white veterans were trying to sideline the divisive issue of slavery, Watts did his best to keep the story of black freedom alive. At the same time, like so many other people of color in Gettysburg, he worked for the "other" war – the white man's war. And how could he not? The establishments that promoted the popular battle history – the history that increasingly skirted black experience – were some of the biggest employers around. (222)

Watts and other Gettysburg blacks persevered, honorably toiling in the grassy fields and raising gargantuan monuments of men who did not look like them, to be adored for the ages:

> He helped transform green fields and rock inclines into one of the largest monument parks in the world. He helped erect statues to brave white men – men whom he believed were fighting in a war about slavery, but whom others argued fought for nothing of the sort. Watts did this work almost into his sixties, and hard labor hurt him, literally. In the early 1890s, while laboring on the monuments, he suffered chest and joint pain. Soon afterward, he said, he became disabled.
>
> In 1918, he died, a man steeped in the Civil War past, and bound up in the ironies of wartime memory. (222-223)

Perhaps there's no greater example of a Camp William Penn soldier symbolizing giving all that he could to fight for America's ideals, despite dealing virtually every day with racial challenges that had to hurt him to the core. Yet, it was not beneath Watts to exhaust his dwindling physical strength and last breaths in hope of realizing the promise of America – liberty.

THE NEW VERSION

OF THE

Colored Volunteer.

Composed and Dedicated to the 24th Regiment, U. S. C. T.

BY CORPORAL SAM'L NICKLESS, CO. I.

When the Twenty-fourth Regiment first began to form,
The boys kept at a distance, afraid to brave the storm,
But now they're rushing in the ranks without any fear,
To join the noble Twenty-fourth, and be a Volunteer.

CHORUS.—Give us the flag, all free without one slave,
And we will defend it as our fathers did so brave,
Onward! boys, onward! it's the year of Jubilee,
God bless America, the land of Liberty.

It was said sometime ago, that the negro would not fight,
But when they gave us arms, and all a soldier's right;
And sent us to the field, how we made the Rebels stare,
For they could not stand the charge of the Colored Volunteer.
CHORUS.—Give us the flag, &c.

When the Rebels made a dashing raid into our noble State,
We all became impatient, and for orders did not wait,
But went unto the Governer, and took him unawares,
For he did not know he'd find so many Colored Volunteers.
CHORUS.—Give us the flag, &c.

Now over twenty thousand men, we've sent into the field,
Who came from Pennsylvania, their country's flag to shield;
They're crowned themselves with laurels, their memory we revere,
The Nation now will always bless the Colored Volunteer.
CHORUS.—Give us the flag, &c.

Now we've raised another gallant band of brave and noble men,
For the present they are stationed at Camp William Penn;
Colonel Wagner is our leader, with him we'll danger dare,
For his faith will ne'er be shaken in the Colored Volunteer.
CHORUS.—Give us the flag, &c.

Now to the twenty-fourth, my boys, three hearty cheers we'll give,
And to her noble officers, long may their memory live;
They all have proved their courage, and will us onward cheer,
When Johnny Rebs dare to confront the Colored Volunteer.
CHORUS.—Give us the flag, &c.

Johnson, Printer, No. 7 North Tenth st.

This poem would have been honored by soldiers such as Private Watts, dedicated to the 24ᵗʰ USCT and honoring the regiment's fighting spirit. *Courtesy of the Library of Congress.*

Epilogue
Coming Full Circle

At Camp William Penn, the momentous and culminating month of April 1865 started with wonderful optimism, as the Union Army racked up victory after victory and Confederate forces were pushed toward Appomattox, ultimately surrendering in front of some of the very soldiers trained at the camp.

In fact, as reflected in the following *Christian Recorder* correspondence dated April 29, 1865, written by a soldier identified as A.B., most likely of the 24th USCT, that hopefulness reached a "crescendo" with the surrender of Gen. Robert E. Lee and his Confederate forces on April 9, 1865:

> Sunday, April 9th, was quite an interesting day, being the day of Thanksgiving for our recent victories. Our services were commenced at the usual hour, and after our Chaplain, the Rev. Henry Austice, had read to the soldiers and congregation the Proclamation issued by Governor Curtin; the choir sang, "My country 'tis of the'[thee] after which, the minister continued his discourse on the atonement, which was listened to with much interest. In the evening, the Rev. R. Faucett gave us a short but interesting sermon from Hebrews 12:1, 2; and, after the services, we all retired to rest. About midnight, the cry was heard in the camp, that Lee and his whole army had surrendered. You can judge of the feelings among the soldiers, when the distant sound of booming cannon was heard, and the ringing of bells throughout town and country.[1]

That mood of elation flowed from what had weeks earlier been anticipated to be a glorious Easter, representing the resurrection of Christ as well as the rebirth of the nation. The local minister of the St. Paul's Episcopal Church, Rev. Robert J. Parvin, not more than a mile northeast of Camp William Penn's grounds, was set to deliver a tremendous sermon that revolved around news that was beyond shocking, according to *The Christian Recorder*:

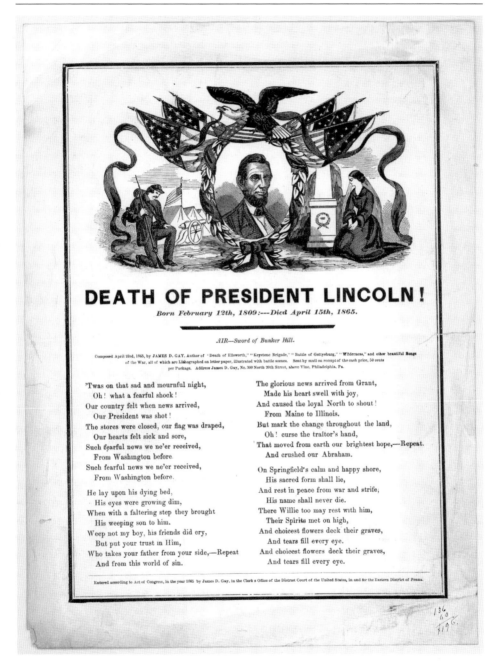

President Abraham Lincoln's death was so devastating that a wide range of remembrances, such as this funeral poster, were distributed. It was created by James D. Gay on April 23, 1865, about two weeks after Lincoln's death. *Courtesy of the Library of Congress.*

Sunday, April 16th, being Easter Sunday, we had an extraordinary sermon by the Rev. Dr. Parvin, from the 28th chapter of Matthew, on the Resurrection, which was delivered in an impressive manner. In the course of which, the Doctor compared the death of our Saviour, to the martyrdom of our noble President, and while he was eulogizing the life and death of our beloved President, there seemed to be the greatest sorrow throughout the entire congregation, many eyes being wet with tears, among officers and soldiers.[2]

Several days later, on April 19th, the scene at Camp William Penn was also devastating, despite being very moving. Again officiated by Rev. Parvin, the preacher during a sermon even recounted touching anecdotes of how he had personally associated with the bygone commander-in-chief, according to a 24th Regiment soldier who wrote to the editor of *The Christian Recorder*:

But, Mr. Editor, the most solemn occasion we have witnessed for years, was on Wednesday morning, April 19th. At about half-past ten o'clock, the drums beat for the soldiers to fall into ranks, and, after the regiment was drawn up in front of head quarters, Col. Wagner, whose heart is in the right place, had the orders of the War Department read to the 24th regiment U.S. colored troops, in reference to the obsequies of our lamented Chief. These were read by Adjutant Mulliken,

Harriet Tubman married a former private of the 8th USCT of Camp William Penn, Nelson Davis (sitting near her with a hat and cigar), who was said to be 20 years younger than the great Underground Railroad icon. She shared Nelson's pension before he died, and was later able to eventually get her own well-deserved pension. *Courtesy of the Library of Congress.*

and listened to with profound respect; after which, the regiment was drawn up in close order, according to military rule. Dr. Parvin, who is an exemplary Christian minister whose works speak for him, then delivered a most heartfelt, impressive, and soul-touching sermon, on the life, sufferings and death, of Abraham Lincoln; he spoke of the many private moments he had spent in the President's society, and how often he had disclosed to him his deep concern for the welfare of his country in this war. He also spoke of one interview, in particular, in which the President wept like a child. "But," said the Doctor, "soldiers, he has gone! You must endeavor to do your duty! God, for some wise purpose, has allowed him to be slain! But, the day is not far distant when there will be a Moses raised up to conduct you through the sea of sorrow which now surrounds you." He said, also, that the time had now come, when soldiers, white and black, were known only as soldiers, without any distinction, as he had seen it through out the army. After the sermon, the Doctor concluded with a very solemn prayer to Almighty God, by which every officer and soldier seemed much affected [...]. Yours, &c., A.B. Chelton Hill, Pa. April 21st, 1865.[3]

Despite Rev. Parvin's wishes for racial equality, the end of the war meant that blacks were merely set on the path to liberation, but by no means translated to certain upward mobility, including many of those associated with Camp William Penn. Nelson Davis, the private of the 8th USCT of Camp William Penn, and his soon-to-be bride who was 20 years his senior, the great Harriet Tubman, were no different.

After retiring to Auburn, New York, following the war:

Tubman also took in boarders. One of these boarders was a young Civil War veteran, Nelson Davis. Davis, a member of Company G, Eighth USCT that fought so valiantly at the Battle of Olustee, Florida, had been honorably discharged on November 10, 1865, at Brownsville, Texas [...]. Nelson Charles, as he was known then, was only twenty-one years old when he was discharged from the army. He followed a fellow soldier, Albert Thompson, from Company G to Auburn, where he found a room at Tubman's home and a job nearby, probably at a local brickyard abutting Harriet's property. (Larson 2004, 239)

And as if Providence itself was working its magic, Tubman received very interesting, but tragic, news: "Not too long after Davis had settled into Tubman's home [as a boarder], she received word that her husband, John Tubman, had been murdered in Dorchester County. On September 30, 1867, John Tubman and a white man named Robert Vincent, a neighbor of Tubman's, had some sort of disagreement, and Vincent shot Tubman dead" (ibid.). Apparently Tubman's relationship with Davis developed over the next two years.

However, Davis was not healthy, likely suffering from the effects of long hours of work and drudgery in extremely adverse conditions, including in places such as the Florida swamps around Olustee, where so many of his comrades had perished. Larson wrote, "Suffering with tuberculosis, he probably could not work consistently, so support of the household often fell on Tubman's shoulders. Some people believed Tubman married Davis in order to take care of him" (253).

Yet Davis, at first, was certainly not completely feeble. At times he "worked in the brickyard, helped farm Tubman's property, and was also an active member of the community, joining the Board of Trustees of St. Mark's AME Church at its founding in March 1870 along with several former Marylanders" (253). Regardless, the ex-warrior's health was definitely on a down slope: "Nelson's health continued to deteriorate, requiring more and more care and leaving the financial responsibilities of the household more fully on Tubman's shoulders" (261). Then sadly, according to Larson, "Nelson Davis died at the age of forty-five, probably as a result of the ravages of tuberculosis," on the 18th of October, 1888. Davis was buried at the nearby Fort Hill cemetery (276).

After Davis' death, Tubman had a very hard time making ends meet because the government would not recognize her as an eligible beneficiary of her deceased mate's pension; nor would they immediately grant Tubman a pension for her stellar work for the Army during the war:

> A Civil War pension would have helped her financial situation, and Harriet continued to press her claim for her war service as a nurse and a spy. In 1887 she petitioned Congress to release the file containing her application for back pay, with the intention, it seems, to reinstate her petition once again. No action was taken, however, and after her husband's death, Tubman applied for a widow's pension under the Dependent Pension Act of 1890. Designed to provide benefits to any disabled war veterans or their widows and dependents, the new pension act greatly expanded the original pension plan, which provided compensation only to veterans suffering with disabilities directly related to war service. Within a month of the enactment of the act in June 1890, Tubman filed her first claim; five years later, on October 16, 1865, she was finally granted an $8-per-month pension as the widow of Nelson Davis. She received a lump-sum retroactive payment of approximately $500 in late October 1895, covering the sixty-odd months from the time she first applied for the widow's pension until it was finally approved. (277)

To compound the pension issue, Davis' past slave identity became a very cumbersome problem:

> The lengthy process to obtain a widow's pension must have been frustrating for Tubman. Her right to Davis's pension would seem incontrovertible. But the bureaucratic process, which all widows had to negotiate, worked against African American soldiers and their dependents in ways that it did not for white applicants. In the case of Nelson Davis, as for many other former slaves who joined the Union army, his identity was at first difficult to ascertain in the military records because he had changed his name after the war from Nelson Charles to Nelson Davis. When Tubman first applied for the pension under the name Nelson Davis, it was denied because the claims office could not find a Nelson Davis on the muster rolls of the Eighth USCT. It took at least eighteen months before the mix-up was straightened out, and then it was another three years before all the supporting documentation, including sworn testimonies of relatives, friends, fellow soldiers from the Eighth USCT, and Auburn lawyers and other officials, was gathered

to the satisfaction of the Pension Bureau. After it was determined that Nelson Charles, who had served with the Eighth USCT, was the same person as Nelson Davis, the bureau required Tubman to provide documentation of their marriage, obtain sworn testimony that her first husband, John Tubman, had died before she married Davis, and demonstrate her worthiness to receive the pension. (277-278)

As a matter of fact, Tubman had to get various government officials and Army officers who knew of her war contributions as a scout, nurse, and spy to write letters of recommendation and verification. The following letter, written by Brigadier General Rufus Saxton on March 21, 1868, is an example, backing a petition sent to Congress by the "Hon. Wm. H. Seward, Secretary of State," supporting "a pension to Harriet Tubman, for services rendered in the Union Army during the late war. I can bear witness to the value of her services in South Carolina and Florida. She was employed in the hospitals and as a spy. She made many a raid inside the enemy's lines, displaying remarkable courage, zeal, and fidelity," Saxton wrote. "She was employed by General Hunter, and I think by Generals Stevens and Sherman, and is as deserving a pension from the Government for her services as any other of its faithful servants" (Bradford 1994, 142).

After dozens of letters and the congressional petition, Tubman eventually received relief via Nelson's pension, as well as benefits from her own until her death in 1913. But it was a hard fought and sad battle, given her great notoriety and stupendous record, as well as top government support.

Tubman certainly was not the only person associated with Camp William Penn who had great difficulties receiving pensions.

There was Benjamin Johnson, a former slave from Maryland who may have escaped in 1845. However, he likely did not experience much action during the war. And although military and government records conflict about the length of his service, his Army pension records indicate:

> At [Camp] William Penn […] near Jenkintown, Penn., about Sept. 1863 he […] strained his back by lifting musket Boxes – That he was not in the military service after Nov. 28, 1863 – That he was in the Hospital at Camp William Penn and discharged therefrom by reason of disability for which he claims pension

As Harriet Tubman aged she still remembered the Civil War days, and opened facilities to help the poor and elderly African Americans in and around Auburn, New York, where she retired. *Courtesy of the Library of Congress.*

[...] that while lifting said musket boxes – and piling them on top of each [,] the pile not being regular [,] the top or one of the said Musket Boxes with muskets (inside) fell on him. (Meier 1994, 100)

Another account, an affidavit likely testifying to Johnson's service, indicates that he was "a rough carpenter at the camp at Chelten Hills," and that the heavy case of muskets somehow was accidentally dropped by a coworker, somehow causing Johnson to fall on his back. He then was confined to a hospital bed, presumably at first at the camp. However, by the time authorities began to investigate the story the surgeon was reportedly deceased (100).

There were even horrific problems following the war regarding the care for wounded black veterans, including many from Camp William Penn, as indicated in "AN APPEAL" that was placed in the September 9, 1865, edition of *The Christian Recorder*. The article describes efforts to raise funds for the establishment of a "home for the disabled" due to the many wounded soldiers formerly of Camp William Penn walking the streets without adequate shelter:

> HOME FOR DISABLED COLORED SOLDIERS.
> AN APPEAL.
> We take peculiar pleasure in calling attention to the letter published below, which has been sent [to] us by a lady well known to many of our brave soldiers, who have experienced the benefits of her kind consideration while in the hospital at Camp William Penn. We have often thought, while looking at the numerous cripples constantly passing along our streets, whether it were not practicable to secure for them, at once, the establishment of such a home as is now designed; and surely there should not be found one, among our own people who is unwilling to contribute his mite to the erection of a monument so enduring as this would prove, – one which would show to the world how much we appreciate pure patriotism, and unflinching bravery which impelled these men to exemplify the manhood existing not less vigorously in the colored American than in the white.[4]

The writer, obviously upset with the veterans' demise, made a direct appeal to the African American community:

> Notwithstanding the fact that this war added largely to the demands made upon the charitable, there is no reason why the enterprise now proposed should fail of success. It is well, too, that the colored people themselves should show their devotion to their race, and to the cause of humanity, by co-operating at once, and efficiently in this good work. Let every one without delay hasten to contribute something, however small, and deem it a privilege to aid in advancing, by this and every other means, the cause which we profess to hold so dear. With so many friends among the ruling class to interest themselves in matters relating to our comfort and elevation, we must unite among ourselves, and unite with them, to illustrate practically our fitness for the enjoyment of the higher benefits of civilization. This enterprise is directed by those who are tried friends of our

people, and we must, by all means, get to work now and secure its success beyond contingencies of whatever nature.[5]

The paper also highlighted a letter from a woman, Anne de B. Mears, long-associated with Camp William Penn and aiding its soldiers, addressed to the editor, Rev. Elisha Weaver:

> SIR: – Through the columns of your widely circulated paper among the colored population of Philadelphia and elsewhere, I wish to make an appeal in behalf of the disabled colored soldiers who have been discharged from the service – many of them have no homes or any one to care for them. It is now our duty to speak and act in their behalf, that such an institution as a home for disabled colored soldiers should at once be established among us.
>
> Having had the opportunity of knowing many of these men who were at Camp William Penn, I feel particularly interested in their behalf, and know that they have received their wounds in a cause in which they have, in full faith, entered to sustain the honor and perpetuate the liberty of our common country, especially to unloose the fetters of their enslaved race – a victory so gloriously won. Let the colored men [now] come and be the first to contribute to such an undertaking, and I feel satisfied that it will succeed, as they have many friends who will aid the cause when the example is once set before them. The winter months are drawing near, and it is time to think of these poor cripples. I ask that the sum of ten thousand dollars ($10,000) shall be subscribed as a beginning to the work, and all donations shall be acknowledged through the papers whenever received. It is the intention to establish this home for the use of the soldiers during their natural life, and after they have passed away to be continued as an institution for aged colored men. Donations can be sent to my address through the Milestown P.O., 22nd Ward, or left with Col. R.R. Corson, 133 Walnut St., Philadelphia. Trusting this appeal will not be in vain, I remain yours, &c., ANNE de B. MEARS. Philadelphia, Aug. 9th, 1865.[6]

And it seems that the Camp William Penn veterans were afflicted with a variety of illnesses, including William Lewis, who served as a private in Company C of the 127th Regiment USCT. He lived in the Norristown area following the war, applying "for a disability pension in 1892 because of an injured back, impaired sight, and rheumatism," as well as "a slight heart murmur" that "was not considered debilitating." Lewis "died January 30, 1903, and was buried in Treemount Cemetery (Lot E-14). The Coroner's Death Docket recorded that he was a 58-year old widower, last employed as a hod carrier, and had been sick with pneumonia for two days before dying" (Meier 1994, 88-89).

Indeed, too many of the young black soldiers from Camp William Penn succumbed to illnesses, as indicated in the death of Private John Boyer, 26, of the 24th USCT, in 1866, according to a short obituary in the *Christian Recorder*:

> BOYER – At Harrisburg, August 4th, of consumption. John Boyer, aged 26 years and 9 months. He was born-in Adams Co., Penna. In Feb. 1865 he entered

into the service of his country, serving as a private in Co. D of 24th Regiment of United States Colored Troops. He leaves a wife and many relatives to mourn his death. His battle is fought. Just in the prime of manhood, he has been stricken down like the bud in the breath of the tempest.[7]

Charles Palmer was mustered in early December 1863 "as a corporal, in Co. A, 22nd Regiment, U.S. Volunteer Infantry, and was honorably discharged at Philadelphia on October 22, 1865." He stated that "he was 'hurt in the perineum [membrane lining the abdominal cavity] whilst climbing a fence in front of Petersburg and a fistula resulted which bothered him ever since. Also contracted rheumatism whilst in the service.'" Apparently, during "February 1864 he was 'absent – sick at Yorktown, Va." (Meier 1994, 96)

However, the end of the war meant more illness for Palmer: "After the war he worked in a livery stable for some years but had to give it up because of his rheumatism and did 'stray jobs' such as whitewashing, cleaning cellars, and beating carpets," before he applied for a pension. "At the time of his pension claims he was a heavy-set man, between 5 feet 8 ¾ inches and 5 feet 9 ½ inches tall and weighing between 202 and 220 pounds. He complained of a fistula, rheumatism, heart disease, lumbago, vision problems, deafness in the left ear, and asthma [...]. Charles Palmer died on October 28, 1904, at the age of 63" (97-98). There is no evidence that he had ever received a pension.

Then there was Henry Johnson, a private in Co. A of the 3rd Regiment, "who mustered in December 14, 1864, as a substitute" (78), likely leaving service on a surgeon's discharge in Tallahassee on June 6, 1865. The surgeon of the 3rd, a.m. Barnes, noted that Johnson suffered from diarrhea and chronic kidney disease for most of a year, causing him to be "unfitted for all soldierly duties, and is disqualified for Veteran Reserve Corps by reason of color. (80)" In describing his own condition, Johnson said the pain started with his kidneys and diarrhea simultaneously, noting that he was not capable of doing a full day's work (79).

Furthermore, compounding his problems and evidence that he certainly had not received a petition:

> Johnson had become an inmate of the Montgomery County Almshouse, in the words of J. Warren Royer, M.D., "in consequence of a severe injury to his left knee from the cut of an axe. This unfortunate accident, complicated with the usual strenuous habit so common to the colored race, conjoined with previous Rheumatism, eventually brought about [tears] of portions of the bones about the knee and extensive ulceration of the lymphatic glands below the knee. Complete anchylosis of the knee joint has taken place within the past two years. This unfortunate has also been afflicted for several winters past with Chronic Bronchitis, which adds not a little to his physical discomfort and general debility. His physical disability is henceforth without the pale of remedies, and will always totally disqualify him from performing any manual labor whatever." (80)

Mournfully, wrote Meier, Johnson died July 25, 1889, at age 68, without the funds for a decent burial. Originally scheduled to be buried at the Montgomery Cemetery, those plans were changed once authorities found out that Johnson was an African American. He

Octavius V. Catto, a black activist, was killed by whites associated with the Democratic Party and local law enforcement organizations, likely due to his civil rights initiatives concerning voting rights and desegregation. *Courtesy of the Library of Congress.*

A group of blacks vote, including a United States Colored Troops soldier, following the Civil War, a long awaited right for African Americans that would be road blocked by such anti-black groups as the Ku Klux Klan. *Courtesy of the Library of Congress.*

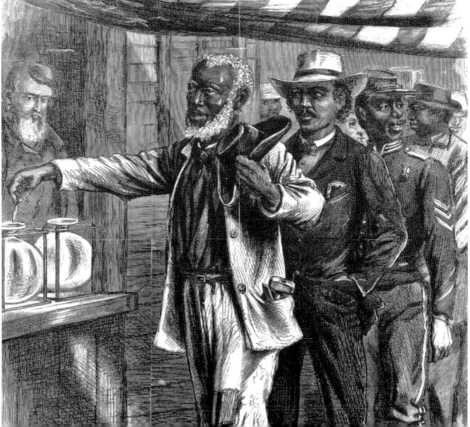

was ultimately buried at the Treemount Cemetery, associated with the African American Mount Zion Church in Norristown that accepted "indigent" whites and blacks, such as Johnson (80).

However, some members of Johnson's 3ʳᵈ USCT never made it out of the state of Florida due to a terrible racial incident that sparked their so-called mutiny and subsequent executions, the last time in U.S. history that such deaths occurred. Their deaths, in so many ways, symbolized the woes of Reconstruction during the late 1800s through the early 1900s, when countless blacks were killed by lynchings, maimed, and not permitted to vote.

The Death of Octavius Catto
The October 1871, the death of the black activist Octavius Valentine Catto in Philadelphia was a prime example of how area racists were determined to impede the temporary rising power of African Americans economically and at the ballot box. Already an exceptionally well known black leader in the region due to his scholarly involvement with the Institute for Colored Youth, where he was a respected faculty member and administrator, as well as civil rights orator and activist who organized a semi-professional black baseball team – the first to officially take on a white team – Catto would have made an attractive target for racists aiming to shatter the black community. "In 1871, with no federal troops on hand and the election of a mayor and city council on the ballot, whites mobbed black voters, killing three and wounding dozens. One of the victims was Octavius V. Catto, one of the first black Philadelphians to volunteer for the U.S. Colored Infantry in 1863. The first black Philadelphian elected to the Franklin Institute, he was feared by white racists as a brilliant young black leader" (Nash 2002, 253).

With the city already inflamed due to riots brought on by fears that blacks seeking to exercise their newly-acquired suffrage rights would upset the pro-racist Democratic power base in the city, blacks had been targeted for at least several days before election day, October 10, 1871. In fact, "Richard Greener, the Harvard grad and I.C.Y. teacher, could not believe what he was seeing – a white man shooting at an unarmed colored man at Tenth and Bainbridge. Greener immediately reported the incident to police but was told that the white man in everyday clothes was Thomas Moran, a 'special policeman.' Police offered no other explanation" (Biddle, Dubin 2010, 422-423).

The east Lombard Street area began to erupt with racial hostilities. Police were called from all parts of the city to the area. Even the military was summoned. "Panic soaked the streets like Indian summer humidity, and white men, often policemen, chased and shot down Negroes, even pursuing them into their houses. Older men like Stephen Smith [the noted anti-slavery abolitionist from Lancaster County] had not seen this kind of violence since the 1840s." And people who were quite familiar with Catto were dying. For instance, that "early afternoon, Levi Bolden, age twenty-two … was standing on Seventh Street, thirty paces north of South Street, when he was shot by a man in a police uniform coat and a white hat. He was carried to Pennsylvania Hospital three blocks away. The hospital treated his wound, but Bolden died three weeks later. Mary Ann Bolden told friends her husband said the shooter was police sergeant John Duffy." According to Biddle and Dubin, soon the conflagration would engulf Catto (424-425).

Although the streets were still very tense on October 17th, the long-awaited day of the election, Catto trekked to his school, the Institute for Colored Youth at Tenth and Bainbridge streets, as usual that morning. "During the twelve thirty school recess, Catto left the institute, walked home, and saw the crowds and the fear in people's eyes." He returned to school by 1 p.m., but very concerned about the students' safety, school authorities closed the school before the normal dismissal time. Catto, a major in the local Fifth Brigade, was asked "to arm himself" and summoned to headquarters at Broad and Race streets at 6 p.m. to "protect the city and its inhabitants as night fell." Catto already had the required sword, but would have also been provided with a horse. While returning from a bank at 919 Lombard Street, where he had withdrawn twenty dollars to purchase a handgun, Catto "was accosted by a white man with a gun on Chestnut Street," but was able to escape unharmed. After briefly meeting a friend and purchasing the gun at a pawn shop, the two parted ways about 3 p.m. at Sixth and Chestnut streets, noted Biddle and Dubin (428).

On his way back home he bumped into at least two acquaintances, careful to avoid the rioting just blocks away. Conflicting reports indicated that he may, or may not have, just voted. Regardless, Catto was just moments away from an awful fate:

> Continuing up Lombard, he turned south at Ninth and walked the one more square to South Street. His home at 814 was now a minute away. The street was becoming more crowded.
>
> He passed 825 South and nodded to his neighbor Thomas Bolling, who had been his pupil at the I.C.Y. and who had heard the 1864 "Alma Mater" speech. Bolling saluted his teacher. It was a little past three thirty.
>
> As Catto walked east on South Street, a white man with a bandaged head and a Kossuth hat was walking west. They were both on the south side of the street. No sign of recognition was apparent as they passed each other in front of Annie Howard's house at 822. Just a few more strides.
>
> A moment after they passed each other, the man with the bandage stopped and turned as if he suddenly realized whom he had just walked by. The damned colored Republican.
>
> The man crouched, pulled out a pistol, and pointed it at Catto. Annie Howard hallooed a warning to the man she knew as Professor: "Look out for that man!"
>
> The clip-clop of a horse drawing a streetcar west on South Street at Eighth did not drown out the sound of the pistol firing.
>
> The first shot struck Catto as he was retreating, his arms "spread out and shaking." Then Bolling's father saw him cross his arms and squeeze himself. He said to his attacker, who was about to shoot again, "What are you doing?"
>
> He ran injured toward the cover of the rear of the streetcar as it pulled to a stop. The conductor Theodore Stratton had heard that first shot. He saw the bandaged man follow behind the car.
>
> Onlookers on the sidewalk gaped. Streetcar passengers looked on aghast. Despite the witnesses, despite the police station at the corner, the bandaged man proceeded with no haste, as if his task were yet undone. Catto turned and faced him. The man fired again at close range. And again. And again. Catto staggered,

turned, and fell into the arms of a police officer who arrived on the scene. (428-429)

Catto's demise, at just 32 years old, was riveting and devastating to the city, and especially the black community, including soldiers that he recruited for Camp William Penn, as well as the former commander of Camp William Penn, Louis Wagner. Leading four black regiments and "a detachment of cavalry" during Catto's October 16th funeral procession that drew thousands of black and white onlookers along Broad Street (436), Brigadier General Louis Wagner had to be thinking of the many black soldiers who had given their lives in the field and the tragic death of Catto. How much more would they have to give their lives for what seemed to be a fleeting equality? How many more noble souls must be sacrificed?

A backlash against the violence turned out a large majority for the Republican ticket that year, which swept to victory due to the ultimate sacrifice of one dedicated to his principles, thereby validating his cause.

Several days after the fatal attack, a large and impassioned meeting of Catto's friends was held at National Hall on Twelfth and Market Streets. Numerous prominent speakers extolled the virtues of Catto's life and denounced the treacherous murders in stark terms. At this time, a large public funeral was planned and paid for at city expense.

The largest public funeral in the city since that of Abraham Lincoln was held for Octavius Catto on October 16, 1871. Because Catto was at the time serving in the Pennsylvania National Guard as a major and inspector general of the 5th Brigade, and, in fact, was on duty at the time of his murder, a full military funeral was authorized. Catto was laid in state in the city armory at Broad and Race Streets. His bier was guarded by troops of the 5th Brigade of the National Guard. Thousands thronged the streets to gain access and a view of the martyred hero. (Waskie 2011, 171)

Services were held throughout the region, even in Washington, D.C., with graduates of the Institute for Colored Youth coming "from as far away as Mississippi and New York" to Philadelphia. Once the procession "reached its destination just before 2:00 p.m." at Lebanon Cemetery, several clergymen offered comforting condolences and prayers. They included the Rev. William J. Alston of the African Episcopal Church of St. Thomas (where Catto and his father were members), led by the legendary Absalom Jones in 1792, who with Bishop Richard Allen (founder of the African Methodist Episcopal Church) had founded the pioneering civil rights group, the Free African Society. Indeed, the AME's then current bishop, Jabez Campbell, also spoke just before Catto's fiancé, Caroline Le Count, moved towards the casket. Her voice, rising above the somber funeral timbre, cried out to the heavens: "Octavius, Octavius! Take me with you" (Biddle, Dubin 2010, 440).

And although she would survive and continue to ascend in position at the I.C.Y., where she taught, Catto's frail father, William Catto, the well known Charleston, South Carolina, preacher who had brought his family to Philadelphia decades earlier, could not overcome his tremendous grief. He died December 7th, "about seven weeks after his son's death" (ibid.).

And as Catto's body was lowered into the ground, the finality of the moment was overwhelming to many. However, perhaps deceased black Civil War patriots gave him a warrior's welcome in the Hereafter. That's because in that "resting place" were also "339 soldiers of the U.S. Colored Troops" (ibid.), including Sergeant-Major Robert Bridges Forten of the 43rd USCT of Camp William Penn, the son of the venerable black sailmaker James Forten who co-founded the Free African Society with other elite Philadelphia black leaders during the late 1700s. Robert sadly died of disease not long after joining the ranks of Camp William Penn, receiving full military honors during his funeral. Lucretia Mott, the famous anti-slavery abolitionist who lived next door to Camp William Penn, spoke during the service (*Forten, Robert Bridges* 2007-2010).

Third Regiment Debacle

At precisely high noon on December 1, 1866, the United States government turned its fury on the black soldiers from the first regiment to march through the gates of Camp William Penn: the 3rd USCT. The six doomed soldiers, headed for a firing squad, likely heard the rousing mid-July 1863 speech of the great abolitionist Frederick Douglass a few years earlier, warning them that their actions during the war would impact the destiny of African Americans throughout the country "for generations to come." And although they had generally taken heed of Douglass' words, this tragic incident foretold of the incredible struggles that African American warriors were burdened with despite their exceptional performance during the war. The official charge was mutiny:

> At 1200 hours, on 1 December 1866, six soldiers from the 3d United States Colored Troops (USCT) were led from the guard house at Fort Clinch, Fernandina, Florida, and executed by a firing squad drawn from white troops at the garrison. The six soldiers – Privates David Craig, Joseph Green, James Allen, Jacob Plowden, Joseph Nathaniel, and Thomas Howard – were executed for the offense of mutiny. They were the last servicemen in the American Armed Forces to be executed exclusively for this offense. The mutiny leading to these convictions occurred on 29 October 1866 – just thirty-three days earlier. It resulted in an armed fire fight between officers and enlisted men and in fourteen court-martial convictions. (Bennett 1991, 167)

It's evident that the soldiers of the 3rd had fought valiantly, even after "a brief period of basic training," embarking in "August 1863 for Morris Island, South Carolina, where they served in the trenches before Fort Wagner," where the 54th Massachusetts, composed of more than a few Philadelphians, had fought so courageously as depicted in the motion picture *Glory*:

> Having suffered substantial casualties during this campaign, the regiment was transferred in February 1864 to Jacksonville, Florida, which by then was occupied by Union forces. From then until the end of the war, the regiment served

on outpost duty, continually fighting skirmishes, mounting raids, and launching expeditions into the Confederate-held interior of the state. After the cessation of hostilities, the regiment continued to be stationed in Florida on occupation duty. (138)

As their comrade, Josiah Walls, was destined to make great strides in what he'd coin the "sunny state" of Florida as a congressman and entrepreneur, the 3ʳᵈ had "the unenviable chore of trying to re-establish and uphold federal authority in a hostile environment," characterized "with endless hours of boredom and frustration." That was a very bad combination, since they were not able to expend energy in combat, causing "many of the soldiers" to turn "to alcohol and chafed under the continuing restrictions of military life and discipline," similar to white regiments following the war. Yet permanent relief was on the horizon. The 3ʳᵈ USCT soon, according to Bennett, received the long-awaited orders to "muster out on October 31, 1866, and the regiment concentrated at Jacksonville to muster out and ship home" (158-159).

The incident on the horizon would certainly dampen spirits, caused by several unfortunate circumstances that included the 3ʳᵈ being commanded by a relatively inexperienced 23-year-old officer, Lieutenant Colonel John L. Brower. The New York City native, in fact, "had no previous enlisted military experience when he obtained a direct commission as a captain in August 1863." His assignments were primarily due to "political connections," with his latest promotion commanding the 3ʳᵈ effective September 12, 1866. That was after the previous commander, "a Colonel Bardwell," moved on to become "military district commander" (159). However, wrote Bennett, Brower's inexperience was not the only problem:

> Unfortunately for the enlisted rank and file, in addition to his inexperience, Brower apparently was something of a martinet. Despite the fact that the 3d USCT had served honorably as a combat regiment and was shortly due to muster out, Brower seemed determined not to let military discipline slack off. While this was understandable and accepted by the troops during hostilities – when strict discipline and control were necessary to keep troops in

Josiah Walls of the 3ʳᵈ USCT eventually became one of the richest landowners and farmers in Florida, rising to serve in state and national politics as a U.S. congressman, and publishing a newspaper that employed a couple of his former Union commanders. That was quite a feat for an ex-slave who had been forced to fight for the Confederates. *Courtesy of the Library of Congress.*

line during battle – Brower's inflexible discipline only served to exacerbate an already strained relationship between most of the officers and the enlisted men of the 3d USCT. (ibid.)

Some of Brower's black soldiers were so upset that one penned a letter to *The Christian Recorder*, published in the August 6, 1864, edition, complaining about the discourteous treatment of black laundresses by white officers in the regiment. The complainants seemed to be particularly concerned about sexual overtones. "We have a set of officers here who apparently think that their commissions are licenses to debauch and mingle with deluded free women under the cover of darkness. The conduct of these officers is such that their presence among us is loathsome in the extreme" (ibid.).

Adding to the strain between the officers and men were the latter's concern "about growing insubordination and drunkenness on the part of their troops." And despite those white officers volunteering to lead black troops, and "negative connotations attached to such an assignment," such men certainly were products of their environments, wrote Bennett: "While they may have desired the abolishment of [s]lavery and respected the fighting qualities of their black troops, rarely was the individual officer untainted by some form of racism" (159-160). Indeed, some of the white officers thought of blacks as virtual heathens:

> Letters and journals indicate that most white officers considered blacks just one step removed from barbarism. As descendants of primitive peoples, these black soldiers – so their white officers felt – lacked self-control and discipline. "The Negro is very fanciful and instable in disposition" stated one officer. Because they perceived their black troops to be inherently savage and lacking self-discipline, white officers greatly feared that their troops could go wild and riot at any time. (160)

Furthermore, such white officers were comparable to Southerners who feared black insurrections before, as well as after the war, Bennett noted:

> Just as the fear of brutal violence in slave revolts terrified Southerners, so too it made the Northern white officers uneasy with the possibility of armed mutiny. One Union officer in a black regiment wrote his wife, "I do not believe we can keep the Negroes from murdering everything they come to once they have been exposed to battle." Additionally, it seems that some white officers were at a loss on how to teach and administer discipline to their black troops. As one enlightened regimental commander pointed out, "Inexperienced officers often assumed that because these men had been slaves before enlistment, they would bear to be treated as such afterwards. Experience proved to the contrary. Any punishment resembling that meted out by overseers caused irreparable damage." Given then, the volatile environment which existed within the regiment, it did not require much for the long-simmering discontent to explode into confrontation. (ibid.)

So, given the circumstances, perhaps it was inevitable that sooner or later something would give. Sadly, the "incident providing the spark occurred on Sunday, October 29, 1865 – two days before the regiment was to be mustered out" (ibid.). The men had come such a very long way and had persevered, only for the proverbial goal posts to be set back, and for some, out of reach forever.

It all started, according to court-martial transcripts, when "it appears that during the midmorning hours of Sunday, October 29th, an unnamed black soldier was apprehended while attempting to pilfer molasses from the unit kitchen," Bennett wrote. However, the soldier was arrested by a Lieutenant Greybill, "acting as officer of the day" (ibid.). Greybill's next move would trigger a chain of events that went well beyond human control:

> Lieutenant Greybill then undertook to have the soldier summarily punished by having him tied up by his thumbs in the open regimental parade ground. The prisoner resisted the efforts of Lieutenant Greybill and a Lieutenant Brown, the regimental Adjutant, to tie him up. At this juncture Lieutenant Colonel Brower arrived on the scene and the prisoner was bound "after some difficulty."
>
> During the time that the prisoner was being strung up, a crowd of enlisted men gathered in the general area and began to manifest a disposition to cut the prisoner down and free him. Private Jacob Plowden, a forty-four year-old ex-slave from Tennessee, began "talking loudly" and disputed the authority of the officers to punish a man by tying him up by the thumbs. Plowden, who was alleged to "have been considerably in his liquor," stated "That it was a damn shame for a man to be tied up like that, white soldiers were not tied up that way nor other colored soldiers, only in our regiment." He further announced that "There was not going to be any more of it, that he would die on the spot but he would be damned if he wasn't the man to cut him down." (160-161)

Plowden and his compatriots certainly had great reason for concern, since the rarely-used punishment required the so-called "offender to be stripped to the waist and be strung up by the thumbs for several hours so that only his toes were touching the ground." So, the many former slaves watching their comrade's torture were likely very disturbed and growing furious, especially given all that they had gone through in risking their lives and health for the Union. "In the Civil War, even though blacks were subordinate to white officers and within the structured environment of the army, they were able to assert themselves and develop individual and collective identities. There were natural bonds among them forged through the institution of slavery, racial discrimination and, most importantly, combat. They were, therefore, highly sensitive to acts by whites that smacked of unfairness or physical brutality. Even such punishments as tying up unruly soldiers were perceived as excessive. Time after time black troops responded by cutting comrades free, and on numerous occasions they launched full-scale mutinies against this sort of mistreatment" (Glatthar 1991, 475-485).

So, it's not surprising that other black soldiers began to side with Plowden. Too many degrading memories of their slave pasts as they risked their very lives for the country made most very adverse to such so-called punishment, Bennett wrote:

Plowden was not alone in his attempts to incite the crowd as Private Jonathan Miller began moving among the crowd shouting, "Lets take him down, we are not going to have any more of tying men up by the thumbs." According to an eyewitness account by another officer, a group of twenty-five to thirty-five unarmed enlisted men started advancing toward the three officers and the prisoner. A Private Richard Lee was in the lead, telling the crowd to "Come on, the man has been hanging there long enough." At this point, Lieutenant Colonel Brower stood by the side of the prisoner, waited until the group was within fifteen feet, and then – drawing his revolver – fired into the crowd. Two of the shots struck a Private Joseph Green in the elbow and side, and he fell wounded in the parade ground. Pandemonium then broke loose and the crowd retreated with a number of soldiers yelling "Go get your guns, lets shoot the son of a bitch." While a number of the black enlisted troops dispersed after the firing, around fifteen to twenty actually obtained their weapons from their respective tents and returned to the parade area[.] There, they opened fire on Lieutenant Colonel Brower and the other officers. (161-162)

As if the situation could not have been more explosive, Lieutenant Greybill decided to get help from the nearby town, presumably from whites, with "several shots whistling close behind him." Meanwhile Lieutenant Brown, serving then as adjutant, "mounted his horse and proceeded to the section of camp where Company 'K' was located" (162). According to Bennett, he tried to calm the soldiers and get them to fall into formation, hoping to head off the rebellion:

There he attempted to have the company fall in so as to quell the mutiny. As the company was forming, several of the armed mutineers – Privates Harley, Howard, and Nathaniel – also arrived in the area. Shots allegedly were fired at Lieutenant Brown, whereupon several soldiers forcibly subdued Privates Nathaniel and Howard and took their muskets away. By this time, the company was gathering about Lieutenant Brown, querying him as to what was going on. During this confusion, Private Harley took Lieutenant Brown's service revolver from its holster and attempted to take him prisoner. In a matter of minutes, however, the noncommissioned officers of Company "K" had restored order in that area. (ibid.)

However, the incident was far from over. Apparently, when a Lieutenant Fenno left his quarters to investigate the raucous, he was surrounded by several enraged black soldiers:

He met with curses and "improper language" from a Private Calvin Dowery. Lieutenant Fenno responded by drawing his saber and slashing Private Dowrey on the left arm, slightly wounding him. While Lieutenant Fenno's attention was distracted by several other of the enlisted soldiers, Dowrey returned with a fence rail and walloped Lieutenant Fenno on the right side of his head. While he was attempting to pick himself off the ground, another unknown soldier forced him down again into the dirt with a buttstroke of his musket. The soldier with the musket then disappeared into the crowd and several soldiers took the fence rail away from Dowrey. (ibid.)

Meanwhile, the turmoil had even spread to a place of normal order, as well as pomp and circumstance: the parade grounds. There, "a fairly brisk fight took place at the regimental parade ground between Lieutenant Colonel Brower and several of the armed mutineers." Bullets whizzed by in every direction. Bennett reported:

> It was estimated that thirty to forty shots were exchanged, until the gunfire abruptly ended when Brower's finger was shot off. Private Richard Lee, one of the original investigators – but one who had not taken up arms – rushed over to Lieutenant Colonel Brower. With the help of several others, he escorted Brower to the relative safety of the cookhouse. Several of the mutineers followed close behind, including Private James Allen, who yelled, "Let me at him, let me shoot the son of a bitch." Private Lee tried to ward the pursuers off, warning them to "stop their damn foolishness." (163)

Apparently though, according to Bennett, a number of the so-called mutineers were apprehended and already held in custody. And during the debacle, the soldier who had been initially hung by his thumbs was almost freed by a sympathizing compatriot, Private James Thomas:

> As Lieutenant Colonel Brower was seeking refuge in the cookhouse, a Captain Walrath arrived with a number of troops who immediately began to disarm the mutineers and quell the disturbance. Brower then left the cookhouse and started for town, aided by several enlisted soldiers. A number of mutineers who had not been apprehended began to follow him a short distance behind, shouting threats and insults. The mutiny pretty much had spent its force at this point although Private Allen did take a Captain Parker prisoner at gunpoint and tied him up in the officer's tent. Colonel Bardwell, the former regimental commander, arrived as the mutiny was winding down. Inasmuch as Colonel Bardwell was well respected by the troops, he was quickly able to settle the situation, obtain aid for the wounded, and effect the immediate release of Captain Parker. With respect to the immediate cause of the mutiny, it appears that a Private James Thomas took advantage of the confusion and worked furiously to release the prisoner [originally hung by the thumbs]. Just when he had succeeded in cutting the post down, however, he was apprehended at gunpoint by a Captain Barker. (ibid.)

The Army wasted no time in establishing cases against "fifteen of the suspected mutineers," who were confined as charges were filed and the trial commencing a startling one day later. "With a speed that would please many a modern day trial counsel, a court-martial convening order was issued on 30 October 1865 with the court-martial scheduled to convene on 31 October 1865." The individual trials commenced on October 31st and ended on November 3rd (163-164).

A general court-martial was convened consisting of seven officers led by, notably, the provost marshal of the 3rd USCT, Major Sherman Conant. The prosecutor and judge advocate was "a Lieutenant A.A. Knight – a line officer from the 34th USCT." None of the accused accepted the assistance of attorneys. They decided to represent themselves (164).

Fourteen of the fifteen soldiers slated to stand trial faced charges of mutiny, clearly "a violation of the 22d Article of War," and "defined as the unlawful resistance or opposition to superior military authority, with a deliberate purpose to subvert the same, or to eject that authority from office." Private Archibald Roberts, meanwhile, was charged with violating the 99th Article – "conduct prejudicial to the good order and military discipline." Although Private Roberts was not charged with actively participating in the mutiny, he was accused of saying following the incident: "Lieutenant Colonel Brower, the God-damned son of a bitch, he shot my cousin. Where is he? Let me see him" (164-165).

And there were other factors that made the cases quite ominous for the accused, noted Bennett, besides their black skin color:

> The maximum punishment for mutiny in time of "war, rebellion or insurrection" was death by shooting. Unfortunately for the accused, Florida still was considered to be in a state of rebellion at the time of the incident, notwithstanding the fact that the last organized Confederate forces had surrendered in May, 1865. This legal fiction not only impacted upon the ability of the court-martial to assess the death penalty but also limited the amount of appellate review that would be afforded any death penalty that was adjudged. In times of peace, any death sentence was required to be transmitted to the Secretary of War, who would review it and present it to the President for his consideration along with his recommendation. In a period in which a state of war or rebellion existed, the division or department commander had the power finally to confirm and execute sentences of death. He could, if he so desired, suspend the execution of a death sentence so as to allow review by the President and to permit the condemned soldier an opportunity to petition for clemency. This, however, was optional while a state of war existed. (165)

But black troops facing court-martial did have one thing in their favor. Major General Benjamin Butler allowed them to be "tried by officers assigned to black regiments." His objective was to "shield the black troops from abuse and prejudice." Yet, given the details of these particular mutiny cases, such an advantage would have been very much minimized, since "most prosecution witnesses were fellow officers from the same regiment" (ibid.).

And there was the matter of the trials being tremendously expedited, with the testimony of an accusatory and "damning" officer. According to Bennett:

> Typically, the trials were models of expedience. Evidently, the longest was four hours in length and the shortest was one hour long. Starting with four courts-martial on 31 October, three were held on November 1, three on November 2, and five on November 3. A total of twenty-two witnesses provided testimony in the various courts-martial, the most appearances being logged by Lieutenant

Brown, the prosecution's star witness. Indeed, Lieutenant Brown seems to have possessed an uncanny ability to remember the faces and mutinous acts of quite a number of individuals who stood trial. From the testimony offered, Lieutenant Brown apparently was most eager to provide damning evidence against the various accused soldiers. In the case of Private Joseph Nathaniel in particular, his questionable testimony that Nathaniel fired upon him cost Private Allen any chance of escaping the death penalty. (166)

Given that the death penalty was likely for a defendant labeled as picking up arms and shooting during the incident, "it was crucial to show that the accused had not fired his weapon at the white officers during the mutiny. This act clearly was the dividing line between a death sentence and a lengthy prison term." Unfortunately for Private Nathaniel, Lieutenant Brown's sworn testimony indicated that a shot from Nathaniel's gun barely missed his head (166-167).

However, two black officers contradicted Brown's story, according to Bennett:

The two black noncommissioned officers who had apprehended Private Nathaniel and stripped him of his weapon testified differently. They indicated that they had not witnessed Nathaniel discharging his musket. Further, they checked his musket for evidence of firing but could not detect signs that it had been discharged. They found his musket capped and loaded. Despite the obviously exculpatory nature of this evidence, however, the court-martial panel either discounted or disregarded it and found Private [Nathaniel] guilty of firing at Lieutenant Brown. (167)

And that was not the only glaring contradiction pertaining to the trial:

Another troubling feature of Lieutenant Brown's and several other officers' testimonies was the issue of Lieutenant Colonel Brower firing into the unarmed group of soldiers. During the first few courts-martial, all the officers – including Brown – testified that Brower actually had fired into the crowd and that the soldiers in the crowd were unarmed at the time. By the second day of the proceedings, however, Brown was asserting that Brower instead had fired warning shots into the air. Perhaps realizing the inconsistency of this testimony with the wounds suffered by Private Green, both Brown and Lieutenant Greybill later claimed that the crowd was armed at the time Brower opened fire. (ibid.)

Meanwhile, although Brower played such a prominent role in the episode, he testified in only one trial – the one concerning Private Joseph Green. "He testified that Private Green advanced upon him with a musket, along with the crowd, and that he had fired to disable Green." However, Green countered by saying he took up arms only after being shot. Strangely enough, just "after testifying, Brower was mustered out and quickly shipped back home to New York City" (ibid.). The black soldiers, given the pattern of inconsistencies and obvious fabrications, didn't stand a chance. "In light of this, one cannot help but wonder what transpired between Lieutenant Colonel Brower and his superiors in the two days between the court-martial and his mustering out," wrote Captain Kevin Bennett in his Fall 1991 article for the Military Law Review. "Considering his incredible overreaction by opening fire, combined with his allowing punishments which, while not specifically prohibited, were looked upon with great disfavor, one has to suspect that the command was anxious to be rid of an embarrassment" (167-168).

Sadly, even those – with the exception of one officer – who were traditionally supposed to help the doomed soldiers, despite their refusal to have legal representation, were ineffective and even hostile:

> Because of the expedited nature of the proceedings and the sentences handed down, one readily might conclude that the trials were nothing more than "kangaroo courts." Notwithstanding the length of the trials and the fact that the accused were not represented by counsel, it appears that the president, Major Conant, endeavored to ensure each accused a full and fair hearing. Conant, a former noncommissioned officer with the 39th Massachusetts Volunteers, consistently asked questions of the various witnesses in an effort to ascertain facts and resolve inconsistencies. Unfortunately, the same balanced approach was lacking with the judge advocate, Lieutenant Knight. Procedurally, he was required to assist the accused soldiers in eliciting favorable testimony when they were not represented by counsel. Throughout the courts-martial, his questions were leading and designed to elicit only incriminating evidence. (168)

A few days into November the devastating verdict was back, wrote Bennett:

> When the last court-martial had adjourned on November 3d, thirteen of the accused had been found guilty of mutiny. Another – Private Roberts – was convicted of conduct prejudicial to good order. Only one accused – Private Theodore Waters – was acquitted of the charge of mutiny. Of the sentences handed down, six – Privates Plowden, Craig, Allen, Howard, Green, and Nathaniel – were sentenced to execution by shooting. Private Dowrey received a sentence of fifteen years at hard labor while Privates Morie and Harley each received ten years. A sentence of two years at hard labor was adjudged against Privates Richard Lee, Alexander Lee, Miller, and Thomas. Private Roberts received a relatively light sentence of two month's confinement. All received dishonorable discharges and total forfeiture of pays. (ibid.)

Perhaps the saddest and most alarming aspect of the cases involved Private David Craig who was shot dead by the firing squad. Although the court proceedings' records were forwarded to the Bureau of Military Justice in Washington, D.C. on November 13, 1865, that might have exonerated Craig, "no actual legal review of the cases appears to have taken place until after the executions" (169). A request for a delay in his trial may have allowed for the introduction of possible facts that pointed towards his innocence, surmised Bennett:

342 Camp William Penn 1863-1865

Contained within Craig's service file is a letter from a H.C. Marehand, dated 10 December 1865, to a Senator Cowan. The letter requested that the sentence of execution be suspended pending a review and investigation of the case. Craig, a twenty-one year-old laborer from Pennsylvania, had been raised as a child by Mr. Marehand. The letter indicated that Marehand had received correspondence the previous day from Craig indicating his dilemma and proclaiming his innocence in that "[Craig] had been excused to take guns from some of the mutineers and in doing so was arrested." In response to the congressional inquiry, a telegraph was sent to General Foster to suspend the sentence and to transmit the record for review. Unfortunately, the telegraph and suspension were too late because the executions had been carried out nine days earlier. General Foster replied back by telegraph on 16 December, informing the War Department of the execution and the fact that the court records had been forwarded on 13 November. (169)

And very suspicious are the missing documents concerning Craig's court martial. "Among all the records arising from the Jacksonville Mutiny, his record alone has been lost, misplaced, or destroyed" (170).

Yet, noted Bennett, there was a bit of semblance of fairness regarding some of the others accused of mutiny, despite the obvious rush to justice and prejudices that seem to have marred the proceedings and destroyed impartiality:

Fortunately for the imprisoned soldiers, the legal process did not end with the deaths of their six comrades. In December 1865, a review of the court-martial records was accomplished by The Judge Advocate General of the Army, Joseph Holt. Although his review as limited to strictly procedural matters, a further review on the merits was conducted by the Bureau of Military Justice in late 1866. That review resulted in the commutation of the prison sentences of the surviving mutineers. Private Jonathan Miller was released in November 1866 and the others – Privates Calvin Dowrey, Morie, Harley, Thomas, and Alexander Lee – were discharged in January 1867. Private Richard Lee previously had died from typhoid fever. (ibid.)

In the end, a couple of the primary white officers involved in the sad case "slipped into obscurity." Interestingly, "no further record of Lieutenant Colonel Brower remains because he failed to file for a pension." In the interim, the primary accuser, "Lieutenant Brown returned to Indiana, married, and died in 1912," while Major Conant departed the service "immediately after the trials." Commendably, Conant began to work for "the welfare of newly freed blacks," accepting a job with the Freedman's Bureau in Florida. "He later returned to New England and died in Connecticut in 1924" (ibid.).

And what was the fate of the so-called "black mutineers?"

"Of the black mutineers who survived prison, even less is known." Since they were "dishonorably discharged, they were ineligible to apply for a military pension; thus no recorded information is available. The only postscript is a letter contained within the file of Private Jacob Plowden. Dated in 1878, it was written

This Frederick Douglass funeral poster is emblematic of his life – rising from an abused slave to the primary spokesperson and leader of African Americans during the Civil War. *Courtesy of the Library of Congress.*

by his brother on behalf of Private Plowden's minor son Jesse, attempting to collect any arrears in pay due Private Plowden." (170)

On a broader scale, what implications did the Jacksonville episode have on the legacy of blacks in the U.S. military that Frederick Douglass and other black abolitionists believed would be a ticket to emancipation and equality? The answer is reflective of the immense struggles that lay just ahead. Bennett wrote:

> In retrospect, the Jacksonville Mutiny serves as a tragic illustration of the turbulent introduction of the black soldier to the military justice system. Clearly, black soldiers had achieved remarkable gains through their noteworthy participation in the Civil War – not the least of which was the end of slavery. While their gains in the administration of military justice were significant in comparison to the arbitrary slave codes, they still had far to travel to achieve parity with their white counterparts. Accordingly, the Jacksonville Mutiny was but the first stop on a long, painful road. (171-172)

The great Douglass, who had ventured through Camp William Penn's gates several years earlier in 1863, generally lived a personally and professionally rewarding life, but had to be hurt by the degradations that continued for most African Americans. That was despite his ongoing civil rights writing, speaking and government appointments – including as U.S. marshal for the District of Columbia, as well as the district's recorder of deeds and U.S. minister to Haiti. "The end of Reconstruction dashed Douglass's hopes for a meaningful emancipation. Even so, he never abandoned the fight for African Americans." Douglass persevered, even after his wife Anna died in 1882 and he married his former secretary Helen Pitts, who was white, sparking much controversy (Gates, Higginbotham eds. 2004, 240).

Before he married Pitts, a decade earlier Douglass had even returned to Pennsylvania, giving a speech in Carlisle on March 2, 1872. While there, however, the Republican owner of the Bentz House, George Z. Bentz, "refused to let Douglass eat his dinner in [a] hotel dining room with the white guests," prompting democratic cries of hypocrisy among the Republicans. The incident likely left Douglass wondering about the still festering wounds of the great war and ongoing racism. Would the black veterans, even those at Camp William Penn, receive ultimate equality and justice (*Visit to Carlisle in 1872* 2010)?

It's very likely that Douglass believed true equality was one day forthcoming, based on his persistence and the passing of crucial constitutional amendments, including the Thirteenth Amendment that officially abolished slavery in 1865, the Fourteenth Amendment of 1868, giving blacks long-awaited citizen rights, as well as the Fifteenth Amendment, guaranteeing voting rights in 1870.

Still, not long before his untimely death of an apparent heart attack, Douglass spoke about the need for anti-lynching laws, as virulent groups such as the Ku Klux Klan became immensely popular throughout the United States. "He personally appealed to [President Benjamin] Harrison for an anti-lynching law and used his position as the only African American official at the 1893 World's Columbian Exposition to bring the issue before an international audience." Yet others would have to pick up the fight. "He had just returned from another lecture tour when he died at his Washington home" February 20, 1895 (Gates, Higginbotham eds. 2004, 240).

Douglass' tremendous legacy shall always be intertwined with the hopes and aspirations of the black soldiers he encouraged and even admonished at Camp William Penn on that July day in 1863.

Warriors Grabbing the Baton

It would be up to such past Camp William Penn warriors as the former captain in the 43rd USCT, Atlanta College President Horace Bumstead, to pick up the fight. Indeed, Bumstead was the white liberal from New England who'd carry on the banner of justice and equality with the help and dynamic leadership of one of the young black professors that he recruited in 1897, just two years after Douglass' death.

At first working very closely with Bumstead and initiating ground breaking studies concerning black culture, William Edward Burghardt Du Bois would ascend to Frederick Douglass' position as the premiere black American leader and intellectual. And with Bumstead's backing, Du Bois would co-found in 1909 the NAACP (National Association for the Advancement of Colored People), as well as become a primary architect of the Niagara Movement.

Born just several years after the Civil War on February 23, 1868, in Great Barrington, Massachusetts, Du Bois was "the son of Mary Silvina Burghardt, a domestic worker, and Alfred Du Bois, a barber and itinerant laborer." And it seems that his father had dubious ties to the Civil War: "Born in Haiti and descended from mixed race Bahamian slaves, Alfred Du Bois enlisted during the Civil War as a private in a New York regiment of the Union army but appears to have deserted shortly afterward," thus setting a pattern that would greatly impact Du Bois. "He also deserted the family less than two years after his son's birth, leaving him to be reared by his mother and the extended Burghardt kin." Meanwhile Alfred's son, William, became the first African American to graduate from his high school in 1884 and then attended the historically black Fisk University in Tennessee starting in September 1885, which was among "the best of the southern colleges for newly freed slaves founded after the Civil War" (Gates, Higginbotham eds. 2004, 246-247).

Remarkably, after leaving Fisk and matriculating to Harvard as a junior and then graduating from there with a doctorate in 1895, Du Bois agreed in 1896 to conduct a study of Philadelphia's Seventh Ward, where the likes of Jeremiah Asher's family had resided in that predominately black area. "There, after an estimated 835 hours of door-to-door interviews in 2,500 households, Du Bois completed the monumental study, the Philadelphia Negro (1899)," consisting of methodology that would be the hallmarks of his upcoming Atlanta studies leading to his future civil rights endeavors that would ultimately conflict with another black leader, Booker T. Washington of the Tuskegee Institute (248-249).

Du Bois, likely learning various details about the establishment of Camp William Penn via conversations with Bumstead at Atlanta University, wrote about the historic facility in his book:

> Steps toward raising Negro troops in the city were taken in 1863, as soon as the efficiency of the Negro soldier had been proven. Several hundred prominent

citizens petitioned the Secretary of War and were given permission to raise Negro regiments. The troops were to receive no bounties, but were to have $10 a month and rations. They were to rendezvous at Camp William Penn, Chelten Hills. A mass meeting was soon held attended by the prominent caterers, teachers and merchants, together with white citizens, at which Frederick Douglass, W.D. Kelley and Anna Dickinson spoke […]. The first three regiments, known as the Third, Sixth and Eighth United States Regiments of Colored Troops, went promptly to the front, the Third being before Fort Wagner when it fell. The other regiments followed as called, leaving still other Negroes anxious to enlist. (Du Bois 1899, 1967, 38-39)

And Du Bois seemed to acknowledge the disappointment of the post-war years, even focusing on the assassination of Octavius V. Catto and massive riots:

In the spring elections of 1871 there was so much disorder, and such poor police protection, that the United States marines were called on to preserve order […].

In the fall elections street disorders resulted in the cold-blooded assassination of several Negroes, among whom was an estimable young teacher, Octavius V. Catto. The murder of Catto came at a critical moment; to the Negroes it seemed a revival of the old slavery-time riots in the day when they were first tasting freedom; to the better classes of Philadelphia it revealed a serious state of barbarism and lawlessness in the second city of the land; to the politicians it furnished a text and example which was strikingly effective and which they did not hesistate to use. (39-40)

The great scholar believed that the immense outrage concerning those post-war riots and the death of Octavius Catto, who had earnestly recruited for Camp William Penn, eventually led to the knocking out of Jim Crow era laws, including segregation on trolleys and other public facilities. In a way, the late 19th century battle for justice and equality in Philadelphia started and ended with Camp William Penn, especially given the incredible magnitude of anti-slavery activists associated with the facility that was situated in a neighborhood that was an epicenter of the Underground Railroad.

The Rise and Legacy of a Star

Perhaps there is no greater example of a rising star from Camp William Penn coming into his own than Josiah Walls of the 3rd USCT. The dynamic young congressman of Florida at the start of the war was, as a slave, forced to serve the Confederacy before falling into the hands of Union forces. Regardless, he was destined to make history in so many remarkable ways.

In fact, Walls "was suspected to be the son of his [Winchester, VA] master, Dr. John Walls, and maintained contact with him throughout his life." He had to have very mixed feelings, and was even likely outraged, when he "was forced to be the private servant of a Confederate artilleryman until he was captured by Union soldiers in May 1862." Fortunately, Walls then matriculated into a "normal school in Harrisburg, Pennsylvania," for about a year (*Black Americans in Congress* 2008).

The future congressman would join the 3rd Infantry Regiment USCT by July 1863, about the time when Union and Rebel forces clashed in the bloody fields and woodlands of Gettysburg. By February 1864, Walls had moved with his fellow soldiers to Northern Florida. "The following June, he transferred to the 35th Regiment USCT, where he served as the first sergeant and artillery instructor." (ibid.)

Romance and prosperity was soon to follow: "While living in Picolota, Florida, Walls met and married Angie Fergueson, with whom he had one daughter, Nettie." And then the war came to an end. "He was discharged in October 1865 but decided to stay in Florida, working at a saw mill on the Suwanee River and, later, as a teacher with the Freedmen's Bureau in Gainesville. By 1868, Walls had saved enough money to buy a 60-acre farm outside the city" (ibid.).

Apparently, in addition to his schooling in Harrisburg, Walls must have been self-taught, but also could have studied with others holding higher degrees as he became more upwardly mobile. "One of the few educated black men in Reconstruction-Era Florida, Walls was drawn to political opportunities available after the war," soon to represent Florida's Alachua County in Florida's constitutional convention of 1868, during the early stages of Reconstruction. "That same year, Walls ran a successful campaign for state assemblyman. The following fall, he was elected to the state senate and took his seat as one of five freedmen in the 24-man chamber in January 1869." He also attended "the Southern States Convention of Colored Men in 1871 in Columbia, South Carolina" (ibid.). Walls fought in the trenches for the hotly-contested political seats of Florida, along the way combating elements of the Ku Klux Klan and even various politicians who abhorred blacks obtaining political, economic, and suffrage power or rights during Reconstruction:

> The 1870 nominee of the Republican Party for Florida's only seat in the U.S. House of Representatives, Walls defeated Silas Niblack after a bitter contest, riddled with charges of fraud and intimidation. Josiah T. Walls thus became the State's first black congressman. Although unseated by the House near the end of his term, Walls was re-elected in 1872. In another contested election in 1874, Walls defeated J.J. Finley, a former Confederate General, but, in 1876, was again removed from office. Walls was elected to the Florida Seneate that year (ibid.).

His intense political activities did not hamper Walls from purchasing a very comfortable home, as well as in 1873 buying an 1175-acre "plantation," and a weekly newspaper, *The New Era*. At one point, Walls was hailed as one of the largest property holders in the state who had employed at the newspaper a couple of his former white commanding officers. Walls was also admitted to the Florida Bar and "served at various times as mayor of Gainesville, a member of the Board of Public Instruction, and County Commissioner" (ibid.).

As the years passed Walls suffered many setbacks, including political and personal, regarding his frail health mostly due to war injuries. "On New Year's Day 1885, Angie

Fergueson Walls died, leaving her husband a widower after nineteen years of marriage, with Nettie, their six-year-old child." He then married 14-year-old "Ella Angeline Gass, his first wife's cousin, on July 5, 1885." That relationship was described by observers as "distant and formal; he seemed much closer to Nettie," his daughter (Klingman 1976, 141).

Over time Walls was "struck down by the physical ailments that had plagued him since the Civil War. He filed for and received a $12 per month pension in 1891." One neighbor described Walls as very ill:

> Walls at this time was "unable to do anything like an able-bodied man's work, in fact he can do about 1/3 as much […]. The symptoms [...] are of the most serious and violent nature. He is unable to breathe clearly, and has the most excruciating pains." A.J. Parker, who had also attended the first Mrs. Walls, testified that he was suffering from "chronic disease of the stomach and eyes, occasioned by degenerated liver." (142)

And then, as if nothing else could possibly go wrong, almost total financial disaster struck. Indeed, "the severe freeze of February 1895 ruined him financially." Walls had many orange trees that were destroyed. He was forced to move "to Tallahassee where he became the director of the farm at Florida Normal College" that ultimately became what is today Florida A&M University. Yet, despite his immense troubles, Walls was still a man of great pride and ingenuity. According to Klingman:

> He spent most of his time in the fields that lay below the Tallahassee hills on which the college was built. He never wore farm clothes or coveralls, but rather preferred to dress in "working suits," the attire of a large and successful man. However, soon after he arrived he instituted techniques of farming new to the college: most important were terrace farming and a new way of plowing to prevent soil erosion. (ibid.)

As Walls continued to age, it seems that he was caught between two worlds: "While in the fields Walls would sometimes talk of his farming days in Gainesville, but he never mentioned his past political career. Nor did he become involved in local Tallahassee affairs, either politically or socially," perhaps just plainly drained from those cumbersome years. He also had to be keeping in the painful memory of several of his 3rd USCT compatriots being executed for mutiny following the war. "He was looked upon as 'a race-pride man'; as such, he was thought too black for the white community and too intelligent for the black. As a result he spent his leisure time at home, primarily reading." Those studious, quiet days would be the proverbial calm before his final storms of life (142-143).

More tragedy was soon to strike. His daughter, Nettie, was accused of murdering a neighbor's child after becoming suddenly withdrawn and acting peculiar, noted Klingman:

> Then, on a bright and sunny day sometime around the turn of the century, Nettie killed a little girl, Maggie Gibbs. According to Mrs. E. R. Jones, an elderly

Tallahassee woman who had been one of Nettie's "children," on that particular day Walls had gotten up early and headed down the hill to the blacksmith's shop with a scythe which needed fixing slung over his shoulder. On his way he passed Mrs. Jones, then a young girl "not yet ten," who was outside playing in her own yard. Soon after he disappeared, and after Ella had gone to her job teaching school, a shot rang out from the Walls home. Nettie rushed out, passed by the bewildered Mrs. Jones and others who quickly gathered at the sound, and ran down the hill. Inside it was discovered that Maggie Gibbs, daughter of a minister, had been stabbed and shot in one of the closets. A short while later, Walls and Nettie came home. He was in a state of shock, apparently refusing to believe that such a thing happened.

One aspect of the murder was revenge; Nettie had been seeing Maggie's father, a widower, for some time. However, they had broken up their relationship shortly before the murder. In any event, based upon her peculiar behavior, she was sent to the state mental institution at Chattahoochee, where she died "six weeks, or six months," after her arrival. Her death took its toll on Walls, who never recovered. (142)

Josiah T. Walls' "own death came on May 15, 1905, around noon." The former congressman, wrote Klingman, "was buried in a Negro cemetery in Tallahassee, most likely after a small funeral service attended by close friends and his widow. There are no published accounts of his death, no will probated, and no death certificate filed with the state of Florida. Thus, in much the same way as he was born and spent his life, Josiah Walls died – surrounded by incomplete details and gaps in the historical record" (143-144). But he did leave behind a tremendous legacy:

> Overcoming deep political divisions in the Florida Republican Party, Josiah Walls became the first African American to serve his state in Congress. The only black Representative from Florida until the early 1990s [...] When he was not fiercely defending his seat in Congress, Walls fought for internal improvements for Florida. He also advocated compulsory education and economic opportunity for all races: [Walls once said regarding black rights:] "We demand that our lives, our liberties, and our property shall be protected by the strong arm of our government, that it gives us the same citizenship that it gives to those who it seems would [...] sink our every hope for peace, prosperity, and happiness into the great sea of oblivion.' (*Black Americans in Congress* 2008).

There was one thing for sure, Josiah Thomas Walls had been a warrior on and off of the battlefield, like so many of his fellow Camp William Penn combatants.

The Buffalo Soldiers and Indian Wars

Many of the black USCT regiments, including some from Camp William Penn, were ultimately sent to the West in order to combat Native Americans and protect U.S. borders. Some historians have postulated that it was an overall strategy for commanders to send so many armed black men to such distant locales because they were perceived to be a threat to the American Republic. Were they capable of leading an armed revolt against the U.S.? Such questions were certainly fueled by pro-Rebel forces following the war, as well as some Northerners.

After all, there were more than a few rank-and-file military blacks who certainly weren't taking abuse from white superiors – military or civilian – especially since they had just risked their lives for the Union. The so-called mutiny of the 3rd Regiment USCT would have been held up as a prime example.

Yet, more than a few of the black soldiers, and some veterans, found staying in the armed forces to be an attractive choice, especially given their prospects of finding virtually no meaningful employment in a society that still had racist tendencies in many quarters. Soldiers serving in such post-war units might earn about $13 a month with room and board. Indeed, some white officers and veterans opted to remain in the military too for similar economic reasons:

> No doubt, some men had grown to like military life during their Civil War service and found the prospect of continued soldiering more appealing than the uncertainties they faced if they returned home. Whatever their reasons for staying in the army, these veterans facilitated the formation of new black regiments in the regular army, providing a cadre of experienced soldiers who could teach raw recruits the ways of military life. Called "buffalo soldiers" by Native Americans, because the black troops' hair reminded them of the buffalo's curly coat, African American cavalry and infantry units played an important role in the Indian wars that lasted from the end of the Civil War into the late 1880s. (Shaffer 2004, 38-39)

One white officer who hailed from Camp William Penn's 127th USCT was Lieutenant Charles Lawrence Cooper, whose daughter, Florrestine Cooper Hooker, wrote about his exploits in the 9th and 10th cavalries, consisting of Buffalo Soldiers following the Civil War. And although it's unclear about whether USCT's black veterans systematically joined the Buffalo Soldier units, it's apparent that several from Camp William Penn did serve as Buffalo Soldiers. In fact, a couple of sources indicate that the 24th and 25th USCT units that fought during the Civil War and hailed from Camp William Penn evolved into Buffalo Soldier units, while some historians say there's not enough evidence to indicate such.

The units were formed at "the end of July 1866," when "Congress passed Public Act No. 181 to increase and fix the military peace establishment, the Army of the United States," according to the military historian William A. Gladstone. "This act initiated through War Department General Orders No. 56, August 1, 1866, and stated that all cavalry regiments would include two regiments of black soldiers, and all infantry regiments would include four regiments of black soldiers." Meanwhile, "General Orders No. 92, dated November 23, 1866, identified the two black cavalry regiments as the 9th and 10th, and the four black infantry regiments as the 38th, 39th, 40th, and 41st." Furthermore, "General Orders No. 16, dated March 11, 1869, further modified this situation by merging the 38th and 41st regiments to form the 24th U.S. Infantry, and the 39th and 40th to form the 25th Infantry" (Gladstone 1993, 182).

Gladstone further noted that black soldiers serving in such units "earned a total of 18 Medals of Honor, and seven black sailors were graced with the same honor" (ibid.).

Regardless, the jobs of those black soldiers would have been quite varied once arriving on the Texas frontier and other far-flung places:

> The duties of the regiments would not be limited to fighting Indians. Law and order were little more than a hope in the post-Civil War Southwest, and civil authorities were compelled constantly to call upon the army to assist in rounding up border scum. The region swarmed with cattle thieves as well as men who killed with little or no provocation. Petty, scheming, and sometimes murderous politicians, combined with greedy land and cattle barons, crooked government contractors, heartless Indian agents, and land-hungry homesteaders, were the sources of civil broils of a scope far beyond the control of local or state authority. The result was inevitable involvement in civil affairs for the Ninth and Tenth, with often little hope or expectation of gratitude regardless of outcome or contribution. (Leckie and Leckie 2003, 18)

One of the Camp William Penn soldiers to join the Buffalo Soldiers was Benjamin F. Davis, born in West Chester, Pennsylvania in 1849 and a veteran of the 32nd USCT. Davis joined the Calvary in 1867, serving a couple of enlistments in the 10th Calvary and then five years as a sergeant major in the 9th Cavalry. He then rose to become post quartermaster sergeant in 1885, and apparently was married the next year in 1886 at the home of a friend, Sergeant John H. Ferguson of the 9th Cavalry. He retired on April 23, 1895, following almost 20 years as a "regimental sergeant major and post quartermaster sergeant," eventually residing at age 69 in the 1600 block of 17th Street in northwest Washington, DC. Davis died November 9, 1921, and was buried with military honors at the Soldiers Home Cemetery in Washington. He was survived by a widow, three daughters, and three grandchildren, and was a member of the National Association for the Advance of Colored People (NAACP) (Schubert and Schubert 2004, 72).

At least one of Davis' 32nd USCT compatriots also joined the 9th Cavalry; Private George Bruce, who also fought with the 40th Infantry. Bruce had difficulty obtaining his Civil War pension because on an application he had mistakenly identified his unit as the "32nd Pennsylvania Infantry," instead of the 32nd U.S. Colored Infantry (43).

Finally Benjamin Helm, formerly a sergeant major in the 6th USCT, joined the 10th Cavalry of the Buffalo Soldiers in Louisville, Kentucky, in February 1867. He obtained the rank of first sergeant in Company C of the 10th (132).

Although the estimated percentage of black USCT soldiers joining "the regular army after the war" was "probably no more than 1 to 2 percent (approximately 2,000 to 3,000 men)," their continued service had a positive historical impact on the American armed forces, according to historian-writer Donald R. Shaffer:

> Whatever the circumstances of their reenlistment and service, the presence of black soldiers in the postwar U.S. Army represented a significant achievement for African American troops that had fought in the Civil War. The formation of

black infantry and cavalry regiments in the postwar army was a tangible signal of the shift in attitude of the Northern public about African Americans and military service. Although the Civil War had by no means eliminated prejudice on the part of white Northerners (after all, the buffalo soldiers served in segregated units), the enlistment of black men was at least a partial recognition of their manhood. In the eyes of the federal government, they were now men enough to fight Native Americans on the frontier, men enough to be given a permanent place in the military structure of the United States. (Shaffer 2004, 39)

The Twilight of Commander Wagner's Life
A year after the war, in 1866 the former commander of Camp William Penn, Louis Wagner, opened an insurance business in Philadelphia, working with a partner and brother George Wagner, a veteran of the camp's 8th USCT. He also continued to be active in the Union League of Philadelphia, the organization that raised much of the initial funds to establish Camp William Penn in early 1863.

Brevetted as a brigadier general on March 13, 1865, for "Meritorious services" during the Civil War, Wagner led a brigade during the funeral of the black rights' leader Octavius Catto, and on the national level served as commander-in-chief of the Grand Army of the Republic. In fact, just before his assassination in October 1871, "Catto was placed on active duty with the National Guard and ordered by his commanding officer, General Louis Wagner, to call out his regiment for service in quelling" the city's race riots that left many blacks dead, including Catto (Waskie 2011, 171).

Also interested in politics following the war, Wagner became a city council person, as well as "was appointed a member of the Board of Education." He must have been very highly respected, because Wagner was elected president of the council three times. In addition, he continued to participate in auxiliary military groups. By 1878 Wagner was elected Recorder of Deeds and a member of the Board of City Trusts (Taylor 1945, 49).

Next, Wagner was appointed by Philadelphia Mayor Edward H. Fitler to organize and implement the city's Department of Public Works. "Tireless in his labors, giving minute attention to all details, knowing neither favor or influence, [Wagner] naturally was not popular with the political element. Beyond question General Wagner was the logical candidate to have been Mayor Fitler's successor, but to his deep disappointment he was turned down, as not 'available' politically." In other words, General Wagner had scruples. He also worked to establish facilities for the less fortunate, as well as helped to oversee Girard College, a facility that would be desegregated during the Civil Rights movement by the black activist and attorney, Cecil Moore (48-49).

On top of all that, Wagner "was keenly interested in Masonic work, and with others organized the Masonic Home, of which body he was its President until his death," often maintaining an exhaustive schedule. "He was also very active in Church work, organizing a Bible class in Market Square Presbyterian Church, which (next to John Wanamaker's) was the largest Bible class in Philadelphia." And it seems, according to Taylor (50), that the great general kept up his searing pace until he died on a cold winter day in January 1914, despite, like many other Camp William Penn veterans, suffering much pain from his leg injury:

Suffering daily from that old wound, he never tired, and his last day was one of his busiest. Arriving at 7:25 a.m. at the office of the Third National Bank, of which he was President, he disposed of his mail, caught the eight o'clock, train for New York; attended a meeting of the New York Life Insurance Company, of which he was a Director; caught the twelve o'clock train for Philadelphia, lunching on the train; presided at a meeting of the Board of City Trusts; went to the Elkins Home, presided at a meeting, taking supper there, and went to preside at the payer meeting at the Market Square Presbyterian Church; reached home at 9:30, and quietly passed away at 10:45 on January 15, 1914. (ibid.)

Corporal Norman Marcell, First Sergeant Frederick Minus, Sergeant Major Joseph H. Lee, and Corporal Albert El are noteworthy re-enactment members of the 3rd USCT, based in Philadelphia, honoring the legacy of that first regiment to be raised at Camp William Penn. The group honored past USCT warriors during a 2010 Grand Review in Harrisburg, PA, featuring parading re-enactors from all over the U.S. *Courtesy of Kristopher H. Scott.*

Lucretia Mott's "Roadside" home stood near this spot in what is today's Cheltenham Township, Pennsylvania, on Old York Road, a few blocks north of Cheltenham Avenue at the entrance of an exclusive housing community, Latham Park. Her mansion was razed in 1911 to clear the way for that development. *Courtesy of Donald Scott, Jr.*

LUCRETIA C. MOTT

Nearby stood "Roadside." the home of the ardent Quakeress, Lucretia C. Mott (1793-1880). Her most notable work was in connection with antislavery women's rights. temperance and peace.

PENNSYLVANIA HISTORICAL AND MUSEUM COMMISSION

The LaMott African Methodist Episcopal Church, built in the late 1800s with the financial support of the transportation magnate George D. Widener, is a centerpiece of the modern community of LaMott, formerly known as Camptown, where Camp William Penn was located. *Courtesy of Kristopher H. Scott.*

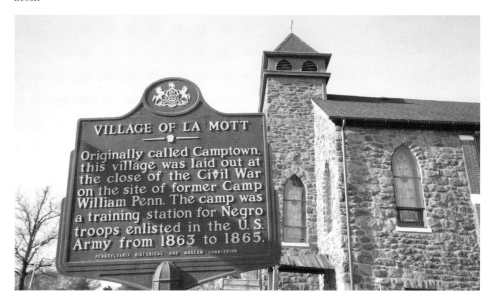

This historic sign is one of several near the LaMott African Methodist Episcopal Church honoring the legacy of Camp William Penn and the surrounding community of LaMott. *Courtesy of Kristopher H. Scott.*

Third Regiment re-enactors pose with this state marker near the refurbished front gates of Camp William Penn, commemorating the almost 11,000 black soldiers who trained there. *Courtesy of Kristopher H. Scott.*

This Camp William Penn stone monument at Willow Avenue and Sycamore Avenue, the center of the LaMott community for more than 65 years, honors the warriors and officers stationed at the facility from 1863 to 1865. *Courtesy of Donald Scott, Jr.*

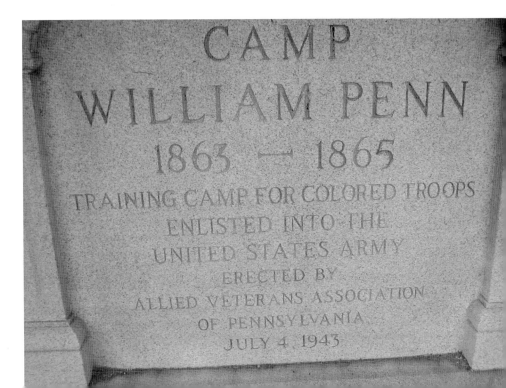

The front gates of Camp William Penn have been refurbished by the Citizens for the Restoration of Historical LaMott (CROHL), a local community group dedicated to establishing monuments, a library, and museum concerning the history of the facility. *Courtesy of Donald Scott, Sr.*

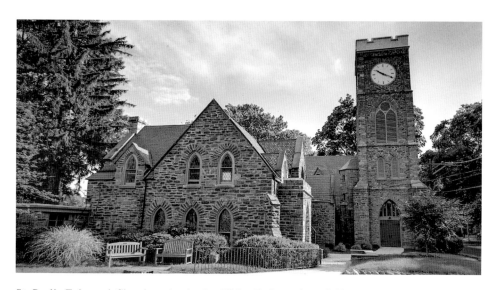

St. Paul's Episcopal Church, today in the Elkins Park section of Cheltenham Township, and its members were instrumental in helping the Camp William Penn regiments with food, supplies, and religious sustenance during the Civil War. *Courtesy of Kristopher H. Scott.*

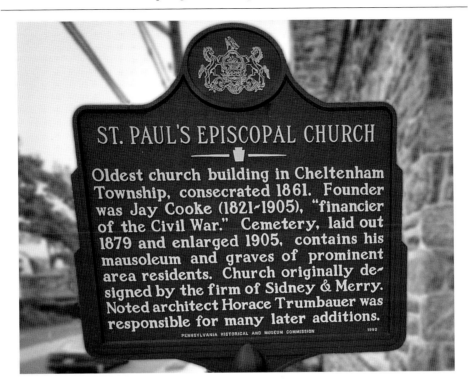

Jay Cooke, the "financier of the Civil War," was a noted member of St. Paul's Episcopal Church on Old York Road in Cheltenham Township. This sign commemorates the tremendous history of the church attended by such Gilded Age families as the Wideners and Elkinses. *Courtesy of Kristopher H. Scott.*

Jay Cooke was buried in a mausoleum in the graveyard of St. Paul's Episcopal Church. When Cooke was alive, Ulysses S. Grant visited Cooke at his mansion when the famous general transported his son Jesse to and from the nearby Cheltenham Military Academy. *Courtesy of Kristopher H. Scott.*

Jay Cooke worked at this desk during the Civil War, drafting documents that would finance the Union's cause during the war. *Courtesy of Kristopher H. Scott.*

William Still, the "father of the Underground Railroad," is buried at the historic Eden Cemetery among the graves of warriors from Camp William Penn. *Courtesy of Joshua Roderick Scott.*

The USCT Grand Review Emerges from Racial Discrimination

Even two decades after the war, in 1886, black regiments in the Civil War did not receive the recognition they deserved, according to various observers. For instance, they were excluded from the Grand Review of troops six months after the war in Washington, DC. As white troops routinely held reunions and parades, to the exclusion of black regiments, African American veterans began to organize such commemorations, according to a June 15, 1886, opinion letter published in the *Christian Recorder* by the former 43rd USCT soldier of Camp William Penn and Philadelphia-based black minister Rev. Jno. C. Brock, including their own Grand Review:

> A few weeks ago the colored veterans of the 54th and 55th Regiments of Infantry and the 5th Cavalry held a reunion in Worcester, Massachusetts. It was to them a delightful occasion. The first time since the war that these heroes had enjoyed the opportunity of being together, recalling the thrilling events of those memorable days when they were in the fierce charge of Wayne or on the bloody fields of Olustee and Honey Hills. Several of the line and staff officers were with them – the heroic Sergeant Carney [the first African American to earn the Medal of Honor]. It was a glorious gathering. It was proposed at that meeting to have a national renunion of colored veterans of the U.S. of America. This movement, I think, ought to be encouraged. The white troops in the several states have their regimental, and ofttimes, brigade reunions. This they can be quite easily, for in

General Louis Wagner, commander of Camp William Penn, is buried in the Ivy Hill Cemetery in Northwest Philadelphia with various family members. Historical records indicate that he died 10:45 p.m. on January 15, 1914, after a very long workday of commuting between New York City and Philadelphia. *Courtesy of Donald Scott, Jr.*

many instances regiments were organized in one town or city and brigades formed in the same locality. They were all recognized as state troops and the relationship established amidst the dangers of the battle-field they have never allowed to be obliterated. But with the colored soldiers, Massachusetts was the only state that accredited her sable braves as state troops.[8]

Reverend Brock even pinpointed what he believed to be the problem with the lack of such recognitions and commemorations for African American regiments, including those formed at Camp William Penn:

> Prejudice prevented the others from recognizing the colored troops recruited within their boarders as state troops [...]. I know that in my native state, Pennsylvania, at Camp William Penn, eleven regiments were organized in the following order, namely: the 3rd, 6th, 8th, 22nd, 25th, 32nd, 41st, 43rd, 45th, 127th, 24th. Yet not one of these were called Pennsylvania Volunteers. 'Tis true, the men composing these regiments came from the different parts of the Union, but that was no reason why the state, whose quota was filled by these very men, should have hesitated to recognize them as state troops. But the fact that the colored regiments were recruited from all portions of this country makes it extremely difficult to have regimental or even brigade reunions. But might there not be a national one? Representatives from the different regiments might possibly be present. An opportunity would be afforded to collect facts for historical information that will never be published by a prejudiced historian. If we wish to have proper credit let us furnish historians from among ourselves to furnish the facts connected with our own history. Examine our school histories, if you please, and you will find very little, if any, reference made to the fact that nearly 200,000 colored men shouldered the musket and went forth to so and die, that the foul blot of slavery might be forever erased from our national banner.[8]

It is then that the Reverend Brock makes his strongest point, perhaps realizing that his proposal would have a lasting impact. After all, he was a man of words and God:

> By all means let us have a reunion. I would suggest some railroad center easy of access from all parts of the country, like Harrisburg, Pa., as a proper place, where the officers and men who still survive of what was known as the United States Colored Troops may assemble and recall those days when the "rejected," at the beginning of the rebellion, eventually became the forlorn hope that came to the rescue in the hour of danger to preserve the unity of the nation when its fate hung trembling in the balance.[9]

Today, in Harrisburg, the tradition of holding a grand review for the black USCT re-enactor regiments continues, with the last one held November 4 to 7, 2010, commemorating the 145th anniversary of the first recognition held in Harrisburg following the war. The famed *Philadelphia Press* correspondent and Harrisburg native who'd go on to work as an attorney, politician, teacher, and diplomat, Thomas Morris Chester, served as the grand marshal of that original parade, organized by the black residents of Harrisburg.

Black veterans and their regiments from all over the country attended the original Harrisburg celebrations, and most recently, the Third USCT re-enactor group, based in Philadelphia, as well as the 22nd and 6th United States Colored Troops from New Jersey participated in the 2010 Grand Review in Harrisburg. Those regiments, and many others, have marched in the Harrisburg commemorations over the years, as well as during the dedication of the African American Civil War Memorial in Washington, DC, where the names of all the Camp William Penn soldiers are inscribed. Their names appear among more than 180,000 of their USCT brethren who served in the war. And included on that monument is the name of the Baptist preacher, the Reverend Jeremiah Asher, who took leave of the Shiloh Baptist Church in Philadelphia to spiritually guide as chaplain his 6th USCT black warriors, only to die in Wilmington, NC, and leave his beloved family behind.

The Surviving Asher Family

As the years passed, U.S. census reports indicate that Reverend Asher's family struggled, but surely survived after his death. And that certainly was not easy for an African American family during the post-Civil War era in Philadelphia, or in many parts of the country for that matter.

The 1870 Federal Census[10] shows that his wife, 49-year-old "Abbigail [*sic*] Asher," – described as an unemployed "Mulatto," and her two sons, Thomas, age 23, an "Upholsterer," and John, 15 – were living in the 7th Ward of the city with a pastor of the Shiloh Baptist Church, the Reverend John P. Wills. The Ashers resided, likely as boarders, in a household headed by "Clergyman" Wills, age 29. He was described as a "Mulatto" from Virginia and living with his likely wife, Julia, age 24 (characterized too as a "Mulatto" from Canada and "keeping house"). Reverend Wills was also listed in a city directory as serving at Shiloh, a "colored" church on South Street between "Tenth and Eleventh" streets (*William Penn Public Ledger Almanac* 2011). There was also the couple's daughter, one-year-old Ada D. Wills. Other people living in the residence included Pennsylvania natives Margaret Dawson, 36 (a private cook), and hotel-waiter Isaac Dawson, 19. There were Maryland natives Jane Palmer, 31, a domestic worker, and John H. Palmer, 23 (a porter), as well as laborer Arthur Johnson (born in Virginia), 23, and Mary Viros, 13 years old, born in Virginia and also described as a "Mulatto."

A decade later, the 1880 United States Federal Census[11] reveals that Reverend Asher's wife, "Abigal [*sic*] Asher," was living in Philadelphia and 58 years old, serving as the head of a household consisting of her two sons, as well as their wives and children. The census documents also show that she was born about 1822 in Connecticut and "Keeping House" in 1880 when the census taker arrived.

Abigail's eldest son, Thomas P. Asher, 34 years old and born in Rhode Island about 1846, is listed as living with her and employed as a "porter" in a local store. Thomas' wife was identified as Sallie Asher, age 26 (born about 1854), and originally from Virginia, where her parents were born. Their son and Abigail's grandson, William T. Asher, was born in Philadelphia about 1878 and was listed as just two years old in the 1880 census.

Abigail's other son, John I. Asher, 24, also resided with Abigail and worked as a "porter." His wife, Ella, 21 years old, was also a Virginia native whose parents hailed from that state. Also carrying the reverend's legacy into the future was John P. Asher, the couple's one month old son, and mother Abigail's grandson.

Abigail died April 14, 1895, at age 79 in Philadelphia, according to her death certificate. She lived in the 1000 block of Rodman Street. The matriarch's occupation was listed as "House Keeper", and she was buried April 18, 1895, at the Lebanon Cemetery – the same segregated burial site where so many black warriors of Camp William Penn and black anti-slavery abolitionist leaders rested, including her husband, the Reverend Jeremiah Asher. Her marital status was characterized as "Widowed" ("Philadelphia, Pennsylvania, Death Certificate Index, 1803-1915 about Abigial [*sic*] Asher," 2011).

Abigail Asher died 31 years after she attended her husband's funeral at the Shiloh Baptist Church, services that were noted in the August 9, 1864, edition of *The Philadelphia Inquirer*:

> FUNERAL SERVICES. – The funeral services of Rev. Jeremiah Asher, of this city, who died at Wilmington, N.C., July 27th, of typhoid [or Yellow] fever, took place yesterday afternoon, in the Shiloh Church. Quite a large number of colored persons were present on the occasion, and among them were many white people who had known the deceased, and desired to show their respect for his memory by attending the funeral services. The exercises were in the usual form of the church to which he belongs, and were solemn in their character. The deceased was in the fifty-third year of his age, and had been pastor of the Shiloh Church about fourteen years.[12]

A follow-up article in the *North American and United States Gazette* several months later and dated November 9, 1865, indicates Reverend Asher's body was transported "in a metallic case" before funeral services were held at the Shiloh Baptist Church. The article noted that Asher had "served nearly two years" as "the Chaplain of the 6th regiment U.S. colored troops." With the "church edifices" described as "crowded on a Tuesday afternoon," a "vast concourse of the friends" of Rev. Asher was among approximately "thirty ministers – white and colored." Soldiers of the 6th USCT also attended the service, according to the obituary. "A letter of thrilling interest, describing his death" was read by a presiding minister. "Several appropriate hymns were sang by a large choir. A long procession followed the remains of their beloved pastor to the Lebanon Cemetery, and there committed his body to the grave in joyful hope of the resurrection and a blessed immortality."[13]

Sheila Jones, historian of Eden Cemetery, southwest of Phildelphia in Colingdale, PA, says Asher's remains were reinterred there (Lebanon Section, Lot 19) and "did not have a headstone," (via email).

Undoubtedly, the Reverend Jeremiah Asher would have been proud of his sons for remaining devoted and close to their mother, Abigail. It seems they harbored in their hearts the goodness of an African ancestor, Gad Asher, who was snatched three generations earlier for enslavement in America, sacrificing his blood and eyesight during the Battle of Bunker Hill to help give birth to the American dynasty. Indeed, the African had given most of his life's energy as an enslaved child of Africa to a brutal system of slavery that made America the most powerful nation on the globe for generations to come. His grandson, Jeremiah, gave all that he could during the Civil War, completing a full circle of liberating the American spirit. Jeremiah's sons' dedication to family was a great tribute to their father's life and radiance lit by the holiness, as well as family values, of the old African.

For the reverend himself would pay the ultimate price – give his own life – so that America might survive and not be destroyed by its greatest contradiction – chattel slavery. The sons' dedication to the family, when all is said and done, was a testament concerning the warriors who gave so much, but tragically received so little after training at Camp William Penn. They had indeed donated plenty for America's future and their elusive liberation that is still fleeting for too many black ancestors of those valiant soldiers. By marching in step with the great Frederick Douglass' vision to sacrifice during the Civil War for the future freedom of generations to come, the warriors of Camp William Penn and other USCT fighters became the antiseptic that began to heal the country's ghastly wounds. If the war would not have been fought and the slavery issue settled, "it's unlikely that there could have been a stable, tranquil coexistence between an independent North and South [...]. There never would have been the sort of roisterous hodgepodge of wide-open energy that America became," writes David Von Drehle in a cover article that appeared in the April 18, 2011, edition of *Time* magazine. "Secession was about making more borders. At its best, Americanism is about tearing them down," concludes Von Drehle in his story, "The Civil War 1861-2011: The Way We Weren't."[14]

And as Asher's family survived and persevered in a society that was sometimes very hostile to blacks, they must have realized that their bygone patriarch, the Reverend Jeremiah Asher, and the Camp William Penn warriors, left behind an enduring message they'd need to keep knocking down those "borders," one right after the other. The 1864 song (composed by a "contraband," likely an ex-slave) and momentous lyrics of the "Hymn of the Freedman," penned by George H. Boker in memory of the deceased 8th Regiment USCT Colonel William Fribley, who was killed with hundreds of black soldiers and stripped naked on the battlefield of Olustee, Florida, epitomizes what the anti-slavery activist and Camp William Penn nurse, Anne de B. Mears, once described as "a victory so gloriously won":

Surely God himself has risen
Over all the wakened world;
Burst the darkness of the prison,
Into hell the shackels hurled;
For we hear a mighty rattle
Fill the valleys and the hills,
As the freedmen march to battle
As the God of freedom wills.

Then rally, rally, rally
round the flag of liberty,
We are men at last and soldiers,
We are free, are free, are free.

God has said make free your brother,
As you now yourselves are free;
Strike for wife and sire and mother,
And for children on the knee.
We are worse than Pagan scoffers
If we fail to do the deed
That God's grace so freely offers
To our people's trampled seed.

God has put the sword and rifle
Into labor-hardened hands,
And we dare not stop or trifle
When our God Himself commands.
We have cut our bonds asunder,
As the mower cuts the grain,
And the land shall fill with wonder
Ere they find them on again.

In the name of God, who heeds us,
We will crush the tyrant's power,
And we trust to Him who leads us
In the battle's bloody hour.
He will take us safely over,
He will heal our wounds with balm,
And the blessed dead He'll cover
In the hollow of his palm.
(Boker 1864, 2008)

Endnotes

Introduction: The proudest moment of my life

[1] "THIRD DECADE OF THE AMERICAN ANTI-SLAVERY SOCIETY." *The Liberator.* June 15, 1864. (Accessible Archives)

[2] "Mr. William Still, of this city, has been elected post sutl[er]," *The Christian Recorder.* January 30, 1864. (Accessible Archives) William Still was one of the most well known and respected black citizens of Philadelphia as the principal operator of the Underground Railroad in the city. With both of his parents being "former slaves," Still "became an active abolitionist, taking a position as clerk in the Philadelphia Anti-slavery Society and later serving as secretary of the Philadelphia Vigilance Committee," according to historian Charles L. Blockson's 2001 book, *African Americans in Pennsylvania: Above Ground and Underground* (35-36). "In his classic book The Underground Railroad, published in 1872, Still provided his readers with numerous accounts of heroism of escapees and those who helped them flee from bondage at the risk of their own lives." Some of Blockson's ancestors escaped via the Underground Railroad and served at Camp William Penn. As post sutler, however, all was not smooth sailing for Still. At one point, members of the 25th USCT at Camp William Penn accused him of short-changing them, sparking a major disturbance and the vandalizing of Still's post store. Although there are conflicting reports concerning the incident, some historical observers contend the problems revolved around a misunderstanding. Others believe class friction between recently liberated African Americans and such upwardly mobile blacks as Still, a prolific and very successful businessperson, contributed to the disturbance.

[3] Records of the Provost Marshal General (National Archives, Philadelphia) Letters Received, RG 110. This Dec. 21st 1863 letter to Louis Wagner regarding two "white" men who were initially serving as post sutlers was deemed illegal by commanders. Suspicious activities sometimes surfaced at such facilities as Camp William Penn since criminals targeted the soldiers and officers who received pay from the government. There were even problems with prostitution at such Civil War camps.

[4] Ibid. This November 18, 1863 letter from Commander Louis Wagner that was sent to Major Lewis Foster of the Adjutant General's Office in Washington indicates his intention to appoint a post sutler.

[5] Ibid. Initially, Commander Wagner's superiors in Washington, D.C. believed a post sutler was not needed, perhaps aggravated by reports of suspicious characters trying to fulfill that role. Major Lewis Foster of the Adjutant General's Office in Washington contended that since Camp William Penn was initially a temporary facility, such an enterprise was not needed. Wagner, obviously, eventually convinced his superiors otherwise since William Still, who had been selling coal to the facility, was appointed to the post.

Chapter One: Emotions ran very high

[1] "Philadelphia Advertisements." *National Anti-Slavery Standard*, May 16, 1863. Edward M. Davis, the son-in-law of the famed women's rights advocate and anti-slavery abolitionist, Lucretia Mott, published the referenced advertisement concerning his "STOCK AND EXCHANGE BROKER" enterprise, located at 39 South Third Street in Philadelphia. "Although he was also a merchant who operated a store at 16 South Eighth Street in Philadelphia featuring 'Hats, Caps, and Straw Goods, also Full Line of Fur Goods,' according to an advertisement in the July 1877

edition of the Cheltenham Record (published by the *Cheltenham Military Academy*), Davis was much more. Born in 1812, he married Lucretia Mott's daughter Maria on October 26, 1836, permanently moving to Cheltenham about 1854 on a property that he called Oak Farm, likely due to the large number of oak trees in the area," according to this writer's 2009 book, *Remembering Cheltenham Township*, for The History Press (87-88). "In addition to leasing the land to the federal government for Camp William Penn, following the North Penn Railroad arrival 'to the northern suburbs in 1854, Davis formed the Chelten Hills Land Association which bought 1000 acres of farm land from neighboring Cheltenham Quakers, and then enticed many prominent Philadelphians to construct handsome country residences' in the area," according to Elaine Rothschild in her 1991 Old York Road Historical Society article, "Historic LaMott." Interestingly, Davis had also been a captain under General John C. Frémont when commanded the Missouri territory and issued a proclamation that essentially freed the enslaved Africans there, causing President Lincoln to dismiss Frémont from that command. One of the rich entrepreneurs who'd soon purchase some of Davis' Cheltenham land was the "financier of the Civil War" for the Union's cause, Jay Cooke. And as a member of the Union League of Philadelphia, Davis likely donated substantial funds to help establish Camp William Penn.

[2] An absorbing account of how Commander Edward Hallowell, a native of Philadelphia and officer of the famous Massachussetts 54th Regiment, was injured appears in the Saturday, August 8, 1863 edition of *The National Anti-Slavery Standard*, in a column entitled, "Personal."

[3] Ibid. Following the July 18, 1863 battle for Fort Wagner on South Carolina's Morris Island, the Saturday, August 22, 1863 edition of the *National Anti-Slavery Standard*, reported, that Hallowell was promoted following the killing of Colonel Robert Gould Shaw, the commander of the Massachusetts 54th regiment, during the battle. The native-Philadelphian replaced Shaw as the commander of the regiment.

[4] Ibid. The Bureau of Colored Troops was established via Special Order No. 143, according to the Saturday, June 6, 1863 edition of the *National Anti-Slavery Standard*. "On May 22, 1863, the War Department announced the establishing of a Bureau of Colored Troops whose functions embraced all matters pertaining to the recruiting, organization and service of black regiments and the officers thereof," notes Benjamin Quarles in his 1989 book, *The Negro in the Civil War* (195). "Provision was made for the appointment of field inspectors, and for the examining of candidates for officers' commissions. By this order the use of the Negro as a soldier became a fixed and permanent policy of the national government."

[5] Ibid. The Saturday, June 20, 1863 edition of the *National Anti-Slavery Standard*, noted in the column, "The Army and the Negroes," that black, state-sponsored soldiers had fought valiantly in Louisiana at Port Hudson. "As a military operation the assault was entirely unsuccessful. Yet the behavior of the black regiments was one bright spot. Their conduct had been under especial scrutiny since Port Hudson was the first real battle in which Negro soldiers were engaged," wrote Benjamin Quarles in his 1989 book, *The Negro in the Civil War*, for Da Capo Press Inc. "Had they flinched under fire, the future of the Negro soldier would have been jeopardized. But they had not flinched. 'No body of troops – Western, Eastern or rebel – have fought better in the war,' editorialized the *New York Times* on June 13, 1863."

[6] Ibid. With reports appearing in such papers as the *National Anti-Slavery Standard*, Camp William Penn was in the national spotlight as some of the nation's first federal black soldiers were recruited and white officers assigned to command regiments after passing examinations and training. The training facility was at 1210 Chestnut Street in Philadelphia; however, occasionally, officers would also complete training exercises on the grounds of Camp William Penn and various areas near central Philadelphia.

[7] Ibid. The June 20, 1863 edition of the *National Anti-Slavery Standard*, noted in an article, "BLACK ENLISTMENTS – PHILADELPHIA," that George L. Stearns, "a Massachusetts abolitionists

who had been a confidant of John Brown," according to Benjamin Quarles in his 1989 book, *The Negro in the Civil War*, was working hard and with the help of the journalist and anti-slavery abolitionist, J.M. McKim, a correspondent for the *Standard*. "In June 1863 Stearns had completed his work of organizing the two Massachusetts regiments, and Stanton prevailed upon hm to become a recruiting commissioner for Negro troops, with the rank of major." Stearns was not only instrumental in recruiting black soldiers in such places as Maryland, Missouri and Tennessee, but also in Philadelphia and for Camp William Penn.

[8] Ibid. The July 4, 1863 edition of the *National Anti-Slavery Standard*, summarized a "private" correspondence, including that Camp William Penn had been established. The routine correspondent, J.M. McKim, apparently was so busy with abolitionist activities that he was not able to file his normal report as the newspaper's Philadelphia correspondent.

[9] Ibid.

[10] Ibid.

[11] Descriptive Book (National Archives and Records Administration, or NARA) record of Charles Jones, 24th USCT, RG 94. Jones, 25 years old, and standing about five feet, five inches, was one of the Camp William Penn recruits who came from distant places, in his case Barbadoes in the "West Indies." He joined the 24th USCT at Norristown, Pennsylvania, not far from Philadelphia, on March 25, 1865, just before the war ended.

[12] Ibid. Charles J. Johnson, 43, was one of many soldiers from New Jersey who joined the 22nd USCT. He enlisted on March 16, 1865 into Company I, but died at a post hospital in Richmond, Virginia that July.

[13] Ibid. Herbert Dull, an 18-year-old from Lancaster, Pa., had been a "sailor" before the war. It wasn't all that unusual for former black sailors to join the Army since they could obtain provisions, as well as pay, for their service. Furthermore, they were afforded a certain amount of stability and protection from slave catchers, especially if they had been formerly enslaved or ran away from so-called owners. (December 25, 2011 interview with Wesley A. Brown, the first African American to Graduate from the U.S. Naval Academy)

[14] "THIRD DECADE OF THE AMERICAN ANTI-SLAVERY SOCIETY." *The Liberator*. January 15, 1864. (Accessible Archives) William Lloyd Garrison, a white Bostonian and journalist, was perhaps the most recognized abolitionist of the Civil War period, with the exception of Frederick Douglass. Garrison had actually visited and befriended Lucretia and James Mott at their previous "Sansom Street home" in Philadelphia, as far back as 1830, according to Margaret Hope Bacon, a descendant of Mott, in her book, *Valiant Friend: The Life of Lucretia Mott*, published 1980 by Walker and Company. "At the Mott dinner table Garrison poured out a tale of woe. He had just completed seven weeks in prison as the result of a libel suit brought against him by a prominent slave trader for an intemperate editorial Garrison had written for the *Genius*." Once returned to "Boston from his Philadelphia visit, Garrison set to work establishing his own antislavery newspaper to advocate immediate emancipation. On January 1, 1831, the first issue of the Liberator was published. He declared, 'I am in earnest, I will not equivocate, I will not excuse, I will not retreat a single inch, and I will be heard.'"

[15] Ibid. Commander Louis Wagner eloquently addressed the audience of the American Anti-Slavery Society, in Boston, during the conference, also attended by members of the 8th USCT regiment of Camp William Penn. Wagner's anti-slavery sentiment is crystal clear in the following excerpt of his speech that appeared in the January 15, 1864 edition of Garrison's paper, *The Liberator*: "And now, with three hundred thousand graves between us and slavery, with the industry and economy of the country disarranged, and with mourning and lamentation in every household in the land, in Heaven's name, may we not end this conflict by amending the Constitution so that it may be as explicitly in the interest of liberty, as in the beginning it was proposed to make it in the interest of slavery? (Applause)"

[16] "FLAG RAISING AT CAMP WILLIAM PENN," *The Christian Recorder*. August 1, 1863. (Accessible Archives)

[17] Ibid.

[18] Adjutant General's Office (Descriptive) Book Records of Volunteer Union Organizations (National Archives and Records Administration or NARA) file of Jacob Wilson, 25th USCT, RG 94. Although Jacob Wilson of the 25th USCT's Company A, was at one point described as deserting in February 1865, just one month after enlisting, the rate of such departures by African Americans was comparatively low. "Despite the indignities they faced, African American soldiers remained committed to the Union Cause. They deserted less often than their white comrades did. More than 14 percent of Northern white soldiers deserted during the war, compared with less than 5 percent of black soldiers," notes Donald R. Shaffer in his 2004 University of Press Kansas book, *After the Glory: The Struggles of Black Civil War Veterans* (16).

[19] Ibid.

[20] Records of the Provost Marshal General (National Archives, Philadelphia) Letters Received, RG 110. Commander Wagner received a November 9, 1863 letter from Maj. Lewis Foster of the Adjutant General's Office in Washington, regarding the need to retrieve a horse and flag that were involved in a desertion.

[21] Ibid. Wagner received another Nov. 17, 1863 letter from "Maj. Lew Foster" concerning the need to stop Camp William Penn officers from living off of camp grounds.

[22] The July 7, 1863 edition of *The Philadelphia Inquirer* reported that Commander Wagner was very pleased with the training progress of the initial recruits for the 3rd Regiment of Camp William Penn, the first to be organized at the facility.

[23] "COLORED TROOPS FOR THE WAR," *Delaware County Republican*. July 10, 1863. (Accessible Archives) Frederick Douglass made appearances in the Philadelphia area during the last half of July, 1863, likely speaking at Camp William Penn on July 18 or the 24, depending on the source.

[24] Adjutant General's Office (Descriptive) Book Records of Volunteer Union Organizations (NARA) file of "J Rickets," 25th USCT, RG 94. "J. Rickets" of Company D, was confined at the guardhouse the entire day for "theft" on February 21, 1864. His harsh punishment, being "bucked & gagged two hours on and two hours off for 4 days," would have not been well-received by his black compatriots, many of them former slaves who had received such treatment.

[25] "HARD TACK AT CAMP WILLIAM PENN," *The Christian Recorder*, August 29, 1863, (Accessible Archives). Initially, the food at Camp William Penn was not cooked well and even unsanitary, according to several letters that recruits wrote to *The Christian Recorder*. A few even wrote top government officials about their disgust.

[26] "SOLDIERS' CIRCLE SOCIETY OF BETHEL AME. CHURCH, PHILADELPHIA." *The Christian Recorder*. October 15, 1864. (Accessible Archives) Church auxiliary groups, such as one from the Mother Bethel AME. Church, the first congregation of the worldwide African Methodist Episcopal Church, often took fresh food and other items to the sick soldiers.

[27] Ibid.

[28] "COLORED PEOPLE AND THE WAR. A Visit to Camp Wm. Penn," *The Christian Recorder*. October 1, 1864. (Accessible Archives) Retrieved May 4, 2011.

[29] Ibid.

[30] Ibid.

[31] Ibid.

[32] Ibid.

[33] "THE PASSENGER CARS OF PHILADELPHIA," *The Christian Recorder*. December 27, 1863. (Accessible Archives) William Still fought against the segregation of streetcars and other

discrimination in Philadelphia, although he never "suffered personally under slavery." Yet, "Still faced discrimination throughout his life and was determined to work for improved race relations," according to Larry Garra's article about Still in the 2004 Oxford University Press book, *African American Lives,* edited by Henry Louis Gates, Jr. and Evelyn Higginbotham. "His concern about civil rights in the North led him in 1859 to write a letter to the press, which started a campaign to end racial discrimination on Philadelphia streetcars, where African Americans were permitted only on the unsheltered platforms. Eight years later the campaign met success when the Pennsylvania legislature enacted a law making such discrimination illegal (pg. 791)."

[34] Ibid.

[35] Ibid.

Chapter Two
The 3rd United States Colored Troops: 'Fortunes of the whole race'

[1] *The New York Times*' August 4, 1863 edition (ProQuest) reported that some of the early recruits of the 3rd USCT participated in a flag-raising, one of the first for federal black troops in the country's history. Commander Louis Wagner must have been at least a decent public speaker because over the course of the war, he would give at least two major addresses at major national anti-slavery conventions. And it had to be quite a proud moment for many of the black recruits, armed and in uniform, and singing the country's national anthem, the "Star-Spangled Banner."

[2] "PRESENTATION OF A FLAG," *The Christian Recorder.* November 21, 1863. (Accessible Archives) A correspondent of the newspaper, published by the African Methodist Episcopal Church, was obviously impressed with a flag-raising ceremony at Camp William Penn, especially the formation of so many black soldiers witnessed by whites and African American spectators. Many of the onlookers traveled by segregated trains or trolleys from Philadelphia to Chelten Hills where the camp was located.

[3] "The Philadelphia Colored Regiment. ITS DEPARTURE FOR CHARLESTON," *The New York Times.* (ProQuest) The white abolitionist, John Brown, who was executed just before the war for leading the October 16, 1859 anti-slavery raid on the arsenal at Harper's Ferry in Virginia, was highly regarded by abolitionists, black citizens and soldiers. In fact, for several years he reportedly resided as a boarder with David Bustill Bowser, the African American designer and creator of at least 10 of the Camp William Penn regimental flags.

[4] "ARMY CORRESPONDENCE," *The Christian Recorder.* October 15, 1864. (Accessible Archives) Relatives and friends of soldiers in Philadelphia relished reading about activities in the field via letters that were sent to *The Christian Recorder*, published by the African Methodist Episcopal (AME) Church in the "City of Brotherly Love." The editor during the Civil War period, the Reverend Elisha Weaver, was educated at Oberlin College and a staunch abolitionist. As a pastor, Rev. Weaver served several congregations throughout the Ohio Valley, East and Mid-Atlantic regions. The reverend even traveled to the deepest parts of the South with other AME ministers. The writer, Sergeant Thomas B. Rockhold, was a frequent contributor to the publication.

[5] "For the *Christian Recorder*. FLORIDA CORRESPONDENCE," *The Christian Recorder.* April 29, 1865. (Accessible Archives) The deaths of Private Samuel Brown and Sergeant Joel Ben were surely unwanted news to relatives and friends. Sergeant Thomas B. Rockhold, who often sent correspondence to *The Christian Recorder*, was also injured. Sergeant Ben's death, while trying to "shield a helpless woman and her child," was likely very touching for folks with anti-slavery sentiments, including the "ladies of the Sanitary Commission." Obviously, the clerk of the 3rd USCT, William B.D. Johnson, continued corresponding with the newspaper during Rockhold's incapacitation.

Chapter Three: The 6ᵗʰ United States Colored Troops: 'This momentous struggle'

[1] The September 5, 1863 edition of the *National Anti-Slavery Standard*, Vol. XXIV. No. 17, Whole No. 1,213, showed that the recruitment of the 6ᵗʰ USCT was vigorous from the start. In fact, the 6ᵗʰ USCT was the first black regiment allowed to officially march in full uniform through the streets of Philadelphia on its way to battle.

[2] "FLAG PRESENTATION AT CAMP WILLIAM PENN," *The Christian Recorder*. September 5, 1863. (Accessible Archives) The elaborate regimental colors of the 6ᵗʰ USCT, one of about 10 designed and created by the black artist, David Bustill Bowser, for Camp William Penn regiments, was bold and audacious. As a correspondent for *The Christian Recorder* described: "It was a beautiful banner, made of the finest silk, with the American eagle in front, over it the words, 'freedom for all,' and under it the inscription, 'Sixth United States Colored Troops,'" an undeniable demand for black emancipation.

[3] Ibid.

[4] Ibid.

[5] Ibid.

[6] Ibid.

[7] Ibid.

[8] Ibid. *The National Anti-Slavery Standard* subsequently reported in its Saturday, September 10, 1863, edition, Vol. XXIV., No. 19, Whole No. 1,215, that recruiting for the 6ᵗʰ USCT was brisk.

[9] Ibid.

[10] The September 12, 1863 edition of *The Christian Recorder,* via Accessible Archives, details the contributions (collected by black community leader Jacob C. White) from some of the region's most prominent citizens. The donations allowed organizers to pay for the services of David B. Bowser, the designer and creator of the Camp William Penn regimental colors.

[11] According to the September 26, 1863 edition of the *National Anti-Slavery Standard*, Vol XXIV, No. 20, Whole No. 1,216, plans were being made to construct barracks for incoming recruits, in a very brief story, "MUSTERING CAMP FOR COLORED SOLDIERS."

[12] "SIXTH U.S. COLORED REGIMENT AT CAMP WILLIAM PENN," *The Christian Recorder*, October 3, 1863 (Accessible Archives) Capt. J.P. Riley of the 6ᵗʰ USCT is supported by the writer as someone who's empathetic and sensitive to black soldiers.

[13] "MARRIED," *The Christian Recorder*. October 17, 1863. (Accessible Archives) Captain Riley of the 6ᵗʰ USCT was apparently very much respected by the black recruits. In fact, the officer also conducted marriages, perhaps one of the reasons for his popularity.

[14] "CAMP WILLIAM PENN," *The Christian Recorder*. October 10, 1863. (Accessible Archives) This report indicates that activities at Camp William Penn were of great interest to the local populace. In fact, the novelty of black soldiers in uniform and carrying weapons, was quite a spectacle as they often paraded on weekends in tight formations.

[15] "COLORED TROOPS' PARADE IN PHILADELPHIA," *The Christian Recorder*. October 10, 1863. (Accessible Archives) With the 6th and 8ᵗʰ USCT regiments of Camp William Penn parading in Philadelphia, racial hostilities must have calmed a bit. Earlier, the 3ʳᵈ USCT of the facility, were not allowed to parade in Philadelphia for fear that it would incite white rioters.

[16] Ibid.

[17] Ibid.

[18] Ibid.

[19] Ibid.

[20] "THE DEPARTURE OF THE 6ᵀᴴ U.S. COLORED REGIMENT," *The Christian Recorder*. October 17, 1863. (Accessible Archives). After parading to the Washington Street area, the 6ᵗʰ USCT were undoubtedly given refreshments and food at one of the massive saloons near the water

before departing by steamer for war. They reportedly saluted Commander Wagner, as well as Governor Curtin. Cheers also were heard for the skipper of the steamer, Captain Sullivan.

[21] Ibid.

[22] "For *the Christian Recorder*. FROM HAMPTON, VA.," *The Christian Recorder*. May 21, 1864. (Accessible Archives) Many Camp William Penn soldiers were furious about the lower pay that they received compared to white soldiers. The pay difference was often as much as $13 for white recruits, compared to just $7 to $10 for black soldiers.

[23] "EMANCIPATION IN MARYLAND," *The Liberator*. November 11, 1864. (Accessible Archives) The officers' training school at 1210 Chestnut Street in Philadelphia as 1864 ended was brilliantly decorated with bright signage and other adornments to mark the end of slavery in Maryland.

[24] Ibid.

[25] "The Court of Appeals today dismissed the application," *The Liberator*. November 4, 1864. (Accessible Archives) An observer and writer to William Lloyd Garrison's newspaper, *The Liberator*, was very pleased with Maryland's emancipation of slaves in late 1864: "We earnestly hope the clergy may open the churches, and give expression to the religious sentiment of the people on this glorious triumph of Liberty, Justice, and Progress in Maryland." The Maryland development led to an optimism concerning the long-awaited military victory among supporters of the Union. They hoped that the judicial defeat of slavery in Maryland would lead to pro-slavery dominoes falling throughout the Confederacy.

Chapter 4: The 8th United States Colored Troops: A most terrific shower of musketry

[1] Records of the Provost Marshal General (National Archives, Philadelphia) Letters Received, RG 110. This letter, sent by Major Lewis Foster to Commander Wagner and dated October 21, 1863, warned him that he did not have the authority to discharge men due to medical reasons. Regarding another matter, provisions to pay certain men bounties would be made. However, perhaps indicating a bit of tension between Wagner and Foster, the major also directs Wagner not to send correspondence that makes multiple requests.

[2] Ibid. The letter of October 27 1863 sent to Commander Louis Wagner indicates about 180 recruits received at Riker's Island, where other black United States Colored Troops regiments were being raised, would be sent to Camp William Penn.

[3] Ibid. This follow-up letter of Nov. 2, 1863 from Maj. Lewis Foster of the Adjutant General's Office to Commander Wagner confirms the black men from New York would arrive at Camp William Penn. Notably, such regiments as the 20th USCT and 26th USCT were soon raised on Riker's Island. The Camp William Penn regiments, during various engagements, would fight alongside those New York units.

[4] "THE AMERICAN ANTI-SLAVERY SOCIETY," *The Liberator*. December 25, 1863. (Accessible Archives) Indicative of Camp William Penn's prominence and importance to the national abolitionist movement, members of the 8th USCT received much recognition during a Boston anti-slavery convention that featured such dynamic speakers or attendees as the camp's neighbor, Lucretia Mott, Frederick Douglass, Robert Purvis, Susan B. Anthony, William Lloyd Garrison, John Greenleaf Whittier, Abby Kelley Foster and Lucy Stone. The program commemorated the Thirtieth Anniversary of the American Anti-Slavery Society in Boston.

[5] Ibid.

[6] Ibid.

[7] "FLORIDA EXPEDITION," *The Christian Recorder*. May 7, 1864. (Accessible Archives) The unpredictability of when a company or regiment might be required to move to another camp or into battle was always on the minds of recruits. This passage indicates that the soldiers certainly took notice when they were able to stay at an idyllic location, despite the drudgery and horrors

of war. And although some soldiers were certainly frustrated when required to move, most took such maneuvering in stride.

[8] Ibid.
[9] Ibid.
[10] Ibid.
[11] Ibid.
[12] Ibid.
[13] Ibid.

Chapter Five: The 22nd United States Colored Troops: 'Phase of hellfire baptism'

[1] Records of the Provost Marshal General (National Archives, Philadelphia) Letters Received, RG 110. The text refers to a December 29, 1864 letter written to Col. James B. Fry alerting him that New Jersey recruits would be assigned to Camp William Penn's 22nd USCT. Many of the soldiers assigned to the 22nd hailed from a wide-range of towns and areas in the Garden State.

[2] Ibid. A letter of October 7, 1864, sent to Commander Louis Wagner, from Major Lewis Foster of the Adjutant General's Office in Washington, D.C., instructs Wagner to choose the smartest and academically prepared soldiers for duty in the southwest of the United States. The men were destined to be clerks, as well as non-commissioned officers.

[3] Adjutant General's Office Book Records of Volunteer Union Organizations (National Archives and Records Administration, or NARA) files of Private John Sullivan, Private Charles Williams and Private John Triplett, 22nd USCT, RG 94. The black soldiers often joined the service at a wide-range of ages, with a few as young as 15-years-old to those reaching near 50. The small sampling of Sullivan, Williams and Triplett, indicates the age differences spanned sometimes 20 or more years.

Chapter Six: The 25th United States Colored Troops: Disease had run its course

[1] "LETTER FROM 25TH U.S.C.T.," *The Christian Recorder.* February 18, 1865. (Accessible Archives) This January 24, 1865 letter written to *The Christian Recorder*, by recruit Nathan Flood, describes the routines of life near the front line, inevitably including illness and death. In fact, most of the casualties of the Civil War were due to disease, many of them contagious. One of the victims, Spencer Bolden of the 25th USCT, must have been a very respected soldier, as well as Philadelphia resident. The writer, Private Flood, also points out that "several" of his other comrades had met similar fates.

[2] Ibid.

[3] "FLORIDA CORRESPONDENCE," *The Christian Recorder.* December 3, 1864. (Accessible Archives) Such correspondence was sent to the editor of The Christian Recorder, Elisha Weaver, due to the publications wide circulation and influence as an organ of the African Methodist Episcopal Church. The writer was apparently very well informed about the importance of diet, as well as educational and religious sustenance.

[4] Ibid.

Chapter Seven: The 32nd United States Colored Troops: A feeling of despair

[1] "*For the Christian Recorder.* FROM MORRIS ISLAND, S.C.," *The Christian Recorder.* July 30, 1864. (Accessible Archives)

[2] Ibid.
[3] Ibid.
[4] Ibid.
[5] Ibid.

[6] Ibid.
[7] Ibid.
[8] Ibid.
[9] Ibid.

Chapter Eight: The 41ˢᵗ United States Colored Troops: We did not falter
[1] "THE 41ˢᵀ U.S.C.T.," *The Christian Recorder*. March 25, 1865. (Accessible Archives)
[2] Ibid.
[3] Ibid.
[4] Ibid.

Chapter Nine: The 43ᵗʰ United States Colored Troops: These redeemed sons of Africa
[1] "LETTER FROM THE FRONT," *The Christian Recorder*. December 17, 1864. (Accessible Archives)
[2] Ibid.
[3] Adjutant General's Office Book Records of Volunteer Union Organizations (National Archives and Records Administration, or NARA) record of Captain Jesse Wilkinson, 43ʳᵈ USCT, RG 94
[4] Ibid. Record of Captain John D. Brown, 43ʳᵈ USCT, RG 94
[5] Ibid. Records of Private William Bundy and Private Asu Augborne, 43ʳᵈ USCT, RG 94
[6] Ibid. Records of Private Sylvester Butcher and Private John Castle, 43ʳᵈ USCT, RG 94
[7] Ibid. Record of Private Joseph Crossman, 43ʳᵈ USCT, RG 94

Chapter Ten: The 45ᵗʰ United States Colored Troops: The Rebs gave way
[1] "THE FLAG PRESENTATION AT CAMP WILLIAM PENN," *The Christian Recorder*. April 17, 1864. (Accessible Archives) The statement by the attorney and activist, Charles Gibbons, "The Government that acknowledges black men as soldiers, at the same time recognizes black men as her citizens," was the essential philosophy of other African American leaders, including Frederick Douglass. They viewed military service, despite the often lower pay and other conditions as compared to whites, as the pathway for equality and liberation.
[2] "CORRESPONDENCE FROM THE FRONT," *The Christian Recorder*. December 31, 1864. (Accessible Archives)
[3] Ibid. Sanitary conditions at Camp William Penn seemed to improve before or by late 1864. Previously, there had been reports of indecent food, as well as latrine conditions. Over the months, though, auxillary groups from outside the camp helped with improving such affairs at Camp William Penn. Officers also issued various directives. However, as the end of the war approached, more complaints apparently surfaced, contributing to the facility's ultimate closing. Simultaneously, as the rank-and-file soldiers perceived the officers as treating them with respect, the morale at such facilities as Camp William Penn improved and likely, so did environmental conditions.
[4] Ibid. A major attraction of black recruits to join the Union army involved the possibility that they would get the opportunity to learn how to read and write. Educational opportunities were available during long hours of idleness, sometimes at Camp William Penn and even near the front lines, depending on the circumstances. Certain buildings or areas (in the field) were often set aside for such lessons.
[5] Ibid. The black recruits were given the opportunity to worship, led often by the regiment's chaplain. Occasionally, local preachers at churches in Philadelphia or near Camp William Penn would conduct services. There were even reports of the Quaker abolitionist and theologian, Lucretia Mott, who lived next door to Camp William Penn, providing such religious nourishment.

Chapter Eleven: The 127ᵗʰ United States Colored Troops: Smiting the reeling rebellion

[1] "ASSAULT ON SERGEANT-MAJOR GREEN (COLORED)," *The Christian Recorder*. October 1, 1864. (Accessible Archives) Black soldiers on leave in Philadelphia often faced the possibility of being attacked by antagonistic whites. The chances of such assaults increased if the soldier, and in some cases black noncommissioned officers, journeyed to a hostile city location alone. The assault on Sergeant-Major Green is a prime example. Some whites were enraged by seeing black men in uniforms and even carrying sidearms. The racial tension in Philadelphia was quite intense before and during the war, as well following the combat years as the period of Reconstruction ensued, since the city was figuratively and realistically a gateway to the South or North.

[2] "DEPARTURE OF COLORED TROOPS FOR THE FIELD," *The Christian Recorder*. October 1, 1864. (Accessible Archives) Due to segregationist policies in Philadelphia, such businesses as the Cooper Shop Saloon were not always welcoming to blacks. However, such behavior began to change as the soldiers from Camp William Penn on their way to war were served there in mass, likely prompted by excellent economic incentives that the proprietor could not pass up. Furthermore, there was clearly brisk competition with other nearby establishments. The Cooper establishment "was founded in a two-story brick building on Otesgo Street about fifty yards south of Washington Avenue, near the Camden Ferry, and the Union Volunteer Refreshment Saloon was located on Swanson Street a short distance below Washington Avenue at Delaware Avenue," according to the book (70), *Philadelphia and the Civil War: Arsenal of the Union*, written by Anthony Waskie, PhD., for The History Press, 2011.

[3] "BANNEKER INSTITUTE," *The Christian Recorder*. December 31, 1864. (Accessible Archives) The Banneker Institute was founded in 1854 and named "in honor of African American astronomer and scientist Benjamin Banneker," according to "African Americans in Pennsylvania: Above Ground and Underground," by Charles L. Blockson., "During the 1700s, he published an almanac for the States of Pennsylvania, Delaware, Maryland, and Virginia" (53). Starting off as a one-room schoolhouse, the Banneker Institute also became a well-known African American literary society, notes Blockson, that was "originally located in Central Hall on Walnut Street above Sixth Street."

[4] "PRESENTATION OF A FLAG," *The Christian Recorder*. November 21, 1863. (Accessible Archives)

Chapter Twelve: The 24ᵗʰ United States Colored Troops: The last to leave

[1] Descriptive Book (National Archives and Records Administration or NARA) record of John Antonia, 24ᵗʰ USCT, RG 94

[2] Descriptive Book (NARA) record of John Jackson and Simon Caulsberry, 24ᵗʰ USCT, RG 94

[3] Descriptive Book (NARA) record of William Brewster, 24ᵗʰ USCT, RG 94

[4] Descriptive Book (NARA) record of Brinmonde Willis, 24ᵗʰ USCT, RG 94

[5] Descriptive Book (NARA) records of Robert Battese, John Baptist, John Liverpool and Peter N. Matthews, 24ᵗʰ USCT, RG 94

[6] Descriptive Book (NARA) records of Lewis F. Moore, 24ᵗʰ USCT, RG 94

[7] "HON. WM. D. KELLY'S LECTURE." *The Christian Recorder*. April 1, 1865. (Accessible Archives)

[8] "PRESENTATION OF COLORS TO THE 24ᵀʰ REGT. U.S.C.T." *The Christian Recorder*. April 22, 1865. (Accessible Archives)

[9] Ibid.

[10] "Entertaining Lecture at Camp William Penn given by Miss. Harriet Tubman." *The Christian Recorder*. April 8, 1865. (Accessible Archives) Following the war, Tubman married a former

soldier, Private Nelson Davis, who joined the 8th USCT of Camp William Penn. After becoming a boarder in Tubman's Auburn, New York, residence, a relationship apparently developed and they were ultimately married. The couple operated several enterprises together, including a farm and home for the aged, as well as for the disadvantaged. Tubman also lived off of Davis' military pension until she received her own after 25 years of fighting for it from the federal government. About 20 years younger than Tubman, Davis died years before Tubman expired in 1913.

[11] "FRED. DOUGLASS," *The Christian Recorder*. February 11, 1865. (Accessible Archives)

[12] THE LECTURE AT CONCERT HALL ON MONDAY NIGHT," *The Christian Recorder*. March 4, 1865. (Accessible Archives)

[13] "For the *Christian Recorder*. H'd. Q'rs. Camp William Penn [Sword Presentation])," *The Christian Recorder*. April 15, 1865. (Accessible Archives)

[14] "Camp William Penn." *The Christian Recorder*. April 8, 1865. (Accessible Archives)

[15] "For the *Christian Recorder* - CAMP WM. PENN." *The Christian Recorder*. April 15, 1865. (Accessible Archives)

[16] "THE UNION VICTORIES." *The Christian Recorder*. April 8, 1865. (Accessible Archives) The praise for Gen. Ulysses S. Grant was likely very intense in the Chelten Hills area, near Camp William Penn, since he occasionally visited the mansion of his friend, Jay Cooke, who financed the Union's cause during the Civil War via his brokerage houses in Philadelphia, Washington, D.C. and New York City. Grant's son, Jesse, attended the Cheltenham Military Academy quite close to where Camp William Penn was located, as noted in the author's 2009 book (134-135), *Remembering Cheltenham Township* for The History Press. However, on at least one occasion, Grant and Cooke had to deal with a very important visitor: the influential Quaker, Lucretia Mott, who requested that they stop the government's brutal policy against Native Americans.

[17] "THE PROCESSION OF FRIDAY LAST," *The Christian Recorder*. April 22, 1865. (Accessible Archives) Octavius Vallentine Catto, who delivered the speech during the referenced ceremony, was a well-known black orator, scholar, educator and civil rights leader. Catto "was a member of the first graduating class at the Institute for Colored Youth and later taught there," according to page 74 of historian Charles L. Blockson's 2001 book, *African Americans in Pennsylvania: Above Ground and Underground*. "Actively involved in organizing black voters in Philadelphia, he was assassinated while rallying African American support for the Republican Party during the 1871 elections. The U.S. Marines were called in after the assassination to prevent [further] race riots. The militia at the Armory, Broad and Race Streets, guarded Catto's body, and he was buried with full military honors [led by the former commander of Camp William Penn, Gen. Louis Wagner] in one of the largest funerals ever held in Philadelphia."

[18] "Camp William Penn," *The Christian Recorder*. April 8, 1865. (Accessible Archives)

[19] Ibid. Although there were likely improvements to conditions at the hospital on the post of Camp William Penn as the war ended, various recruits complained of earlier conditions there. Furthermore, National Archives' service records indicate more than a few soldiers died in the hospital or infirmary, likely of infectious diseases or infections. Some soldiers also complained about the bedside manners of "surgeons," sometimes described as racist. The soldiers relished the opportunity to be treated well, socially and medically, by such volunteer assistants as "Mrs. Mears," a religious woman who apparently also gave religious instructions.

[20] "LETTER FROM LIEUTENANT-COLONEL TRIPE," *The Christian Recorder*. June 3, 1865. (Accessible Archives)

Epilogue: Coming full circle

[1] "Camp William Penn," *The Christian Recorder*. April 29, 1865. (Accessible Archives)

[2] Ibid.

[3] Ibid.

[4] "HOME FOR DISABLED COLORED SOLDIERS. AN APPEAL," *The Christian Recorder.* September 9, 1865. (Accessible Archives)

[5] Ibid.

[6] Ibid.

[7] "DIED. BOYER," *The Christian Recorder*. August 18, 1866. (Accessible Archives)

[8] "REUNION OF COLORED TROOPS," *The Christian Recorder.* July 15, 1882. (Accessible Archives)

[9] Ibid.

[10] The United States 1870 Federal Census, www.ancestry.com

[11] The United States 1880 Federal Census, www.ancestry.com

[12] "FUNERAL SERVICES," *The Philadelphia Inquirer.* August 9, 1864.

[13] "FUNERAL OF REV. J. ASHER." *North American and United States Gazette*. November 9, 1865.

[14] "The Civil War 1861-2011: The Way We Weren't," David Von Drehle, *Time Magazine*, April 18, 2011.

Bibliography

Accessible Archives. Online database of nineteenth-century newspapers. http://www.accessible.com/accessible/.

"American Civil War Soldiers about Jeremiah Asher," Ancestry.com [database online]. Provo, UT. Operations, Inc., 2011. http://search.ancestry.com/cgi-bin/sse.dll?rank=1&new=1& MSAV=1&msT=1&gss=angs-g&gsfn-Jeremiah&msddy=1864. Accessed December 28, 2011.

Asher, Jeremiah. *Incidents in the Live of The Rev. J. Asher*, Freeport, New York: Books for Libraries Press, 1850, 1971.

Bacon, Margaret Hope. *Valiant Friend: The Life of Lucretia Mott*. New York: Walker and Company, 1980.

Bates, Samuel P. *History of the Pennsylvania Volunteers, 1861-5*. Wilmington, North Carolina: Broadfoot, 1871, 1993.

Bennett, Captain B. Kevin. "The Jacksonville Mutiny" *Military Law Review*, Volume 134 (Fall 1981), 157-172.

Biddle, Daniel R. and Murray Dubin. *Tasting Freedom: Octavius Catto and the Battle for Equality in Civil War America*. Philadelphia, Pennsylvania: Temple University Press, 2010.

Billington, Ray Allen. *The Journal of Charlotte L. Forten*. New York and London, England: W.W. Norton & Company, 1953.

Binder, Frederick M. "Philadelphia's Free Military School," *Pennsylvania History*, Vol. 17, no. 4 (October, 1950), 281-291. Penn State University Press. http://www.jstor.org/stable/27769155. Accessed December 30, 2011.

Blackett, R.J. M., ed. *Thomas Morris Chester, Black Civil War Correspondent: His Dispatches from the Virginia Front*. Baton Rouge, Louisiana: Da Capo Press, Inc., 1989.

Blockson, Charles L. *African Americans in Pennsylvania Above Ground and Underground: An Illustrated Guide*. Harrisburg, Pennsylvania: RB Books, 2001.

Boker, George H. "Hymn of Freedman." The Lester S. Levy Collection of Sheet Music: J Scholarship. Johns Hopkins University, 1864, 2008. https://jscholarship.library.jhu.edu/handle/1774.2/5689. Accessed November 16, 2011.

Bradford, Sarah. *Harriet Tubman: The Moses of Her People*. Secaucus, New Jersey: Carol Publishing Group, 1994.

Calderhead, William L. "PHILADELPHIA IN CRISIS: JUNE-JULY, 1863." *Pennsylvania History*, vol. 28, no. 2. (April 1961), 142-155. Penn State University Press. http://www.jstor.org/stable/27770024. Accessed May 5, 2011.

"Bumstead, Horace, 1841-1919. Horace Bumstead collection of documents concerning ordnance of the 43rd regiment of the U.S. Colored Troops: Guide," Houghton Library, Harvard College Library. Harvard University, Cambridge, MA 02138, 2003. http://oasis.lib.harvard.edu/oasis/deliver/~hou00185. Accessed October 31, 2011.

Claxton, Melvin and Mark Puls. *Uncommon Valor: A Story of Race, Patriotism, and Glory in the Final Battles of the Civil War.* Hoboken, New Jersey: John Wiley & Sons, Inc., 2006.

Colimore, Edward. *Eyewitness Reports: The Inquirer's Live Coverage of the American Civil War.* Philadelphia, Pennsylvania: Philadelphia Newspapers, Inc., 2004.

Cornish, Dudley T. *The Sable Arm: Black Troops in the Union Army, 1861-1865.* Lawrence, Kansas: The University Press of Kansas, 1956, 1987.

Creighton, Margaret S. *The Colors of Courage: Gettysburg's Forgotten History.* New York, New York: Basic Books (Perseus Books Groups), 2005.

"David Bustill Bowser Historical Marker," ExplorePAhistory.com, 2010. http://explorepahistoroy.com/hmaker.php?markerid=1=A-18D. Accessed December 2, 2011.

Davis, William C., Brian C. Pohanka and Don Troiani. *Civil War Journal: The Legacies.* Nashville, TN Thomas Nelson Inc. 1998.

"Diary of a Black Soldier, 1863-1864." The Gilder Lehrman Institute of American History 2009-2012. http://www.gilderlehrman/.org/collection/doc_archive.php. Accessed July 29, 2011)

"Diary of Sergeant Major Christian A. Fleetwood: U.S. Colored Infantry Fourth Regiment, Company G." National Humanities Center Resource Toolbox.The Making of African American Identity: Volume 1, 1500-1865, 2007. http://nationalhumanitiescenter.org/pds/maai/identity/ text7/fleetwooddiary.pdf. Accessed September 23, 2011.

("Directors & Members: George H. Boker (Director) 1892," 2008. Accessed November 16, 2011, http://mechanicsnationalbank.com/members/george-boker/. Accessed December 30, 2011.

Dobak, William A. *Freedom by the Sword: The U.S. Colored Troops, 1862-1867,* Government Printing Office, 2011. books.google.com. Accessed September 18, 2011.

Drehle, David Von. "The Civil War 1861-2011: The Way We Weren't, " *Time* Vol. 177, no. 15 (2011), 40-51.

Du Bois, W. E. B. *The Philadelphia Negro: A Social Study.* New York: Benjamin Blom, Inc., 1899, 1967.

Dyer, Frederick H. *A Compendium of the War of the Rebellion Compiled and Arranged from Official Records of the Federal and Confederate Armies, Reports of he Adjutant Generals of the Several States, the Army Registers, and Other Reliable Documents and Sources.* Des Moines, Iowa: The Dyer Publishing Company, 1908.

Fisher, Sydney George. A Philadelphia Perspective: The Civil War Diary of Sidney George Fisher. New York: Fordham University Press, 2007. http://www.scribd.com / doc/34098494/A-Philadelphia-Perspective. Accessed May 28, 2010.

Foner, Philip S. "The Battle To End Discrimination Against Negroes on Philadelphia Streetcars: (Part I) Background and Beginning of the Battle. *Pennsylvania History*, vol. 40. no. 3 (July 1973), 260-290. Penn State University Press. http://www.jstor.org/stable/27772133. Accessed: May 5, 2011.

Frank, Lisa Tendrick. *Women in the American Civil War.* Volume 1, Santa Barbara, California: ABC-CLIO, 2008.

"Frederick Douglass – Visit to Carlisle in 1872," Dickinson University. 2010. http://housedivided.dickinson.edu,. Accessed December 12, 2011.

Gates, Henry Louis Jr. and Evelyn Brooks Higginbotham, eds. *African American Lives.* New York: Oxford University Press, 2004.

Gayley, Alice J. "8th United States Colored Regiment Pennsylvania Volunteers," www.pa-roots.com). 2011. http://www.pa-roots.com/pacw/usct/8thusct/8thusctorg.html. Accessed December 30, 2011.

Gayley, Alice J. "3rd United States Colored Regiment Pennsylvania Volunteers," pa-roots.com. 2011. http://www.pa-roots.com/pacw/usct/8thusct/8thusctorg.html. Accessed December 30, 2011.

Geffert, Hannah N. "John Brown and His Black Allies: An Ignored Alliance." *The Pennsylvania Magazine of History and Biography*, Vol. 126, No. 4. October, 2002. 591-610. http://www.jstor.org/stable/20093575. Accessed May 5, 2011.

Gladstone, William A. *Men of Color.* Gettysburg, Pennsylvania: Thomas Publications, 1993.

Glatthar, Joseph T. *Glory*, the 54th Massachusetts Infantry, and Black Soldiers in the Civil War." *The History Teacher*, vol. 24, no. 4. August, 1991. 475-485. Society for History Education. http://www.jstor.org/stable/494706. Accessed May 5, 2011.

Hahn, Steven. *A Nation Under Our Feet: Black Political Struggles in the Rural South from Slavery to the Great Migration.* Cambridge, Massachusetts and London, England: The Belknap Press of Harvard University Press, 2003.

Hartwig, Robert Norman. *A Recollection of Chaplain Thomas Scott Johnson of the 127th United States Colored Troops and 36th United States Colored Troops During and After the Civil War*, 1970. books.google.com. Accessed December 30, 2011.

Heist, Sharon. "Rev. Jeremiah Asher, Chaplain of the 6th USCT." Afrigeneas.com. AfriGeneas Military Research Forum Archive. 2005. www.afrigeneas.com/forum-militaryarchive/index.cgi/md/read/id/1914/sbj/come-usct-geneological-connections. Accessed November 16, 2011.

Higginson, Thomas Wentworth. *Army Life in a Black Regiment.* New York: Barnes & Noble, Inc., 1869, 2009.

Hine, Darlene Clark. *Black Women in America: An Historical Encyclopedia.* Brooklyn, New York: Carlson Publishing, 1993.

Holzer, Harold and Craig L. Symonds, eds. *The New York Times: Complete Civil War 1861-1865.* New York: Black Dog & Leventhal Publishers, Inc., 2010.

Hooker, Clorrestine Cooper and Steve Wilson. *Child of the Fighting Tenth: On the Frontier with the Buffalo Soldiers.* Oxford University Press, November 20, 2003. books.google.com. Accessed December 2, 2011.

Hopkins, Leroy T., "Now Balm in Gilead: Lancaster's African American Population and the Civil War Era."

Eric Ledell Smith and Joe Williamn Trotter Jr.,eds. *African Americans in Pennsylvania: Shifting Historical Perspectives.* University Park, PA: The Pennsylvania State University Press and The Pennsylvania Historical and Museum Commission, 177-197. 1997.

"Horace Bumstead Records: 1879-1919." Manuscript Archival Collections. Robert W. Woodruff Library. Atlanta University Center. 2009. http://www.auctr.edu/rwwl/Home/tabid/407/Default.aspx. Accessed October 31, 2011.

Horigan, Michael. *Elmira: Death Camp of the North.* Mechanicsburg, Pennsylvania: Stackpole Books, 2008, 1864.

Johnson, James Elton. "A HISTORY OF CAMP WILLIAM PENN AND ITS BLACK TROOPS IN THE CIVIL WAR, 1863-1865." PhD diss., University of Pennsylvania, 1999.

Johnson, James Weldon. "To Horace Bumstead." PoemHunter.com. Friday, April 2, 2010. http://www.poemhunter.com/poem/to-horace-bumstead/. Accessed October 31, 2011.

"Josiah Thomas Walls." Black Americans in Congress. Office of History and Preservation, Office of the Clerk, Black Americans in Congress, 1870–2007. Washington, D.C.: U.S. Government Printing Office, 2011. *http://baic.house.gov/member-profiles/profile. html?intID=17.* Accessed February 21, 2011.

"JOSIAH T. WALLS." Alachua County Historical Commission. 2008-2011. http//growth-management.alachua.fl.us/historic/historic_ commission/historical_markers/. Accessed February 24, 2010.

Kaplan, Sidney and Emma Nogrady Kaplan. *The Black Presence in the Era of the American Revolution.* Revised ed. Amherst, Massachusetts: The University of Massachusetts Press, 1989.

Klingman, Peter D. *Josiah Walls: Florida's Black Congressman of Reconstruction.* Gainesville: The University Press of Florida, 1976.

Lardas, Mark. *African American Soldier in the Civil War: USCT 1862-66.* Botley, Oxford, United Kingdom: Osprey Publishing, Ltd., 2006.

Larson, Kate Clifford. *Harriet Tubman – Portrait of an American Hero: Bound for the Promised Land.* New York: The Random House Publishing Group, 2004.

Leckie, William H. with Shirley A Leckie. *The Buffalo Soldiers: A Narrative of the Black Calvary in the West.* Revised ed. Oklahoma: University of Oklahoma Press, 2003.

Logan, Rayford W. and Michael R.Winston, eds. *Dictionary of American Negro Biography.* 1st ed. New York and London, England: W. W. Norton & Company, 1982.

Mayer, Henry. *All On Fire: William Lloyd Garrison and the Abolition of Slavery.* New York: Henry Mayer, 1998.

McPherson, James M. *Battle Cry of Freedom: The Civil War Era.* New York: Oxford University Press, Inc., 1988.

Meier, Judith A. H. "Citizens of Color: Biographical Sketches of Montgomery County's Black Soldiers in the Civil War," *The Bulletin of the Historical Society of Montgomery County* Volume 29, nos. 2, 3 (Spring & Fall 1994), 3-145.

Miller, John Chester. *The Wolf by the Ears: Thomas Jefferson and Slavery.* Charlottesville and London: Rector and the University of Virginia and Thomas Jefferson Memorial Foundation, Inc., 1991.

Nash, Gary B. *First City: Philadelphia and the Forging of Historical Memory.* Philadelphia, PA: University of Pennsylvania Press, 2002.

Norton, Oliver W. *Army Letters 1861-1865.* Chicago, Illinois: O.L. Deming., 1903.

Oakes, James. *The Radical and The Republican*. New York and London: W.W. Norton & Company, 2007.

Paradis, James M. *Strike the Blow for Freedom*. Shippensburg, Pennsylvania: White Mane Publishing Company, Inc., 1998.

Pearson, Elizabeth Ware, ed. *Letters from Port Royal 1862-1868*. New York: Arno Press and *The New York Times*, 1969.

"Philadelphia, Pennsylvania, Death Certificate Index, 1803-1915 about Abigial [sic] Asher." Ancestry.com. [database on-line]. Provo, UT: Ancestry.com Operations, Inc., 2011. http://search.ancestry.com/cgi-bin/sse.dll?rank=1&MSAV=1&msT=1&gss=angs-g&gsfn=Abigail&gsln=Asher&msbdy. Accessed December 28, 2011.

Quarles, Benjamin. *The Negro in the Civil War*. New York: Da Capo Press, Inc., 1953, 1989.

Price, Jimmy. "Profile in Courage: Sergeant-Major Thomas R. Hawkins, 6th USCI." Sable Arm. 2010. http://sablearm.blogspot.com. Accessed August 3, 2011.

Redkey, Edwin S., ed. *A Grand Army of Black Men: Letters from African American Soldiers in the Union Army*. Cambridge University Press, 1992. http://books.google.com. Accessed April 17, 2011.

Redpath, James. *The Public Life of Capt. John Brown*. Thayer and Eldridge. 1860. http://books.google.com. Accessed April 17, 2011.

Rockhold, T.R. "3rd USCT Letter," *Christian Recorder*, June 25, 1864. Accessible Archives. http://battleofolustee.org. Accessed November 25, 2011.

Roper, Robert. *Now the Drum of War: Walt Whitman and his Brothers in the Civil War*. New York: Walker & Company, 2008.

Sailer, Don. "Forten, Robert Bridges." House Divided. Dickinson College, 2007-2010. http://hd.housedivided.dickinson.edu/node/32480. Accessed December 29, 2011.

Sailer, Don. "Pennsylvania Grand Review," House Divided. Dickinson College, 2007-2010. http://hd.housedivided.dickinson.edu. Accessed November 25, 2011.

"Sergeant Major Hawkins, Thomas R., U.S. Army." COMOHS.org., 2011 http://www.cmohs.org/recipient-detail/592/hawkins-thomas-r.php. Accessed August 3, 2011.

("Lieutenant/Adjutant EDGERTON, NATHAN H., U.S. ARMY. CMOHS.org. http://www.cmohs.org/recipient-detail/399/edgerton-nathan-h.php. Accessed August 3, 2011.

Schubert, Irene and Frank N. Schubert, *On the Trail of the Buffalo Soldier II: New and Revised Biographies of African Americans in the U.S. Army*, 1866-1917. The Scarecrow Press, Inc. Lanham, Maryland, Toronto – Oxford, 2004, 72. books.google.com. Accessed June 14, 2011.

————. "Camp William Penn." Pennsylvania Civil War 150. Pennsylvania Heritage Society and Pennsylvania Historical & Museum Commission, 2011. http://www.pacivilwar150.com/war/camp-william-penn.aspx. Accessed April 13, 2011.

————. *Images of America: Camp William Penn*. Charleston, South Carolina: Arcadia Publishing, 2008.

————. *Remembering Cheltenham Township*. Charleston, South Carolina and London, England: The History Press, 2009.

————. "Courageous Hallowells risked everything," The Journal-Register Co. www.montgomerynews.com. Accessed November 23, 2011.

_____. "Camp William Penn Black Soldiers in Blue." *America's Civil War*. Primedia. November, 1999.

_____. "Camp William Penn's Black Soldiers In Blue," *November 1999, America's Civil War*. www.HistoryNet.com. Accessed August 3, 2011.

_____. "Alexander Kelly: From the coal mines to the front lines." http://www. pacivilwar150.com/people/africanamericans/Story.aspx?id=31. Accessed August 3, 2011.

_____. "Tracing legacy of a black Civil War soldier," www.afrigeneas.com. Accessed October 24, 2011.

Shaffer, Donald R. *After The Glory: The Struggles of Black Civil War Veterans*. Lawrence, Kansas: The University Press of Kansas, 2004.

Silcox, Harry. *Nineteenth-Century Philadelphia Black Militant: Octavius V. Catto (1839-1871)*, 1997, 203.

Slawson, Roberrt G. *Prologue to Change: African Americans in Medicine in the Civil War Era*. Frederick, Maryland: The NMCWM Press, 2006.

Smedley, R.C. *History of the Underground Railroad in Chester and Neighboring Counties of Pennsylvania*. First Edition. Mechanicsburg, Pennsylvania: Stackpole Books, 1883, 2005.

Still, William. *The Underground Rail Road*. Medford, New Jersey: Plexus Publishing, Inc., 1872, 2005.

Switala, William J. *Underground Railroad in Pennsylvania*. 1st ed. Mechanicsburg, Pennsylvania: Stackpole Books, 2001.

Taggart, John H. "Free Military School for Applicants for Command of Colored Troops, No. 1210 Chestnut Street, Philadelphia," Access Pennsylvania Digital Repository. http://www.accesspadr.org/cdm4/document.php?CISOROOT=/sstlp-cw&CISOPTR=1322&REC=15 1864. Accessed September 18, 2011.

Taylor, John C. "A Sketch of General Louis Wagner." Jenkintown, Pa. Old York Road Historical Society (OYRHS). Old York Road Historical Society Bulletin, Volume 9 1945, 49.

"The American Revolution: Lighting Freedom's Flame: African Americans in the Revolution," National Park Service. 2008. www.nps.gov. Accessed December 30, 2011.

"The American Revolution: Lighting Freedom's Flame: Salem Poor: 'A Brave and Gallant Soldier.'" National Park Service, 2008. www.nps.gov. Accessed December 30, 2011.

"Thomas Day Timeline," 2010. The Apprend Foundation. Caswell County Historical Association. http://www.slideshare.net/caswellhistorian/thomas-day-timeline. Accessed December 30, 2011.

"The Annual of Washington and Jefferson College for 1883," A.T. Zeising & Co., Printers. Philadelphia. 1884. 171-172. books.google.com/books?idThe+Annual+of+Washingto n+and+Jefferson+College+for+1883. Accessed December 30, 2011.

Trotter, Joe William Jr. and Eric Ledell Smith, eds. *African Americans in Pennsylvania: Shifting Historical Perspectives*. University Park: The Pennsylvania State University, 1997.

Trudeau, Noah Andre. *Like Men of War: Black Troops in the Civil War 1862-1865*. Toronto, Canada: Little, Brown and Company, 1998.

_____. *Gettysburg: A Testing of Courage*. First Edition. New York: HarperCollins Publishers, Inc., 2002.

Tucker, Phillip Thomas. *From Auction Block to Glory: The African American Experience*. New York: Michael Friedman Publishing Group, Inc., 1998.

Vermilyea, Peter, C. "The Effect of the Confederate Invasion of Pennsylvania on Gettysburg's African American Community," Gettysburg Discussion Group, 1996. www.gdg.org/gettysburg20magazine/. Accessed December 30, 2011.

Waskie, Anthony. *Philadelphia and the Civil War: Arsenal of the Union*. Charleston and London: The History Press, 2011.

"W.B. Johnson 3rd USCT Letter." *The Christian Recorder*, July 6, 1864. Accessible Archives. http://battleofolustee.org. Accessed November 25, 2011.

Wert, Jeffrey D. "Camp William Penn and the Black Soldier," Pennsylvania History, vol. 46, no. 4 (October 1979), 335-346. http://www.jstor.org/stable/27772625. Accessed May 5, 2011.

William Penn Public Ledger Almanac. Volume 1870/1878, 2011. http://www.ebooksread. com/authors-eng/william-penn/public-ledger-almanac-volume-18701878. Accessed December 12, 2011.

"Who They Were... What They Did," Historic La Mott, Pennsylvania. The Canton Group and Chambres & Associates. 2007. www.historic-lamott-pa.com. Accessed September 18, 2011.

About the Author

Donald "Ogbewii" Scott, a history columnist for the *Journal-Register Co.* and an assistant professor of English at the Community College of Philadelphia, has written two history books focusing on Camp William Penn, as well as the history of the township where he resides: Cheltenham, a northwest suburb of Philadelphia, PA. He has also contributed to two major anthologies, including the *African American National Biography*, published by Oxford University Press and edited by Harvard professors Henry Louis Gates, Jr., and Evelyn Higginbotham. Scott also contributed stories to the *Encyclopedia of Jim Crow*, a Houghton Mifflin publication edited by Grambling State University professors Nikki L.M. Brown and Barry M. Stentiford.

A graduate of Cheyney University (formerly known as the historic Institute for Colored Youth) and Columbia University Graduate School of Journalism in New York, Scott has served as a reporter, columnist and editor for several newspapers in Miami and southeastern Pennsylvania. He has written about a variety of African American history, archaeology, and genealogy topics for such national magazines as *America's Civil War*, *Everton's Family History,* and *American Visions,* in addition to regional newspapers, including *The Philadelphia Inquirer.*

As a history columnist for the *Journal-Register Co.*, Scott (whose middle name moniker "Ogbewii" is Nigerian for "one who honors ancestors") has often focused on black genealogy, investigating and writing about the ancestry of modern descendants of the United States Colored Troops (USCT), soldiers who fought during the Civil War, and black families with roots to colonial America and beyond. He has also researched his own family history with Gullah origins on St. Helena Island, off the coast of South Carolina, and Abbeville County in that state.

Scott has also taught at Cheyney University, Temple University and Peirce College. He has researched and written about the African traits of Pennsylvania's colonial blacks, and lectured widely about the topic for the Pennsylvania Humanities Council and Pennsylvania Historical & Museum Commission. He was featured on the Pennsylvania Cable Network's televised lecture series, *Humanities On the Road.* Further, Scott was interviewed by Judith Gay, Ph.D., Vice President for Academic Affairs for the Community College of Philadelphia's cable television series *Dialogues,* concerning Camp William Penn. Via his research about various Pennsylvania estates where slave labor was used, Scott has written many articles about that topic and the prevalence of slave-holding Quakers in Pennsylvania, including the commonwealth's founder William Penn, and other notables, such as Benjamin Franklin and George Washington.

Scott resides with his wife Billie, a human resources executive, in Elkins Park, Cheltenham Township, PA.

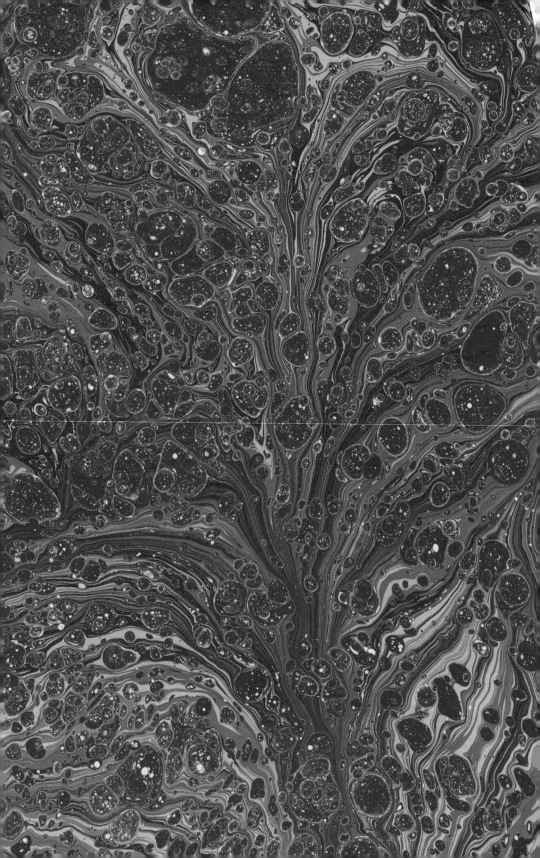